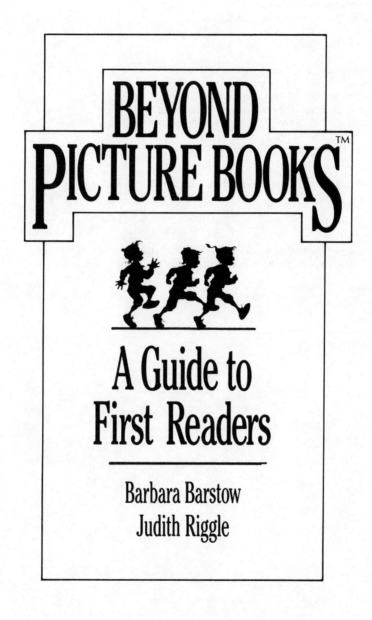

BEYOND PICTURE BOOKS™

A Guide to First Readers

Barbara Barstow
Judith Riggle

R. R. BOWKER
New York

Published by R. R. Bowker Company
a division of Reed Publishing (USA) Inc.
Copyright © 1989 by Reed Publishing (USA) Inc.
All rights reserved
Printed and bound in the United States of America

Library of Congress Cataloging-in-Publication Data

Barstow, Barbara.
  Beyond picture books: a guide to first readers / Barbara Barstow,
Judith Riggle.
    p.   cm.
  Includes indexes.
  ISBN 0-8352-2515-1
  1. Readers (Primary)—Bibliography. 2. Children's literature—
Bibliography. 3. Libraries, Children's—Book lists. I. Riggle,
Judith. II. Title.
Z5818.E5B37 1989
[PE1119.3]
011'.6250543—dc19   89-30798
                                                  CIP

ISBN 0-8352-2515-1

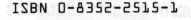

9 780835 225151

TO RALPH
        –Barb

TO MY HUSBAND, TOM
        –Judy

CONTENTS

PREFACE

I n preparing this selective annotated bibliography, we relied on our knowledge and experience with first readers as children's librarians with the Cuyahoga County Public Library (CCPL).

First readers are defined here as books intended for children at a first or second grade level (occasionally third) that have a recognizable format and generally belong to a series. The standard format for a first reader has large print, short sentences, a limited amount of print per page, and usually at least one illustration on each double-page spread. The vocabulary can be, but is not always, controlled and is generally limited to sight words, words of few syllables, and a familiar spoken vocabulary.

In order to be included in this bibliography the following criteria were used. The book had to be well-written, contain accurate information, have stories or subjects of interest to children in the primary grades, and have illustrations that complement the text and are attractive to children. Both in- and out-of-print books are included here. Excluded were books that had a very limited vocabulary but seemed more suitable to toddlers than first or second graders and books that were too sophisticated for first or second graders in spite of their format or vocabulary.

In locating the books for this bibliography, the collections of five CCPL branches were used: Berea, Brook Park, Fairview Park, Middleburg Heights, and North Olmsted. The collections at four other Ohio libraries were also extensively used: Cleveland Public Library; Lakewood Public Library; Avon Lake Public Library; and Boulevard Elementary School, Shaker Heights; as well as many other state libraries via interlibrary loan. For titles that might have been missed, reference was made to publishers' catalogs, *The Elementary School Library Collection, The Children's Catalog,* and a computer printout of all first readers maintained at Maple Heights Regional Library of CCPL. Publication dates of titles span 1951 to 1989. The 1989 titles were included when prepublication copies were available.

From the 1,610 titles in the Annotated Bibliography a list of 200 Outstanding First Readers has been selected. These outstanding titles were chosen on the basis of exceptional language and treatment of subject. This list includes both old and new titles, some standard in most library collections, and all currently in print according to *Children's Books in Print 1988–1989*.

The Annotated Bibliography is arranged alphabetically by author surname. Each title has been assigned an entry number. Where applicable each annotation contains the following information: title, illustrator, publisher, date, out-of-print (o.p.) status, paperback data (publisher, if different from hardbound edition; date), ISBN (not given for o.p. titles), subjects, readability level, and a brief annotation.

One ISBN number has been used for each title that is still in print. Wherever possible the library binding ISBN has been used; however, in instances where the library binding is o.p. the hardbound ISBN is used. When both the library binding and hardbound editions are o.p. the paperback edition ISBN is used. The annotations are short, give a brief plot synopsis, occasionally provide critical information, and offer a few words about the illustrations.

The most challenging task was to provide meaningful subject headings. The *Sears List of Subject Headings*, 10th edition, provided the first and most useful source. Library of Congress subject headings from the copyright pages of more recent titles were also helpful. In addition we relied on our experience with patron requests to create subject headings; for example, "Babies, new" rather than just "Babies." Five Cuyahoga county area children's librarians evaluated the proposed subjects and made helpful suggestions for the final list.

Probably the most controversial part of this bibliography was the assignment of readability level. Researchers have consistently questioned the reliability of the available tests (for example, Fry and Spache), and for many of the same reasons we do too. The formulas used for testing readability do not take into consideration the sophistication of the information they are dealing with, do not guarantee comprehension of information, have not been based on real statistical investigations of children and their reading, and do not consider cultural differences in language usage. Further, research has shown that sections of books can vary greatly in readability level. This was noticed when we used what we found to be the best computer readability program for Spache—Minnesota Educational Computing Corporation's 1982 program for the Apple IIe. Three 100-word passages chosen at random from the beginning, middle, and end of each book were entered into the computer and then evaluated by the readability program. Reading levels varied according to which passages were entered and the judgment of the person entering the passages in dividing compound sentences or in designating a word like astronaut as "known" to a reader.

The intention is that the reading level assignments be used in the most general way to identify books on the low, middle, and high range of difficulty for children beginning to read. The objective is to *encourage* children to read by providing access to quality material within their reach and by helping children *stretch* their skills, not stifle their interest.

The most dramatic finding is that there is a large body of fine literature classified as "first readers." Outstanding writers of books for older children like Jane Yolen, Virginia Hamilton, Eleanor Coerr, William Sleator, Marjorie Weinman Sharmat, and Betsy Byars also write creatively for this age level. Outstanding picture book writers and illustrators such as Russell Hoban, Pat Hutchins, Arnold Lobel, Aliki, Lillian Hoban, Ann Rockwell, Marc Simont, Steven Kellogg, and Tomie dePaola also share their talents with this group. The language these writers use is simple but natural, nonpatronizing, varied, and inventive. Their nonfiction is accurate, clear, and makes complex subjects surprisingly understandable. Much of the nonfiction would be useful for adults just beginning to explore a new field of interest. Their illustrations offer the visual extension of a text, often in a humorous way, by providing a bridge between profusely illustrated picture books and the books for upper elementary schoolchildren.

Thanks are due to the following people for their help with the preparation of this book: Margaret Skiff, former Coordinator of Children's Services of the Cuyahoga County Public Library; Larry Swinburn of Swinburn Readability Laboratories; for their help in proofreading, numbering of pages, and other miscellaneous tasks, Mary Ashbrook, Joyce Bell, Ralph Bertonaschi, John Birmingham, Carol Burns, Jo Crabtree, Rebecca Croom, Priscilla Drach, Ruth Hadlow, Leslie Molnar, Tom Riggle, Doris Robinson, Wade Spafford, Ellen Stepanian, Carol Strama, Rebecca Thomas, Janet Warren, and Albie Weiss. And for their willingness to try to get us books and to help us in finding materials, the staffs of the Cuyahoga County Public Library Interloan Department; the Berea Branch Library, especially its circulation department; the Brook Park, Fairview Park, Middleburg Heights, and Olmsted Falls branch libraries; other branches of CCPL; and the staff of the Avon Lake Public Library.

We also thank the staff at R. R. Bowker: Marion Sader, publisher, for encouraging us to do this project; Sheck Cho, Managing Editor, for helping us in the preparation of the manuscript; and Iris Topel, Editing Supervisor, for catching many discrepancies that somehow got by us.

Finally, we recognize that there may be omissions in our list and would appreciate suggestions for books to include in a future edition.

OUTSTANDING FIRST READERS

The following is a selected list of 200 outstanding first readers. This list is a mix of old and new titles, fiction and nonfiction, all currently in-print according to *Children's Books in Print 1988–1989* and all worthy of purchase for school or public library collections. Many of what we considered to be the very best first readers were out-of-print and therefore ineligible for this list. All of these books are well-written, contain accurate information when dealing with nonfiction subjects, are of interest to primary age children, and have attractive illustrations that complement the text. No attempt was made to present a balanced list of fiction and nonfiction works or of first, second, and third grade books. For books in a series like those of Arnold Lobel's Frog and Toad series and Marjorie Sharmat's Nate the Great series, only one title is listed.

Alexander, Sue
  World Famous Muriel
Aliki
  At Mary Bloom's
  Corn Is Maize
  Dinosaurs Are Different
  My Five Senses
  My Hands
Baker, Betty
  The Turkey Girl
Bang, Molly G.
  Wiley and the Hairy Man
Bartlett, Margaret
  Where the Brook Begins
Baynton, Martin
  Fifty Saves His Friend
Benchley, Nathaniel
  George the Drummer Boy

  A Ghost Named Fred
  Strange Disappearance of Arthur Cluck
Berenstain, Stan, and Berenstain, Jan
  The Berenstain Bears and the Spooky Old Tree
Berger, Melvin
  Why I Cough, Sneeze, Shiver, Hiccup, and Yawn
Boegehold, Betty
  Hurray for Pippa!
Bonsall, Crosby
  And I Mean It, Stanley
  Case of the Dumb Bells
  Mine's the Best
  Tell Me Some More
Brandenberg, Franz

*Aunt Nina and Her Nephews and
  Nieces*
Leo and Emily and the Dragon
Branley, Franklyn M.
  Beginning of the Earth
  The Sky Is Full of Stars
  Snow Is Falling
  Tornado Alert
  Volcanoes
Brenner, Barbara
  A Dog I Know
  Wagon Wheels
Bulla, Clyde R.
  Daniel's Duck
Bunting, Eve
  The Big Red Barn
Burton, Jane
  Freckles the Rabbit
Carlson, Nancy
  Arnie Goes to Camp
  Harriet and Walt
Carrick, Carol
  The Longest Float in the Parade
Carter, Anne
  Bella's Secret Garden
Cazet, Denys
  Saturday
Cerf, Bennett A.
  More Riddles
Chenery, Janet
  Toad Hunt
Chorao, Kay
  Oink and Pearl
Christian, Mary B.
  Penrod Again
  The Toady and Dr. Miracle
Clinton, Patrick
  I Can Be a Father
Coerr, Eleanor
  Chang's Paper Pony
  The Josefina Story Quilt
Cole, Joanna
  Bony-Legs
  Plants in Winter

Coville, Bruce, and Coville,
Katherine
  Sarah's Unicorn
Cromie, William J.
  Steven and the Green Turtle
Delton, Judy
  A Birthday Bike for Brimhall
  Two Good Friends
dePaola, Tomie
  The Quicksand Book
Dorros, Arthur
  Ant Cities
Eastman, Philip D.
  Are You My Mother?
Ehrlich, Amy
  *Leo, Zack and Emmie Together
    Again*
Fisher, Aileen
  The House of a Mouse
Freedman, Russell
  Dinosaurs and Their Young
Frith, Michael K.
  *I'll Teach My Dog One Hundred
    Words*
Gackenbach, Dick
  Hattie Rabbit
  Hound and Bear
Gage, Wilson
  Down in the Boondocks
  *Mrs. Gaddy and the Fast-
    Growing Vine*
Gauch, Patricia L.
  *Aaron and the Green Mountain
    Boys*
Giff, Patricia R.
  Today Was a Terrible Day
Graham, Bob
  Crusher Is Coming
Greene, Carol
  Snow Joe
Haddad, Helen R.
  Truck and Loader
Hancock, Sibyl
  Old Blue

Harrison, Virginia
The World of a Falcon
Hasler, Eveline
Winter Magic
Heilbroner, Joan
*This Is the House Where Jack
Lives*
Hoban, Lillian
Arthur's Honey Bear
Hoff, Syd
Danny and the Dinosaur
Holl, Adelaide
Wake Up, Small Bear
Holland, Marion
Big Ball of String
Hurd, Edith T.
Johnny Lion's Bad Day
Hutchins, Pat
The Best Train Set Ever
Jacobs, Francine
Supersaurus
Johnson, Crockett
Picture for Harold's Room
Johnson, Jean
Librarians A to Z
Kessler, Leonard
Hey Diddle Diddle
Kick, Pass and Run
Old Turtle's Winter Games
Komaiko, Leah
Earl's Too Cool for Me
Kowalczyk, Carolyn
Purple Is Part of a Rainbow
Kraske, Robert
Daredevils Do Amazing Things
Landshoff, Ursula
Cats Are Good Company
Lauber, Patricia
Snakes Are Hunters
Lawrence, James
*Binky Brothers and the Fearless
Four*
Leech, Jay, and Spencer, Zane
Bright Fawn and Me

LeSieg, Theo
Come Over to My House
Eye Book
Wacky Wednesday
Lewis, Thomas P.
Clipper Ship
Hill of Fire
Lobel, Arnold
Days with Frog and Toad
Grasshopper on the Road
Mouse Soup
Small Pig
Lopshire, Robert
I Am Better Than You!
Lowery, Janette S.
Six Silver Spoons
McCully, Emily A.
The Grandma Mix-Up
McKissack, Patricia
The Maya
Our Martin Luther King Book
McNulty, Faith
Woodchuck
Madsen, Ross M.
*Perrywinkle and the Book of
Magic Spells*
Maestro, Betsy
Ferryboat
Marshall, Edward
Four on the Shore
Fox in Love
Marzollo, Jean
Cannonball Chris
Marzollo, Jean, and Marzollo,
Claudio
Blue Sun Ben
Meddaugh, Susan
Too Short Fred
Minarik, Else H.
Little Bear
Percy and the Five Houses
Monjo, F. N.
Drinking Gourd

Mooser, Stephen
  Funnyman and the Penny Dodo
Morris, Robert
  Dolphin
Muschg, Hanna
  Two Little Bears
Myrick, Mildred
  The Secret Three
Newman, Nanette
  That Dog!
O'Connor, Jane
  Lulu and the Witch Baby
Oneal, Zibby
  Maude and Walter
Osborne, Mary P.
  Mo to the Rescue
Palmer, Helen M.
  A Fish Out of Water
Parish, Peggy
  Amelia Bedelia
  Good Hunting, Blue Sky
  Scruffy
Parker, Philip
  The Life Cycle of a Sunflower
Phillips, Joan
  Tiger Is a Scaredy Cat
Platt, Kin
  Big Max
Porte, Barbara Ann
  Harry's Dog
Posell, Elsa
  Whales and Other Sea Mammals
Prager, Annabelle
  The Spooky Halloween Party
Prall, Jo
  My Sister's Special
Prelutsky, Jack
  It's Halloween
  What I Did Last Summer
Pringle, Laurence
  Twist, Wiggle, and Squirm
Quackenbush, Robert
  Detective Mole

Rabinowitz, Sandy
  How I Trained My Colt
Robins, Joan
  Addie Meets Max
Rockwell, Anne
  Thump Thump Thump!
Rockwell, Anne, and Rockwell, Harlow
  The Night We Slept Outside
Rockwell, Harlow
  I Did It
Roop, Peter, and Roop, Connie
  Keep the Lights Burning Abbie
Rosenbloom, Joseph
  Deputy Dan and the Bank Robbers
Ross, Pat
  M and M and the Haunted House Game
Ryder, Joanne
  White Bear, Ice Bear
Rylant, Cynthia
  Henry and Mudge in Puddle Trouble
Sandin, Joan
  The Long Way to a New Land
Schick, Eleanor
  Home Alone
Schulman, Janet
  The Big Hello
  Jenny and the Tennis Nut
Schwartz, Alvin
  In a Dark, Dark Room and Other Scary Stories
  There Is a Carrot in My Ear and Other Noodle Tales
Scott, Geoffrey
  Egyptian Boats
Seixas, Judith S.
  Drugs
  Water
Selsam, Millicent E.
  Greg's Microscope

Selsam, Millicent E., and Hunt, Joyce
  A First Look at Leaves
Seuss, Dr.
  Cat in the Hat
  Fox in Socks
  Great Day for Up!
  Green Eggs and Ham
  Hop on Pop
Shannon, George
  The Gang and Mrs. Higgins
Sharmat, Marjorie W.
  Griselda's New Year
  Nate the Great
  The Story of Bentley Beaver
Shaw, Evelyn
  Alligator
Shecter, Ben
  Hester the Jester
Showers, Paul
  What Happens to a Hamburger
Shub, Elizabeth
  Clever Kate
  The White Stallion
Simon, Seymour
  Soap Bubble Magic
Sleator, William
  Once, Said Darlene
Solomon, Chuck
  Our Soccer League
Springstubb, Tricia
  My Minnie Is a Jewel
Stadler, John
  Snail Saves the Day
Stevens, Carla
  Anna, Grandpa, and the Big Storm
Stolz, Mary
  Emmett's Pig

Tangborn, Wendell V.
  Glaciers
Thaler, Mike
  Pack 109
Thomson, Pat
  Thank You for the Tadpole
  Can You Hear Me, Grandad?
Tobias, Tobi
  Marian Anderson
Trier, Carola S.
  Exercise
Van Leeuwen, Jean
  Amanda Pig and Her Big Brother Oliver
Waddell, Martin
  The Tough Princess
Weiss, Leatie
  Heather's Feathers
Wheeler, M. J.
  Fox Tales
Wiseman, Bernard
  Morris and Boris
Wood, Audrey
  Three Sisters
Wyler, Rose, and Ames, Gerald
  Magic Secrets
Yolen, Jane
  Commander Toad and the Planet of the Grapes
  Sleeping Ugly
Zemach, Harve, and Zemach, Kaethe
  The Princess and Froggie
Ziefert, Harriet
  Jason's Bus Ride
  Strike Four!
Zion, Gene
  Harry and the Lady Next Door
Zweifel, Frances W.
  Bony

ANNOTATED BIBLIOGRAPHY

A

Abisch, Roz

1 *Do You Know What Time It Is?* Ill. by Boche Kaplan. Prentice-Hall, 1968, o.p. SUBJECTS: Clocks; Concepts—Time; Science. RL 3.0.
Information about telling time is followed by instructions for making a clock with which to practice. The information is clearly and logically presented, and the illustrations contribute well to the story.

Adams, Florence

2 *Mushy Eggs.* Ill. by Marilyn Hirsch. Putnam, 1973, o.p. SUBJECTS: Baby-sitting—Fiction; Family life—Fiction; Parents, working—Fiction. RL 2.8.
The new baby-sitter is nice and bakes good cookies, but cannot make the mushy eggs like the boys' previous baby-sitter, their beloved Fanny. Homely details warm this tale of special relationships.

Adler, David A.

3 *The Carsick Zebra and Other Animal Riddles.* Ill. by Tomie dePaola. Holiday House, 1983; Bantam, pap., 1985. ISBN 0-8234-0479-X. SUBJECTS: Animals—Fiction; Jokes and riddles. RL 2.4.
Wordplay employing familiar situations and animals is used in an extremely inventive manner. Line drawings are of humorous animals.

4 *My Dog and the Birthday Mystery.* Ill. by Dick Gackenbach. Holiday House, hb and pap., 1987. ISBN 0-8234-0632-6. SERIES: First Mystery. SUBJECTS: Animals—Dogs—

Fiction; Birthdays—Fiction; Mystery and detective stories. RL 2.0.
Jennie's friends, having arranged a surprise party for her birthday, trick her into working on a mystery that leads her to the party. The story is accompanied by pictures with red, orange, yellow, and gray washes with black outlining.

5 *My Dog and the Green Sock Mystery.* Ill. by Dick Gackenbach. Holiday House, 1986. ISBN 0-8234-0590-7. SERIES: First Mystery. SUBJECTS: Animals—Dogs—Fiction; Mystery and detective stories. RL 2.6.
Jennie's astute observations and My Dog's contributions help locate Andy's missing belongings. Characteristic mishaps of childhood add humor and warmth to the tale. My Dog, curious and appealingly shaggy, is the focus of the ink drawings.

6 *My Dog and the Knock Knock Mystery.* Ill. by Marsha Winborn. Holiday House, 1985. ISBN 0-8234-0551-6. SERIES: First Mystery. SUBJECTS: Animals—Dogs—Fiction; Mystery and detective stories. RL 2.2.
This gently humorous mystery is solved with the intuitive help of My Dog. A slightly sick shaggy white pup lying on marbleized avocado grass surrounded by the remains of the apples he has consumed—in the course of duty—is typically appealing.

7 *Redwoods Are the Tallest Trees in the World.* Ill. by Kazue Mizumura. Crowell, 1978. ISBN 0-690-01368-X. SERIES: Let's-Read-and-Find-Out Science. SUBJECTS: Nature; Plants—Trees; Science. RL 2.8.
The size and growth of redwoods are contrasted with more familiar trees. Brown and green watercolors are fairly dull.

Adler, David A. (cont.)

8 *The Twisted Witch and Other Spooky Riddles.* Ill. by Victoria Chess. Holiday House, 1985; Bantam, pap., 1986. ISBN 0-8234-0571-0. SUBJECTS: Holidays—Halloween—Fiction; Jokes and riddles. RL 3.2.

Riddles include topics such as witches. Illustrations are in gray and black.

Alexander, Sue

9 *Marc the Magnificent.* Ill. by Tomie dePaola. Pantheon, 1978, o.p. SUBJECTS: Imagination—Fiction; Magic—Fiction. RL 2.9.

A boy's fantasy of fame as a magician contrasts with his first clumsy attempts at magic—but finally ends in success. Fantasy and reality are humorously contrasted through the use of language and simple pictures. Illustrations are primarily in plum, tan, and dull gold.

10 *More Witch, Goblin, and Ghost Stories.* Ill. by Jeanette Winter. Pantheon, 1978. ISBN 0-394-83933-1. SERIES: I Am Reading. SUBJECTS: Friendship—Fiction; Ghost stories; Witches—Fiction. RL 2.8.

An indoor picnic, a faked illness, a tall tale, a day spent observing nature, all bring these three friends closer. Soft pencil drawings complement the theme well.

11 *Seymour the Prince.* Ill. by Lillian Hoban. Pantheon, 1979, o.p. SERIES: I Am Reading. SUBJECTS: Clubs—Fiction; Plays—Fiction. RL 2.5.

Does Seymour want to be part of the Maple Street club badly enough to be laughed at as the prince in *Sleeping Beauty*? Soft pencil drawings are warm and appealing.

12 *Witch, Goblin, and Ghost Are Back.* Ill. by Jeanette Winter. Pantheon, 1985. ISBN 0-394-86296-1. SERIES: I Am Reading. SUBJECTS: Friendship—Fiction; Ghost stories; Witches—Fiction. RL 3.2.

Lessons about friendship—and the consequences of eating nothing but fudge—are gently relayed in five chapters. Another book in a series about three friends. Illustrations are low-key and in soft pencil.

13 *Witch, Goblin, and Ghost in the Haunted Woods.* Ill. by Jeanette Winter. Pantheon, 1981. ISBN 0-394-84443-2. SERIES: I Am Reading. SUBJECTS: Friendship—Fiction; Ghost stories; Witches—Fiction. RL 3.1.

Through a story, two friends help Goblin learn how to swim. Warm, supportive friends are very different from one another. Soft pencil drawings convey the feelings.

14 *Witch, Goblin, and Sometimes Ghost: Six Read-Alone Stories.* Ill. by Jeanette Winter. Pantheon, 1976. ISBN 0-394-93216-1. SERIES: I Am Reading. SUBJECTS: Friendship—Fiction; Ghost stories. RL 2.5.

These six tales include friends telling stories so that fear of lightning is allayed, and friends collaborating in writing a book. Pencil drawings underscore the relationship of the three.

15 *World Famous Muriel.* Ill. by Chris Demarest. Little, Brown, 1984; Dell, pap., 1988. ISBN 0-316-03131-3. SUBJECTS: Humorous stories; Mystery and detective stories. RL 2.3.

Muriel follows clues, including footprints, to discover who has stolen the decorations for the queen's party. Tongue-in-cheek humor is appropriately illustrated with comic watercolor drawings.

16 *World Famous Muriel and the Scary Dragon.* Ill. by Chris Demarest. Little, Brown, 1985; Dell, pap., 1988. ISBN 0-316-03134-8. SUBJECTS: Humorous stories; Mythical creatures—Fiction. RL 2.1.

When the King of Pompandcircumstance sends for Muriel to rid the neighborhood of a dragon, she takes her tightrope and her favorite peanut butter cookies. Delightful humor is immeasurably heightened with cartoon drawings in watercolors.

Aliki

17 *At Mary Bloom's.* Ill. by author. Greenwillow, 1976. ISBN 0-688-02481-5. SUBJECTS: Cumulative tales; Pets—Fiction. RL 2.4.

Mary Bloom helps a small girl celebrate her mouse's new babies. Marvelous animal ink drawings range from tiny mice to wall-to-wall pets and a story rebus.

18 *Corn Is Maize: The Gift of the Indians.* Ill. by author. Crowell, 1976; Harper & Row, pap., 1976. ISBN 0-690-00975-5. SERIES: Let's-Read-and-Find-Out Science. SUBJECTS: Food; Native Americans. RL 3.2.

The history of Native American corn cultivation going back 5,000 years is traced, as well as the ways it has been used and valued. Fascinating illustrations in gray, yellow, and green add immeasurably to the story. Illustrated instructions for making a corn husk wreath are appended.

19 *Digging Up Dinosaurs.* Ill. by author. Harper & Row, 1988. ISBN 0-690-04716-9. SERIES: Let's-Read-and-Find-Out Science. SUBJECTS: Dinosaurs; Science. RL 2.5.

Of utmost interest in this story is the transporting of the dinosaur fossil finds to the museum and their preparation for exhibit. The dainty soft colored pencil drawings are augmented by cartoon comments from children, scientists, and museum buffs.

20 *Dinosaur Bones.* Ill. by author. Crowell, 1988. ISBN 0-690-04549-2. SERIES: Let's-Read-and-Find-Out Science. SUBJECTS: Dinosaurs; Fossils; Science. RL 3.6.

A child visiting a museum wonders how people know so much about dinosaurs and what they looked like, leading into a look at the history of fossil discoveries. Aliki's simple, colorful illustrations work well here as they do in her other dinosaur books.

21 *Dinosaurs Are Different.* Ill. by author. Crowell, 1985; Harper & Row, pap., 1986. ISBN 0-690-04456-9. SERIES: Let's-Read-and-Find-Out Science. SUBJECTS: Dinosaurs; Science. RL 3.0.

Exceptionally well presented information on how one can distinguish the families of dinosaurs by their teeth and hips is illustrated with accurate sketches, color-coding, and cartoons of children. Length and weight, the name of each dinosaur, and the cartoons are hand-lettered.

22 *Fossils Tell of Long Ago.* Ill. by author. Crowell, 1972; Harper & Row, pap.,

1983. ISBN 0-690-31379-9. SERIES: Let's-Read-and-Find-Out Science. SUBJECTS: Fossils; Science. RL 2.9.

After relating how fossils are formed, Aliki suggests that children can look for fossils in limestone buildings, or create their own casts. Lively, detailed drawings enhance this fascinating text.

23 *Green Grass and White Milk.* Ill. by author. Crowell, 1974, o.p. SERIES: Let's-Read-and-Find-Out Science. SUBJECTS: Animals—Cows; Food. RL 2.7.

Aliki's sense of wonder is conveyed in language and lighthearted ink drawings showing how grass becomes milk. A child's recipe for yogurt is integral to the text.

24 *How a Book Is Made.* Ill. by author. Crowell, 1985. ISBN 0-690-04498-4. SUBJECTS: Books and reading; Careers. RL 3.8.

Aliki likes how a book feels, looks, and smells. She details the stages of a book's creation to publication. Cat characters in soft pastel cartoons even show details of color separation and printing.

25 *Long-Lost Coelacanth and Other Living Fossils.* Ill. by author. Crowell, 1973. ISBN 0-690-50478-0. SERIES: Let's-Read-and-Find-Out Science. SUBJECTS: Animals—Fish, prehistoric; Fossils, living. RL 3.1.

The drama of the 1938 discovery that the coelacanth was not extinct 70 million years ago is captured in simple language. Horses, starfish, algae, and horseshoe crabs are some of the other living fossils introduced. Children are asked to guess what living fossil the author does *not* save!

26 *My Five Senses.* Ill. by author. Crowell, 1962; Harper & Row, pap., 1984. ISBN 0-690-56763-4. SERIES: Let's-Read-and-Find-Out Science. SUBJECTS: Science; Senses. RL 2.5.

A stimulating variety of sensory experiences presented in simple black and white ink drawings and prints alternating with green and turquoise.

27 *My Hands.* Ill. by author. Crowell, 1962. ISBN 0-690-56834-7. SERIES: Let's-Read-

Aliki (cont.)

and-Find-Out Science. SUBJECTS: Human body—Hands. RL 2.8.

To illustrate the usefulness of hands, readers are asked to put their hands on their heads to see how long they can go before they have to use them. Interesting format is enlivened by ink sketches, alternately colored with yellow, orange, and red.

28 *My Visit to the Dinosaurs.* 2nd ed. Ill. by author. Crowell, hb and pap., 1985. ISBN 0-690-04423-2. SERIES: Let's-Read-and-Find-Out Science. SUBJECTS: Dinosaurs; Science. RL 3.6.

A small boy visits the natural history museum and learns about 15 common dinosaurs, as well as the work of paleontologists. Information is well presented and appealingly illustrated with ink sketches having green, turquoise, and gray washes.

29 *Story of Johnny Appleseed.* Ill. by author. Prentice-Hall, 1963, o.p. SUBJECTS: Biographies; Plants—Trees. RL 2.9.

The outline of Johnny Appleseed's life and legend is given in sympathetic terms. Bold, decorative sketches underline his friendly relations with Native Americans and animals.

30 *A Weed Is a Flower: The Life of George Washington Carver.* Ill. by author. Simon & Schuster, hb and pap., 1988. ISBN 0-671-66118-3. SUBJECTS: Biographies; Science. RL 3.0.

A laudatory outline of this talented man's life and accomplishments.

31 *Wild and Woolly Mammoths.* Ill. by author. Crowell, 1977; Harper & Row, pap., 1983. ISBN 0-690-01276-4. SERIES: Let's-Read-and-Find-Out Science. SUBJECTS: Animals, extinct. RL 3.7.

In 1901 a frozen 10,000-year-old woolly mammoth was found with 30 pounds of flower, pine needles, moss, and pine cones in its stomach. Facts about Stone Age culture relating to mammoths is woven skillfully into this fascinating account. Ink and pencil sketches are in turquoise and brown.

Allard, Harry

32 *There's a Party at Mona's Tonight.* Ill. by James Marshall. Doubleday, 1979, o.p.

SUBJECTS: Animals—Pigs—Fiction; Parties—Fiction. RL 3.0.

Potter Pig repeatedly tries to inveigle an invitation to Mona's party; however, he's not invited because of his lack of tact. Arched-framed solid colors in sketches are in pig-pink, black, yellow, and turquoise.

Allen, Laura J.

33 *Ottie and the Star.* Ill. by author. Harper & Row, 1979. ISBN 0-06-020108-8. SERIES: Early I Can Read. SUBJECTS: Animals—Otters—Fiction. RL 2.2.

A small otter encounters a shark, a dolphin, and a starfish trying to reach a star. Watercolor washes fit the watery setting well.

34 *Where Is Freddy?* Ill. by author. Harper & Row, 1986. ISBN 0-06-020098-7. SERIES: I Can Read. SUBJECTS: Animals—Mice—Fiction; Imagination—Fiction; Mystery and detective stories. RL 2.5.

When rich Mrs. Trumbly's grandson Freddy is missing, Rollo and Tweedy follow the clues of missing coat hangers, sheets, and laundry basket to track him down. This story of imagination and logic is illustrated with ink and wash drawings of expressive mice characters.

Allen, Marjorie N.

35 *One, Two, Three—Ah-Choo!* Ill. by Dick Gackenbach. Coward, McCann, 1980. ISBN 0-698-30718-6. SERIES: Break-of-Day. SUBJECTS: Allergies—Fiction; Pets—Fiction. RL 2.3.

Because of allergies, Wally cannot have the usual furry pets. Readers learn with him about hermit crabs. Gackenbach's warm, fuzzy drawings are in pumpkin and gray.

Allen, Marjorie N., and Allen, Carl

36 *Farley, Are You for Real?* Ill. by Joel Schick. Coward, McCann, 1976, o.p. SUBJECTS: Humorous stories; Magic—Fiction. RL 2.6.

The misadventures of an inept genie named Farley give Archie a taste of fear and wonder when he shrinks to two inches in height. Excellent pen and ink drawings give perspective, humor, and drama.

Allington, Richard L.

37 *Colors.* Ill. by Noel Spangler. Raintree, 1979. ISBN 0-8172-1280-9. SERIES: Beginning to Learn About. SUBJECTS: Concepts—Color. RL 2.5.
In a very didactic manner, a girl introduces colors by drawing an item that is characteristically that color. Large drawings of an apple, bluebells, a mushroom, and so forth are shown on white with a border that matches the color of the item depicted.

38 *Hearing.* Ill. by Wayne Dober. Raintree, 1980. ISBN 0-8172-1291-4. SERIES: Beginning to Learn About. SUBJECTS: Senses—Hearing; Sound. RL 2.1.
The sounds of vehicles and animals are drawn with onomatopoeic words such as "caroo," "moo," and "crackle." Collages in soft colors draw attention to a myriad of familiar sounds.

Allington, Richard L., and Krull, Kathleen

39 *Reading.* Ill. by Joel Naprstek. Raintree, 1980. ISBN 0-8172-1322-8. SERIES: Beginning to Learn About. SUBJECTS: Books and reading. RL 2.4.
A didactic text relates that one should learn to read for fun, to learn new things, to get around, and to avoid danger. Colored drawings are enclosed in large circles.

40 *Spring.* Ill. by Lynn Uhde. Raintree, 1981. ISBN 0-8172-1342-2. SERIES: Beginning to Learn About. SUBJECTS: Seasons—Spring. RL 2.1.
The reader is asked about feelings, sounds, sports, and other signs of spring. Soft watercolors show the play, flora, and fauna of the season.

41 *Time.* Ill. by Yoshi Miyake. Raintree, 1983. ISBN 0-8172-1388-0. SERIES: Beginning to Learn About. SUBJECTS: Concepts—Time. RL 2.4.
Minimal information about time is given; half of the text asks the reader didactic questions about when time goes slowly or what one would like to do in the future. Watercolor washes emphasize the patterns of clothing, walls, and a striped cat.

Anders, Rebecca

42 *Dolly the Donkey.* Orig. French by Anne-Marie Pajot, trans. by Dyan Hammarberg. Photos by Antoinette Barrere, drawings by L'Enc Matte. Carolrhoda, 1976. ISBN 0-87614-062-2. SERIES: Animal Friends. SUBJECTS: Animals—Donkeys; Pet care; Pets. RL 4.0.
Four children acquire Dolly the donkey and her cart. They learn about the joys and aggravations of caring for a new pet. Color photos alternate with black and white. Occasional drawings give close-ups of hooves or carrying baskets.

43 *Lorito the Parrot.* Orig. French by Anne-Marie Pajot, trans. by Dyan Hammarberg. Ill. by Colyann, and L'Enc Matte. Carolrhoda, 1976. ISBN 0-87614-068-1. SERIES: Animal Friends. SUBJECTS: Animals—Parrots; Pet care; Pets. RL 3.6.
Children visiting their neighbor who owns a parrot learn about its habits, beak, toes, diet, eyes, and native habitat. Black and white close-up photos alternate with color photos in this easy nonfiction book.

44 *Winslow the Hamster.* Orig. French by Anne-Marie Pajot, trans. by Dyan Hammarberg. Ill. by Rank, and L'Enc Matte. Carolrhoda, 1977. ISBN 0-87614-078-9. SERIES: Animal Friends. SUBJECTS: Animals—Hamsters; Pet care; Pets. RL 3.6.
Well-presented facts about hamster habits, history, and charm. Excellent photos with some drawings.

Anderson, Peggy P.

45 *Time for Bed, the Babysitter Said.* Ill. by author. Houghton Mifflin, 1987. ISBN 0-395-41851-8. SUBJECTS: Animals—Frogs and toads—Fiction; Baby-sitting—Fiction; Bedtime—Fiction. RL 1.6.
Joe is *very* elusive, and the baby-sitter unimaginative, when it is time for bed. A "please" finally turns the tables in this simplistic bedtime saga. Three-tone drawings have plenty of action and nice froglike touches.

Applebaum, Stan

46 *Going My Way: Nature's Hitchhikers.* Ill. by Leonard Shortall. Harcourt Brace,

Applebaum, Stan (cont.)

1976, o.p. SERIES: Let Me Read. SUBJECTS: Nature; Science. RL 2.8.

Suckerfish, oxpeckers, burrs, fleas, and bee-eaters are some of the hitchhikers introduced. Illustrative sketches have a hint of color.

Archbold, Tim

47   *The Race.* Ill. by author. Holt, 1988. ISBN 0-8050-0954-X. SUBJECTS: Concepts—Space—Fiction; Stories in rhyme. RL 2.0.

A huge dog accompanies a gloved and helmeted boy on a headlong, crazy cart ride home for dinner. This outrageous adventure is underscored by ink washed sketches of a cart whose wheels rarely touch the ground. Very limited vocabulary is expanded by the illustrations.

Arnott, Kathleen

48   *Dragons, Ogres, and Scary Things: Two African Folktales.* Ill. by Cary. Garrard, 1974. ISBN 0-8116-6978-5. SUBJECTS: Folklore—Africa; Mythical creatures. RL 2.6.

In the first tale Gatsha saves the village girls from a dragon and wild animals with his magic drum. A gnome-woman's ingenuity saves Imtali from ogres in the second tale. The charcoal colored pen and wash drawings are highlighted in gold, which detracts from their quality.

49   *Spiders, Crabs, and Creepy Crawlers: Two African Folktales.* Ill. by Bette Davis. Garrard, 1978. ISBN 0-8116-4412-X. SERIES: Imagination. SUBJECTS: Animals—Crabs—Fiction; Animals—Spiders—Fiction; Folklore—Africa. RL 2.6.

Why Flamingo stands on one leg (to escape the notice of crabs angry that he ate the King of Crabs) and why Spider lives under a stone (because he stole the magic grinding stone) are well told in simple language. The colored drawings, however, are static and dull.

Asch, Frank

50   *Bread and Honey.* Ill. by author. Parents Magazine Press, 1982; Crown, pap., 1988. ISBN 0-8193-1077-8. SERIES: Read Aloud

and Easy Reading. SUBJECTS: Animals—Bears—Fiction. RL 2.2.

Ben's picture of his mother is modified by all his animal friends until it has features taken from many animals, but his mother likes it anyway. A warm story is illustrated with large drawings in flat primary colors.

Aseltine, Lorraine; Mueller, Evelyn; and Tait, Nancy

51   *I'm Deaf and It's Okay.* Ill. by Helen Cogancherry. Whitman, 1986. ISBN 0-0075-3472-2. SERIES: Concept. SUBJECTS: Physically and mentally impaired; Senses—Hearing. RL 2.1.

The way in which ordinary situations at home or school become scary or threatening to a deaf child is most sensitively told. Excellent pencil drawings help relay the emotional impact of deafness on the child.

Averill, Esther

52   *Fire Cat.* Ill. by author. Harper & Row, 1960; pap., 1983. ISBN 0-06-020196-7. SERIES: I Can Read. SUBJECTS: Animals—Cats—Fiction. RL 2.0.

Pickles makes up for some of his mischief when he becomes a fire cat. Stylized drawings are highlighted in red, black, and sunshine yellow.

B

Baker, Barbara

53   *Digby and Kate.* Ill. by Marsha Winborn. Dutton, 1988. ISBN 0-525-44370-3. SERIES: Easy Reader. SUBJECTS: Animals—Dogs—Fiction; Friendship—Fiction. RL 1.8.

Digby and Kate, a dog and cat respectively, are very different in temperament but still best friends. Pastel patterned drawings are somewhat stylized and romantic.

54   *Digby and Kate Again.* Ill. by Marsha Winborn. Dutton, 1989. ISBN 0-525-44477-7. SUBJECTS: Animals—Cats—

Fiction; Animals—Dogs—Fiction; Friendship—Fiction. RL 1.9.
Four chapters show the relationship between the cat and dog friends—in the garden, with a new bicycle, raking leaves, and procrastinating about letter writing. Jewel-like colored drawings show the mishaps and antics of the pair.

Baker, Betty

55 *All-by-Herself*. Ill. by Catherine Stock. Greenwillow, 1980, o.p. SERIES: Read-alone. SUBJECTS: Giants—Fiction. RL 2.1.
The villagers still do not welcome All-by-Herself after she kills the ice giant because she is different. Three-tone washes on ink sketches are striking.

56 *The Big Push*. Ill. by Bonnie Johnson. Coward, McCann, 1972, o.p. SERIES: Break-of-Day. SUBJECTS: Native Americans—Hopi. RL 2.3.
The Big Push was the final break between those Hopi who accepted white influence, however reluctantly, and those who did not. Sympathetic historical treatment is illustrated with shadowy pencil drawings.

57 *Little Runner of the Longhouse*. Ill. by Arnold Lobel. Harper & Row, 1962. ISBN 0-06-020341-2. SERIES: I Can Read. SUBJECTS: Cumulative tales; Native Americans—Fiction. RL 2.5.
Little Runner tries to trade his baby brother for some adventure in imitation of his elders on New Year's Day. Lobel adds authentic details of life in the longhouse.

58 *No Help at All*. Ill. by Emily Arnold McCully. Greenwillow, 1978, o.p. SERIES: Read-alone. SUBJECTS: Folklore—Mexico; Mexico—Fiction. RL 2.4.
The West Wind puts a Mayan boy to work after rescuing him from a man-eating "thing," but returns him home when all his own efforts to escape end in disaster. Simple expressive drawings are well suited to this Mayan legend.

59 *Partners*. Ill. by Emily Arnold McCully. Greenwillow, 1978, o.p. SERIES: Read-

alone. SUBJECTS: Animals—Fiction; Friendship—Fiction. RL 2.6.
Badger and Coyote have an imperfect friendship as they hang stars, grow crops, and hunt prairie dogs. Themes and humor have a folktale base. Pastel pencils color the excellent ink drawings.

60 *Pig War*. Ill. by Robert Lopshire. Harper & Row, 1969. ISBN 0-06-020333-1. SERIES: I Can Read History. SUBJECTS: Historical fiction; United States—1783–1865—Fiction. RL 2.5.
A squabble about whether Britain or America owns a Puget Sound island is settled when a pig is paid for. Three-color comic illustrations are simple, yet effective.

61 *Rat Is Dead and Ant Is Sad*. Ill. by Mamoru Funai. Harper & Row, 1981. ISBN 0-06-020347-1. SERIES: I Can Read. SUBJECTS: Cumulative tales; Native Americans—Legends; Native Americans—Pueblos. RL 3.0.
An unusual cumulative tale includes a rat, an ant, a jay, a cottonwood tree, a sheep, a Pueblo family, and a horse. Illustrations pick up the patterns and colors of the Southwest and Pueblo culture.

62 *Three Fools and a Horse*. Ill. by Glen Rounds. Macmillan, 1975, o.p.; pap., 1987. ISBN 0-689-71123-9. SERIES: Ready-to-Read. SUBJECTS: Folklore—Native Americans; Humorous stories; Native Americans—Fiction. RL 2.4.
The Apaches' Foolish People have trouble locating a buffalo, cooking food, and staying on a horse. Rounds' comic ink drawings emphasize the People's potbellies and the looks of disgust on the horses' faces. This nonsense tale is effectively told and illustrated.

63 *The Turkey Girl*. Ill. by Harold Berson. Macmillan, 1983. ISBN 0-02-708260-1. SERIES: Ready-to-Read. SUBJECTS: Animals—Turkeys—Fiction; Behavior—Brave—Fiction. RL 2.4.
Elements of the Cinderella story are woven into this tale of an orphan girl's devotion to her turkeys. Her bravery, protecting them from a wolf, earns her a family at last. Berson's graceful line drawings have a folktale flavor.

Baker, Betty (cont.)

64 *Worthington Botts and the Steam Machine.* Ill. by Sal Murdocca. Macmillan, 1981. ISBN 0-02-708190-7. SERIES: Ready-to-Read. SUBJECTS: Books and reading—Fiction; Robots—Fiction. RL 2.7.

Worthington Botts reads *all* the time—until he builds a labor-saving robot. His continuing temptations to read are especially creative. Murdocca's four-color cartoon drawings complement the text perfectly.

Baker, Donna

65 *I Want to Be a Pilot.* Ill. by Richard Wahl. Childrens, 1978, o.p. SUBJECTS: Careers. RL 2.8.

Jimmy visits the airport with his neighbor, Captain Richards. Large print, stiff language, and full color drawings are slightly dated.

66 *I Want to Be a Police Officer.* Ill. by Richard Wahl. Childrens, 1978, o.p. SUBJECTS: Community helpers. RL 2.5.

An overview of the types of police work and training is given. Pencil and wash characters are multicultural and nonsexist.

Baker, Eugene

67 *I Want to Be a Basketball Player.* Ill. by Richard Wahl. Childrens, 1972, o.p. SUBJECTS: Sports—Basketball. RL 2.8.

From the point of view of Larry and Craig, basketball novices, basic information about technique and skill-building drills is presented. Ink and wash sketches illustrate this fairly dry text. No girls are shown in the gym class.

68 *I Want to Be a Tennis Player.* Ill. by Richard Wahl. Childrens, 1973, o.p. SUBJECTS: Sports—Tennis. RL 2.9.

As Dave and Diane get their first tennis lessons, technique and rules are introduced. Figures are drawn against an abstract background.

69 *Outdoors.* Ill. by Tom Dunnington. Creative Education, 1980, o.p. SERIES: Safety First. SUBJECTS: Safety. RL 2.4.

Basil and Rover play in dangerous situations as the reader is asked what is wrong. Rules are then stated. They are restated in three black pages at the end. Animal characters are large and colorful.

Balestrino, Philip

70 *Fat and Skinny.* Ill. by Pam Makie. Crowell, 1975, o.p. SERIES: Let's-Read-and-Find-Out Science. SUBJECTS: Science. RL 2.7.

Differences in body weight, activity, calories, and metabolism are discussed simply. Line drawings show children of all sizes eating, exercising, and playing.

71 *Hot as an Ice Cube.* Ill. by Tomie dePaola. Crowell, 1970. ISBN 0-690-40415-8. SERIES: Let's-Read-and-Find-Out Science. SUBJECTS: Science; Science experiments. RL 3.1.

Household items provide a way to test many concepts relative to temperature. Well-presented facts are illustrated in turquoise and cocoa.

72 *The Skeleton Inside You.* Ill. by True Kelley. Harper & Row, 1989. ISBN 0-690-04733-9. SERIES: Let's-Read-and-Find-Out Science. SUBJECTS: Human body—Skeleton. RL 3.0.

The function, parts, and connectors of human bones are outlined in a clear, understandable way. Large colorful framed drawings enliven the text.

Bancroft, Henrietta

73 *Down Come the Leaves.* Ill. by Nonny Hogrogian. Crowell, 1961. ISBN 0-690-24313-8. SERIES: Let's-Read-and-Find-Out. SUBJECTS: Nature; Plants—Trees; Seasons—Fall. RL 2.0.

Bancroft, from the point of view of two children playing in the leaves, focuses on the variety and wonder of trees, as she gives information about the life cycle of trees. The pencil silhouettes and leaf patterns are deceptively simple, drawn by a master illustrator.

Banel, Joseph

74 *Lee Wong, Boy Detective.* Ill. by Ed Malsberg. Garrard, 1972. ISBN 0-8116-

6967-X. SERIES: Venture. SUBJECTS: Mystery and detective stories. RL 2.6.
The boy detective finds out by observation that the naughty new neighbor, Betty, has a twin. Gray and blue highlight simple pencil drawings in this rather obvious tale.

Bang, Betsy

75 *Cucumber Stem.* Ill. by Tony Chen. Greenwillow, 1980, o.p. SERIES: Read-alone. SUBJECTS: India—Fiction. RL 2.7.
A Bengali tale of a magic cucumber and a brave man who is two fingers tall. There are stylized Indian design details.

76 *Tuntuni the Tailor Bird.* Ill. by Molly G. Bang. Greenwillow, 1978, o.p. SERIES: Read-alone. SUBJECTS: Folklore—India; India—Fiction. RL 2.7.
In the first cumulative tale, mosquitoes set off a chain of events in order to get the barber to remove a thorn from the bird Tuntuni's foot. In costume, design, characters, and vegetation, Molly Bang (daughter of the author) captures the flavor of Bengal and the humor of the tiny bird's escapades.

Bang, Molly G.

77 *Tye May and the Magic Brush.* Ill. by author. Greenwillow, 1981, o.p. SERIES: Read-alone. SUBJECTS: Folklore—China; Magic—Fiction. RL 2.2.
Although the emperor tries to steal Tye May's magic brush, he gets his just reward. Satisfying tale of magic is illustrated by delicate pencil and ink drawings.

78 *Wiley and the Hairy Man: Adapted from an American Folktale.* Ill. by author. Macmillan, 1976; pap., 1987. ISBN 0-02-708370-5. SERIES: Ready-to-Read. SUBJECTS: Folklore—Black Americans; Folklore—United States; Magic—Fiction. RL 2.8.
Following his mother's instructions, Wiley tricks the powerful Hairy Man who lives in the swamp near the Tombigbee River. Based on a well-known American folktale, this version is suitable for telling. Charcoal grays of pencil and paint are superbly apt for the Tennessee tale.

Barr, Catherine

79 *Bears In—Bears Out.* Ill. by author. Henry Z. Walck, 1967, o.p. SUBJECTS: Animals—Bears—Fiction. RL 2.9.
At Yellowstone National Park two bear cubs get a car ride unbeknownst to the family. Credible story has child appeal. Crayon and ink drawings and hand-lettered text are very effective.

80 *Gingercat's Catch.* Ill. by author. Henry Z. Walck, 1970, o.p. SUBJECTS: Animals—Cats—Fiction; India—Fiction. RL 3.3.
The competition is fierce when Gingercat tries out for a job as a watchcat at the state office in India. Hand-lettered text goes well with the yellow and gray pencil illustrations.

Barr, Jene

81 *What Will the Weather Be?* Ill. by P. J. Hoff. Whitman, 1965, o.p. SERIES: Community Helpers. SUBJECTS: Community helpers; Weather. RL 2.8.
The importance and methods of weather forecasting are preceded by a picture dictionary. Ink drawings are a little dated.

Barrett, Judi

82 *I'm too small. YOU'RE TOO BIG.* Ill. by David Rose. Atheneum, 1981, o.p. SUBJECTS: Concepts—Size; Fathers. RL 2.8.
Contrasts between father and small son are pleasantly exaggerated in framed ink and wash drawings.

Barrett, Ron

83 *Hi-Yo, Fido!* Ill. by author. Crown, 1984, o.p. SUBJECTS: Humorous stories. RL 3.3.
This modern tall tale about how dogboys and doggirls become cowboys and cowgirls has many inventive touches. Rock formations include a huge fire hydrant and a bowl for dog biscuits; dog bones are carried on the "Bony Express." Busy four-color illustrations delight the eye.

Bartlett, Margaret

84 *Where Does All the Rain Go?* Ill. by
Patricia Collins. Coward, McCann, 1973,
o.p. SERIES: Science Is What and Why.
SUBJECTS: Science; Water. RL 3.7.
The rain cycle is simply and expertly described. Ink sketches have block printed highlights in gold and royal blue.

85 *Where the Brook Begins.* Ill. by Aldren A.
Watson. Crowell, 1961. ISBN 0-690-88428-
1. SERIES: Let's-Read-and-Find-Out
Science. SUBJECTS: Nature; Science;
Water. RL 2.5.
In terms children can relate to, rhythmic
language conveys good information about the
origin of brooks. Graceful simple pencil drawings have turquoise and orange highlights.

Bason, Lillian

86 *Those Foolish Molboes!* Ill. by Margot
Tomes. Coward, McCann, 1977, o.p.
SUBJECTS: Denmark—Fiction; Folklore—
Denmark; Humorous stories. RL 2.8.
In the first of three tales in this book, the
foolish Molboes mark the watery hiding place
of the village bell on the *boat!* Tomes's excellent illustrations have a homely folk flavor
and interesting detail.

Baynton, Martin

87 *Fifty and the Fox.* Ill. by author. Crown,
1986. ISBN 0-517-56069-0. SERIES: It's
Great to Read! SUBJECTS: Tractors—Fiction. RL 2.6.
When soft-hearted Wally is assigned to rid the
farm of a fox, Fifty the tractor finds a creative
way to help. Comic drawings are bright with
sunshine and help make a tractor protagonist
plausible.

88 *Fifty and the Great Race.* Ill. by author.
Crown, 1987. ISBN 0-517-56354-1. SERIES:
It's Great to Read! SUBJECTS: Animals—
Rats—Fiction; Fairs—Fiction; Tractors—
Fiction. RL 3.4.
Some farmers make fun of the old-fashioned
tractor, Fifty, at the fair, so it is up to Fifty to
win the big tractor race to redeem himself. In
a surprise ending, Fifty's friend Norris the rat

saves the day. Colored pencil drawings are in
pale pastels.

89 *Fifty Gets the Picture.* Ill. by author.
Crown, 1987. ISBN 0-517-56355-X. SERIES:
It's Great to Read! SUBJECTS:
Friendship—Fiction; Humorous stories;
Tractors—Fiction. RL 2.8.
It turns out that Fifty the tractor has more
than one talent! He gets help from his animal
friends with his artistic triumphs. Intriguing
perspective is relayed as much by soft pastel
drawings as by text.

90 *Fifty Saves His Friend.* Ill. by author.
Crown, 1986. ISBN 0-517-56022-4. SERIES:
It's Great to Read! SUBJECTS: Animals—
Cats—Fiction; Animals—Rats—Fiction;
Tractors—Fiction. RL 3.2.
Fifty the tractor's ingenious trick scares the
cat away from his friend Norris the rat
permanently. Sunshine yellow predominates
in soft pastel drawings.

Beckman, Beatrice

91 *I Can Be a Teacher.* Photos. Childrens, hb
and pap., 1985. ISBN 0-516-41843-2.
SERIES: I Can Be. SUBJECTS: Careers.
RL 3.2.
A picture dictionary and an index accompany
information about the variety of teaching
positions, including the responsibilities both
inside and outside the classroom. Color photos are plentiful, but occasionally they look
static and posed.

Behrens, June

92 *How I Feel.* Photos by Vince Streano.
Childrens, 1973, o.p. SUBJECTS: Emotions.
RL 2.2.
Examples of situations demonstrating feelings of anger, loneliness, pride, and love are
given simply. Some of the situational photos
look posed, and the language is somewhat
stilted.

93 *I Can Be a Truck Driver.* Ill. by author.
Childrens, hb and pap., 1985. ISBN 0-516-
01848-5. SERIES: I Can Be. SUBJECTS:
Careers; Trucks. RL 3.7.
"If you've got it . . . a truck brought it."
Training and techniques are illustrated with

large sharp color photos that include women. Includes a picture dictionary, a glossary, and an index.

94 *I Can Be an Astronaut.* Photos. Childrens, hb and pap., 1984. ISBN 0-516-01837-X. SERIES: I Can Be. SUBJECTS: Careers; Science; Space travel. RL 2.6.
The need for teamwork and specialized training is emphasized in this basic career book. Excellent photos underline the opportunities in this exciting profession.

95 *Juliette Low: Founder of the Girl Scouts of America.* Photos. Childrens, 1988. ISBN 0-516-04171-1. SUBJECTS: Biographies. RL 2.8.
The creative eccentricities, organizing ability, vision, and enthusiasm of this founder of the Girl Scouts of America are well portrayed. Historic black and white photos document the text.

96 *Look at the Sea Animals.* Photos by Vince Streano. Childrens, 1975, o.p. SUBJECTS: Animals; Nature; Oceans and ocean life. RL 2.8.
A sea turtle, an octopus, a hermit crab, a dolphin, and a stingray are some of the sea animals introduced. Full color photos are faced by basic information.

Benchley, Nathaniel

97 *George the Drummer Boy.* Ill. by Don Bolognese. Harper & Row, 1977; pap., 1987. ISBN 0-06-020500-8. SERIES: I Can Read. SUBJECTS: Historical fiction; United States—Revolution—Fiction. RL 2.6.
A most unusual perspective on the beginning of the Revolutionary War told from the point of view of a British drummer boy. His feelings prior to and during the events at Concord are sketched. Red, blue, and gray drawings convey the flavor of the period.

98 *A Ghost Named Fred.* Ill. by Ben Shecter. Harper & Row, 1968; pap, 1979. ISBN 0-06-020474-5. SERIES: I Can Read Mystery. SUBJECTS: Ghost stories; Imagination—Fiction; Mystery and detective stories. RL 2.1.

George's solitary, imaginative play directs him to a deserted house while he is still dressed as an astronaut. This leads to a treasure hunt with a gentle ghost named Fred. Four-color illustrations enhance this satisfying tale.

99 *Oscar Otter.* Ill. by Arnold Lobel. Harper & Row, 1966; pap., 1980. ISBN 0-06-020471-0. SERIES: I Can Read. SUBJECTS: Animals—Otters—Fiction. RL 2.1.
Oscar's fancy slide takes him far from home—and his enemies spot him! He is chased by a procession of animals. Lively animal drawings are in earth tones against white.

100 *Red Fox and His Canoe.* Ill. by Arnold Lobel. Harper & Row, 1964; pap., 1985. ISBN 0-06-020476-1. SERIES: I Can Read. SUBJECTS: Animals—Fiction; Humorous stories; Native Americans—Fiction. RL 2.3.
Red Fox is satisfied with a small canoe after three bears, two otters, a raccoon, and a moose wreck his larger one. Action illustrations concentrate on animal misadventures and add to the tongue-in-cheek humor.

101 *Running Owl the Hunter.* Ill. by Mamoru Funai. Harper & Row, 1979. ISBN 0-06-020454-0. SERIES: I Can Read. SUBJECTS: Growing-up—Fiction; Humorous stories; Native Americans—Fiction. RL 3.2.
When all his independent hunting schemes go astray, Running Owl is assisted by an eagle who takes pity on him. Two-tone washes warm humorous ink sketches.

102 *Sam the Minuteman* Ill. by Arnold Lobel. Harper & Row, 1969; pap., 1987. ISBN 0-06-020479-6. SERIES: I Can Read History. SUBJECTS: Historical fiction; United States—Revolution—Fiction. RL 2.7.
A bare and unromanticized account of the unintentional beginning of the Revolutionary War. It is told from the point of view of the young son of a Minuteman, who tells of the suspense, fear, excitement, and pain of the encounter. Pencil drawings are historically accurate in feeling and detail.

103 *Several Tricks of Edgar Dolphin.* Ill. by Mamoru Funai. Harper & Row, 1970.

Benchley, Nathaniel (cont.)

ISBN 0-06-020468-0. SERIES: I Can Read.
SUBJECTS: Animals—Dolphins—Fiction.
RL 2.1.

Edgar the dolphin escapes his captors after adding water to his shallow tank aboard a ship. The conclusion is satisfying without creating villains. Pencil drawings have two-tone washes.

104 *Small Wolf.* Ill. by Joan Sandin. Harper
& Row, 1972. ISBN 0-06-020492-3.
SERIES: I Can Read History. SUBJECTS:
Native Americans; United States—
Colonial period—Fiction. RL 2.3.

From the perspective of a Native American boy, the consequences of the encroachment of Europeans are portrayed. Well-researched, unsentimental view of history is shown with expressive drawings.

105 *Snorri and the Strangers.* Ill. by Don
Bolognese. Harper & Row, 1976. ISBN 0-
06-020458-3. SERIES: I Can Read
History. SUBJECTS: Adventure stories;
Canada; Historical fiction. RL 2.1.

Snorri, the first white child born in North America, encounters some hostile natives before returning to Greenland with his family. Adventurous history is told in simple terms and illustrated with ink drawings having red and pale lemon washes.

106 *Strange Disappearance of Arthur Cluck.*
Ill. by Arnold Lobel. Harper & Row,
1967; pap., 1979. ISBN 0-06-020478-8.
SERIES: I Can Read Mystery. SUBJECTS:
Mystery and detective stories. RL 2.3.

Ralph the owl identifies the missing chick, Arthur, because he is the only chick who rides on someone's head. Wonderful animal expressions add zest to the pumpkin and green highlighted pencil drawings.

Bendick, Jeanne

107 *A Place to Live.* Ill. by author. Parents
Magazine Press, 1970, o.p. SERIES:
Stepping-Stone. SUBJECTS:
Communities. RL 2.3.

The needs and interrelatedness of communities—of people, plants, and animals—are discussed. This concept of community is introduced in 13 short chapters with questions interspersed to involve the reader. Lively ink drawings have avocado highlights.

108 *Shapes.* Ill. by author. Watts, 1968, o.p.
SUBJECTS: Concepts—Shape. RL 3.2.

Some shapes are flat, some three-dimensional; some names for shapes are specific and some general; shapes evoke a range of feelings. Fascinating ideas about shapes are interspersed with thought-provoking questions. Heavy ink and red drawings are somewhat dated, however.

Berenstain, Stan, and Berenstain, Jan

109 *After the Dinosaurs.* Ill. by Michael
Berenstain. Random House, 1988. ISBN
0-394-90518-0. SERIES: First Time
Readers. SUBJECTS: Animals—
Prehistoric; Stories in rhyme. RL 3.6.

Ancestors of horses, birds, elephants, sloths, and camels as well as Man are introduced, along with the exhortation that whether *we* become extinct or not is up to modern man. Information is trivialized by cartoon-like stone age people.

110 *The Bear Detectives.* Ill. by authors.
Beginner, 1975. ISBN 0-394-93127-0.
SERIES: I Can Read It All by Myself.
SUBJECTS: Animals—Bears—Fiction;
Humorous stories; Mystery and
detective stories. RL 2.5.

Pa and Snuff the sniff hound lead the Bear detectives astray repeatedly. Cartoon illustrations exaggerate the miscues.

111 *Bear Scouts.* Ill. by authors. Random
House, 1967. ISBN 0-394-90046-4.
SUBJECTS: Animals—Bears—Fiction;
Camps and camping—Fiction; Stories
in rhyme. RL 2.5.

The Scouts end up rescuing boastful Pa again and again, relying on their trusty guidebook. Cartoon illustrations help point out Pa's follies.

112 *Bears in the Night.* Ill. by authors.
Random House, 1971. ISBN 0-394-92286-
7. SERIES: Bright and Early. SUBJECTS:
Animals—Bears—Fiction; Concepts—

Space—Fiction; Emotions—Fear—
Fiction. RL 1.5.
The path through the woods to Spook Hill
leads the Bear children over, under, and
around obstacles in the landscape leading to
nocturnal adventure. This traditionally for-
matted tale is written with a simple vocabulary. Illustrations are in the blue-blacks and
yellow of night.

113 *Bears on Wheels.* Ill. by authors.
Random House, 1969. ISBN 0-394-90967-
4. SERIES: Bright and Early Counting.
SUBJECTS: Bicycles and bicycling—
Fiction; Concepts—Numbers;
Humorous stories. RL 1.2.
Antics on a unicycle provide a humorous
backdrop to this counting book with a primer
vocabulary. Acrobatic bears perform against
a very plain background.

114 *Bears' Vacation.* Ill. by authors.
Beginner, 1968, o.p. SERIES: I Can Read
It All By Myself. SUBJECTS: Animals—
Bears—Fiction; Safety—Fiction; Stories
in rhyme. RL 2.1.
Papa demonstrates everything *not* to do for
safety at the beach. Cartoon drawings exag-
gerate the action.

115 *The Berenstain Bears and the Big Road
Race.* Ill. by authors. Random House,
hb and pap., 1987. ISBN 0-394-99134-6.
SERIES: First Time Readers. SUBJECTS:
Animals—Bears—Fiction; Concepts—
Color—Fiction; Fables. RL 2.5.
The little red car putt-putts past the overconfi-
dent racers, including the green one with
dirty tricks. Typical cartoon illustrations are
in soft pastels.

116 *Berenstain Bears and the Ghost of the
Forest.* Ill. by authors. Random House,
1988. ISBN 0-394-90565-2. SERIES: First
Time Readers. SUBJECTS: Animals—
Bears—Fiction; Ghost stories; Stories in
rhyme. RL 3.5.
Papa gets more than one scare himself after
trying to scare the bear scouts on a campout
by dressing as a ghost. Forced story is illustrated with typical Berenstain cartoons.

117 *The Berenstain Bears and the Missing
Dinosaur Bone.* Ill. by authors.

Beginner, 1980. ISBN 0-394-94447-X.
SERIES: I Can Read It All By Myself.
SUBJECTS: Animals—Bears—Fiction;
Mystery and detective stories; Stories
in rhyme. RL 3.0.
With a crowd gathering to view the museum's
dinosaur bones, the Bears and their hound
dog scour the museum looking for a missing
thigh bone. The skillfully woven tale of suspense, humor, and mystery has the typical
illustrations of the Berenstains.

118 *The Berenstain Bears and the Missing
Honey.* Ill. by authors. Random House,
hb and pap., 1987. ISBN 0-394-99133-8.
SERIES: First Time Readers. SUBJECTS:
Animals—Bears—Fiction; Mystery and
detective stories; Stories in rhyme.
RL 3.1.
Following clues with Snuff their sniffer
hound in the lead, the Bears have one disaster
after another. Pastel colors catalog this humorous sleuthing.

119 *The Berenstain Bears and the Spooky Old
Tree.* Ill. by authors. Random House,
1978. ISBN 0-394-93910-7. SERIES: Bright
and Early. SUBJECTS: Animals—Bears—
Fiction; Mystery and detective stories.
RL 2.2.
A well-crafted suspense story uses very basic
vocabulary. The hazards are heightened in
cartoon illustrations.

120 *Berenstain Bears Blaze a Trail.* Ill. by
authors. Random House, 1987. ISBN 0-
394-99132-X. SERIES: First Time
Readers. SUBJECTS: Animals—Bears—
Fiction; Hiking—Fiction; Stories in
rhyme. RL 3.0.
Scout Leader Jane awards Papa and the
scouts merit badges despite Papa's failures to
follow the guidebook. Pastel cartoons underline Papa's follies.

121 *The Berenstain Bears on the Moon.* Ill.
by authors. Random House, 1985. ISBN
0-394-97180-9. SERIES: Bright and Early.
SUBJECTS: Animals—Bears—Fiction;
Space travel—Fiction; Stories in rhyme.
RL 2.5.
On the moon the Bears fly their flag, take
moon notes, and collect moon rocks for their
moon rock totes. This light introduction to

Berenstain, Stan, and Berenstain, Jan (cont.)

space travel suggests that the stars are next. Cartoon illustrations are typical of the Berenstains.

122 *The Berenstain Kids: I Love Colors.* Ill. by authors. Random House, 1987. ISBN 0-394-99129-X. SERIES: First Time Readers. SUBJECTS: Concepts—Color; Stories in rhyme. RL 2.4.
Uninspired verse reviews the colors of the rainbow and what primary colors produce each color. Pictures are typical.

123 *The Berenstains' B Book.* Ill. by authors. Random House, 1971. ISBN 0-394-92324-3. SERIES: Bright and Early. SUBJECTS: Alphabet—Fiction; Animals—Bears—Fiction; Nonsense. RL Off Spache scale.
Cumulative nonsense follows big brown bear and friends biking backward who collectively break baby bird's balloon. Flat, colorful cartoon illustrations add lots of noise and action.

124 *Big Honey Hunt.* Ill. by authors. Beginner, 1962. ISBN 0-394-90028-6. SERIES: I Can Read It All By Myself. SUBJECTS: Animals—Bears—Fiction; Stories in rhyme. RL 1.5.
Papa Bear encounters an owl, a porcupine, a skunk, and some angry bees while trying to find his own honey. Cartoon drawings are typical of the Berenstains.

125 *Bike Lesson.* Ill. by authors. Beginner, 1964, o.p. SERIES: I Can Read It All By Myself. SUBJECTS: Animals—Bears—Fiction; Bicycles and bicycling—Fiction. RL 2.0.
Papa's "lessons" end disastrously until Small Bear finally gets his first turn on the new bicycle, and he rides Papa home on his handlebars. Humor is at the expense of sound bicycle safety. Drawings are typical of the Berenstains.

126 *C Is for Clown.* Ill. by authors. Random House, 1972. ISBN 0-394-92492-4. SERIES: Bright and Early. SUBJECTS: Alphabet—Fiction; Nonsense. RL 2.7.
Clarence the clown carries a number of animals carrying things beginning with the letter "C" before the inevitable crash. Nonsense

is illustrated with cartoon characters balancing higher and higher.

127 *The Day of the Dinosaur.* Ill. by Michael Berenstain. Random House, 1987. ISBN 0-394-99130-3. SERIES: First Time Readers. SUBJECTS: Dinosaurs; Stories in rhyme. RL 2.9.
Simplistic treatment of not always accurate basic dinosaur facts has awkward grammar and a little humor. Includes a pronunciation guide. Pastel cartoon sketches are acceptable.

128 *He Bear, She Bear.* Ill. by authors. Random House, 1974. ISBN 0-394-92997-7. SERIES: Bright and Early. SUBJECTS: Animals—Bears—Fiction; Careers; Stories in rhyme. RL 2.5.
Careers for both sexes are discussed and include cowboy, astronaut, and animal trainer. Far-reaching possibilities are presented in rhyme, illustrated with cartoons.

129 *Inside, Outside, Upside Down.* Ill. by authors. Random House, 1968. ISBN 0-394-91142-3. SERIES: Bright and Early. SUBJECTS: Animals—Bears—Fiction; Concepts—Space—Fiction; Stories in rhyme. RL 1.9.
A small bear returns home to tell Mama about his adventures in a box in which he traveled to town inside, outside, upside down. Simple rhythmic language and pictures focusing on the yellow box give this story its appeal.

130 *Old Hat, New Hat.* Ill. by authors. Random House, 1970. ISBN 0-394-90669-1. SERIES: Bright and Early. SUBJECTS: Animals—Bears—Fiction; Humorous stories. RL 1.4.
A bear shopping for a new hat finds himself most satisfied with his old one. Cartoon drawings add humor.

131 *Ready, Get Set, Go!* Ill. by authors. Random House, 1988. ISBN 0-394-90564-4. SERIES: First Time Readers. SUBJECTS: Animals—Bears—Fiction; Sports—Fiction; Stories in rhyme. RL 2.7.
In family Olympic events, Papa is *best* only at sleeping. Stereotypes of Mama as timer and starter and Papa as stupid are dull. Pastel cartoons are typical of the Berenstains.

Berg, Jean

132 *Nobody Scares a Porcupine*. Ill. by
    Robert L. Jefferson. Westminster, 1969,
    o.p. SUBJECTS: Animals—Porcupines—
    Fiction; Behavior—Brave—Fiction.
    RL 3.0.
The mouse, squirrel, muskrat, beaver, and
even the porcupine are all afraid of something, but still go about their everyday tasks.
Some information about porcupines emerges.
Pencil drawings are warmed with turquoise
and yellow colored pencil.

Berger, Melvin

133 *Atoms*. Ill. by Arthur Schaffert. Coward,
    McCann, 1968, o.p. SERIES: Science Is
    What and Why. SUBJECTS: Energy;
    Science. RL 3.7.
Simple comparisons hint at possibilities for
nuclear power: The atoms in one drop of
water exceed the number of leaves on trees in
the world! Berger suggests uses for nuclear
power in transportation and electricity but
lists none of the drawbacks. Broad-stroked
drawings are in varied media.

134 *Energy from the Sun*. Ill. by Giulio
    Maestro. Crowell, 1976. ISBN 0-690-
    01056-7. SERIES: Let's-Read-and-Find-
    Out Science. SUBJECTS: Energy; Science
    experiments. RL 2.8.
Berger traces the broad outlines of how necessary energy in its various forms is to our
world. Some simple solar experiments are
included. Graphically appealing drawings alternate gray tones with four colors.

135 *Germs Make Me Sick!* Ill. by Marylin
    Hafner. Crowell, 1985; Harper & Row,
    pap., 1987. ISBN 0-690-04429-1. SERIES:
    Let's-Read-and-Find-Out Science.
    SUBJECTS: Diseases; Illness. RL 3.2.
The causes and treatment of common illnesses are discussed in this book written by a
former teacher. Lively, bright illustrations
include some cartoon humor.

136 *Simple Science Says: Take One Mirror*.
    Ill. by G. Brian Karas. Scholastic, 1989.
    ISBN 0-590-41613-8. SUBJECTS: Science
    experiments. RL 3.1.
Science experiments such as being able to
look around corners, making a rainbow or a
kaleidoscope, reading backward writing, or
doing word magic are intriguingly presented.
Pencil drawings with turquoise highlights
add humor and expand the text.

137 *Stars*. Ill. by Marilyn Miller. Coward,
    McCann, 1971, o.p. SERIES: Science Is
    What and Why. SUBJECTS: Astronomy;
    Science. RL 2.6.
In simple terms, questions about the size and
composition of stars, how far from earth they
are, and why they shine and twinkle are
answered. Red, white, and blue illustrations
are effective.

138 *Storms*. Ill. by Joseph Cellini. Coward,
    McCann, 1970, o.p. SERIES: Science Is
    What and Why. SUBJECTS: Science;
    Weather—Storms. RL 3.3.
An excellent introduction to the causes of
storms is given, as well as some simple home
observations. Black crayon and blue wash
drawings are a bit dated.

139 *Switch On, Switch Off*. Ill. by Carolyn
    Croll. Harper & Row, 1989. ISBN 0-690-
    04786-X. SERIES: Let's-Read-and-Find-
    Out Science. SUBJECTS: Electricity;
    Energy; Science experiments. RL 3.2.
Excellent well-presented information about
how electricity is generated. Bright drawings
feature familiar household scenes and pets.
There are also diagrams of distribution systems.

140 *Why I Cough, Sneeze, Shiver, Hiccup,
    and Yawn*. Ill. by Holly Keller. Crowell,
    1983. ISBN 0-690-04254-X. SERIES: Let's-
    Read-and-Find-Out Science. SUBJECTS:
    Human body—Reflexes; Science. RL 3.1.
Comic sketches show how and why the re-
flexes work, using children and a cat as
models. Well-presented information, with illustrations that lighten the tone.

Bishop, Ann

141 *Merry-Go-Riddle*. Ill. by Jerry Warshaw.
    Whitman, 1973. ISBN 0-8075-5072-8.
    SUBJECTS: Jokes and riddles. RL 2.8.
Interesting word play uses themes from the
circus and circus performers so that the
humor is cumulative. Illustrations are red
and black ink cartoons.

Bishop, Bonnie

142 *No One Noticed Ralph.* Ill. by Jack Kent. Doubleday, 1978, o.p. SERIES: Reading On My Own. SUBJECTS: Animals— Parrots—Fiction. RL 2.8.

Ralph the parrot is noticed when he gives a fire alert. Lively drawings of Ralph and people are in browns and reds.

143 *Ralph Rides Away.* Ill. by Jack Kent. Doubleday, 1979, o.p. SERIES: Reading On My Own. SUBJECTS: Animals— Parrots—Fiction; Lost, being—Fiction. RL 2.6.

Ralph gets lost in the zoo on his first adventurous picnic in the park with Mr. and Mrs. Muggs. The creative solution to his restitution to the family is matched by bright, comic four-color illustrations.

Bishop, Claire

144 *Georgette.* Ill. by Ursula Landshoff. Coward, McCann, 1973, o.p. SERIES: Break-of-Day. SUBJECTS: Animals— Chickens—Fiction. RL 2.5.

Georgette the chicken saves her neck with her dancing abilities in a tale of romance and suspense in a Paris apartment. Ink sketches add flavor to the setting.

145 *Truffle Pig.* Ill. by Kurt Wiese. Coward, McCann, 1971, o.p. SERIES: Break-of-Day. SUBJECTS: Animals—Pigs—Fiction; France—Fiction. RL 3.0.

The marvelous piglet Marcel saves his skin by his ability to dig for the elusive and costly truffles. The tale is told in simple language but not a controlled vocabulary. Distinctly French in character, illustrations are in ink with blue and yellow colored pencil.

Blakely, Cindy, and Drinkwater, Suzanne

146 *The Look Out! Book: A Child's Guide to Street Safety.* Ill. by Barbara Klunder. Scholastic, 1988. ISBN 0-590-40962-X. SUBJECTS: Safety. RL 2.9.

Bright and action-filled sketches of animal children lighten the lists of rules for personal and traffic safety. There are a lot of "don'ts," and the illustrations are almost too busy.

Blassingame, Wyatt

147 *Bowleg Bill, Seagoing Cowboy.* Ill. by Herman Vestal. Garrard, 1976, o.p. SUBJECTS: Humorous stories; Tall tales. RL 3.0.

Sailing with 10,000 rabbits he had lassoed, Bowleg Bill has his hands full when they reproduce faster than the ship is moving. Bowleg Bill also discovers the thrill of whale riding. Runaway rabbits provide the most visual interest. The illustrations are in turquoise, orange, and gray.

148 *How Davy Crockett Got a Bearskin Coat.* Ill. by Mimi Korach. Garrard, 1972. ISBN 0-8116-4035-3. SERIES: Tall Tales. SUBJECTS: Folklore—United States; Humorous stories; Tall tales. RL 2.3.

While trying to replace his moth-eaten coat, Davy ends up being chased by his quarry, a bear. When he catches the bear and knots his tail through a hole in a tree, the bear runs on, skinless! Comic pencil drawings add to the fun of this tall tale.

149 *Pecos Bill and the Wonderful Clothesline Snake.* Ill. by Herman Vestal. Garrard, 1978. ISBN 0-8116-4046-9. SERIES: American Folktales. SUBJECTS: Folklore—United States; Humorous stories; Tall tales. RL 3.7.

Glass snakes that shatter and reassemble attached to other snakes, snakes with bells instead of rattles, snakes wild as broncos, and pancake snakes sunning under syrup and blueberries—these are some of the inventions of a tall tale enhanced by turquoise and gold drawings.

150 *Pecos Bill Catches a Hidebehind.* Ill. by Herman Vestal. Garrard, 1977. ISBN 0-8116-4045-0. SERIES: American Folktales. SUBJECTS: Folklore—United States; Humorous stories; Tall tales. RL 2.8.

After a roperite and a telescopo help Pecos Bill and Sluefoot Sue capture a hidebehind for a zoo, they feel sorry for the shy animal and send a roperite instead. Simple turquoise and orange illustrations add to the humor of this outrageous tall tale.

Blocksma, Norma

151 *Best Dressed Bear*. Ill. by Sandra Kalthoff. Childrens, 1984, o.p. SERIES: Just One More. SUBJECTS: Animals—Bears—Fiction; Animals—Fiction; Stories in rhyme. RL 1.9.
Bear is dressed formally for a dance—but forgets his pants. Language is rhythmic and simple, but not predictable. Full color drawings of friendly animals add humor to a tale that uses an 80 word vocabulary.

Boegehold, Betty

152 *Chipper's Choices*. Ill. by Jim Arnosky. Coward, McCann, 1981, o.p. SUBJECTS: Animals—Chipmunks—Fiction; Animals—Fiction. RL 3.0.
Chipper the chipmunk tells stories about his friends Mole, Jay, Toad, and Squirrel in which the animals argue about who is boss, encounter a scary noise, and share riddles and some poems. Soft pencil drawings focus on nuts and individual animals.

153 *Here's Pippa Again*. Ill. by Cyndy Szekeres. Knopf, 1975. ISBN 0-394-83090-3. SERIES: Read-aloud/Read-alone. SUBJECTS: Animals—Fiction; Animals—Mice—Fiction; Growing-up—Fiction. RL 2.3.
Pippa is often restless and ready for adventure. She wants to learn how to swim, play in the snow, find a pet, and have a party. Her animal friends' antics are shown in charming pencil drawings.

154 *Hurray for Pippa!* Ill. by Cyndy Szekeres. Knopf, 1980, o.s.i. SERIES: Read-aloud/Read-alone. SUBJECTS: Animals—Fiction; Animals—Mice—Fiction. RL 2.3.
Testing under the chin with a buttercup, cleaning out old toys, teaching a rabbit to play games, and playing dress-up occupy Pippa and her animal friends. Joyful pencil drawings suit the homely adventures.

155 *Pippa Pops Out!* Ill. by Cyndy Szekeres. Knopf, 1979, o.s.i.; pap., 1980. ISBN 0-440-46865-5. SERIES: Read-aloud/Read-alone. SUBJECTS: Animals—Mice—Fiction; Friendship—Fiction; Growing-up—Fiction. RL 2.8.
The fears and feelings of inadequacy, as well as the warmth of friendship, are celebrated. Pencil drawings show expressive mice, squirrels, ducklings, and crickets.

156 *Small Deer's Magic Tricks*. Ill. by Jacqueline Chwast. Coward, McCann, 1977, o.p. SERIES: Break-of-Day. SUBJECTS: Animals—Deer—Fiction; Folklore—Indonesia. RL 2.5.
Four traditional Indonesian trickster tales about the tiny mouse deer, Kanchil. In one tale he outwits a tiger, some crocodiles, a wild pig, and an elephant. Comic-style ink drawings are mediocre.

157 *Three to Get Ready*. Ill. by Mary Chalmers. Harper & Row, 1965. ISBN 0-06-020551-2. SERIES: I Can Read. SUBJECTS: Animals—Cats—Fiction; Sibling rivalry—Fiction; Siblings—Fiction. RL 1.9.
Mother Cat rescues and comforts her children Gigi, George, and Ginger as they explore the world at night outside their yard. Soft drawings in gray, green, and rose accompany this reassuring tale.

Bonsall, Crosby

158 *The Amazing, the Incredible, Super Dog*. Ill. by author. Harper & Row, 1986. ISBN 0-06-020591-1. SUBJECTS: Animals—Cats—Fiction; Animals—Dogs—Fiction. RL 2.7.
Willy the cat and his mistress do all sorts of tricks trying to train Super Dog, a cuddly puppy who yawns, watches butterflies, and "plays dead." Meanwhile poor Willy's accomplishments go unrecognized. Simple ink sketches are colorful with intriguing design and laced with humor.

159 *And I Mean It, Stanley*. Ill. by author. Harper & Row, 1974, o.p.; pap., 1984. ISBN 0-06-444046-X. SERIES: Early I Can Read. SUBJECTS: Animals—Dogs—Fiction; Imagination—Fiction. RL 1.7.

Bonsall, Crosby (cont.)

A small boy's creations using things found in an alley are ruined when his pet, Shaggy Stanley, finally appears. Delightful ink drawings add warmth to an inventive tale.

160 *The Case of the Cat's Meow.* Ill. by author. Harper & Row, 1965, o.p.; pap., 1978. ISBN 0-06-444017-6. SERIES: I Can Read. SUBJECTS: Friendship—Fiction; Mystery and detective stories. RL 2.2.

Four friends try to find the missing cat, Mildred, using cats, dogs, food, and alarms. Characters in this series are interesting individuals. Line drawings are colored with gray, red, salmon, and pumpkin.

161 *Case of the Dumb Bells.* Ill. by author. Harper & Row, 1966, o.p.; pap., 1982. ISBN 0-06-444030-3. SERIES: I Can Read. SUBJECTS: Friendship—Fiction; Mystery and detective stories. RL 2.2.

Wizard, Skinny, Tubby, and Snitch have some difficulties with their phone system, cleverly conveyed by one-sided telephone conversations with irate parents. Excellent ink drawings convey relationships sympathetically.

162 *The Case of the Hungry Stranger.* Ill. by author. Harper & Row, 1963, o.p.; pap., 1980. ISBN 0-06-444026-5. SERIES: I Can Read Mystery. SUBJECTS: Clubs—Fiction; Friendship—Fiction; Mystery and detective stories. RL 2.4.

After agreeing that the blueberry pie thief would have a blue smile, the gang gives the smile test to the mailman, paper boy, ice cream man, a policeman, and a neighbor without success. Dialogue, personality, humor, and action are enhanced by expressive line drawings.

163 *Case of the Scaredy Cats.* Ill. by author. Harper & Row, 1971, o.p.; pap. 1984. ISBN 0-06-444047-8. SERIES: I Can Read. SUBJECTS: Friendship—Fiction; Mystery and detective stories. RL 1.7.

During the fight between the boys in the gang and the girls who try to take the clubhouse over, little scaredy-cat Annie is lost and all join in to try to find her. Warm, reassuring, realistic ending is enhanced by ink drawings with marvelous cross-hatched patterns.

164 *The Day I Had to Play with My Sister.* Ill. by author. Harper & Row, 1972, o.p.; pap., 1988. ISBN 0-06-444117-2. SERIES: Early I Can Read. SUBJECTS: Siblings—Fiction. RL 1.6.

A small sister's way of playing hide-and-seek does not satisfy her older brother. Appealing cross-hatched ink drawings with pale rose and gray show the antics of a devoted shaggy dog.

165 *Mine's the Best.* Ill. by author. Harper & Row, 1973; pap., 1984. ISBN 0-06-020578-4. SERIES: Early I Can Read. SUBJECTS: Behavior—Argumentative—Fiction; Friendship—Fiction. RL 1.5.

This classic argument between friends is resolved with the boys aligned together against a new antagonist—a girl. Visually fascinating inked patterned drawings of a parade of boardwalk people are in green and brown.

166 *Piggle.* Ill. by author. Harper & Row, 1973. ISBN 0-06-020580-6. SERIES: I Can Read. SUBJECTS: Dreams—Fiction; Imagination—Fiction; Nonsense. RL 1.6.

Bear teaches Homer how to play "Piggle" (making nonsense rhymes), after his overtures are rejected by Duck, Rabbit, Pig, and his sisters. Charming, witty nonsense is illustrated with warm cross-hatched ink drawings during Homer's dream, and pale pink and brown while he is awake.

167 *Tell Me Some More.* Ill. by Fritz Siebel. Harper & Row, 1961. ISBN 0-06-020601-2. SERIES: I Can Read. SUBJECTS: Books and Reading—Fiction; Imagination—Fiction; Libraries—Fiction. RL 2.0.

Andrew captures Tim's imagination with tales of elephants, camels, mountains and fountains, moons and spoons, rings and kings—which can be held in the hand or carried under his arm (in books)! The boys are drawn in ink, the imaginings are in color in this captivating tale.

168 *What Spot?* Ill. by author. Harper & Row, 1963, o.p.; pap., 1980. ISBN 0-06-444027-3. SERIES: I Can Read. SUBJECTS: Animals—Birds—Fiction; Animals—Walruses—Fiction. RL 2.3.

Some polar animals puzzle over a mysterious black spot in the snow. This imaginative tale is illustrated with textured tones in pencil.

Bourne, Miriam A.

169 *Four-Ring Three.* Ill. by Cyndy Szekeres. Coward, McCann, 1973, o.p. SUBJECTS: Historical fiction; Plays—Fiction; Telephones—Fiction. RL 3.3.

Frank and his sister Martha, with her friend Jean, convince their father to get a new-fangled telephone by producing a play. Characterizations, dialogue, and historical detail all ring true. The antics of cats and children enliven the period drawings.

170 *Second Car in Town.* Ill. by Ray Burns. Coward, McCann, 1972, o.p. SERIES: Break-of-Day. SUBJECTS: Cars—Fiction; Historical fiction. RL 2.4.

Garbed in a duster, Ellen felt like a princess on her first car ride. A feeling for the fear, wonder, and hazards of the new contraption is conveyed. Good ink sketches capture the action and humor.

Bowden, Joan C.

171 *Bean Boy.* Ill. by Sal Murdocca. Macmillan, 1978, o.p. SERIES: Ready-to-Read. SUBJECTS: Cumulative tales. RL 1.9.

The adventures of a child carved from a bean by a childless couple are told in original cumulative fashion. Green and orange drawings have some folk flavor.

172 *Strong John.* Ill. by Sal Murdocca. Macmillan, 1979, o.p. SERIES: Ready-to-Read. SUBJECTS: Folklore. RL 1.9.

John's hard work is repaid by worthless gifts; when he uses them to help a queen, he is richly rewarded. The characters are more flat and the rhythm of the tale less rich than in traditional tales. Turquoise and orange drawings are mediocre.

Bozzo, Maxine Z.

173 *Toby in the Country, Toby in the City.* Ill. by Frank Modell. Greenwillow, 1982. ISBN 0-688-00917-4. SUBJECTS: City and town life—Fiction; Farm and country life—Fiction. RL 2.0.

The similarities between the life-style of a country boy and a city boy are emphasized, from school and play to enjoyment of the seasons. Excellent comic watercolor illustrations add sparkle to the simple text.

Bram, Elizabeth

174 *Woodruff and the Clocks.* Ill. by author. Dial, hb and pap., 1980. ISBN 0-8037-9633-1. SERIES: Easy-to-Read. SUBJECTS: Animals—Cats—Fiction; Clocks—Fiction. RL 2.6.

Woodruff finds out that his neglected cat, Muffin, is more important to him than his fascination with clocks in the first of four stories in this book. Flat colors highlight simple ink drawings.

Brandenberg, Franz

175 *Aunt Nina and Her Nephews and Nieces.* Ill. by Aliki. Greenwillow, 1983. ISBN 0-688-01870-X. SUBJECTS: Animals—Cats—Fiction; Birthdays—Fiction; Family life—Fiction. RL 2.5.

Aunt Nina's house provides more adventure than the zoo, the toy shop, the theater, the haunted house, and a treasure hunt combined when her nieces and nephews come to celebrate her cat's birthday. Lively watercolor and ink drawings add to the action.

176 *Everyone Ready?* Ill. by Aliki. Greenwillow, 1979, o.p. SERIES: Read-alone. SUBJECTS: Animals—Mice—Fiction; Family life—Fiction. RL 2.2.

The Fieldmouse family is so busy they have trouble catching the train all at the same time. Delicate pen and ink drawings with washes of pink and green match the warmth and humor with human parallels.

177 *Leo and Emily and the Dragon.* Ill. by Aliki. Greenwillow, 1984. ISBN 0-688-02532-3. SERIES: Read-alone. SUBJECTS: Baby-sitting—Fiction; Hiking—Fiction; Imagination—Fiction. RL 2.1.

Leo and Emily have a long hike, complete with picnic, cave, sleeping bags, and sunbathing. When "boring" Harold baby-sits that night, they have another exhausting and imaginative hike indoors! Lively drawings in spring green and orange capture the delights, fears, and exhaustion well.

Brandenberg, Franz (cont.)

178 *Leo and Emily's Big Ideas*. Ill. by Aliki. Greenwillow, 1982. ISBN 0-688-00755-4. SERIES: Read-alone. SUBJECTS: Friendship—Fiction; Play—Fiction. RL 2.3.

Leo and Emily's escapades include dressing up to scare people and making wet tracks and "back" marks all over the garage. The imaginative text and delicate, lively illustrations capture the spirit of adventure in everyday neighborhood play.

179 *Leo and Emily's Zoo*. Ill. by Yossi Abolafia. Greenwillow, 1988. ISBN 0-688-07457-X. SUBJECTS: Family life—Fiction. RL 2.5.

Leo and Emily's backyard zoo is disappointing until some "zoo animals" appear next door. This is a very refreshing story enhanced by lively watercolors of children and animals.

180 *Nice New Neighbors*. Ill. by Aliki. Greenwillow, 1977; Scholastic, pap., 1980. ISBN 0-688-84105-8. SERIES: Read-alone. SUBJECTS: Animals—Mice—Fiction; Friendship—Fiction; Moving, household—Fiction. RL 2.4.

Rejected by the other children on the street, the mice children decide to put on a play to attract their new neighbors' attention. Diminutive ink and wash drawings add to the charm of this book.

181 *A Robber! A Robber!* Ill. by Aliki. Greenwillow, 1976, o.p. SUBJECTS: Animals—Cats—Fiction; Emotions—Fear—Fiction. RL 3.1.

The sound of snoring from their bottom bunk beds scares Edward and Elizabeth, who are in their respective rooms. In the morning they find out that visitors Uncle Peter and Aunt Ann were sharing their room. Darker penciled night scenes convey just enough feeling of fear.

182 *Six New Students*. Ill. by Aliki. Greenwillow, 1978, o.p. SERIES: Read-alone. SUBJECTS: Animals—Mice—Fiction; School stories. RL 2.6.

Ferdinand the mouse's creative first-grade teacher introduces him to all the subjects he does not expect to enjoy in first grade. Gentle humor has marvelous small pastel watercolor mice illustrations.

183 *What Can You Make of It?* Ill. by Aliki. Greenwillow, 1977, o.p. SERIES: Read-alone. SUBJECTS: Animals—Mice—Fiction; Circuses—Fiction; Moving, household—Fiction. RL 3.7.

The Fieldmouse family moves in seven vans because of all their "rubbish": magazines, toilet paper tubes, milk and egg cartons, and so on. However, they find creative uses for all their treasures. Whimsical ink sketches have yellow, orange, gray, and green colored pencil highlights.

Branley, Franklyn M.

184 *Beginning of the Earth*. Rev. ed. Ill. by Giulio Maestro. Crowell, hb and pap., 1972. ISBN 0-690-12988-2. SERIES: Let's-Read-and-Find-Out. SUBJECTS: Astronomy; Geology; Science. RL 2.9.

Dark, abstract designs with ink and washes of black and gray with highlights of fuchsia and blue aptly illustrate Branley's speculation.

185 *North, South, East, and West*. Ill. by Robert Galster. Crowell, 1966. ISBN 0-690-58609-4. SERIES: Let's-Read-and-Find-Out. SUBJECTS: Concepts—Direction; Science. RL 2.5.

After beginning with right and left, up and down, Branley invites children to learn compass directions by using their shadows. The printed graphics illustrate concepts extremely well and have excellent eye appeal.

186 *Oxygen Keeps You Alive*. Ill. by Don Madden. Crowell, 1971, o.p.; Harper & Row, pap., 1972. ISBN 0-06-445021-X. SERIES: Let's-Read-and-Find-Out Science. SUBJECTS: Air; Science; Science experiments—Air. RL 3.0.

The text underlines the importance of oxygen to animals, birds, fish, and plants, but especially people—at high altitudes, in space, or under the sea—at every moment of life. Drawings complement the text to show how the lungs work.

187 *The Planets in Our Solar System*. Rev. ed. Ill. by Don Madden. Crowell, hb and pap., 1987. ISBN 0-690-04581-6. SERIES: Let's-Read-and-Find-Out. SUBJECTS: Astronomy; Science. RL 2.8.

Basic size and distance between the planets in our solar system are introduced, with patterns and suggestions for making two models. Children and pets are included in the ink drawings to humanize the science facts.

188 *Rain and Hail.* Ill. by Harriett Barton. Crowell, 1983. ISBN 0-690-04353-8. SERIES: Let's-Read-and-Find-Out. SUBJECTS: Science; Weather. RL 3.2.
Information about both rain and hail is logically presented. Illustrations and type are in royal blue.

189 *The Sky Is Full of Stars.* Ill. by Felicia Bond. Crowell, 1981; Harper & Row, pap., 1983. ISBN 0-690-04123-3. SERIES: Let's-Read-and-Find-Out Science. SUBJECTS: Astronomy; Science. RL 2.7.
Branley takes children out at night—with pet and blanket—to observe four common constellations, and gives directions for reproducing the configurations with a coffee can and a flashlight. Blue, light green, and various shades of gray show the children and the stars.

190 *Snow Is Falling.* Rev. ed. Ill. by Holly Keller. Crowell, hb and pap., 1986. ISBN 0-690-04548-4. SERIES: Let's-Read-and-Find-Out. SUBJECTS: Seasons—Winter; Weather—Snow. RL 2.1.
The benefits as well as the hardships of snow to plants, animals, and people are presented. Details of wildlife winters and playing in the snow are drawn in ink against a sparkling blue sky.

191 *The Sun: Our Nearest Star.* Rev. ed. Ill. by Don Madden. Crowell, hb and pap., 1988. ISBN 0-690-04678-2. SERIES: Let's-Read-and-Find-Out. SUBJECTS: Astronomy; Science. RL 2.8.
Besides information about the sun, a simple plant experiment and the idea that coal and oil are stored-up solar energy are introduced. Ink drawings in sky blue, apple green, and gray highlight and lighten the text.

192 *Sunshine Makes the Seasons.* Rev. ed. Ill. by Giulio Maestro. Crowell, 1985; Harper & Row, pap., 1986. ISBN 0-690-04482-8. SERIES: Let's-Read-and-Find-Out Science. SUBJECTS: Seasons; Science. RL 2.7.
Good information about seasonal change is logically presented and related to a child's experience. Textured crayon against black is very effective.

193 *Tornado Alert.* Ill. by Giulio Maestro. Crowell, 1988. ISBN 0-690-04686-3. SERIES: Let's-Read-and-Find-Out. SUBJECTS: Weather—Storms. RL 3.3.
Exceptionally well presented information about tornados is included along with simple safety precautions to follow during a tornado. Softly textured colored drawings are also factual but reassuring.

194 *Volcanoes.* Ill. by Marc Simont. Crowell, 1985; Harper & Row, pap., 1986. ISBN 0-690-04431-3. SERIES: Let's-Read-and-Find-Out Science. SUBJECTS: Geology; Science. RL 3.2.
The examples of Pompeii, Krakatoa, and Mount St. Helen's provide good information about the movement of tectonic plates and associated earthquake/volcanic activity. Excellent watercolors show the above events, simple diagrams, and geologists at work.

195 *Weight and Weightlessness.* Ill. by Graham Booth. Crowell, 1971. ISBN 0-690-87329-8. SERIES: Let's-Read-and-Find-Out Science. SUBJECTS: Concepts—Weight; Science. RL 2.6.
Well-described concepts of weight and weightlessness are illustrated with simple, decorative ink sketches.

196 *What Makes Day and Night.* Rev. ed. Ill. by Helen Borten. Crowell, hb and pap., 1986. ISBN 0-690-04524-7. SERIES: Let's-Read-and-Find-Out Science. SUBJECTS: Astronomy; Science. RL 2.2.
As a child turns in a circle before a lamp, so the earth turns in relation to the sun, creating light and dark periods we call day and night. Basic information is well illustrated with strong black prints on white or a solid color.

197 *What the Moon Is Like.* Rev. ed. Photos. Ill. by True Kelley. Crowell, 1986; Harper & Row, pap., 1986. ISBN 0-690-87860-5. SERIES: Let's-Read-and-Find-Out. SUBJECTS: Astronomy; Science. RL 2.7.
Updated basic information about the moon is excellent. Illustrations are cutesy pastels, smudgy sketches, and mediocre photos.

Brenner, Barbara

198 *Baltimore Orioles.* Ill. by J. Winslow Higginbottom. Harper & Row, 1974. ISBN 0-06-020665-9. SERIES: I Can Read. SUBJECTS: Animals—Birds. RL 1.8.
Besides mating and nesting habits, Brenner includes hazards in the lives of young orioles. Well-presented information is accompanied by appealing illustrations.

199 *Beef Stew.* Ill. by John E. Johnson. Knopf, 1965, o.p. SERIES: Read-alone. SUBJECTS: Grandparents—Fiction. RL 2.5.
Nicky cannot seem to get any friends to come over for dinner for beef stew, but he gets a nice surprise. Four-color illustrations show Nicky's friends in school and in the neighborhood.

200 *A Dog I Know.* Ill. by Fred Brenner. Harper & Row, 1983. ISBN 0-06-020685-3. SUBJECTS: Animals—Dogs—Fiction; Pets—Dogs—Fiction. RL 2.3.
The special qualities of a boy's shaggy mutt are told in the first person. Brown pencil with washes focus on the brave-with-bear, scared-of-paper beloved pet.

201 *Nicky's Sister.* Ill. by John E. Johnson. Knopf, 1966, o.p. SERIES: Read-alone. SUBJECTS: Behavior—Running away—Fiction; Sibling rivalry—Fiction. RL 2.3.
Nicky prefers a hamster to a pesky baby sister until she is threatened by a bully. Details of home life are in ink with a three-color wash.

202 *Wagon Wheels.* Ill. by Don Bolognese. Harper & Row, 1978; pap., 1984. ISBN 0-06-020669-1. SERIES: I Can Read History. SUBJECTS: Behavior—Brave; Frontier and pioneer life; Historical fiction. RL 2.7.
This amazing adventure story of homesteading in the Kansas Territory was based on events in the lives of the Muldie boys and their father. Their resourcefulness and courage in facing starvation, grief, and a prairie fire are depicted. Effective pencil drawings have three-tone washes.

Brinkloe, Julie

203 *Gordon Goes Camping.* Ill. by author. Doubleday, 1975, o.p. SUBJECTS: Animals—Bears—Fiction; Camps and camping—Fiction. RL 2.1.
Gordon needs his friend Marvin's advice—and company—when he goes on his first camping trip. Patterned ink drawings have a green contrasting wash.

Broekel, Ray

204 *Experiments with Air.* Photos. Childrens, hb and pap., 1988. ISBN 0-516-01213-4. SERIES: New True. SUBJECTS: Science experiments—Air. RL 2.5.
A narrative describing the properties of air leads into simple experiments that clarify the text. The experiments are usually very simple, although two require adult supervision. Full color photos help readers follow the experiment instructions.

205 *Experiments with Water.* Photos. Childrens, hb and pap., 1988. ISBN 0-516-01215-0. SERIES: New True. SUBJECTS: Science experiments—Water; Water. RL 3.0.
Experiments exploring a dozen properties of water, from magnification to capillary action, are introduced in separate short chapters. Photos are exceptional.

Bronin, Andrew

206 *Gus and Buster Work Things Out.* Ill. by Cyndy Szekeres. Coward, McCann, 1975, o.p. SERIES: Break-of-Day. SUBJECTS: Animals—Raccoons—Fiction; Siblings—Fiction. RL 2.4.
Squabbling over toys or the top bunk, or even how to eat properly, two brothers settle their differences by playing each other's favorite games—football and checkers. Soft pencil drawings with pale yellow warm this reassuring tale.

207 *I Know a Football Player.* Ill. by Charles Dougherty. Putnam, 1973, o.p. SERIES: Community Helpers. SUBJECTS: Careers;

Community helpers; Sports—Football.
RL 2.9.
A boy's neighbor, Jim, is a professional football player and takes him behind the scenes. Bare-bones information is given. Illustrations in gray and red are static.

Brown, Marc

208 *The Silly Tail Book.* Ill. by author.
Parents Magazine Press, 1983; Crown, pap., 1987. ISBN 0-8193-1109-X.
SUBJECTS: Mythical creatures—Fiction; Stories in rhyme. RL 2.2.
Whimsical animals with unexpected tails in unexpected places provide the humor. Simple language has a pleasing cadence. Illustrations are in flat pastel colors.

Brownell, M. Barbara

209 *Busy Beavers.* Photos and drawings.
National Geographic, 1988. ISBN 0-87044-0074-2. SERIES: Books for Young Readers. SUBJECTS: Animals—Beavers; Nature. RL 3.6.
This photoessay has good information about beavers. Especially well done are photos of a beaver swimming in clear water and of a beaver nursing her kit.

Bulla, Clyde R.

210 *Daniel's Duck.* Ill. by Joan Sandin.
Harper & Row, 1977; pap., 1982. ISBN 0-06-020909-7. SERIES: I Can Read.
SUBJECTS: Family life—Fiction; Wood carving—Fiction. RL 2.2.
Everyone in Daniel's family spends long winter nights making crafts for the spring fair. When Daniel's carved duck evokes laughter, he thinks, at first, that people are laughing *at* him. Watercolor illustrations primarily in grays and green give rich details of Tennessee Appalachian life.

211 *Poor Boy, Rich Boy.* Ill. by Marcia Sewell. Harper & Row, 1979. ISBN 0-06-020897-X. SERIES: I Can Read. SUBJECTS: Orphans—Fiction. RL 1.7.
Orphaned by war, Coco is raised by a baker, Rosa, but later claimed by a rich and doting

uncle. An unusual and touching story about worldly values is simply illustrated with light tones highlighting expressive ink drawings by a noted illustrator.

212 *A Tree Is a Plant.* Ill. by Lois Lignell.
Crowell, 1960. ISBN 0-690-83529-9.
SERIES: Let's-Read-and-Find-Out.
SUBJECTS: Nature; Plants—Trees; Science. RL 2.0.
Children follow an apple tree through the seasons. Boldly outlined sketches with apple green, gray, and red are in tune with the simply outlined information.

Buller, Jon, and Schade, Susan

213 *Space Rock.* Ill. by Jon Buller. Random House, 1988. ISBN 0-394-99384-5. SERIES: Step into Reading. SUBJECTS: Science fiction. RL 2.5.
Dogged, trite story of a purple glob from the planet Kal-dor that helps a boy do homework and provides a "space rock" concert before returning home. Stiff cartoon drawings have bright watercolors.

Bunting, Eve

214 *The Big Red Barn.* Ill. by Howard Knotts. Harcourt Brace, 1979, o.p.; pap., 1979. ISBN 0-15-611938-2. SERIES: Let Me Read. SUBJECTS: Barns—Fiction; Farm and country life—Fiction; Stepparents—Fiction. RL 3.0.
The hayloft is where a boy mourned his mother's death, so the barn fire represents a big loss to which he must adjust—with the help of an understanding grandpa. Knotts's sympathetic pencil drawings add to the feelings of home.

215 *Goose Dinner.* Ill. by Howard Knotts. Harcourt Brace, 1981, o.p. SERIES: Let Me Read. SUBJECTS: Animals—Geese—Fiction; Farm and country life—Fiction. RL 3.4.
Because Goose rules the barnyard, the family does not appreciate her until she—and Dad—fend off a marauding raccoon. Warm pencil drawings glow.

Bunting, Eve (cont.)

216 *The Robot Birthday*. Ill. by Marie
DeJohn. Dutton, 1980. ISBN 0-525-38542-
8. SERIES: Smart Cat. SUBJECTS:
Birthdays—Fiction; Moving,
household—Fiction; Robots—Fiction.
RL 2.3.

A birthday with a new house and sitter turns
out to be the most exciting one ever, thanks to
a robot birthday present. Pencil drawings
have a turquoise wash.

Burt, Denise

217 *Our Family Vacation*. Photos by
Haworth Bartram. Gareth Stevens,
1985. ISBN 0-918831-29-6. SERIES:
Growing Up. SUBJECTS: Seashore—
Fiction; Vacations—Fiction. RL 2.8.

Luis is shown packing for a trip; on the next
page he is catching crabs on the beach, with
no textual or visual transition. The full page
color photos are somewhat posed looking, but
give some feeling of sandcastles and shells.

Burton, Jane

218 *Caper the Kid*. Photos by author.
Random House, 1988. ISBN 0-394-99962-
2. SERIES: How Your Pet Grows!
SUBJECTS: Animals—Goats; Nature.
RL 3.1.

The growth of a pair of white-socked kids is
detailed, from their food and play to exploration and climbing abilities. Excellent color
photos capture the glint of sunlight, the sparkle of an eye, and the texture of a furry coat.

219 *Chester the Chick*. Photos by author.
Random House, hb and pap., 1988. ISBN
0-394-99640-2. SERIES: How Your Pet
Grows! SUBJECTS: Animals—Chickens;
Pets. RL 3.3.

The first year of a chick's life is described.
Exceptional photos depict each stage in
growth.

220 *Dabble the Duckling*. Photos by author.
Random House, 1988. ISBN 0-394-99960-
6. SERIES: How Your Pet Grows!
SUBJECTS: Animals—Ducks; Nature.
RL 2.7.

With excellent color photos the step-by-step

development of a duck from egg to adulthood
is illustrated.

221 *Fancy the Fox*. Photos by author.
Random House, 1988. ISBN 0-394-99963-
0. SERIES: How Animals Grow! SUBJECTS:
Animals—Foxes; Nature. RL 3.4.

The development of three orphan kits brought
up in an animal shelter is traced with excellent
color photos and interesting details of their
learning to fend for themselves in the woods.

222 *Freckles the Rabbit*. Photos by author.
Random House, hb and pap., 1988. ISBN
0-394-99639-9. SERIES: How Your Pet
Grows! SUBJECTS: Animals—Rabbits;
Pets. RL 2.9.

The development of Freckles the rabbit is
followed, from naked newborn to having her
first litter. Exceptional photos of the lop-
eared black and white rabbit are included,
along with pictures of the cat, dog, and wild
rabbit she encounters.

223 *Ginger the Kitten*. Photos by author.
Random House, hb and pap., 1988. ISBN
0-394-99638-0. SERIES: How Your Pet
Grows! SUBJECTS: Animals—Cats; Pets—
Cats. RL 3.3.

The weekly growth and exploration of a
kitten are described in words and incredibly
appealing color photos. Feast your eyes on the
three backlit six-week-old ginger kittens
among the ferns!

224 *Jack the Puppy*. Photos by author.
Random House, hb and pap., 1988. ISBN
0-394-99641-0. SERIES: How Your Pet
Grows! SUBJECTS: Animals—Dogs;
Pets—Dogs. RL 2.9.

Jack's monthly growth from a groping newborn to a playmate for his mother's next litter
is described in words and excellent color
photos of puppies at play.

Busch, Phyllis

225 *Cactus in the Desert*. Ill. by Harriett
Barton. Crowell, 1979. ISBN 0-690-
03136-1. SERIES: Let's-Read-and-Find-
Out. SUBJECTS: Nature; Science. RL 3.2.

Although the text concentrates on how cacti
conserve water, their uses by animals and
people are touched on. Illustrations are apt.

Butterworth, Christine

226 *Ants.* Photos and drawings by Paula
Chasty. Silver Burdett, 1988. ISBN 0-
382-09553-7. SERIES: My World—Blue.
SUBJECTS: Animals—Ants; Nature.
RL 2.9.
Pastel drawings of ant tunnels augment the
information given by excellent photos in this
photoessay. Several types of ants are depicted, which is a bit confusing.

227 *Beavers.* Photos and drawings by Paula
Chasty. Silver Burdett, 1988. ISBN 0-
382-09555-3. SERIES: My World—Blue.
SUBJECTS: Animals—Beavers; Nature.
RL 2.6.
Marvelous photos of beavers cutting trees,
building dams, defending and feeding themselves, and raising their babies are accompanied by simple text. Drawings show the inte-
rior of the lodge.

228 *Bees.* Photos by Paula Chasty. Silver
Burdett, 1988. ISBN 0-382-09554-5.
SERIES: My World—Blue. SUBJECTS:
Animals—Bees. RL 2.5.
Outstanding close-up photos provide the best
information on bees. Language and drawings
are somewhat stilted.

229 *Rabbits.* Photos and drawings by Paula
Chasty. Silver Burdett, 1988. ISBN 0-
382-09588-8. SERIES: My World—Blue.
SUBJECTS: Animals—Rabbits. RL 2.1.
With exceptional photos and some second-
rate drawings, the first year of life of a young
buck and doe is outlined. Habits, enemies,
fast maturity, and habitat are covered.

230 *Squirrels.* Photos and drawings by Paula
Chasty. Silver Burdett, 1988. ISBN 0-
382-09556-1. SERIES: My World—Blue.
SUBJECTS: Animals—Squirrels; Nature.
RL 2.5.
Some photos are exceptional, some less
sharp, and some drawings are poor. There is
confusion over types of squirrels being discussed, and neither the text nor the illustrations flow smoothly.

231 *Swallows.* Photos and drawings by
Paula Chasty. Silver Burdett, 1988. ISBN
0-382-09552-9. SERIES: My World—Blue.

SUBJECTS: Animals—Swallows; Nature.
RL 2.0.
The life cycle of migrating swallows is detailed. Text is illustrated with acceptable
drawings and excellent color photos. One
photo of a swallow drinking on the fly and
another photo showing a swallow scooping
up mud for a nest are exceptional.

Byars, Betsy

232 *The Golly Sisters Go West.* Ill. by Sue
Truesdell. Harper & Row, 1985. ISBN 0-
06-020884-8. SERIES: I Can Read.
SUBJECTS: Frontier and pioneer life—
Fiction; Humorous stories; Western
stories. RL 2.3.
May-May and Rose's naiveté and arguing
lead to impromptu concerts, unnecessary
nighttime fears, and an unmanageable dancing horse. Six zany adventures are illustrated in full color, capturing the humor and
action.

C

Carley, Wayne

233 *Charley the Mouse Finds Christmas.* Ill.
by Ruth Bagshaw. Garrard, 1972. ISBN
0-8116-6953-X. SERIES: Venture.
SUBJECTS: Animals—Mice—Fiction;
Holidays—Christmas—Fiction. RL 2.2.
By Christmas, a mouse living in a department
store has lost all his toys, food, and compan-
ions. When a child spots the mouse in a
window, the child tells Santa. Appealing
mouse drawings are against a watercolor
background.

234 *Here Comes Mirium, the Mixed-Up
Witch.* Ill. by Ted Schroeder. Garrard,
1972, o.p. SUBJECTS: Magic—Fiction;
Witches—Fiction. RL 2.8.
Mirium's magic leads to adventures with an
overfriendly dinosaur, a knight, a mummy,
and a dog in the closed museum. Black and
rose drawings are pedestrian.

235 *Mixed Up Magic.* Ill. by David Stone.
Garrard, hb and pap., 1971. ISBN 0-

Carley, Wayne (cont.)

8116-6711-1. SERIES: Venture. SUBJECTS: Witches—Fiction. RL 1.8.

Mirium's magic mistakes turn a dog show into pandemonium. Her cloak looks mysterious in black finger-painted design against the royal blue and orange of the policeman and dogs, respectively.

236 *Percy the Parrot Passes the Puck.* Ill. by Art Cumings. Garrard, 1972, o.p. SUBJECTS: Animals—Parrots—Fiction; Humorous stories; Sports—Ice hockey—Fiction. RL 2.9.

Hockey fan Percy the Parrot appears on a television commercial for a food he dislikes in order to have a chance to see his home hockey team in action. This lively and imaginative story is simply illustrated with apple green and orange highlights.

237 *Percy the Parrot Yelled Quiet!* Ill. by Art Cumings. Garrard, 1974; ISBN 0-8116-6058-3. SERIES: Easy Venture. SUBJECTS: Animals—Parrots—Fiction; Pets—Fiction. RL 2.4.

Percy turned out not to be the quiet pet Mrs. Gray originally wanted, but he sure was fun! Simple story is illustrated with comic watercolor drawings.

238 *Puppy Love.* Ill. by Erica Merkling. Garrard, hb and pap., 1971. ISBN 0-8116-6716-2. SERIES: Venture. SUBJECTS: Pets—Dogs—Fiction; Sibling rivalry—Fiction. RL 1.5.

Leslie discovered that looking after her new baby brother was like taking care of her puppy, Lickins. The analogy is satisfactory. Ink drawings show Leslie's pride in accomplishment.

239 *The Witch Who Forgot.* Ill. by Lou Cunette. Garrard, 1974, o.p. SUBJECTS: Witches—Fiction. RL 1.2.

Mirium forgets where she put her shoe, hat, cat, and coat—even where she was going with a cake. Humor comes from unlikely places, as she looks for lost items. Cartoon drawings.

Carlson, Nancy

240 *Arnie and the Stolen Markers.* Ill. by author. Viking Kestrel, 1987. ISBN 0-

670-81548-9. SUBJECTS: Behavior—Stealing—Fiction. RL 2.8.

Arnie feels bad after stealing some markers until he confesses and has a chance to work off the cost. Full color drawings accompanying this straightforward moral seem to show the shopkeeper and mother angrier than the text indicates.

241 *Arnie Goes to Camp.* Ill. by author. Viking Kestrel, 1988. ISBN 0-670-81549-7. SUBJECTS: Animals—Fiction; Camps and camping—Fiction. RL 2.7.

Despite his misgivings and homesickness, Arnie enjoys the accomplishments and the camaraderie of summer camp. Bright colored drawings show action-filled days and nights.

242 *Harriet and the Garden.* Ill. by author. Carolrhoda, 1982; Penguin, pap., 1985. ISBN 0-87614-184-X. SUBJECTS: Animals—Dogs—Fiction; Behavior—Honest—Fiction. RL 2.6.

After a sleepless night struggling with her conscience, Harriet, a dog, confesses to trampling Mrs. Hoozit's prize garden—and feels better. Colorful drawings focus on Harriet's long day.

243 *Harriet and the Roller Coaster.* Ill. by author. Carolrhoda, 1982; Penguin, pap., 1984. ISBN 0-87614-183-1. SUBJECTS: Amusement parks—Fiction; Animals—Dogs—Fiction; Emotions—Fear—Fiction. RL 2.4.

Taunted by George, a rabbit, Harriet, a dog, reluctantly tries a roller coaster—and finds she likes it! Carlson's books challenge children to broaden their experiences and outlook. Bright colors convey feelings of fear and excitement.

244 *Harriet and Walt.* Ill. by author. Carolrhoda, 1982; Penguin, pap., 1984. ISBN 0-87614-185-8. SUBJECTS: Animals—Dogs—Fiction; Siblings—Fiction. RL 2.1.

Harriet, originally burdened by her little brother when they go to play in the snow, ends up defending him against the impatience of her friend George. Quietly moral tale is illustrated with ink and colored pencil.

245 *Harriet's Halloween Candy.* Ill. by author. Carolrhoda, 1982; Penguin,

pap., 1984. ISBN 0-87614-182-3.
SUBJECTS: Animals—Dogs—Fiction;
Behavior—Sharing—Fiction;
Holidays—Halloween—Fiction. RL 2.4.
Harriet shares her overabundance of Halloween candy only when she is sick from eating too much. Details of how she sorts her candy by color, size, and favorites add authenticity and humor. Pastel drawings have interesting patterns of clothes and candy.

246 *Loudmouth George and the Big Race.* Ill. by author. Carolrhoda, 1983; Penguin, pap., 1986. ISBN 0-87614-215-3.
SUBJECTS: Animals—Rabbits—Fiction;
Behavior—Excuses—Fiction. RL 2.3.
George is too tired, too full, or too busy to train for the big race that Harriet ends up winning. His fatigue is graphically captured by corduroy legs and dragging limbs. Full color illustrations are on green or royal blue backgrounds.

247 *Loudmouth George and the Cornet.* Ill. by author. Carolrhoda, 1983; Penguin, pap., 1985. ISBN 0-87614-214-5.
SUBJECTS: Animals—Rabbits—Fiction;
Behavior—Excuses—Fiction; Musical instruments—Fiction. RL 2.7.
George thinks he is too good at playing the cornet to take lessons, and when asked to leave the band, he has excuses and a better idea—he will take up the tuba. Colored pencil drawings show his family's consternation clearly.

248 *Loudmouth George and the Fishing Trip.* Ill. by author. Carolrhoda, 1983; Penguin, pap., 1985. ISBN 0-87614-213-7.
SUBJECTS: Animals—Rabbits—Fiction;
Behavior—Bragging—Fiction; Fishing—Fiction. RL 2.4.
George's bragging is brought up short when Harriet's family takes him fishing. She is then on hand to keep his reports of success accurate. George in sky-blue pajamas with carrots on them is a nice touch.

249 *Loudmouth George and the Sixth-Grade Bully.* Ill. by author. Carolrhoda, 1983; Penguin, pap., 1985. ISBN 0-87614-217-X. SUBJECTS: Animals—Rabbits—Fiction; Behavior—Bullying—Fiction; School stories. RL 2.4.
When a bully steals George's lunch every day, George's friend Harriet helps him prepare an unpleasant surprise in the next day's lunch! All who have suffered at the hands of a bully will be able to identify with George's creative revenge. Pencil drawings are in full color.

250 *Making the Team.* Ill. by author. Carolrhoda, 1985. ISBN 0-87614-281-1. SERIES: Louanne Pig. SUBJECTS: Animals—Pigs—Fiction; Sex roles—Fiction; Sports—Football—Fiction. RL 2.6.
Louanne and Arnie, two pigs, practice together for cheerleading and football tryouts—but Louanne makes the football squad and Arnie the cheerleading. Pencil drawings are in red, blue, and green.

251 *The Mysterious Valentine.* Ill. by author. Carolrhoda, 1985. ISBN 0-87614-282-X. SERIES: Louanne Pig. SUBJECTS: Animals—Pigs—Fiction; Holidays—Valentine's Day—Fiction. RL 2.8.
The reader finally figures out who Louanne the pig's secret admirer is, but Louanne never does. Familiar characters are drawn in full color with pencil.

252 *The Perfect Family.* Ill. by author. Carolrhoda, 1985. ISBN 0-87614-280-3. SERIES: Louanne Pig. SUBJECTS: Animals—Pigs—Fiction; Family life—Fiction; Siblings—Fiction. RL 2.7.
Louanne the pig finds out that living in a family of ten siblings is not for her when she spends the weekend at her friend George's house. Colored pencil drawings add humor.

253 *The Talent Show.* Ill. by author. Carolrhoda, 1985. ISBN 0-87614-284-6. SERIES: Louanne Pig. SUBJECTS: Animals—Pigs—Fiction; Self-esteem—Fiction. RL 2.8.
Louanne the pig gets involved in the talent show even though she thinks she has nothing to contribute. Bright colored drawings add to the sympathetic treatment of feeling left out.

254 *Witch Lady.* Ill. by author. Carolrhoda, 1985. ISBN 0-87614-283-8. SERIES: Louanne Pig. SUBJECTS: Animals—Pigs—Fiction; Haunted houses—Fiction; Scary stories. RL 3.0.
When Louanne the pig twists her ankle in the witch lady's yard, she finds out what *really* goes on in that scary house—but she may not tell her friends. Colored pencil drawings are in flat primary colors.

Carona, Philip

255 *Numbers*. Photos and drawings. Childrens, hb and pap., 1982. ISBN 0-516-01634-2. SERIES: New True. SUBJECTS: Concepts—Numbers; Mathematics. RL 2.4.
Watercolor illustrations and colored photos show a simple history and the uses of numbers.

Carrick, Carol

256 *Empty Squirrel*. Ill. by Donald Carrick. Greenwillow, 1981, o.p. SERIES: Read-alone. SUBJECTS: Pets—Fiction; Pets—Wild animals—Fiction. RL 2.1.
Paul returns a fish he caught to the pond and a neglected toy squirrel that lost its stuffing outside over the winter to its owner, and keeps a turtle when he discovers it likes tuna. Soft pencil drawings are in brown and orange.

257 *The Longest Float in the Parade*. Ill. by Donald Carrick. Greenwillow, 1982. ISBN 0-688-00919-0. SERIES: Read-alone. SUBJECTS: Camps and camping—Fiction; Parades—Fiction. RL 2.7.
At summer camp, Jimmy and Pinky's imaginative parade entry, a Chinese dragon, rivals all others. Warmly realistic from dialogue to atmosphere and characters, the text is complemented beautifully by the soft watercolor illustrations.

Carrick, Malcolm

258 *Happy Jack*. Ill. by author. Harper & Row, 1979. ISBN 0-06-021122-9. SERIES: I Can Read. SUBJECTS: Folklore. RL 1.9.
The tale of foolish Jack who wins the princess is retold in simple language. Sepia drawings have avocado and peach washes.

259 *Mr. Tod's Trap*. Ill. by author. Harper & Row, 1980. ISBN 0-06-021114-8. SERIES: I Can Read. SUBJECTS: Animals—Foxes—Fiction. RL 2.8.
Mr. Tod's ingenious rabbit traps work to Weasel's advantage, so Mrs. Tod takes over hunting and Mr. Tod takes over the housework. A houseful of appealing fox kits and lumpy clever rabbits enrich the tale.

260 *Today Is Shrew Day*. Ill. by author. Harper & Row, 1978, o.p. SERIES: I Can Read. SUBJECTS: Animals—Frogs and toads—Fiction; Animals—Shrews—Fiction; Friendship—Fiction. RL 2.6.
Bullfrog gets all sorts of advice for babysitting—for a doll. Unusual perspectives add interest; illustrations are in gloomy, muddy colors.

Carter, Anne

261 *Bella's Secret Garden*. Ill. by John Butler. Crown, 1986. ISBN 0-517-56308-8. SERIES: It's Great to Read! SUBJECTS: Animals—Rabbits; Nature. RL 2.9.
Human paws move Bella the rabbit from a suburban garden to a field away from the danger of cats, dogs, and machinery. Full page artwork is outstanding. From expressive eyes, fur that invites petting, down to the rabbit endpapers, there is a consistent rabbit perspective.

262 *Molly in Danger*. Ill. by John Butler. Crown, 1986. ISBN 0-517-56534-X. SERIES: It's Great to Read! SUBJECTS: Animals—Moles—Fiction; Nature. RL 3.0.
When Molly is forced out of her hole by floodwaters, she faces danger from a heron and an owl before finding new burrowing ground. Exceptional close-up full page drawings give a mole's view of the world.

263 *Ruff Leaves Home*. Ill. by John Butler. Crown, 1986. ISBN 0-517-56068-2. SERIES: It's Great to Read! SUBJECTS: Animals—Foxes; Nature. RL 2.1.
A year of exploration and danger in the life of a young fox is exceptionally well portrayed in language and in effective full page drawings. Other wildlife is shown, as well as the dangers to which a fox on the fringe of a suburban area is exposed.

264 *Scurry's Treasure*. Ill. by John Butler. Crown, 1986. ISBN 0-517-56535-8. SERIES: It's Great to Read! SUBJECTS: Animals—Squirrels; Nature. RL 2.4.
The content of finely drawn full color illustrations of the world from a young squirrel's perspective is well reflected in the text, as a squirrel mistakes a brooch for a nut.

Cartwright, Sally

265 *Sunlight*. Ill. by Marylin Hafner. Coward, McCann, 1974, o.p. SUBJECTS: Rainbows; Science experiments; Shadows. RL 2.7.
Simple experiments with rainbows, reflections, and shadows are suggested. Visual interest is high with soft pencil drawings, varied in their use of space.

266 *The Tide*. Ill. by Marilyn Miller. Coward, McCann, 1970, o.p. SERIES: Science Is What and Why. SUBJECTS: Oceans and ocean life; Science. RL 3.6.
At the simplest level, Cartwright presents information about different kinds of tides and their causes. Interesting effects with printing and overlaid washes add visual appeal.

267 *Water Is Wet*. Ill. by Marylin Hafner. Coward, McCann, 1973, o.p. SUBJECTS: Science experiments—Water; Water. RL 1.8.
Ideas for simple science projects with water are appealingly presented. Illustrations are well suited to the text.

Caseley, Judith

268 *Molly Pink*. Ill. by author. Greenwillow, 1985. ISBN 0-688-04005-5. SUBJECTS: Emotions—Fear—Fiction; Music—Fiction. RL 3.3.
Despite Molly's singing practice, she freezes when she has a solo on stage—until members of her family turn their backs. Framed pictures in pink and yellow are well suited to the text.

Castiglia, Julie

269 *Jill the Pill*. Ill. by Steven Kellogg. Atheneum, 1979, o.p. SUBJECTS: Siblings—Fiction. RL 2.7.
Jill's teenage behavior has nothing in common with her small brother's. Expressive, detailed ink drawings add authenticity to this story.

Catton, Chris, ed.

270 *Matchmaking*. Ill. by Oxford Scientific Films. Putnam, 1987. ISBN 0-399-21451-

8. SUBJECTS: Nature. RL Off Spache scale.
A variety of mating activities is briefly described, from attracting mates with dramatic coloration or scent to presenting "gifts," to calling mates, or to fighting for them. Excellent color photos take the reader to woods, water, the Arctic, and garden.

Cauley, Lorinda B.

271 *Bake-Off*. Ill. by author. Putnam, 1978, o.p. SERIES: See and Read. SUBJECTS: Animals—Fiction; Bakers and baking—Fiction; Contests—Fiction. RL 3.9.
Knowing sweets win votes, but committed to nutritious recipes, Mr. Hare wins the autumn bake-off with a surprise entry (recipe appended). Forest animals are given individual character through expressive ink drawings alternately colored in two-tone washes.

Cazet, Denys

272 *Saturday*. Ill. by author. Bradbury, 1985; Macmillan, pap., 1988. ISBN 0-02-717800-5. SUBJECTS: Animals—Dogs—Fiction; Grandparents—Fiction; Humorous stories. RL 3.7.
Grandpa is always ready to leave work to play—or do a science project—with his grandson, Barney. Grandma's pancakes, cocoa, or a pillow help when Barney is unhappy. Humorous story illustrated with gray ink drawings captures the warmth of these relationships.

Cebulash, Mel

273 *Basketball Players Do Amazing Things*. Photos. Random House, 1976. ISBN 0-394-93184-X. SERIES: Step-Up. SUBJECTS: Sports—Basketball. RL 2.8.
Outstanding basketball players discussed include the traveling female All American Red Heads, a trick shooter, and record foul shooters. The disputed 1972 Olympic game between the Soviet Union and the United States is covered. Brief, well-told stories are illustrated with black and white action photos.

Cerf, Bennett A.

274 *Bennett Cerf's Book of Animal Riddles.* Ill. by Roy McKie. Random House, 1964. ISBN 0-394-90034-0. SERIES: I Can Read It All By Myself. SUBJECTS: Animals—Fiction; Jokes and riddles. RL 2.0.

Dogs, turtles, hummingbirds, snails, and rabbits are some of the subjects of these clever, simple riddles. They are masterfully illustrated with McKie's bold line drawings.

275 *Bennett Cerf's Book of Laughs.* Ill. by Carl Rose. Beginner, 1959. ISBN 0-394-90011-1. SERIES: I Can Read It All By Myself. SUBJECTS: Jokes and riddles. RL 1.9.

Standard jokes relying on wordplay are retold using a vocabulary of 232 words, well geared to second-grade humor. Dated drawings nevertheless illustrate the misconceptions of the words, thus adding humor.

276 *Bennett Cerf's Book of Riddles.* Ill. by Roy McKie. Random House, 1960. ISBN 0-394-90015-4. SERIES: I Can Read It All By Myself. SUBJECTS: Jokes and riddles. RL 1.9.

Not too familiar standard riddles about dogs, cats, horses, pigs, and children are illustrated by a cartoon master of expressive line.

277 *More Riddles.* Ill. by Roy McKie. Random House, 1961. ISBN 0-394-90024-3. SERIES: I Can Read It All By Myself. SUBJECTS: Jokes and riddles. RL 2.0.

Traditional riddles are retold simply. Comic illustrations extending the riddles are in primary colors.

Chandler, Edna W.

278 *Cowboy Sam and Freddy.* Ill. by Jack Merryweather. Benefic, 1959, o.p. SUBJECTS: Cowboys—Fiction; Western stories. RL 1.7.

Freddy is eager to become a cowboy, but he needs to be outfitted and learn a few things first. Blue, yellow, and red illustrations convey the action.

279 *Pony Rider.* Ill. by Jack Merryweather. Benefic, 1966, o.p. SERIES: Tom Logan.

SUBJECTS: Cowboys—Fiction; Frontier and pioneer life—Fiction; Western stories. RL 2.5.

Using a 60-word vocabulary, the author introduces a beginning reader to the West, including the Pony Express. Colored ink sketches are good.

Chapin, Cynthia

280 *Healthy Is Happy.* Ill. by Joann Daley. Whitman, 1971, o.p. SERIES: Community Helpers. SUBJECTS: Community helpers; Doctors and nurses. RL 2.1.

Medical specialists in various fields help Joe and Beth's family. Ink drawings have washes with a marbelized look.

Charles, Donald

281 *Calico Cat's Exercise Book.* Ill. by author. Childrens, hb and pap., 1982. ISBN 0-516-03457-X. SERIES: Calico Cat. SUBJECTS: Animals—Cats; Exercise. RL 2.6.

Exuberant decorative cat drawings encourage exercise, as does the very abbreviated text.

Chase, Catherine

282 *Pete, the Wet Pet.* Ill. by Gail Gibbons. Elsevier-Dutton, 1981, o.p. SUBJECTS: Animals—Dogs—Fiction; Pets—Dogs—Fiction. RL 1.5.

A simple story of the mess a big cuddly dog makes in the house when he comes in to get dry. Ink sketches with crayon and wash coloring add to the warmth of the tale.

Chenery, Janet

283 *Toad Hunt.* Ill. by Ben Shecter. Harper & Row, 1967. ISBN 0-06-021263-2. SERIES: Science I Can Read. SUBJECTS: Animals—Reptiles and amphibians; Nature; Science. RL 2.7.

Teddy and Peter learn about turtles, salamanders, and frogs as they search for a toad. Soft colored pencil and ink drawings show humor and reverence for wild animals.

284 *Wolfie.* Ill. by Marc Simont. Harper & Row, 1969. ISBN 0-06-021264-0. SERIES: I Can Read. SUBJECTS: Animals—Spiders; Nature. RL 2.5.

Good information about wolf spiders is spiced with a younger sister's desire to feed "Wolfie"; she turns out to be a dead shot stunning flies for Wolfie's meals with a rubber band. Two-color illustrations are plain, yet expressive.

Chittenden, Margaret

285 *When the Wild Ducks Come.* Ill. by Beatrice Darwin. Follett, 1972, o.p. SERIES: Beginning to Read. SUBJECTS: Animals—Ducks; Seasons. RL 3.1.

A boy observes a pair of ducks through the seasons. Colorful, impressionistic block prints are exceptional.

Chlad, Dorothy

286 *In the Water . . . On the Water.* Ill. by Lydia Halverson. Childrens, 1988. ISBN 0-516-01974-0. SERIES: Safety Town. SUBJECTS: Safety. RL 2.4.

Some of the safety rules discussed include wearing a life jacket, not throwing sand, not jumping into a pool, using steps and railing, and not playing with faucets. Unimaginative text seems overcautious, for example, always wearing life jackets on the beach. Illustrations are done in watercolor.

287 *Matches, Lighters, and Firecrackers Are Not Toys.* Ill. by Lydia Halverson. Childrens, hb and pap., 1982. ISBN 0-516-01982-1. SERIES: Safety Town. SUBJECTS: Safety. RL 3.0.

The bare facts regarding the benefits and dangers of fire are flanked by a repetition of simple rules. Bright watercolors follow the text.

288 *Playing on the Playground.* Ill. by Lydia Halverson. Childrens, 1987. ISBN 0-516-01989-9. SERIES: Safety Town. SUBJECTS: Playgrounds; Safety. RL 2.0.

Six rules about playground safety begin with "*never* go alone." Following the explanations, the rules are repeated. Large drawings are of multiethnic children.

289 *Stop, Look, and Listen for Trains.* Ill. by Lydia Halverson. Childrens, hb and pap., 1983. ISBN 0-516-01988-0. SERIES: Safety Town. SUBJECTS: Safety; Trains. RL 2.8.

Chlad admonishes the reader to stop, look, and listen; never play near tracks; and wait until the train is gone before crossing tracks. A little information about trains is given as well. Large colorful paintings accompany the text.

290 *When I Ride in a Car.* Ill. by Lydia Halverson. Childrens, hb and pap., 1983. ISBN 0-516-01987-2. SERIES: Safety Town. SUBJECTS: Safety. RL 2.9.

Buckle-up, talk or play quietly, and never bother the driver are the safety rules introduced. Large watercolor drawings soften the presentation slightly.

Chorao, Kay

291 *Oink and Pearl.* Ill. by author. Harper & Row, 1981. ISBN 0-06-021273-X. SERIES: I Can Read. SUBJECTS: Animals—Pigs— Fiction; Siblings—Fiction. RL 2.0.

The pigs Oink and Pearl feel frustrated, but find solace in each other's company. Elements from four chapters are skillfully woven together. Pig-pink and soft apple green color sympathetic illustrations.

292 *Ups and Downs with Oink and Pearl.* Ill. by author. Harper & Row, 1986. ISBN 0-06-021275-6. SERIES: I Can Read. SUBJECTS: Animals—Pigs—Fiction; Sibling rivalry—Fiction. RL 2.5.

Pearl's anger and jealousy of her little brother evaporate with laughter and sharing in this story about pig siblings. Soft pink, orange, and yellow washes warm this gentle tale.

Christian, Mary B.

293 *Devin and Goliath.* Ill. by Normand Chartier. Addison-Wesley, 1974, o.p. SUBJECTS: Animals—Turtles—Fiction; Pets—Wild animals—Fiction. RL 2.4.

Devin finds that capturing a turtle named Goliath is not as satisfying as he expected. Pencil drawings with two-color highlights are especially sympathetic to animals.

Christian, Mary B. (cont.)

294　*Doggone Mystery*. Ill. by Irene Trivas. Whitman, 1980. ISBN 0-8075-1656-2. SERIES: First Read-Alone Mystery. SUBJECTS: Animals—Dogs—Fiction; Mystery and detective stories. RL 2.7.
The kids' dog, Ruffles, helps them uncover the thief. Ink and turquoise washed sketches add humor and help provide clues.

295　*Go West, Swamp Monsters*. Ill. by Marc Brown. Dial, 1985; pap., 1987. ISBN 0-8037-0144-6. SERIES: Easy-to-Read. SUBJECTS: Behavior—Manners—Fiction; Humorous stories; Monsters—Fiction. RL 2.3.
Four swamp monsters in cowboy attire join some child campers visiting their swamp. Humor comes from the monsters' literal interpretation of camping. Brown's illustrations of the monsters make them appear *very* friendly.

296　*Green Thumb Thief*. Ill. by Don Madden. Whitman, 1982, o.p. SERIES: First Read-alone. SUBJECTS: Animals—Dogs—Fiction; Mystery and detective stories. RL 3.0.
The undercover kids and their shedding dog, Hercules, track down a plant thief. Far-fetched mystery has ink with gray and red wash drawings.

297　*J. J. Leggett, Secret Agent*. Ill. by Jacquie Hann. Lothrop, 1978, o.p. SUBJECTS: Mystery and detective stories. RL 3.0.
A boy's walkie-talkie unexpectedly saves the day. Humorous pencil drawings have pumpkin highlights.

298　*Lucky Man*. Ill. by Glen Rounds. Macmillan, 1979. ISBN 0-02-718270-3. SERIES: Ready-to-Read. SUBJECTS: Folklore. RL 2.0.
Felix got poorer and deeper and deeper in trouble for all his hard work until one unexpected day in court. Ink sketches have a folk flavor.

299　*Penrod Again*. Ill. by Jane Dyer. Macmillan, 1987. ISBN 0-02-718550-8. SERIES: Ready-to-Read. SUBJECTS: Animals—Bears—Fiction; Animals— Porcupines—Fiction; Friendship— Fiction. RL 2.1.
Five chapters show the trials and satisfactions of friendship between a bear and a porcupine who have very different personalities. Jewel-like watercolors of the animal characters are outstanding.

300　*Penrod's Pants*. Ill. by Jane Dyer. Macmillan, 1986. ISBN 0-02-718520-6. SERIES: Ready-to-Read. SUBJECTS: Animals—Bears—Fiction; Animals— Porcupines—Fiction; Friendship— Fiction. RL 2.5.
The friendship between a bear and a porcupine is strained when they shop for pants, pull a loose tooth, and decide who is to get the last cookie. Full color watercolors feature emerald greens, royal blues, and sunshine yellows.

301　*Swamp Monsters*. Ill. by Marc Brown. Dial, hb and pap., 1983. ISBN 0-8037-7616-0. SERIES: Easy-to-Read. SUBJECTS: Monsters—Fiction; School stories. RL 2.4.
Swamp monsters Fenny and Crag decide they like snail stew and their own swamp after they go to school with a group of children. Children may gain some perspective on how others might view their everyday behavior. Literal-minded humor is illustrated with watercolors in rose, lemon, and brown.

302　*The Toady and Dr. Miracle*. Ill. by Ib Ohlsson. Macmillan, 1985; pap., 1987. ISBN 0-02-718470-6. SERIES: Ready-to-Read. SUBJECTS: Frontier and pioneer life—Fiction; Humorous stories. RL 2.7.
In this frontier story, Luther proves he is not dumb when he outwits an itinerant medicine man. Vivid language and pen and ink drawings complement each other to set the mood, create interesting characters, and add humor to the story.

303　*Ventriloquist*. Ill. by Mamoru Roland Funai. Coward, McCann, 1982, o.p. SERIES: Break-of-Day. SUBJECTS: Animals—Dogs—Fiction; Pets—Dogs— Fiction. RL 2.6.
Arthur's dog Burford has marvelous gifts that go unrecognized, according to his master.

Three-tone illustrations alternate with gray tones.

Clark, Ann N.

304 *Little Indian Basket Maker*. Ill. by Harrison Begay. Melmont, 1957, o.p. SERIES: Look Read Learn. SUBJECTS: Art and artists; Native Americans—Papagos. RL 3.1.

The basket making of Papago Native Americans involves hands and heart. Illustrations capture the color and texture of that culture with simply colored drawings featuring one little girl and her grandmother.

Claverie, Jean

305 *The Party*. Ill. by author. Crown, 1985. ISBN 0-517-56026-7. SERIES: It's Great to Read! SUBJECTS: Birthdays—Fiction; Costumes—Fiction; Parties—Fiction. RL 2.7.

Some of the difficulties in choosing a costume and the squabbles during a birthday party are suggested in abbreviated text, using a child's perspective. Pale colored pencil drawings fill the pages. Binding is poor.

306 *The Picnic*. Ill. by author. Crown, 1985. ISBN 0-517-56025-9. SERIES: It's Great to Read! SUBJECTS: Family life—Fiction; Picnics—Fiction. RL 2.3.

A family's relaxing day in the country ends up at a fast-food joint, ketchup-spattered, but with sun-yellow balloons with hearts. Muted pastel illustrations contrast adult and child response to events. Binding is poor.

307 *Shopping*. Ill. by author. Crown, 1985. ISBN 0-517-56024-0. SERIES: It's Great to Read! SUBJECTS: Humorous stories; Shopping—Fiction. RL 2.9.

A small child's adventures at the grocery store and in the television department of a store have tongue-in-cheek adult humor. Misty yellows, reds, and blues draw the reader into a child's world. Binding is poor.

308 *Working*. Ill. by author. Crown, 1985. ISBN 0-517-56021-6. SERIES: It's Great to Read! SUBJECTS: Fathers—Fiction; Imag-ination—Fiction; Parents, working—Fiction. RL 2.4.

A small boy's explorations at his father's work place provide varied adult reactions, judging by their expressions. This tale is warmed by the snowball play and hug on the way home. Light pastel drawings have a grainy texture.

Clinton, Patrick

309 *I Can Be a Father*. Photos. Childrens, 1988. ISBN 0-516-01904-X. SERIES: I Can Be. SUBJECTS: Fathers; Parent and child. RL 2.5.

The varied ways in which fathers care for their children, teach them, and provide for them, are described in fluid, nonsexist language. A glossary and a picture glossary, many colored photos, and an index add to this warmly readable factual book.

Clithero, Sally

310 *Beginning-to-Read Poetry*. Ill. by Erik Blegvad. Follett, 1967, o.p. SUBJECTS: Imagination—Fiction; Poetry. RL 3.5.

Poems such as "Holding Hands," "Mrs. Peck-Pigeon," and "The Make-Believe House" sparkle from this unusual collection. Watercolor washes show tiny animals, elves, snow people, and shoes.

Coatsworth, Elizabeth

311 *Bob Bodden and the Seagoing Farm*. Ill. by Frank Aloise. Garrard, 1970, o.p. SUBJECTS: Humorous stories; Tall tales. RL 3.6.

This story explains how Maine sea-captain Bob Bodden's oceangoing farm caused the lakes and islands along Maine's shores. Ink sketches are a bit dated.

Coerr, Eleanor

312 *Chang's Paper Pony*. Ill. by Deborah Kogan Ray. Harper & Row, 1988. ISBN 0-06-021329-9. SERIES: I Can Read. SUBJECTS: Animals—Horses—Fiction; United States—1783–1865—Fiction. RL 2.9.

Coerr, Eleanor (cont.)

A Chinese-American boy, Chang, growing up in a gold mining town, dreams of having a pony. Pencil drawings in turquoise and gold soften the harsh outlines of his life, and celebrate the realization of his dream.

313 *Jane Goodall*. Ill. by Kees de Kiefte. Putnam, 1976, o.p. SUBJECTS: Biographies; Science. RL 2.8.
The outlines of Goodall's dreams, opportunities, and choices are given. Soft pencil sketches are appropriate.

314 *The Josefina Story Quilt*. Ill. by Bruce Degen. Harper & Row, 1986. ISBN 0-06-021349-3. SERIES: I Can Read. SUBJECTS: Frontier and pioneer life—Fiction; Quilting—Fiction; Western stories. RL 2.7.
The hardships and satisfactions of wagon train travel are commemorated in a quilt by a young girl. Pencil outline drawings; each chapter is headed with a quilt patch significant to Josefina's experience.

315 *Mixed-Up Mystery Smell*. Ill. by Tomie dePaola. Putnam, 1976, o.p. SERIES: See and Read. SUBJECTS: Clubs—Fiction; Haunted houses—Fiction; Mystery and detective stories. RL 2.3.
While hunting for a mysterious smell's source, the children nervously follow their noses to a "haunted" house, and discover the source of the delicious smell. Pale cocoa, avocado, and turquoise coloring alternates with pencil in dePaola's distinctive drawings.

316 *Waza Wins at Windy Gulch*. Ill. by Janet McCaffery. Putnam, 1977, o.p. SERIES: See and Read. SUBJECTS: Animals—Camels; Humorous stories; United States—1783–1865—Fiction. RL 3.2.
A true story about the imported Camel Brigade of the 1850s that reads like a tall tale as Dirtyshirt Dan tries to get the camels in trouble to save his mules. Excellent textured drawings are in shades of brown.

Cohen, Caron L.

317 *Three Yellow Dogs*. Ill. by Peter Sis. Greenwillow, 1986. ISBN 0-688-06231-8.

SUBJECTS: Animals—Dogs—Fiction; Concepts—Numbers. RL 1.0.
A five-word text is enlivened with dogs of all shapes and pastel colors. Some are shown close-up and others are seen from a distance.

Cole, Joanna

318 *Bony-Legs*. Ill. by Dirk Zimmer. Four Winds, 1983; Scholastic, pap., 1988. ISBN 0-02-722970-X. SUBJECTS: Folklore—Russia; Magic—Fiction; Russia—Fiction. RL 2.1.
Sasha's kindness to Baba Yaga's creaking gate and a hungry cat and dog helps her escape from the Russian witch. Richly patterned illustrations embroider this simple version of a traditional tale of fear, magic, and kindness.

319 *Golly Gump Swallowed a Fly*. Ill. by Bari Weissman. Parents Magazine Press, 1981; pap., 1987. ISBN 0-8193-1070-0. SERIES: Read Aloud and Easy Reading. SUBJECTS: Cumulative tales; Tall tales. RL 2.7.
Golly Gump's adventures lead him to cover his mouth when he yawns in a tale paralleling "I Know an Old Lady Who Swallowed a Fly." Flat colors and expressive animals have some similarities to dePaola's illustrations.

320 *The Magic School Bus: Inside the Human Body*. Ill. by Bruce Degen. Scholastic, 1988. ISBN 0-590-41416-7. SUBJECTS: Human body. RL 3.2.
The ploy of a school bus shrinking to enter a human body is distracting to the information being presented. Although enlivened by cartoons of children grumbling and mini school reports about the body systems, the watercolor drawings are too busy to allow the reader to focus on learning about the human body.

321 *The Missing Tooth*. Ill. by Marylin Hafner. Random House, 1988. ISBN 0-394-99279-2. SERIES: Step into Reading. SUBJECTS: Friendship—Fiction; Human body—Teeth—Fiction. RL 2.4.
Arlo and Robby had the same pets, liked the same games, and looked alike, down to the same missing teeth. After a bet about

which one was going to lose the next tooth, the friendship becomes strained. Full colors warm this realistic story with a satisfying resolution.

322 *Mixed-Up Magic*. Ill. by True Kelley. Hastings House, 1987; Scholastic, pap., 1987. ISBN 0-8038-9298-5. SUBJECTS: Magic—Fiction; Nonsense; Stories in rhyme. RL 2.2.

Rhyming nonsense is effectively paired with an elf's inept magic. Soft pastels warm the text.

323 *Plants in Winter*. Ill. by Kazue Mizumura. Crowell, 1973. ISBN 0-690-62886-2. SERIES: Let's-Read-and-Find-Out Science. SUBJECTS: Plants; Seasons—Winter. RL 2.4.

A child finds out how various plants survive the winter from a botanist, whose theories do not cover the hardy snowdrop blossom. Pale gray and green washes most appropriately illustrate each type of plant.

Collins, David R.

324 *If I Could, I Would*. Ill. by Kelly Oechsli. Garrard, 1979; ISBN 0-8116-4417-0. SERIES: Imagination. SUBJECTS: Imagination—Fiction; Mothers—Fiction. RL 2.4.

A small boy likes his mother so much he would give her lots of candy; take her for a wagon ride to the moon; give her a haunted house, lots of pets, and a castle—and even eat spinach! Gentle humor is reinforced by four-color cartoon drawings.

Conklin, Gladys

325 *I Caught a Lizard*. Ill. by Artur Marokvia. Holiday House, 1967, o.p. SUBJECTS: Animals—Lizards; Pet care; Pets—Wild animals. RL 3.2.

Conklin conveys her fascination with many small wild animals and tells how to care for them, but she advocates letting them return to their natural environment after observing them for several days. Lightly colored pencil drawings reinforce this message.

Cooke, Ann

326 *Giraffes at Home*. Ill. by Robert Quackenbush. Crowell, 1972. ISBN 0-690-33082-0. SERIES: Let's-Read-and-Find-Out Science. SUBJECTS: Animals—Giraffes; Nature. RL 3.5.

Information about giraffes' mating, birth, feeding, enemies, and herd behavior is presented in an interesting fashion. Excellent four-color illustrations alternate with gray ones.

Corbett, Scott

327 *Boy Who Walked on Air*. Ill. by Ed Parker. Little, Brown, 1974, o.p. SUBJECTS: Humorous stories; Inventors and inventions—Fiction. RL 2.6.

Max's willpower and Morry's inventiveness have disastrous results—most of the time—as they try to become airborne. Cartoon illustrations add humor.

Corey, Dorothy

328 *Everybody Takes Turns*. Ill. by Lois Axeman. Whitman, 1980. ISBN 0-8075-2166-3. SERIES: Self-Starters. SUBJECTS: Behavior—Sharing. RL 1.3.

At the most basic level, the text talks about people, including children, taking turns: in line, when only one toy is available, and crossing the street. Situations have child appeal, as do illustrations with varied patterns, cherry red washes, and pets.

Cossi, Olga

329 *Gus the Bus*. Ill. by Howie Schneider. Scholastic, 1989. ISBN 0-590-41616-2. SUBJECTS: Buses—Fiction. RL 2.9.

After getting new tires, Gus, the school bus, has a day chasing a dog and horses, racing a fire truck, and attempting to take off at the airport. Pastel cartoons show the silly grin on his radiator and the wild flowers on his mirror.

Counsel, June

330 *But Martin!* Ill. by Carolyn Dinan. Faber & Faber, 1984. ISBN 0-571-13349-

Counsel, June (cont.)

5. SUBJECTS: Cultural diversity—Fiction; School stories. RL 2.4.

An intriguing, upbeat story celebrating diversity, play, and cooperative learning focuses on Martin, who is green and flies to school in a saucer. Ink drawings are brightened with washes and colored pencil.

Coville, Bruce, and Coville, Katherine

331 *The Foolish Giant*. Ill. by authors. Lippincott, 1978. ISBN 0-397-31800-6. SERIES: I-Like-to-Read. SUBJECTS: Giants—Fiction. RL 2.7.

A loving portrait of a brave, kind, and friendly giant named Harry is given, along with an explanation of his limitations and powers. All the tears are not Harry's in this evocative story illustrated with soft, detailed pencil drawings.

332 *Sarah's Unicorn*. Ill. by authors. Lippincott, 1979; Harper & Row, pap., 1985. ISBN 0-397-31873-1. SERIES: I-Like-to-Read. SUBJECTS: Mythical creatures—Fiction; Witches—Fiction. RL 2.5.

Sarah's magical adventures with Oakhorn the unicorn nearly come to an end when Mag the evil witch discovers them together. Pencil drawings supply atmosphere and expressive details, especially of the forest animals.

Craig, M. Jean

333 *Spring Is Like the Morning*. Ill. by Don Almquist. Putnam, 1965, o.p. SUBJECTS: Seasons—Spring; Senses. RL 2.8.

Outstanding textured prints in gray, brown, and avocado focus on the sights and feeling of spring.

Cromie, William J.

334 *Steven and the Green Turtle*. Ill. by Tom Eaton. Harper & Row, 1970; ISBN 0-06-021374-4. SERIES: I Can Read Science. SUBJECTS: Animals—Turtles; Nature; Pets—Wild animals. RL 2.5.

Steven's rescue and later release of a tiny green turtle is sympathetically treated in this easy science book. Sketches have a predominantly turquoise wash.

Curran, Eileen

335 *Life in the Meadow*. Ill. by James Watling. Troll, hb and pap., 1985. ISBN 0-8167-0343-4. SUBJECTS: Animals; Animals—Insects. RL 2.2.

A child frolics and observes the abundant life in a meadow. Textual illustrations are bright, with interesting perspectives; however, the cover is dull.

Curren, Polly

336 *I Know a Plumber*. Ill. by Frank Aloise. Putnam, 1976, o.p. SERIES: Community Helpers. SUBJECTS: Careers; Community helpers. RL 2.9.

A picture glossary helps children clarify concepts regarding plumbing. A plumber's typical house call is shown. Ink sketches are good.

Cushman, Doug

337 *Aunt Eater Loves a Mystery*. Ill. by author. Harper & Row, 1987. ISBN 0-06-021327-2. SERIES: I Can Read. SUBJECTS: Animals—Anteaters—Fiction; Mystery and detective stories. RL 2.9.

A missing suitcase, a mysterious shadow, a strange visitor next door, and a cat-sitting adventure are competently dealt with by Aunt Eater. Homey pictures are in turquoise, yellow, and forest green.

338 *Uncle Foster's Hat Tree*. Ill. by author. Dutton, 1988. ISBN 0-525-44410-6. SERIES: Easy Reader. SUBJECTS: Aunts and uncles—Fiction; Tall tales. RL 2.1.

Bored Merle becomes absorbed in the adventure stories attached to Uncle Foster's hats. Bright perky watercolors enliven the imaginative first person tall tales.

D

Dauer, Rosamund

339 *Bullfrog and Gertrude Go Camping*. Ill. by Byron Barton. Greenwillow, 1980; Dell, pap., 1988. ISBN 0-688-84207-0.

SERIES: Read-alone. SUBJECTS: Animals—Frogs and toads—Fiction; Animals—Snakes—Fiction; Camps and camping—Fiction. RL 2.7.
Gertrude and Bullfrog come home a family after adopting Itsa Snake during a camping trip. Four-color framed drawings have shapeless friendly frogs and an expressive snake.

340 *Bullfrog Builds a House.* Ill. by Byron Barton. Greenwillow, 1976, o.p. SERIES: Read-alone. SUBJECTS: Animals—Frogs and toads—Fiction; Friendship—Fiction. RL 2.9.
Bullfrog does not enjoy his new house with the front-porch diving board until he invites Gertrude to share it. Simple humor and a feeling of home regarding these two frogs are conveyed partly through avocado, rust, and cocoa drawings.

341 *Bullfrog Grows Up.* Ill. by Byron Barton. Greenwillow, 1976, o.p.; Dell, pap., 1988. ISBN 0-440-40007-4. SERIES: Read-alone. SUBJECTS: Animals—Frogs and toads—Fiction; Family life—Fiction; Growing-up—Fiction. RL 2.3.
Bullfrog needs a lunch, a pack of cards, and a last bath before setting off on his own from his adopted mouse family (practicing his neglected frog talk). Interesting ideas for presentation to primary-school-age children are illustrated with humor, enhancing individual characters.

Daugherty, Charles M.

342 *Samuel Clemens.* Ill. by Kurt Werth. Crowell, 1970, o.p. SERIES: Crowell Biography. SUBJECTS: Biographies; Writing. RL 3.4.
The zestful life of this famous writer is well portrayed. Werth's expressive drawings give character and flavor to Clemens's adventures.

Davis, Gibbs

343 *Katy's First Haircut.* Ill. by Linda Shute. Houghton Mifflin, 1985. ISBN 0-395-38942-9. SUBJECTS: Haircutting—Fiction; School stories. RL 2.7.
A simple topic, a first haircut, is dealt with sympathetically, especially by Katy's teacher

(a male) and parents, who give her free choice about how her hair is to be cut. Full color illustrations are softened by pencil outlines and shading.

Day, Jenifer W.

344 *What Is a Flower?* Ill. by Dorothea Barlowe. Golden, 1975. ISBN 0-307-61800-5. SERIES: Child's Golden Science. SUBJECTS: Nature; Plants—Flowers. RL 3.1.
A few sentences discuss various plants ranging from wild and garden flowers to vegetables, grasses, vines, and exotic flowers. Good information is illustrated with large, colorful watercolors.

345 *What Is a Fruit?* Ill. by Enid Kotschnig. Golden, 1976. ISBN 0-395-38942-9. SERIES: Child's Golden Science. SUBJECTS: Nature; Plants—Fruit. RL 3.0.
Information is given about tomatoes and melons, grains, peas and berries, and the relationships between them. Word lists are appended. Large watercolor drawings add to the book's appeal.

De Brunhoff, Laurent

346 *Babar's Little Circus Star.* Ill. by author. Random House, 1988. ISBN 0-394-98959-7. SERIES: Step into Reading. SUBJECTS: Animals—Elephants—Fiction; Circuses—Fiction. RL 2.0.
Isabelle cannot climb trees, ride a bike, or go to school, and she must go to bed early. However, small as she is, she has success in the circus. Flat decorative pastel drawings present the typical Babar family.

De Fossard, Esta

347 *Dinah the Dog with a Difference.* Photos by Haworth Bartram. Gareth Stevens, 1985. ISBN 0-918831-22-9. SERIES: Easy-to-Read Animal Adventures. SUBJECTS: Animals—Dogs; Physically and mentally impaired. RL 1.9.
Dinah's curiosity and fearlessness set her apart from her littermates, and fit her for work as a guide dog. Photo close-ups of puppy adventures are captivating.

De Fossard, Esta (cont.)

348 *Tommy the Timid Foal.* Ill. by Haworth Bartram. Gareth Stevens, 1985. ISBN 0-918831-37-7. SERIES: Easy-to-Read Animal Adventures. SUBJECTS: Animals—Horses—Fiction. RL 2.3.
Pedestrian writing about a foal needing friends is very didactic. Anthropomorphism in dialogue and realism in color photos is confusing—is it fiction or not? Notes to grown-ups, questions for discussion, and new words are appended.

Degen, Bruce

349 *The Little Witch and the Riddle.* Ill. by author. Harper & Row, 1980. ISBN 0-06-021415-5. SERIES: I Can Read. SUBJECTS: Friendship—Fiction; Jokes and riddles; Witches—Fiction. RL 2.4.
The Little Witch needs the help of her friend Otto Ogre to solve the riddles that open the "Book of Magic." This witty, gentle story is enhanced by framed pencil drawings of the pair. The drawings are highlighted in rose and gold.

DeJong, David C.

350 *Happy Birthday Egg.* Ill. by Harvey Weiss. Little, Brown, 1962, o.p. SUBJECTS: Mystery and detective stories. RL 2.9.
The nighttime mystery turns out to be an ostrich egg, not a dragon egg. Ink sketches have lavender colored pencil highlights.

DeLage, Ida

351 *ABC Pigs Go to Market.* Ill. by Kelly Oechsli. Garrard, 1977. ISBN 0-8116-4350-6. SERIES: Once Upon an ABC. SUBJECTS: Alphabet—Fiction; Animals—Pigs—Fiction. RL 2.3.
Pig children at the supermarket explore the *dairy*, look at *keys*, buy an *ounce* and a *pound* of nuts, and *wait* for change. Although the parts of speech are inconsistent and the vocabulary is not necessarily familiar, the mischief, curiosity, and setting of watercolor drawings definitely are.

352 *Beware! Beware! A Witch Won't Share.* Ill. by Ted Schroeder. Garrard, 1972, o.p. SUBJECTS: Gypsies—Fiction; Witches—Fiction. RL 3.1.
Both the farmer and the witch have trouble with the gypsies. Pencil drawings are highlighted with chartreuse and yellow.

353 *A Bunny Ride.* Ill. by Tracy McVay. Garrard, 1975. ISBN 0-8116-6065-6. SUBJECTS: Animals—Rabbits—Fiction. RL 2.2.
Baby bunnies want to ride to town as their raccoon and opposum friends do. However, the baby bunnies find a pony ride too bumpy. Pastel drawings of the babies are most appealing.

354 *Farmer and the Witch.* Ill. by Gil Miret. Garrard, 1966. ISBN 0-8116-4050-7. SERIES: Tall Tales. SUBJECTS: Witches—Fiction. RL 3.2.
The witch's marvelous brew includes toadstools, feathers, worms, webs, and lizards. Her magic has the barnyard in chaos until the farmer's ingenuity and Hoppy Toad save the day. Pumpkin and black drawings add lively humor.

355 *Frannie's Flower.* Ill. by Ellen Sloan. Garrard, 1979. ISBN 0-8116-6076-1. SUBJECTS: Imagination—Fiction. RL 1.6.
A doll survives Frannie's milk-feeding, swinging, sleeping, and wagon-riding better than her flower. Soft pastel drawings focus on a small girl's play.

356 *Good Morning, Lady.* Ill. by Tracy McVay. Garrard, 1974. ISBN 0-8116-6051-6. SUBJECTS: Animals—Fiction. RL 1.3.
The possum tinker sells a pot to a mouse to use for an unusual purpose. Pastel colors show the smallest woodland creatures.

357 *Hello, Come In.* Ill. by John Mardon. Garrard, hb and pap., 1971. ISBN 0-8116-6708-1. SUBJECTS: Houses—Fiction. RL 1.7.
Grandma, a witch, a pig, a ghost, a frog, a bird, a pony, a toymaker, and some children invite the reader into their abodes. Thin story line is supported by stylized, two-color drawings.

358 *Old Witch and the Crows.* Ill. by Marianne Smith. Garrard, 1983. ISBN 0-8116-4063-9. SERIES: Old Witch. SUBJECTS: Witches—Fiction. RL 2.9.

When Old Witch helps the crows by chasing away the owl, they return the favor by bringing creepy crawlies for her brew. Bright purple and orange, with some gray and brown, keep the setting spooky.

359 *Old Witch Finds a New House.* Ill. by Pat Paris. Garrard, 1979. ISBN 0-8116-4065-5. SERIES: Old Witch. SUBJECTS: Witches—Fiction. RL 2.9.

A woodcutter returns Old Witch's favor in full after she rescues him when he is trapped under a fallen tree. Comic drawings are in black, red, and green.

360 *Old Witch Goes to the Ball.* Ill. by Gustave E. Nebel. Garrard, 1969. ISBN 0-8116-4055-8. SERIES: Old Witch. SUBJECTS: Witches—Fiction. RL 2.7.

The clever farmer's wife distracts Old Witch from getting even when the angry witch does not win the Halloween costume contest. Gray and gold washes highlight lively ink drawings.

361 *The Old Witch's Party.* Ill. by Mimi Korach. Garrard, 1976. ISBN 0-8116-4061-2. SERIES: Old Witch. SUBJECTS: Witches—Fiction. RL 2.8.

Children mistake Old Witch for Grandma Petticoat twice. Turquoise and fuchsia highlight ink drawings.

362 *Pilgrim Children Come to Plymouth.* Ill. by Herman Vestal. Garrard, 1981. ISBN 0-8116-6084-2. SUBJECTS: Holidays—Thanksgiving; Pilgrims. RL 2.2.

Written from the point of view of Pilgrim children, the book focuses on the contributions and friendship of the Native Americans, without softening the fear and hardships. Warmth is added by watercolor drawings.

363 *Squirrel's Tree Party.* Ill. by Tracy McVay. Garrard, 1978. ISBN 0-8116-6073-7. SUBJECTS: Animals—Squirrels—Fiction. RL 1.9.

Cute animal children celebrate in the rain, sunshine, or wind. Appealing soft watercolors of animals complement the gentle story.

364 *Weeny Witch.* Ill. by Kelly Oechsli. Garrard, 1968. ISBN 0-8116-4052-3. SERIES: Old Witch. SUBJECTS: Fairies—Fiction; Witches—Fiction. RL 2.9.

Weeny Witch does not fit in with those who try to darken the sky by capturing the night fairies. Some imaginative twists and rhymes give substance to the story. Drawings help set the atmosphere with lavender, blue, and pink.

365 *What Does a Witch Need?* Ill. by Ted Schroeder. Garrard, 1971. ISBN 0-8116-4058-2. SERIES: Old Witch. SUBJECTS: Witches—Fiction. RL 2.6.

Old Witch discovers she needs a stray dog as much as a new kitten to make her brew and protect her toadstools from the gnomes. Nice touches of expression, both verbal and facial, enliven this tale.

Delton, Judy

366 *A Birthday Bike for Brimhall.* Ill. by June Leary. Carolrhoda, 1985. ISBN 0-87614-256-0. SERIES: On My Own. SUBJECTS: Animals—Bears—Fiction; Bicycles and bicycling—Fiction; Friendship—Fiction. RL 2.5.

Did Bear trick Brimhall into learning how to ride his birthday bike? (Yes, and it worked!) Finely textured ink drawings add detail and drama to this story.

367 *Brimhall Turns Detective.* Ill. by Cherie R. Wyman. Carolrhoda, 1983. ISBN 0-87614-203-X. SERIES: On My Own. SUBJECTS: Animals—Bears—Fiction; Humorous stories; Mystery and detective stories. RL 1.9.

The antics of two friends that trace monster tracks have exaggerated humor. Ink drawings have sepia pencil accents.

368 *Brimhall Turns to Magic.* Ill. by Bruce Degen. Lothrop, 1979, o.p. SERIES: Fun-to-Read. SUBJECTS: Friendship—Fiction; Magic—Fiction. RL 2.4.

When Roger the rabbit appears in Brimhall's hat by magic, it takes special friends to make him "disappear." Soon Bear regrets his grumpiness when Roger was around. Pencil drawings in gray and brown give detailed characterizations.

Delton, Judy (cont.)

369 *The Goose Who Wrote a Book.* Ill. by Catherine Cleary. Carolrhoda, 1982. ISBN 0-87614-179-3. SERIES: On My Own. SUBJECTS: Writing—Fiction. RL 2.6.
"Cheese Louise" says Goose when her friends want her absentminded fictional character to be a different animal. Pencil drawings are highlighted with turquoise and orange.

370 *Groundhog's Day at the Doctor.* Ill. by Giulio Maestro. Parents Magazine Press, 1981. ISBN 0-8193-1042-5. SUBJECTS: Animals—Fiction; Holidays— Groundhog Day—Fiction. RL 3.2.
After Groundhog wakes up a day early feeling stiff and tired, he finds himself giving advice to animals he meets in the doctor's waiting room—and ends up going skiing with the doctor. Full color drawings have a textured background.

371 *I Never Win!* Ill. by Cathy Gilchrist. Carolrhoda, 1981. ISBN 0-87614-139-4. SERIES: On My Own. SUBJECTS: Self-esteem—Fiction. RL 2.6.
Although a boy does not win birthday prizes or games, he takes his frustrations out on his piano practicing and eventually gets recognition for his talent. Ink drawings with black and red highlights are expressive of feelings.

372 *No Time for Christmas.* Ill. by Anastasia Mitchell. Carolrhoda, 1988. ISBN 0-87614-327-3. SERIES: On My Own. SUBJECTS: Animals—Bears—Fiction; Holidays—Christmas—Fiction. RL 2.3.
Bear and Brimhall are so busy working to buy each other Christmas presents that they don't see each other. Bright watercolors warm the friendship.

373 *Two Good Friends.* Ill. by Giulio Maestro. Crown, 1974, o.p.; pap., 1986. ISBN 0-517-55949-8. SUBJECTS: Animals— Bears—Fiction; Animals—Ducks— Fiction; Friendship—Fiction. RL 2.5.
What good are a clean house and wonderful nut pies without an understanding friend? Differences that seem insurmountable are resolved with love. Soft colored pencil drawings complement the mood.

Demers, Jan

374 *What Do You Do with a . . . ?* Ill. by Don Robison. Willowisp, hb and pap., 1985. ISBN 0-87406-034-6. SERIES: Predictable Read Together. SUBJECTS: Stories in rhyme. RL 1.7.
Rhythmic questions about familiar settings are answered in short rhyming phrases. Busy, brightly colored animals illustrate the questions.

Dennis, Wesley

375 *Tumble: The Story of a Mustang.* Ill. by author. Hastings House, 1966, o.p. SUBJECTS: Animals—Horses—Fiction. RL 3.1.
After a spell in a rodeo, Tumble succeeds his father as king of the mustangs. The sympathetic, elegant language has pencil illustrations.

Denzel, Justin

376 *Jumbo: Giant Circus Elephant.* Ill. by Richard Amundsen. Garrard, 1973. ISBN 0-8116-4850-8. SERIES: Famous Animal Stories. SUBJECTS: Animals—Elephants; Circuses. RL 2.6.
A true story tells about a small, gentle elephant who delighted fans for 20 years on both sides of the Atlantic. Full color illustrations show the drama of Jumbo's farewell to the circus.

dePaola, Tomie

377 *Cloud Book.* Ill. by author. Holiday House, 1975. ISBN 0-8234-0259-2. SUBJECTS: Weather—Clouds. RL 3.7.
An index is included in this lively presentation of information and sayings about clouds. Children, animals, and imagination abound in the simple, decorative illustrations.

378 *The Kids' Cat Book.* Ill. by author. Holiday House, 1979. ISBN 0-8234-0365-3. SUBJECTS: Pet care; Pets—Cats. RL 2.8.
Cat history and care is intriguingly presented when a boy visits Granny Twinkle. Add the author's outstanding creamy pastel illustra-

tions to the text for a book that should be owned universally.

379 *Oliver Button Is a Sissy*. Ill. by author. Harcourt Brace, hb and pap., 1979. ISBN 0-15-257852-8. SUBJECTS: Dancing—Fiction; Self-esteem—Fiction; Sex roles—Fiction. RL 2.5.
Oliver likes to draw and read, play jump rope—and dance. Although the boys at school tease him, and his father thinks he is a sissy, Oliver revels in dance lessons and the teasing turns to admiration. Drawings are in turquoise and cocoa.

380 *The Quicksand Book*. Ill. by author. Holiday House, 1977; pap., 1984. ISBN 0-8234-0291-6. SUBJECTS: Nature; Science. RL 2.9.
Jungle Boy corrects misconceptions people have about quicksand while Jungle Girl sinks. When *he* falls in, she is in no hurry to help him out. Good information is presented in an arresting way and ably illustrated with hand-lettered cartoons and fact boxes.

Dewey, Ariane

381 *Laffite, the Pirate*. Ill. by author. Greenwillow, 1985; ISBN 0-688-04230-9. SUBJECTS: Historical fiction; Pirates—Fiction; United States—1783–1865—Fiction. RL 3.2.
Rousing stories of Laffite the pirate's bravado and occasional generosity and legends of treasure troves are retold by Dewey. Her colorful, decorative illustrations have clear lines and flat colors.

Dinardo, Jeffrey

382 *Timothy and the Big Bully*. Ill. by author. Simon & Schuster, 1988. ISBN 0-671-66562-6. SERIES: Books for Young Readers. SUBJECTS: Animals—Frogs and toads—Fiction; Behavior—Bullying—Fiction; Siblings—Fiction. RL 2.4.
Big brother Martin saves Timothy from the bully Big Eddie. Simple story is less imaginative than other stories about bullies such as Nancy Carlson's *Loudmouth George and the Sixth Grade Bully* (Carolrhoda, 1983). Flat and stiff illustrations are in pastels.

Dineen, Jacqueline

383 *Let's Look at Rain*. Ill. by Carolyn Scrace. Bookwright, 1989. ISBN 0-531-18255-X. SERIES: Let's Look At. SUBJECTS: Nature; Water. RL 2.5.
The water cycle, collection and uses of water, weather, and storms related to the water cycle are introduced. Includes glossary and index. Acceptable pastel drawings.

Dines, Glen

384 *John Muir*. Ill. by author. Putnam, 1974, o.p. SERIES: See and Read Biography. SUBJECTS: Biographies; Nature. RL 2.6.
Inventor and naturalist John Muir wrote lovingly about the wilderness. His work helped to save large tracts of land as parks for others to enjoy. This well-told, simple story has forest green, black, and gray colored drawings.

Dolch, Edward W., and Dolch, Marguerite P.

385 *Aesop's Stories*. Ill. by Marguerite P. Dolch. Garrard, 1951. ISBN 0-8116-2602-4. SERIES: Pleasure Reading. SUBJECTS: Animals—Fiction; Fables. RL 2.5.
Fifty-six familiar fables are retold in simple but smoothly flowing language, with morals intact. Drawings with red coloring are dated, however.

386 *Circus Stories*. Ill. by Dee Wallace. Garrard, 1956. ISBN 0-8116-2512-5. SERIES: Basic Vocabulary. SUBJECTS: Circuses—Fiction. RL 2.4.
The quality of stories varies, from the sentimental one of a dog saving the audience from a lion on the loose, to the high drama of a fall by the famous Wallendas. Plain drawings add little.

387 *Folk Stories*. Ill. by Marguerite P. Dolch. Garrard, 1952. ISBN 0-8116-2500-1. SERIES: Basic Vocabulary. SUBJECTS: Folklore—Europe. RL 2.4.
Twenty folktales include nursery tales such as "The Pot That Would Not Walk," "Lazy Jack," and "The Three Wishes." Both the retelling and the drawings are plain, but they make traditional tales accessible to young readers.

Dolch, Edward W., and Dolch, Marguerite P. (cont.)

388 *Lion and Tiger Stories.* Ill. by Charles Forsythe. Garrard, 1957. ISBN 0-8116-2511-7. SERIES: Basic Vocabulary. SUBJECTS: Animals—Lions—Fiction; Animals—Tigers—Fiction; Folklore. RL 2.5.

Traditional tales as well as circus adventures are retold well. Each story begins with an ink drawing with gold highlights.

389 *Lodge Stories.* Ill. by Billy M. Jackson. Garrard, 1957. ISBN 0-8116-2506-0. SERIES: Basic Vocabulary. SUBJECTS: Folklore—Native Americans; Native Americans—Legends. RL 2.1.

This book encompasses 18 authentic Native American tales coming from the Cherokee, Creek, Alabama, Yuchi, Choctaw, Natchez, and Seminole tribes. These well-told tales are headed by ink drawings of animals with orange background.

390 *Once There Was a Bear.* Ill. by Gerald McCann. Garrard, 1962. ISBN 0-8116-2814-0. SERIES: First Reading. SUBJECTS: Animals—Bears; Folklore. RL 2.4.

One hundred and ten sight words plus one new word per page are used to tell eight stories of bears, some true, some folktales. There is a good variety in style and outcome among the stories. The stories are illustrated with ink drawings highlighted in red and blue.

391 *Once There Was a Monkey.* Ill. by Kenyon Shannon. Garrard, 1962. ISBN 0-8116-2813-2. SERIES: First Reading. SUBJECTS: Animals—Monkeys—Fiction; Folklore. RL 2.8.

The end of the book lists the eight stories about monkeys from India, Africa, Tibet, Brazil, and the Philippines. The language used in this book is very abbreviated. Rose and green highlight pedestrian drawings.

392 *Stories from Old Russia.* Ill. by James Lewicki. Garrard, 1964. ISBN 0-8116-2560-5. SERIES: Folklore of the World. SUBJECTS: Folklore—Russia; Russia—Fiction. RL 2.7.

Twenty-one traditional tales, of Vasilisa, Baba Yaga, and Ivan the Fool, are followed by a mini-pronunciation guide. Full color paint-ings are far superior to illustrations in most Dolch readers.

393 *Tepee Stories.* Ill. by Robert S. Kerr. Garrard, 1955, o.p. SERIES: Basic Vocabulary. SUBJECTS: Folklore—Native Americans; Native Americans—Fiction. RL 2.7.

Blackfoot, Pawnee, Cheyenne, Kiowa, Wichita, Sioux, Crow, and Arikara tribal stories are retold in this book. Creation myths, tales of Coyote, and stories of giants, animals, and magic are exceptionally well told, but the drawings in red are very dated.

394 *"Why" Stories.* Ill. by Marguerite P. Dolch. Garrard, 1958. ISBN 0-8116-2502-8. SERIES: Basic Vocabulary. SUBJECTS: Animals—Fiction; Folklore. RL 2.0.

Stories, such as why Bear has a little tail, why Woodpecker looks for bugs, and why Jellyfish has no bones, are told in simple yet fluid, rhythmic language. Green colored drawings are dated.

Dolch, Marguerite P.

395 *Once There Was a Coyote.* Ill. by Carl Hauge and Mary Hauge. Garrard, 1975. ISBN 0-8116-2816-7. SERIES: First Reading. SUBJECTS: Animals—Coyotes—Fiction; Folklore—Native Americans. RL 2.5.

In simple, effective language, these stories tell why Coyote is smart, why he is a dirty color, why he does not crawl, why the volcano smokes, and how Coyote escaped from the Giants. Coyote looks appealingly doglike in simple drawings.

396 *Stories from Africa.* Ill. by Vincent Smith. Garrard, 1975, o.p. SERIES: Folklore of the World. SUBJECTS: Folklore—Africa. RL 2.5.

Sixteen stories include the creation of man and woman, why we have rain, and a story about a "foolish" man who won a bet. Graphically pleasing illustrations are in flat primitive style with deep vivid colors.

Donnelly, Judy

397 *Tut's Mummy: Lost and Found.* Ill. by James Watling. Random House, hb and pap., 1988. ISBN 0-394-89189-3. SERIES: Step into Reading. SUBJECTS: Egypt, ancient. RL 3.3.

The drama of finding of Tutankhamen's tomb is presented factually. Full color pastel drawings are taken from tomb paintings; the poor-quality black and white photos detract.

Donnelly, Liza

398 *Dinosaur Beach*. Ill. by author. Scholastic, 1989. SUBJECTS: Dinosaurs—Fiction; Fantasy. RL 2.5.

A boy and his dog, Bones, are at a beach, where Bones' sand dinosaur creates a panic. The boy and Bones then travel to Dinosaur Beach, viewing a dozen dinosaurs who have created a sand sculpture of *them!* Simple, well-crafted story has soft pastel drawings and a brief description of each dinosaur.

Dorros, Arthur

399 *Ant Cities*. Ill. by author. Crowell, 1987. ISBN 0-690-04570-0. SERIES: Let's-Read-and-Find-Out Science. SUBJECTS: Animals—Ants; Nature. RL 3.1.

An overview of the social organization, food, and types of ants is given, along with such details as how the antennae are used and how to build one's own ant city. Soft watercolors give cutaways and close-up views of ant cities.

400 *Feel the Wind*. Ill. by author. Crowell, 1989. ISBN 0-690-04741-X. SERIES: Let's-Read-and-Find-Out Science. SUBJECTS: Science. RL 2.8.

Beginning by introducing familiar results that demonstrate the characteristics of wind, the text continues by describing the causes and uses of wind. Soft watercolors personalize and enhance this excellent text.

401 *Pretzels*. Ill. by author. Greenwillow, 1981, o.p. SERIES: Read-alone. SUBJECTS: Humorous stories. RL 3.1.

I Freyem Fine's biscuit dough, after being used as an anchor chain, is reconstituted as a pretzel. This tall tale is illustrated with ink and two-tone washes.

Dorsky, Blanche

402 *Harry: A True Story*. Ill. by Muriel Batherman. Prentice-Hall, 1977, o.p. SUBJECTS: Animals—Rabbits—Fiction. School stories. RL 2.9.

Harry, the nursery school's pet rabbit, is "not himself," and it takes a trip to the vet to find out why. Delicate ink sketches are in pastel colors except for the black rabbit.

Dreifus, Miriam

403 *Brave Betsy*. Ill. by Sheila Greenwald. Putnam, 1961, o.p. SERIES: See and Read. SUBJECTS: Lost, being—Fiction; Toys—Dolls and dollhouses—Fiction. RL 2.1.

When Joan is trapped in the empty school, her doll Betsy leads her parents to her rescue. Green colored pencil alternating with red illustrates this simple tale.

Dubowski, Cathy E., and Dubowski, Mark

404 *Pretty Good Magic*. Ill. by Mark Dubowski. Random House, hb and pap., 1987. ISBN 0-394-99068-4. SERIES: Step into Reading. SUBJECTS: Animals—Rabbits—Fiction; Humorous stories; Magic—Fiction. RL 2.7.

The town of Forty Winks is so quiet that Presto decides to learn a new, impressive trick to wake everyone up—and finds himself stuck with dozens of rabbits. Comical pencil and wash drawings successfully complement the text.

E

Eastman, Patricia

405 *Sometimes Things Change*. Ill. by Seymour Fleischman. Childrens, 1983. ISBN 0-516-02044-7. SERIES: Rookie Readers. SUBJECTS: Change. RL 2.0.

Things change: caterpillars, tadpoles, eggs, grapes, seeds, buds, babies, strangers, clouds, and so forth. Some rather complex ideas for beginning readers using a 47 word vocabulary. Simple ink and wash drawings focus on children and animals.

Eastman, Philip D.

406 *Are You My Mother?* Ill. by author. Beginner, 1960. ISBN 0-394-90018-9. SERIES: I Can Read It All By Myself. SUBJECTS: Growing up—Fiction; Mothers—Fiction; Parent and child—Fiction. RL 1.4.

Baby Bird hatches while Mother is out digging worms. He seeks her in the barnyard and is hoisted by a snorting machine—into his own nest just in time to meet his mother. Brown pencil drawings have yellow and red highlights, complementing this reassuring tale.

407 *Best Nest.* Ill. by author. Beginner, 1968. ISBN 0-394-90051-0. SUBJECTS: Animals—Birds—Fiction; Houses—Fiction. RL 2.4.

Mr. Bird's search for a better nest demonstrates that a shoe, a mailbox, and a church steeple all have their drawbacks. Simple comic illustrations underline his relief when he finds his wife safe—back in the old nest.

408 *Flap Your Wings.* Ill. by author. Random House, 1969, o.p.; pap., 1984. ISBN 0-394-83565-4. SERIES: Early Bird. SUBJECTS: Animals—Birds—Fiction. RL 2.2.

Mr. and Mrs. Bird hatch a foundling egg with surprising results. A well-constructed story that is illustrated simply.

409 *Sam and the Firefly.* Ill. by author. Beginner, 1958, o.p. SERIES: I Can Read It All By Myself. SUBJECTS: Animals—Fireflies—Fiction; Animals—Owls—Fiction. RL 2.1.

Gus the firefly's skill at spelling runs amok until he is saved from the consequences of his mischief by his friend Sam, an owl. Inventive humor has turquoise illustrations with yellow owl eyes and firefly writing.

Edwards, Anne

410 *Houdini.* Ill. by Joseph Ciardiello. Putnam, 1977, o.p. SERIES: See and Read. SUBJECTS: Biographies; Magic. RL 3.3.

This true story of the best-known magician ever has great drama and human interest. Ink drawings add interesting details.

411 *P. T. Barnum.* Ill. by Marylin Hafner. Putnam, 1977, o.p. SERIES: See and Read Biography. SUBJECTS: Biographies; Circuses. RL 3.4.

Barnum's colorful career is traced—from the small boy who always had a head for sums to the flamboyant showman. Gray tone drawings capture some of the excitement.

Ehrlich, Amy

412 *Buck-Buck the Chicken.* Ill. by R. W. Alley. Random House, hb and pap., 1987. ISBN 0-394-98804-3. SERIES: Step into Reading. SUBJECTS: Animals—Chickens—Fiction; Humorous stories; Pets—Fiction. RL 2.2.

Won by Nancy's father at the county fair, Buck-Buck is a pampered pet who does not seem to know how to act like a chicken. This delightfully silly story is illustrated with watercolors with ink detailing.

413 *Leo, Zack and Emmie.* Ill. by Steven Kellogg. Dial, hb and pap., 1981. ISBN 0-8037-4761-6. SERIES: Easy-to-Read. SUBJECTS: Friendship—Fiction; School stories. RL 2.6.

Emmie, as the newcomer, upsets the friendship between Leo and Zack. Four episodes of everyday experiences are warm and humorous, enhanced by delicious four-color action-filled illustrations.

414 *Leo, Zack and Emmie Together Again.* Ill. by Steven Kellogg. Dial, 1987. ISBN 0-8037-0382-1. SERIES: Easy-to-Read. SUBJECTS: Friendship—Fiction. RL 2.3.

Four stories tell how the friendship of these three is tested at school and in the neighborhood. The drawings add to the sense of mischief and express the emotions and warmth of childhood.

Elkin, Benjamin

415 *Big Jump and Other Stories.* Ill. by Katherine Evans. Beginner, 1958. ISBN 0-394-90004-9. SUBJECTS: Jokes and riddles—Fiction; Kings and queens—Fiction. RL 2.0.

Ben solves the king's quandaries with creative thinking, but without high drama. Red and green colored pencil illustrations show the action but have minimal appeal except for those of Ben's puppy.

Elliott, Dan

416 *Ernie's Little Lie.* Ill. by Joe Mathieu. Random House, hb and pap., 1983. ISBN 0-394-95440-8. SERIES: Start-to-Read. SUBJECTS: Behavior—Lying—Fiction. RL 2.2.

Ernie did not originally intend to claim someone else's artwork as his own, but he certainly feels better after confessing. Straightforward drawings show "Sesame Street" characters.

417 *Grover Learns to Read.* Ill. by Normand Chartier. Random House, 1985. ISBN 0-394-97498-0. SERIES: Start-to-Read. SUBJECTS: Books and reading—Fiction; Libraries—Fiction. RL 2.2.

Grover is not sure he wants to learn to read if he misses out on his mother's bedtime story. Bright pastel drawings are of "Sesame Street" characters.

Elting, Mary, and Folsom, Michael

418 *Q Is for Duck: An Alphabet Guessing Game.* Ill. by Jack Kent. Houghton Mifflin, hb and pap., 1980. ISBN 0-395-29437-1. SUBJECTS: Alphabet—Fiction; Animals—Fiction. RL 3.2.

This alphabet book is for older readers because the letters represent *verbs* not nouns. "L is for Frog Why? Because a Frog Leaps." However, the verbs used are not predictable or even logical. Drawings are charming.

Epstein, Sam, and Epstein, Beryl

419 *Hold Everything.* Ill. by Tomie dePaola. Holiday House, 1973, o.p. SUBJECTS: Science. RL 3.1.

Sewing, adhesives, saliva, icing, staples, nails, and zippers are some of the ways things are held together. Creative possibilities such as holding hands and using "and" are suggested. Three-color illustrations give detail and humor.

420 *Pick It Up.* Ill. by Tomie dePaola. Holiday House, 1971, o.p. SUBJECTS:

Human body—Hands; Science; Tools. RL 3.3.

Using familiar objects or animals as examples, the many ways things are picked up are discussed. Alternating cocoa and turquoise and black and white drawings add humorous touches.

421 *Who Needs Holes?* Ill. by Tomie dePaola. Hawthorn, 1970, o.p. SUBJECTS: Concepts. RL 2.0.

Armholes, buttonholes, colanders, shower heads, drills, lifesavers, and keyholes are some of the common holes explored in this creative text using a self-discovery experimental approach. DePaola's appealing people and animal drawings alternate ink with lavender and golden brown.

Eugenie, and Olson, Mary C., reteller

422 *Kittens for Keeps.* Ill. by Eugenie. Western, 1987. ISBN 0-307-03678-2. SERIES: Step Ahead Beginning Reader. SUBJECTS: Grandparents—Fiction; Pets—Cats—Fiction; Seashore—Fiction. RL 2.1.

Visiting her grandmother at the seashore, Meg finds two kittens and keeps them until the end of the summer when one stays with her grandmother and the other goes home to the city with Meg. Illustrated with sweet watercolor paintings.

Evans, Katherine

423 *The Boy Who Cried Wolf.* Ill. by author. Whitman, 1960. ISBN 0-8075-0863-2. SUBJECTS: Folklore. RL 2.9.

This traditional tale of a shepherd boy who cries wolf once too often is retold well. Crayon drawings give a folktale flavor.

424 *Camel in the Tent.* Ill. by author. Whitman, 1961, o.p. SUBJECTS: Folklore—Turkey; Turkey—Fiction. RL 3.2.

Traditional moral tale tells how a man lost a sultan's riches by letting a camel get his head in his tent. Textured crayon illustrates this foolish tale well.

Evans, Katherine (cont.)

425 *Maid and Her Pail of Milk.* Ill. by author. Whitman, 1959, o.p. SUBJECTS: Folklore—Netherlands; Netherlands—Fiction. RL 2.3.

"Never count your chickens until they are hatched" is the moral a country maid longing for citified finery discovers. Crayon and pencil drawings are appropriate.

426 *The Man, the Boy, and the Donkey.* Ill. by author. Whitman, 1958, o.p. SUBJECTS: Folklore—Netherlands; Netherlands—Fiction. RL 3.1.

This moral tale is well told with an authentic Dutch flavor. Black and white pencil drawings alternate with full color ones.

427 *One Good Deed Deserves Another.* Ill. by author. Whitman, 1964, o.p. SUBJECTS: Folklore—Mexico; Mexico—Fiction. RL 2.8.

A traditional tale of Señor Coyote and Snake is retold with a boy's wise action saving a family from a ruffian. Ink drawings alternate with color, showing authentic folk details.

Eyles, Heather

428 *A Zoo in Our House.* Ill. by Andy Cooke. Warner, 1988. ISBN 1-55782-002-3. SERIES: Early Reader. SUBJECTS: Zoos—Fiction. RL 3.3.

One by one some zoo animals visit a little boy's house, then *all* come for a party! Large, colorful zany animals and the messes they create are eye-catching.

F

Farley, Walter

429 *Little Black, a Pony.* Ill. by James Schucker. Beginner, 1961. ISBN 0-394-90021-9. SUBJECTS: Animals—Horses—Fiction. RL 1.7.

When his master begins riding a bigger horse, his former riding horse Little Black becomes sad and tries to keep up. Only when the boy is saved by Little Black after falling through the ice does he fully appreciate his faithful pony. This is an absorbing horse story despite its dated illustrations.

Feder, Paula K.

430 *Where Does the Teacher Live?* Ill. by Lillian Hoban. Dutton, 1979, o.p. SUBJECTS: School stories. RL 2.3.

The answer to a question many children ponder—"where does teacher live?"—is discovered by the reader, but not the children of this slight story. Hoban's soft watercolors are suitable.

Fine, Jane

431 *Surprise!* Ill. by Mary Morgan. Viking Kestrel, 1988. ISBN 0-670-82036-9. SERIES: Hello Reading. SUBJECTS: Birthdays—Fiction; Families—Fiction; Mothers—Fiction. RL 2.6.

Three young children get up very early and quietly prepare a tray of juice and cookies for their mother's birthday. The text is very brief, relying on the pictures of the excited children and their rambunctious cat to help tell the story. Illustrations are in bright, vibrant watercolors.

Finsand, Mary J.

432 *The Town That Moved.* Ill. by Reg Sandland. Carolrhoda, 1983. ISBN 0-87614-200-5. SERIES: On My Own. SUBJECTS: Historical fiction. RL 3.2.

In the 1920s, when iron ore was discovered under the town of Hibbing, Minnesota, the buildings were rolled one by one on logs to a nearby location. Pencil drawings show the action.

Firmin, Peter

433 *Basil Brush Gets a Medal.* Ill. by author. Prentice-Hall, 1973, o.p. SUBJECTS: Animals—Foxes—Fiction; Animals—Moles—Fiction; Cumulative tales. RL 2.9.

This original cumulative tale recounts Basil the fox and Harry the mole's adventures getting milk for the princess's porridge before deserved medals can be awarded. Red wash highlights ink animal drawings.

434 *Basil Brush Goes Boating.* Ill. by author. Prentice-Hall, 1969, o.p. SUBJECTS: Animals—Foxes—Fiction; Fishing—Fiction; Friendship—Fiction. RL 2.6.
Basil the fox and his friend Harry the mole manage to leave all of their equipment behind when they go fishing. Gentle humor warms this tale of friendship; blue highlights ink drawings.

435 *Basil Brush Goes Flying.* Ill. by author. Prentice-Hall, 1977, o.p. SUBJECTS: Animals—Foxes—Fiction; Animals—Moles—Fiction. RL 2.4.
Irrepressible optimism fuels Basil the fox and his friend Harry the mole's flying adventures. A blue wash brightens action-filled ink drawings.

436 *Basil Brush in the Jungle.* Ill. by author. Prentice-Hall, 1970, o.p. SUBJECTS: Animals—Foxes—Fiction; Humorous stories; India—Fiction. RL 3.0.
Basil the fox takes the cage he makes to India, where the butterfly, crocodile, snake, and tiger are happier in the jungle than in his cage. Humor is used in this exotic adventure; ink and green wash sketches focus on animals, an unforgettable Indian ferryman, and an umbrella man.

437 *Basil Brush on the Trail.* Ill. by author. Prentice-Hall, 1979, o.p. SUBJECTS: Animals—Foxes—Fiction; Animals—Moles—Fiction; Mystery and detective stories. RL 2.2.
Basil the fox and Harry the mole's bungling attempts do not uncover the real thief of the silver tennis trophies until the owner returns home. Ink drawings have orange highlights.

Fisher, Aileen

438 *The House of a Mouse.* Ill. by Joan Sandin. Harper & Row, 1988. ISBN 0-06-021849-5. SUBJECTS: Animals—Mice—Fiction; Poetry. RL 3.1.
The world of different kinds of mice is explored—the dangers, tracks, nests, and habits—in lighthearted simple verse. Soft pencil drawings beautifully complement this rhythmic celebration of mice.

FitzGerald, Cathleen

439 *Let's Find Out about Words.* Ill. by Georgia Froom. Watts, 1971, o.p. SUBJECTS: English language. RL 2.5.
FitzGerald celebrates the contributions of various cultures to the English language, as well as the history and evolution of our language. Information is well presented. Ink drawings are against a gold or orange background.

Fitz-Gerald, Christine

440 *I Can Be a Mother.* Photos. Childrens, 1989. ISBN 0-516-41914-5. SERIES: I Can Be. SUBJECTS: Mothers; Parent and child. RL 2.8.
Good basic information regarding birth and adoptive mothers and stepmothers is given. A picture glossary precedes the text and a second glossary ends the book. Exceptional color photos brighten the text.

Fleischman, Sid

441 *Kate's Secret Riddle Book.* Ill. by Barbara Bottner. Watts, 1977, o.p.; Avon, pap., 1984. ISBN 0-380-40253-X. SERIES: Easy-Read Story. SUBJECTS: Jokes and riddles. RL 2.5.
Riddles for young readers are woven into a story about some girls trying to find out the answer to their friend Wally's riddle. Yellow and pumpkin colors predominate in illustrations with humor (but weird faces).

Flower, Phyllis

442 *Barn Owl.* Ill. by Cherryl Pape. Harper & Row, 1978, o.p. SERIES: I Can Read Science. SUBJECTS: Animals—Owls; Science. RL 2.3.
The life cycle of a barn owlet is traced, simply and eloquently. Pencil drawings with tan and gray washes show the drama of learning to fly and the first successful hunt.

Fox, Charles P.

443 *When Autumn Comes*. Ill. by author.
Reilly & Lee, 1966, o.p. SERIES: Easy-to-
Read-Photo-Story. SUBJECTS: Animals;
Nature; Seasons—Fall. RL 2.0.
The changes before winter for birds, small
mammals, plants, and trees are described,
emphasizing observing and listening. Black
and white photos include many appealing
close-ups.

444 *When Summer Comes*. Ill. by author.
Reilly & Lee, 1966, o.p. SERIES: Easy-to-
Read-Photo-Story. SUBJECTS: Animals;
Nature; Seasons—Summer. RL 2.2.
The reader is invited to observe frogs, ducks,
snakes, skunks, dragonflies, woodchucks, raccoons, hawks, wasps, owls, and a mystery
egg. Black and white photos include the
young in their nests.

445 *When Winter Comes*. Ill. by author.
Reilly & Lee, 1962, o.p. SERIES: Easy-to-
Read-Photo-Story. SUBJECTS: Animals;
Nature; Seasons—Winter. RL 1.9.
From raccoons and skunks to foxes and opos-
sums, the animals' activities—and tracks—
are described and illustrated with black and
white photo close-ups.

Fradin, Dennis

446 *Cancer*. Photos. Childrens, hb and pap.,
1988. ISBN 0-516-01210-X. SERIES: New
True. SUBJECTS: Diseases. RL 3.4.
Facts about cancer and what is known about
it; also focus on smoking as an avoidable
carcinogen. Excellent photos show healthy
people, hospital procedures, and some diseased organs.

447 *Declaration of Independence*. Photos and
drawings. Childrens, 1988. ISBN 0-516-
01153-7. SERIES: New True. SUBJECTS:
United States—Revolution. RL 3.7.
An index and glossary accompany nine short
chapters in large print giving background
information about the Declaration of Independence as well as its effects on our government.
Photos and many drawings are in color.

448 *The Flag of the United States*. Photos.
Childrens, 1988. ISBN 0-516-01158-8.
SERIES: New True. SUBJECTS: Flags;
United States—History. RL 2.9.
Ten chapters give the history and care of the
American flag, the writing of the Star Span-
gled Banner, and the pledge to the flag. A
glossary and index are appended to basic,
well-presented information, liberally illus-
trated with good photos.

449 *The Pawnee*. Photos. Childrens, 1988.
ISBN 0-516-01155-3. SERIES: New True.
SUBJECTS: Native Americans—Pawnee.
RL 3.7.
The history and life-style of the Pawnee are
described in ten short chapters, with a glossary and index appended. Excellent color
photos give details of symbolism on clothing
and sacred objects.

450 *The Shoshoni*. Photos. Childrens, 1988.
ISBN 0-516-01156-1. SERIES: New True.
SUBJECTS: Native Americans—Shoshoni.
RL 3.6.
The importance of song, dance, and story in
Shoshoni life is added to the history, which
includes Sacajawea. Close-up color photos of
traditional clothing are most captivating.

451 *Thirteen Colonies*. Photos and drawings.
Childrens, 1988. ISBN 0-516-01157-X.
SERIES: New True. SUBJECTS: United
States—Colonial period. RL 3.7.
The reasons the Spanish, English, French,
and Africans came to America, how they lived
and broke away from England, and the fate of
the Indians are introduced in six short chapters. A glossary and index add to its accessibil-
ity. A chart shows population per colony by
decade. Liberally illustrated with excellent
color photos.

452 *The Voyager Space Probes*. Photos.
Childrens, hb and pap., 1985. ISBN 0-
516-01944-9. SERIES: New True.
SUBJECTS: Astronomy; Science; Space
travel. RL Off Spache scale.
Excellent color photos illustrate current information about Jupiter and Saturn gar-
nered by the Voyager space probe, which is
still headed for Neptune. A glossary and
index are appended.

Franchere, Ruth

453 *Cesar Chavez.* Ill. by Earl Thollander.
Crowell, 1970, o.p.; Harper & Row,
pap., 1988. ISBN 0-06-446023-1. SERIES:
Crowell Biography. SUBJECTS:
Biographies. RL 2.9.
Cesar Chavez knew firsthand the hardships of
migrant labor, and worked to organize Mexican Americans to improve their living and
working conditions. Sketches are appropriate, though not exciting.

Freedman, Russell

454 *Dinosaurs and Their Young.* Ill. by
Leslie Morrill. Holiday House, 1983.
ISBN 0-8234-0496-X. SUBJECTS:
Dinosaurs; Science. RL 3.6.
How the recent discovery of a duckbill dinosaur nursery by a Montana high school teacher
has altered scientists' ideas about how dinosaurs lived is detailed by this 1984 Newbery
award winner.

Freeman, Dorothy R.

455 *Friday Surprise.* Ill. by Mary Murphy.
Elk Grove, 1968, o.p. SUBJECTS: Books
and reading—Fiction; Family life—
Fiction; Fathers—Fiction. RL 1.9.
Mario's imaginative school art projects delight each member of the family—especially
his father—when Mario learns to read. The
drawings are of marginal quality and detract
from the story.

Freschet, Berniece

456 *Little Black Bear Goes for a Walk.* Ill. by
Glen Rounds. Scribner, 1977, o.p.
SUBJECTS: Animals—Bears—Fiction.
RL 2.5.
Little Bear's first exploration on his own
introduces him to bugs, porcupines, water,
bees—and *honey.* The expressive ink sketches
add humor.

457 *Lizard Lying in the Sun.* Ill. by Glen
Rounds. Scribner, 1975, o.p. SUBJECTS:
Animals—Lizards; Nature; Science.
RL 2.6.

Good information about lizards is presented
in an absorbing way by focusing on one
lizard. Intriguing ink sketches enhance the
text.

458 *Moose Baby.* Ill. by Jim Arnosky.
Putnam, 1979, o.p. SERIES: See and
Read Nature. SUBJECTS: Animals—
Moose; Nature. RL 3.1.
Encounters with a skunk, a coyote, and fight-
ing bull moose mark a baby moose's first
year. The ink and wash sketches are very
appealing.

459 *Possum Baby.* Ill. by Jim Arnosky.
Putnam, 1978, o.p. SERIES: See and
Read Nature. SUBJECTS: Animals—
Opossum; Growing-up; Nature. RL 3.3.
The trials of growing up are told from the
point of view of a young possum—from birth
to independence. The tale is interrupted
briefly to give information about other mar-
supials. Arnosky's black ink drawings are
very appealing.

Friskey, Margaret

460 *Indian Two Feet and the Wolf Cubs.* Ill.
by John Hawkinson. Childrens, 1971.
ISBN 0-516-03506-1. SUBJECTS: Animals—
Wolves—Fiction; Native Americans—
Fiction; Pets—Wild animals—Fiction.
RL 2.7.
Indian Two Feet spends so much time watching the wolf family that he is included in their
family circle. When he tries to adopt a cub, he
is advised that other wolves will take care of
any orphans. Watercolor drawings are especially good of the animals.

461 *Mystery of the Farmer's Three Fives.* Ill.
by Lucy Hawkinson and John
Hawkinson. Childrens, 1963, o.p. SERIES:
Reading Lab. SUBJECTS: Concepts—
Numbers—Fiction; Farm and country
life—Fiction; Mathematics—Fiction. RL
1.9.
A 145-word vocabulary is used to sketch
arithmetic skills in an imaginative way, using
barnyard animals. Delicate ink and wash
drawings lighten the lesson.

Friskey, Margaret (cont.)

462 *Three Sides and the Round One.* Ill. by
Mary Gehr. Childrens, 1973, o.p.
SUBJECTS: Concepts—Shape;
Mathematics; Stories in rhyme. RL 2.3.
Creative, rhythmic language introduces
shapes of ordinary objects. Striking, simple
shapes stand out on bright solid backgrounds.

463 *The True Book of the Moonwalk
Adventure.* Photos by NASA. Childrens,
1970, o.p. SUBJECTS: Science; Space. RL
2.8.
Information about the moon is gained, along
with some of the drama of the first moon
walk, and the appearance of Earth from
space. Each NASA photo faces relevant text.

Frith, Michael K.

464 *I'll Teach My Dog One Hundred Words.*
Ill. by P. D. Eastman. Beginner, 1973.
ISBN 0-394-82692-2. SERIES: Bright and
Early. SUBJECTS: Humorous stories;
Stories in rhyme. RL 2.2.
Rhythmic humor teaching the reader, as well
as the dog, 100 new words; accented by
excellent comic drawings.

Froman, Robert

465 *Bigger and Smaller.* Ill. by Gioia Fiammenghi. Crowell, 1971, o.p.; pap., 1971.
ISBN 0-690-14197-1. SUBJECTS:
Concepts—Size. RL 2.9.
The relative nature of size is emphasized and
some entertaining relationships are explored. Ink and wash drawings are graphically interesting.

Funai, Mamoru

466 *Moke and Poki in the Rain Forest.* Ill. by
author. Harper & Row, 1971. ISBN 0-06-
021927-0. SERIES: I Can Read. SUBJECTS:
Folklore—Hawaii; Hawaii—Fiction;
Rainbows—Fiction. RL 1.9.
Moke and Poki are six-inch menehunes. With
the help of their friends they build a house,
sing to the moon, sail a bean-pod canoe, and
search for rainbows. Turquoise and rose-
brown colors create a tropical setting for the
wee friends.

G

Gackenbach, Dick

467 *Hattie Be Quiet, Hattie Be Good.* Ill. by
author. Harper & Row, 1977. ISBN 0-06-
021951-3. SERIES: Early I Can Read.
SUBJECTS: Animals—Rabbits—Fiction;
Behavior—Obedient—Fiction. RL 2.4.
Hattie's effort to please her mother by unchar-
acteristically spending time quietly is misinterpreted, as is her effort to help her friend
Shirley feel perkier. Fat, cuddly rabbits with
pumpkin coloring help portray Hattie's zest
for life.

468 *Hattie Rabbit.* Ill. by author. Harper &
Row, 1976. ISBN 0-06-021940-8. SERIES:
Early I Can Read. SUBJECTS: Animals—
Rabbits—Fiction; Friendship—Fiction.
RL 2.2.
Hattie makes two decisions: She likes her
mother because she is warm, soft, and furry,
and the money she won by tricking her
friends is a poor substitute for their friendship. Brown and turquoise drawings are of
appealing rabbits.

469 *Hattie, Tom and Chicken Witch (a play
and a story).* Ill. by author. Harper &
Row, 1980. ISBN 0-06-021959-9. SERIES: I
Can Read. SUBJECTS: Animals—Rabbits—Fiction; Holidays—Easter—Fiction; Plays—Fiction. RL 2.1.
Hattie Rabbit is allowed a part in the Easter
play only when Linda Chicken twists her
ankle. Chickens and rabbits are important to
Easter, they decide. Sympathetic animal characters are drawn in rose, beige, and gray.

470 *Hound and Bear.* Ill. by author. Clarion,
1976. ISBN 0-395-28796-0. SUBJECTS: Animals—Bears—Fiction; Animals—Dogs—
Fiction; Friendship—Fiction. RL 2.7.
Hound loses out on his own birthday when he
tricks Bear into sleeping too long; he loses a
present when he tries another trick. Bear gets
the best present of all when Hound promises
not to play any more tricks. Gentle moral is
illustrated with gray and rust washes.

471 *Hurray for Hattie Rabbit!* Ill. by author.
Harper & Row, 1986. ISBN 0-06-021983-

1. SERIES: Early I Can Read. SUBJECTS: Animals—Rabbits—Fiction; Mothers—Fiction. RL 2.3.

The mischievous, sad, smug, and repentant expressions of two cuddly friends, Hattie Rabbit and Rosie Pig, are captivating. Their mothers find creative solutions for sleeplessness and the girls have a bet for who will get her mother to say "yes" first.

472 *Mother Rabbit's Son Tom.* Ill. by author. Harper & Row, 1977. ISBN 0-06-021948-3. SERIES: Early I Can Read. SUBJECTS: Animals—Rabbits—Fiction. RL 2.5.

Tom's steady diet of a hamburger with onion, ketchup, and pickles on a poppy-seed roll has results even his parents do not expect. It is also clear that Tom's mother should *never* have consented to a dinosaur for a pet! Gentle, simple illustrations are rust and beige with a dark outline.

Gage, Wilson

473 *The Crow and Mrs. Gaddy.* Ill. by Marylin Hafner. Greenwillow, 1984; Scholastic, pap., 1985. ISBN 0-688-02536-6. SERIES: Read-alone. SUBJECTS: Humorous stories. RL 2.8.

Mrs. Gaddy has a running feud with a mischievous crow. Broad humor is enhanced by detailed ink and wash drawings.

474 *Down in the Boondocks.* Ill. by Glen Rounds. Greenwillow, 1977. ISBN 0-688-84085-X. SERIES: Read-alone. SUBJECTS: Humorous stories; Stories in rhyme. RL 3.4.

This sprightly comic story of a robber scared away by the racket in the boondocks that the deaf farmer cannot hear is told in wonderfully repetitive, rhythmic style. Scratchy ink drawings colored with textured brown and avocado are marvelously appropriate.

475 *Mrs. Gaddy and the Fast-Growing Vine.* Ill. by Marylin Hafner. Greenwillow, 1985. ISBN 0-688-04232-5. SERIES: Read-alone. SUBJECTS: Humorous stories. RL 2.6.

The goat Mrs. Gaddy bought as a last resort to trim the vine that grew like lightning was almost as hard to get rid of as the vine. Comic sketches are in green and brown.

476 *Mrs. Gaddy and the Ghost.* Ill. by Marylin Hafner. Greenwillow, 1979. ISBN 0-688-84179-1. SERIES: Read-alone. SUBJECTS: Ghost stories. RL 2.5.

Mrs. Gaddy's inventive devices for getting rid of a noisy ghost all fail, but she changes her mind about getting rid of the ghost when she hears it crying. Excellent illustrations are in rose and brown.

477 *Squash Pie.* Ill. by Glen Rounds. Greenwillow, 1976, o.p. SUBJECTS: Humorous stories; Wordplay. RL 2.7.

The farmer's seeing-eye potatoes, corn ears, and dogwood tree's bark do not catch the thief stealing his squash. When the farmer's wife discovers she *likes* squash pie, no more are stolen. Droll pen and ink drawings have textured light blue and orange highlights.

Gauch, Patricia L.

478 *Aaron and the Green Mountain Boys.* Ill. by Margot Tomes. McDonald, 1987; pap., 1988. ISBN 0-936915-05-6. SUBJECTS: Historical fiction; United States—Revolution—Fiction. RL 2.8.

Although an eager boy wants to help in the fight against the British, his part of chopping wood and washing mugs at first seems very unglamorous. A well-told history from a child's view has exceptional, authentic pen and ink drawings.

Gelman, Rita Golden

479 *Hey, Kid!* Ill. by Carol Nicklaus. Watts, 1977, o.p. SERIES: Easy-Read Story. SUBJECTS: Gifts and gift-giving—Fiction; Stories in rhyme. RL 2.2.

A girl's surprise box holds a friendly critter who talks and sings until she gives it to another curious child. Ink drawings have colored pencil and three-color painted background. The ghostlike visitor is defined with pencil.

Gemme, Leila B.

480 *T-Ball Is Our Game.* Photos by Richard Marshall. Childrens, 1978. ISBN 0-516-03630-0. SUBJECTS: Sports—T-Ball. RL 2.4.

Gemme, Leila B. (cont.)

Abbreviated text accompanies large action color photos underlining the learning and fun aspects of T-ball. The rules are appended.

Gibbons, Gail

481 *Happy Birthday!* Ill. by author. Holiday House, 1986. ISBN 0-8234-0614-8. SUBJECTS: Birthdays. RL 3.5.

Basic information about birthdays is illustrated in full color decorative style with bright blue predominating.

482 *Trains.* Ill. by author. Holiday House, 1987; pap., 1988. ISBN 0-8234-0640-7. SUBJECTS: Trains. RL 3.2.

Information regarding trains, such as types of engines and cars, loading and unloading, and signals for engineers and drivers of cars near tracks, is given. Strong primary-color graphics add appeal.

Gibson, Gertrude

483 *CAT-CAT.* Ill. by Darrell Wiskur. Childrens, 1970. o.p. SUBJECTS: Animals—Cats—Fiction; Pets—Fiction. RL 1.9.

Cat-Cat ruled the roost even after a dog, Butch, came into the household. Chalk sketches give Cat-Cat distinction.

Giff, Patricia R.

484 *The Almost Awful Play.* Ill. by Susanna Natti. Viking, 1984; Puffin, pap., 1985. ISBN 0-670-11458-8. SUBJECTS: Plays—Fiction; School stories. RL 2.3.

Thesbian disaster turns into triumph with Ronald Morgan's quick thinking. Colored drawings help capture the spirit of school rivalries and friendship.

485 *Happy Birthday, Ronald Morgan!* Ill. by Susanna Natti. Viking Kestrel, 1986; Penguin, pap., 1988. ISBN 0-670-80741-9. SUBJECTS: Birthdays—Fiction; Friendship—Fiction; School stories. RL 1.8.

Ronald Morgan has bad news—his birthday comes after school is out, and he lost the friendship of his best friend. His teacher encourages him to make up; he does not notice the surreptitious preparations underway for a party. Full color drawings illustrate very real situations.

486 *Ronald Morgan Goes to Bat.* Ill. by Susanna Natti. Viking Kestrel, 1988. ISBN 0-670-81457-1. SUBJECTS: Self-esteem—Fiction; Sports—Baseball—Fiction. RL 2.1.

Ronald's enthusiasm for baseball is originally outstripped by his skill, but some tips and practice improve his confidence. Bright, lively watercolors warm the sympathetic tale.

487 *Today Was a Terrible Day.* Ill. by Susanna Natti. Viking Kestrel, 1980; Puffin, pap., 1984; ISBN 0-670-71830-0. SUBJECTS: Books and reading—Fiction; School stories; Self-esteem—Fiction. RL 2.3.

One upbeat note from his teacher turns a day full of misery into one of joy for second grader Ronald Morgan. Comic drawings underline the mishaps and teasing of a boy anxious to please.

488 *Watch Out, Ronald Morgan!* Ill. by Susanna Natti. Viking Kestrel, 1985; Puffin, pap., 1986. ISBN 0-670-80433-9. SUBJECTS: Eyeglasses—Fiction; School stories. RL 2.2.

Ronald's teacher encourages him to have his eyes checked when he seems to be tripping and squinting, and has trouble making visual distinctions. This upbeat book has emerald greens and royal blues in lively child-centered drawings.

Gilchrist, Theo E.

489 *Halfway Up the Mountain.* Ill. by Glen Rounds. Lippincott, 1978. ISBN 0-397-31805-7. SUBJECTS: Folklore—United States; Humorous stories. RL 3.1.

Vivid, colorful language spices this traditional tale of a nearly blind old woman scaring off the bandit, Bloodcoe, as she tries to salt and pepper the beef and push the garlic bits inside. Wry pen and ink drawings are masterful.

Gillham, Bill

490 *What's the Difference?* Photos by Fiona Horne. Putnam, 1986. ISBN 0-399-21321-X. SERIES: Look and Talk. SUBJECTS: Concepts; Visual perception. RL 2.6.

The reader is asked to describe the differences between such things as a girl with long hair and one with braids and a big wheel and a bicycle. Basic differentiation is easy with excellent color photos featuring primary colors.

Ginsburg, Mirra

491 *The Night It Rained Pancakes.* Ill. by Douglas Florian. Greenwillow, 1975, o.p. SERIES: Read-alone. SUBJECTS: Folklore—Russia; Russia—Fiction. RL 2.4.

Clever Ivan's trickery enables his simple brother's tale of finding gold to be discredited. A traditional tale is told and illustrated with appropriately plain ink and wash drawings.

Glendinning, Sally

492 *Jimmy and Joe Find a Ghost.* Ill. by Paul Frame. Garrard, 1969. ISBN 0-8116-4701-3. SERIES: Jimmy and Joe. SUBJECTS: Ghost stories. RL 2.1.

The only twist in this pedestrian story is that the "flippety-flops" and objects thrown by the "ghost" are traced to a seal. The realistic drawings place multiracial boys in the city.

Goennel, Heidi

493 *My Day.* Ill. by author. Little, Brown, 1988. ISBN 0-316-31839-6. SUBJECTS: Growing up; Play. RL 2.5.

This tale of a girl's ordinary school day takes on special qualities because of the simple graphics of the artwork.

Goldin, Augusta

494 *Ducks Don't Get Wet.* Ill. by Leonard Kessler. Harper & Row, 1989. ISBN 0-690-04782-7. SERIES: Let's-Read-and-Find-Out Science. SUBJECTS: Animals—Ducks; Nature. RL 3.6.

An introduction to various kinds of ducks and their characteristics. Facts that are included

are: some ducks can dive 100 feet deep and some can fly 70 miles per hour! Charming ducks and neighboring pond animals are in watercolors.

495 *Spider Silk.* Ill. by Joseph Low. Crowell, 1964; pap., 1976. ISBN 0-690-76075-2. SERIES: Let's-Read-and-Find-Out Science. SUBJECTS: Animals—Spiders; Nature. RL 3.9.

Silk is used for navigation and for cocoons. Webs are for catching food. Simple information concentrates on the common grass spider. Ink drawings have two-tone washes on alternate pages.

496 *Straight Hair, Curly Hair.* Ill. by Ed Emberley. Crowell, 1966; pap., 1972. ISBN 0-690-77921-6. SERIES: Let's-Read-and-Find-Out Science. SUBJECTS: Human body—Hair; Science experiments. RL 3.4.

Information about hair is interspersed with simple experiments and suggested observations. Accompanying sketches have touches of humor to lighten the text.

Goldman, Susan

497 *Grandma Is Somebody Special.* Ill. by author. Whitman, 1976. ISBN 0-8075-3034-4. SERIES: Self Starters. SUBJECTS: Grandparents—Fiction. RL 3.2.

The joy and comfort in simple activities with Grandma, such as looking at a fire engine, photos, and her jewelry box; cooking; playing games; telling and reading stories; and singing old songs are clearly conveyed. Full color watercolors also have a homey everyday appeal.

Gordon, Sharon

498 *What a Dog!* Ill. by Deborah Sims. Troll, 1980. ISBN 0-89375-393-9. SERIES: First-Start Easy Reader. SUBJECTS: Animals—Dogs—Fiction; Pets—Dogs—Fiction. RL 1.5.

Only 9 of the 56 words in the book have more than 1 syllable. Bernie walks the eager dog—or is it the other way around? Line drawings focus on a roly-poly pet.

Graham, Bob

499 *Crusher Is Coming.* Ill. by author. Viking Kestrel, 1988. ISBN 0-670-82081-4. SUBJECTS: Friendship—Fiction; Self-esteem—Fiction. RL 2.7.

Peter introduces many activities to impress an older friend, Crusher, but Crusher enjoys most playing with Peter's baby sister. Excellent watercolor and ink sketches underline the contrast between how Crusher looks and how he acts.

Gramatky, Hardie

500 *Bolivar.* Ill. by author. Putnam, 1961, o.p. SUBJECTS: Animals—Donkeys—Fiction; Ecuador—Fiction. RL 3.5.

Despite his spirited mistakes, Bolivar the burro grows into his famous name as he courageously saves the revelers from a raging bull. Pictures are as exuberant as the little donkey.

Granowsky, Alvin, Tweedt, Joy A., and Tweedt, Craig L.

501 *Chicken Salad Soup.* Ill. by Michael L. Denman. Modern Curriculum, 1985, o.p. SERIES: Beginning to Read. SUBJECTS: Computers—Fiction; Cookery—Fiction. RL 2.6.

When Eric follows a computer recipe for lunch, he ends up with chicken salad instead of soup. Only 77 words are used in this story. Cartoon drawings show the kitchen mess.

502 *Computer Park.* Ill. by Michael L. Denman. Modern Curriculum, 1985, o.p. SUBJECTS: Computers—Fiction. RL 2.5.

The chaos in a computer entertainment park when the computers go down is suggested in this 77-word text. Busy cartoons add to the fun.

503 *Robert's Robot.* Ill. by Michael L. Denman. Modern Curriculum, 1985, o.p. SUBJECTS: Robots—Fiction. RL 2.6.

Robert dreams of his very own robot cleaning his room and doing his yard work and his homework! Ninety-two word text is illustrated with busy cartoons.

504 *Who Said That?* Ill. by Michael L. Denman. Modern Curriculum, 1985, o.p. SERIES: Beginning to Read. SUBJECTS: Birthdays—Fiction; Computers—Fiction; School stories. RL 2.1.

With a 77-word vocabulary, some children surprise their teacher with a birthday message from the new talking computer. Large pastel cartoons are action-filled and busy.

Graves, Charles P.

505 *Fourth of July.* Ill. by Ken Wagner. Garrard, 1963. ISBN 0-8116-6550-X. SERIES: Holiday. SUBJECTS: Holidays—Fourth of July. RL 2.9.

In ten short chapters the history, music, symbols, and celebrations of the Fourth of July are presented. Illustrated in red, white, and blue.

506 *Wright Brothers.* Ill. by Fermin Rocker. Putnam, 1973, o.p. SERIES: See and Read Beginning to Read Biography. SUBJECTS: Airplanes; Biographies. RL 2.9.

The author traces the history of the Wright brothers' determined efforts to fly. Good ink sketches give a flavor of the times.

Greene, Carla

507 *Doctors and Nurses: What Do They Do?* Ill. by Leonard Kessler. Harper & Row, 1963. ISBN 0-06-022076-7. SERIES: I Can Read. SUBJECTS: Careers; Community helpers; Doctors and nurses. RL 2.2.

A picture dictionary precedes simple information about (male) doctors and (female) nurses in different roles, especially those most likely to affect children. Fuchsia highlights comic drawings.

508 *Truck Drivers: What Do They Do?* Ill. by Leonard Kessler. Harper & Row, 1967. ISBN 0-06-022099-6. SERIES: I Can Read. SUBJECTS: Careers; Trucks. RL 2.7.

A picture glossary precedes a lively look at the multitude of jobs truck drivers and their trucks perform. A view of the cab and engine is also provided. Simple pen and ink drawings have red and yellow highlights.

509 *What Do They Do? Policemen and Firemen.* Ill. by Leonard Kessler. Harper & Row, 1962, o.p. SERIES: I Can Read. SUBJECTS: Community helpers; Fire fighting; Police. RL 2.4.

Basic facts include equipment, safety, and training in these helpers' most familiar roles. A picture glossary introduces the text. Bold sketches are effective.

Greene, Carol

510 *Benjamin Franklin: A Man with Many Jobs.* Photos by Steve Dobson. Childrens, 1988. ISBN 0-516-04202-5. SERIES: Rookie Biography. SUBJECTS: Biographies; United States—History. RL 2.4.

Aided by a simple, well-illustrated format, the creative accomplishments of Benjamin Franklin are outlined. Five short chapters are augmented by a time line and index.

511 *Hi, Clouds.* Ill. by Gene Sharp. Childrens, hb and pap., 1983. ISBN 0-516-02036-6. SERIES: Rookie Readers. SUBJECTS: Weather—Clouds—Fiction. RL 2.0.

Many shapes are seen in the clouds by two city children. A 27-word vocabulary and simple bright illustrations make this an appealing beginning reader.

512 *Ice Is . . . Whee!* Ill. by Paul Sharp. Childrens, 1983. ISBN 0-516-02037-4. SERIES: Rookie Readers. SUBJECTS: Seasons—Winter—Fiction. RL 1.9.

The beauty of ice and the fun of sliding on it or playing with icicles are celebrated with a 21 word vocabulary. Cartoon drawings are colorful, yet simple.

513 *Please Wind?* Ill. by Gene Sharp. Childrens, 1982. ISBN 0-516-02033-1. SERIES: Rookie Readers. SUBJECTS: Seasons—Spring—Fiction; Stories in rhyme. RL 1.2.

A child's wish for a brisk wind is granted, blowing clothes on the clothesline, a balloon, a hat, and even her kite. Creative story uses only 22 words and has simple watercolor drawings.

514 *Rain! Rain!* Ill. by Larry Frederick. Childrens, 1982. ISBN 0-516-42034-8. SERIES: Rookie Readers. SUBJECTS: Stories in rhyme; Weather—Rain. RL 2.0.

Twenty-nine words celebrate rain (especially puddles to play in). Cheerful, action-filled illustrations feature emerald green and royal blue watercolors.

515 *Shine, Sun!* Ill. by Gene Sharp. Childrens, 1983. ISBN 0-516-02038-2. SERIES: Rookie Readers. SUBJECTS: Play—Fiction; Seasons—Summer—Fiction. RL 1.5.

Twenty-seven words and bright watercolors focus on a little girl dancing and wading on a sunny day, as well as her admiring the flowers, butterflies, and birds singing.

516 *Snow Joe.* Ill. by Paul Sharp. Childrens, hb and pap., 1982. ISBN 0-516-02035-8. SERIES: Rookie Readers. SUBJECTS: Seasons—Winter—Fiction; Stories in rhyme. RL 1.0.

Remarkable interest is generated in snow play using just 15 words. Large comic illustrations are in pastels.

Greene, Laura

517 *I Am an Orthodox Jew.* Ill. by Lisa C. Wesson. Holt, Rinehart, 1978, o.p. SUBJECTS: Religion. RL 2.5.

The weekly rituals and restrictions of Orthodox Jews are shown from the point of view of a boy, his sister, and his gentile friend. Ink drawings underline the warmth of family tradition.

Grey, Judith

518 *What Time Is It?* Ill. by Susan Hall. Troll, 1981. ISBN 0-89375-509-5. SUBJECTS: Animals—Fiction; Books and reading—Fiction; Concepts—Time. RL 1.2.

A boy squirrel asks whether it is time to eat or play. Rhythmic language is used with a basic vocabulary of 25 words. Pastel washes feature cute animals, butterflies, and birds.

Grey, Judith (cont.)

519 *Yummy, Yummy*. Ill. by Joan E.
Goodman. Troll, 1981. ISBN 0-89375-
543-5. SUBJECTS: Animals—Hippos—
Fiction; Bakers and baking—Fiction. RL
1.7.
A hippo makes an apple-carrot-honey-chocol-
ate cake for a yummy treat. Slight story has a
37 word vocabulary and soft pastel illustrations.

Greydanus, Rose

520 *Double Trouble*. Ill. by Roland Rodegast.
Troll, 1981. ISBN 0-89375-529-X.
SUBJECTS: Animals—Raccoons—Fiction;
Siblings—Twins—Fiction. RL 2.4.
Jim and Tim, raccoon twins, blame each
other for messes, but end up doing the cleaning together. Limited story line uses a 34-
word vocabulary. Large textured drawings
are in bright colors.

521 *Let's Pretend*. Ill. by Marsha Winborn.
Troll, hb and pap., 1981. ISBN 0-89375-
545-1. SERIES: Giant First-Start.
SUBJECTS: Imagination—Fiction. RL 2.2
Children "spy" on their dog and cat. A slim
story line and text are expanded by attractive
marbelized watercolors on white.

Gridley, Marion

522 *Osceola*. Ill. by Lloyd E. Oxendine.
Putnam, 1972, o.p. SERIES: See and
Read Beginning to Read Biography.
SUBJECTS: Biographies; Native
Americans—Seminoles. RL 2.3.
The bravery and determination of one man to
preserve his native culture culminates in his
early death. Crude ink sketches have orange
highlights.

Gross, Ruth B.

523 *A Book about Pandas*. Photos. Dial,
1972; Scholastic, pap., 1988. ISBN 0-
8037-0968-4. SUBJECTS: Animals—
Pandas; Nature. RL 3.1.
Habits and characteristics of pandas learned
from studying their behavior in a zoo are
related in this photoessay. Black and white
pictures are numerous, catching pandas in a
variety of poses.

Gruber, Suzanne

524 *The Monster under My Bed*. Ill. by
Stephanie Britt. Troll, hb and pap.,
1985. ISBN 0-8167-0456-2. SERIES: Giant
First-Start. SUBJECTS: Animals—Bears—
Fiction; Bedtime—Fiction. RL 2.9.
A small bear, certain that he hears noises
under his bed, calls his mother repeatedly
for reassurance. He settles down only when
the source of the disturbance is found—his
cat, Fluffy. The reassuring tale has excellent
watercolor drawings with royal blue predominating.

Gunther, Louise

525 *A Tooth for the Tooth Fairy*. Ill. by Jim
Cummins. Garrard, 1978. ISBN 0-8116-
4308-5. SUBJECTS: Tooth fairy—Fiction.
RL 2.4.
When Rose loses her tooth in the grass at the
playground and tries to substitute a fake, she
finds that her trouble was not necessary.
Straightforward story has full color illustrations.

H

Haddad, Helen R.

526 *Truck and Loader*. Ill. by Donald
Carrick. Greenwillow, 1982. ISBN 0-688-
00827-5. SERIES: Read-alone. SUBJECTS:
Trucks. RL 2.7.
The complementary work of loader and dump
truck doing road building, tree removal, and
pond building is well described. Carrick's
exceptional drawings are in muted orange,
beige, and green.

Hall, Katy, and Eisenberg, Lisa

527 *Buggy Riddles*. Ill. by Simms Taback.
Dial, 1986. ISBN 0-8037-0140-3. SERIES:
Easy-to-Read. SUBJECTS: Jokes and
riddles. RL 2.6.

Each of the 41 riddles (with answers) featuring insects is given in a full page. The illustrations are bold, brightly colored, and humorous.

528 *Fishy Riddles*. Ill. by Simms Taback. Dial, hb and pap., 1983. ISBN 0-8037-2431-4. SERIES: Easy-to-Read. SUBJECTS: Jokes and riddles. RL 2.4.

The riddles all have pleasing, but not always predictable, plays on words. Fittingly illustrated in cartoon style with turquoise and orange.

Hall, Lynn

529 *Captain: Canada's Flying Pony*. Ill. by Tran Mawicke. Garrard, 1976. ISBN 0-8116-4857-5. SERIES: Famous Animal Stories. SUBJECTS: Animals—Horses. RL 2.9.

A true story of a mud-colored pony and a girl who outjumped larger horses all over the world is told with drama and humor. Watercolor drawings focus on the pony and girl.

Hall, Malcolm

530 *CariCATures*. Ill. by Bruce Degen. Coward, McCann, 1978, o.p. SERIES: Break-of-Day. SUBJECTS: Animals—Fiction; Jokes and riddles—Fiction; Newspapers—Fiction. RL 2.7.

The Claws and Paws newspaper begins to thrive only when some cat cartoons and riddles are added. Excellent ink and wash drawings of the animal characters enhance the good characterizations.

531 *Derek Koogar Was a Star*. Ill. by Joel Schick. Coward, McCann, 1975, o.p. SUBJECTS: Animals—Cougars—Fiction; Animals—Fiction; Humorous Stories. RL 2.6.

With tongue-in-cheek humor, a tricky potbellied washed-up movie star cougar has the tables turned by Maxine Bear. Expressive ink drawings and good dialogue exaggerate the humor.

532 *Edward, Benjamin and Butter*. Ill. by Tomie dePaola. Coward, McCann, 1981, o.p. SUBJECTS: Animals—Horses—Fiction; Animals—Tapirs—Fiction; Friendship—Fiction. RL 2.2.

The tables are turned when Edward tries to cheer up his gloomy friend Benjamin with a trick. Pencil and yellows illustrate this story with gentle humor and unexpected twists.

533 *Headlines*. Ill. by Wallace Tripp. Coward, McCann, 1973. ISBN 0-698-30482-9. SERIES: Break-of-Day. SUBJECTS: Animals—Fiction; Books and reading—Fiction; Newspapers—Fiction. RL 3.1.

Editor Theodore Cat's newspaper headlines come out wrong because a pack rat family steals type. Good characterization comes from text and Tripp's outstanding ink drawings.

Hamilton, Virginia

534 *Jahdu*. Ill. by Jerry Pinkney. Greenwillow, 1980, o.p. SERIES: Read-alone. SUBJECTS: Fantasy; Shadows—Fiction. RL 2.4.

Accompanied by his independent shadow, Jahdu rolls up the sky to crawl behind, and sticks his finger in the cup of night to taste it. Rich language patterns and pencil drawings on palest lavender stimulate the imagination.

Hamsa, Bobbie

535 *Dirty Larry*. Ill. by Paul Sharp. Childrens, 1983. ISBN 0-516-02040-4. SERIES: Rookie Readers. SUBJECTS: Play—Fiction. RL 3.7.

Larry's dirty anatomy from ears and knees to nose and neck are detailed in 32 familiar words. Cartoons show how much fun he has getting so dirty. (Beginning readers will be able to enjoy this book despite the Spache reading level assignment.)

536 *Fast Draw Freddie*. Ill. by Stephen Hayes. Children, hb and pap., 1984. ISBN 0-516-02046-3. SERIES: Rookie Readers. SUBJECTS: Art and artists; Stories in rhyme. RL 2.2.

The 31-word rhymed text celebrates the possibilities for drawing on paper. Ink sketches of multiethnic children are set in a city environment.

537 *Polly Wants a Cracker*. Ill. by Jerry Warshaw. Childrens, hb and pap., 1986. ISBN 0-516-02071-4. SERIES: Rookie

Hamsa, Bobbie (cont.)

Readers. SUBJECTS: Animals—Parrots—Fiction; Concepts—Numbers; Stories in rhyme. RL 2.7.
A simple 32-word vocabulary is used for a story counting the crackers Polly wants. Lively full color drawings of three children and a dog pampering Polly keep the story moving.

Hancock, Sibyl

538 *Bill Pickett: First Black Rodeo Star.* Ill. by Lorinda B. Cauley. Harcourt Brace, 1977, o.p. SERIES: Let Me Read. SUBJECTS: Biographies; Black Americans; Western stories. RL 2.8.
The rodeo adventures of the first black international rodeo star. The close relationship he had with his horse, Spradley, is also emphasized. Sepia drawings add to the story.

539 *Old Blue.* Ill. by Erick Ingraham. Putnam, 1980. ISBN 0-399-61141-X. SERIES: See and Read. SUBJECTS: Cowboys; Western stories. RL 3.3.
The remarkable true story of a tame lead longhorn steer named Old Blue is told from the point of view of a novice on one particular drive in 1878. This tale is exceptional in its telling, as well as in its soft pencil drawings.

Hare, Norma Q.

540 *Wish Upon a Birthday.* Ill. by Diane Dawson. Garrard, 1979. ISBN 0-8116-4418-9. SUBJECTS: Bakers and baking—Fiction; Birthdays—Fiction; Kings and queens—Fiction. RL 2.5.
The cook's helper, Gabe, makes the very first birthday cake as his gift for Princess Melinda. Busy, bright cartoon-style drawings show the bustle in the castle kitchen.

Harrison, David

541 *Case of the Missing Frog.* Ill. by Jerry Warshaw. Rand McNally, 1972, o.p. SERIES: Fledgling. SUBJECTS: Animals—Frogs and toads—Fiction; City and town life—Fiction; Stories in rhyme. RL 1.7.
A search for their missing pet, Og the frog, leads two boys all over their city neighborhood. Sketches shows expressive animal faces and the flavor of the neighborhood.

542 *Little Turtle's Big Adventure.* Ill. by J. P. Miller. Random House, 1969, o.s.i.; pap., 1985. ISBN 0-394-96345-8. SERIES: Early Bird. SUBJECTS: Animals—Turtles; Nature. RL 2.7.
When road construction forces Little Turtle to relocate, a boy helps him find a new home. The cover is dated, but the other illustrations are excellent, with good graphics, textures, and an interesting variety of techniques.

543 *Wake Up, Sun.* Ill. by Hans Wilhelm. Random House, hb and pap., 1986. ISBN 0-394-98256-8. SERIES: Step into Reading. SUBJECTS: Cumulative tales; Farm and country life—Fiction. RL 1.4.
The animals were very nice to the farmer's baby after her cries coincided with the sunrise. Appealing simple watercolors focus on friendly farm animals.

Harrison, Virginia

544 *The World of a Falcon.* Photos by Oxford Scientific Films. Gareth Stevens, 1988. ISBN 1-55532-308-1. SERIES: Where Animals Live. SUBJECTS: Animals—Falcons; Nature. RL 3.4.
The habitat, life cycle, and special characteristics of kestrels (a kind of falcon), and their adjustment to people are covered. Index and glossary are helpful. Close-up color photos are exceptional, especially of kestrels "hovering" with feathers extended. Adapted from Mike Birkhead's *The Falcon Over the Town* (Gareth Stevens, 1988).

545 *The World of Dragonflies.* Photos by Oxford Scientific Films. Gareth Stevens, 1988. ISBN 1-55532-310-3. SERIES: Where Animals Live. SUBJECTS: Animals—Dragonflies; Nature. RL 4.
The habitat, anatomy, and life cycle of dragonflies are introduced, along with their enemies and relationships with people. Spectacular close-up photos of dragonflies at every stage of their life cycle accompany the informative

text. Adapted from Christopher O'Toole's *The Dragonfly Over the Water* (Gareth Stevens, 1988). (Spache gives the reading level above fourth grade.)

546 *The World of Lizards.* Photos by Oxford Scientific Films. Gareth Stevens, 1988. ISBN 1-55532-307-3. SERIES: Where Animals Live. SUBJECTS: Animals—Lizards; Nature. RL 4.
Information about the variety, habitats, anatomy, and life cycle of lizards, particularly their protective coloration and habits, is given. Exceptional close-up color photos are up to Oxford Scientific Films' standards. Adapted from Mike Linley's *The Lizard in the Jungle* (Gareth Stevens, 1988). (Spache gives reading level above fourth grade.)

547 *The World of Mice.* Photos by Oxford Scientific Films. Gareth Stevens, 1988. ISBN 1-55532-309-X. SERIES: Where Animals Live. SUBJECTS: Animals—Mice. RL 3.9.
The habitat, life cycle, senses, and food, as well as the enemies of mice are described. Mice as pests and pets for people are also discussed. Exceptional close-up color photos add immeasurably to the book. Adapted from Robert Burton's *The Mouse in the Barn* (Gareth Stevens, 1988).

Harshman, Terry W.

548 *Porcupine's Pajama Party.* Ill. by Doug Cushman. Harper & Row, 1988. ISBN 0-06-022249-2. SERIES: I Can Read. SUBJECTS: Animals—Fiction; Friendship—Fiction; Humorous stories. RL 3.3.
Three animal friends share an evening of baking cookies, watching a scary late night television show, and some bedtime fears. Simple ink drawings show Porcupine in glasses and a baseball cap, a big bowl of popcorn, and the only three cookies that did not get eaten before being baked.

Hasler, Eveline

549 *Winter Magic.* Trans. of *In Winterland.* Ill. by Michele Lemieux. Morrow, 1985. ISBN 0-688-05258-4. SUBJECTS: Animals—

Cats—Fiction; Fantasy; Seasons—Winter—Fiction. RL 2.2.
Peter takes a winter ride on his cat, Sebastian, through the caves, forest, and underground. Somewhat impressionistic paintings reinforce the dreamy qualities of his adventure.

Hatch, Shirley C.

550 *Wind Is to Feel.* Ill. by Marilyn Miller. Coward, McCann, 1973, o.p. SUBJECTS: Senses—Touch; Weather. RL 2.2.
The wind is described through a variety of familiar sensory experiences and experiments. Effective pencil sketches have pale blue, yellow, and gray washes.

Hautzig, Deborah

551 *Handsomest Father.* Ill. by Muriel Batherman. Greenwillow, 1979, o.p. SERIES: Read-alone. SUBJECTS: Fathers—Fiction; School stories; Self-esteem—Fiction. RL 2.5.
A child's agonies regarding his father's personal appearance are sympathetically portrayed when the father attends open house at school. Ink and wash sketches blend superbly.

552 *Happy Birthday, Little Witch.* Ill. by Marc Brown. Random House, hb and pap., 1985. ISBN 0-394-97365-8. SERIES: Step into Reading. SUBJECTS: Birthdays—Fiction; Witches—Fiction. RL 2.8.
When Little Witch's Halloween friends surprise her with a birthday party, she plays pin the tail on the devil, it rains black and blue jellybeans, and there are firecrackers. Expectations are gently overturned in this story illustrated with Brown's humorous drawings.

553 *It's a Secret!* Ill. by Tom Leigh. Random House, 1988. ISBN 0-394-99672-0. SERIES: Start-to-Read. SUBJECTS: Concepts—Numbers. RL 2.0.
Bert's feelings are hurt when Ernie tells others that Bert can't count past 100. The Sesame Street group then learns to count together. Characters are in bright colors.

554 *It's Easy!* Ill. by Joe Mathieu. Random House, 1988. ISBN 0-394-91376-0.

Hautzig, Deborah (cont.)

SUBJECTS: Friendship—Fiction; Gardening—Fiction; Puppets—Fiction. RL 1.8.
Big Bird finds he needs help with his sunflower garden after all to keep the birds away. Large colored drawings are of Sesame Street characters.

555 *It's Not Fair!* Featuring Jim Henson's Sesame Street Muppets. Ill. by Tom Leigh. Random House, 1986. ISBN 0-394-98151-0. SERIES: Start-to-Read. SUBJECTS: Friendship—Fiction. RL 2.3.
After Bert does all the work and Ernie gets the credit, Ernie gives Bert an unusual gift—a dustpan and brush. Realistic differences are dealt with sympathetically. Colorful cartoons of familiar television characters illustrate the text.

556 *Little Witch's Big Night.* Ill. by Marc Brown. Random House, hb and pap., 1984. ISBN 0-394-96587-6. SERIES: Step into Reading. SUBJECTS: Witches—Fiction. RL 3.7.
Little Witch, left behind on Halloween because she had been too good, gives some trick-or-treaters a night to remember. Friendly watercolor drawings take away all fear.

557 *Why Are You So Mean to Me?* Ill. by Tom Cooke. Random House, 1986. ISBN 0-394-88060-9. SERIES: Start-to-Read. SUBJECTS: Friendship—Fiction; Self-esteem—Fiction. RL 2.4.
Grover's mother tells him he will always be good at being himself, regardless of how he plays baseball. Feelings are expressed and friends forgiven in another Henson Muppet series book, illustrated in bright pastels.

Hawes, Judy

558 *Why Frogs Are Wet.* Ill. by Don Madden. Crowell, 1968, o.p.; Harper & Row, pap., 1987. ISBN 0-06-445043-0. SERIES: Let's-Read-and-Find-Out Science. SUBJECTS: Animals—Frogs and toads; Science. RL 2.5.
Frogs preceded dinosaurs by 50 million years, have 2,000 varieties, were the first animals to

have a voice. Fascinating frog facts are illustrated by bright, decorative drawings with bold strokes.

Hawkins, Colin, and Hawkins, Jacqui

559 *I'm Not Sleepy!* Ill. by authors. Crown, 1985. ISBN 0-517-55973-0. SERIES: It's Great to Read! SUBJECTS: Animals—Bears—Fiction; Bedtime—Fiction. RL 2.0.
Not until Mommy comes to tuck him in does Baby Bear settle down for the night. Abbreviated dialogue between mother and child is illustrated showing only rotund baby's delaying antics.

560 *Jen the Hen.* Ill. by authors. Putnam, 1985. ISBN 0-399-21207-8. SERIES: Flip-the-Page Rhyming. SUBJECTS: Birthdays—Fiction; Stories in rhyme. RL 2.1.
Ken, Ben, Wren, and a hen called Jen meet in the glen at ten—for a birthday party. Wordplay using basic vocabulary is illustrated with rotund cartoon characters in pastels, and two tiny bookish worms.

561 *Mig the Pig.* Ill. by Colin Hawkins. Putnam, 1986. ISBN 0-399-21061-X. SERIES: Flip-the-Page Rhyming. SUBJECTS: Animals—Pigs—Fiction; Stories in rhyme; Wordplay. RL 2.6.
The beginning consonant of "pig" changes to make "big," "wig," "twig," and five other rhyming words. Zany cartoons include "talking" scallop-edged worms.

562 *Pat the Cat.* Ill. by authors. Putnam, 1983, o.p.; pap., 1986. ISBN 0-399-20957-3. SUBJECTS: Animals—Cats—Fiction; Stories in rhyme. RL 2.4.
Pat the fat cat has a rat named Nat and a bat named Tat in his hat on the mat. Story is as lively as vocabulary allows, brightened by scallop-edged animals and worms.

563 *Tog the Dog.* Ill. by Colin Hawkins. Putnam, 1986. ISBN 0-399-21338-4. SERIES: Flip-the-Page Rhyming. SUBJECTS: Animals—Dogs—Fiction; Stories in rhyme; Wordplay. RL 2.9.
Jog, fog, cog, frog, bog, hog, log, and a dog named Tog are rhyming words produced by changing initial consonants and accenting

them with humorous wordplay. Visual humor is added with lumpy cartoon animals.

564 *Zug the Bug*. Ill. by Colin Hawkins. Putnam, 1988. ISBN 0-399-21556-5. SERIES: Flip-the-Page Rhyming. SUBJECTS: Animals—Insects—Fiction; Stories in rhyme; Wordplay. RL 3.1.

Seven words rhyming with bug are made by changing the initial consonant. Cartoons are enlivened by the humorous commentary of two worms.

Hayes, Geoffrey

565 *The Mystery of the Pirate Ghost: An Otto and Uncle Tooth Adventure*. Ill. by author. Random House, hb and pap., 1985. ISBN 0-394-97220-1. SERIES: Step into Reading. SUBJECTS: Dinosaurs—Fiction; Mystery and detective stories; Pirates—Fiction. RL 2.4.

Dinosaurs Otto and Uncle Tooth uncover a pirate "ghost" with a trumpet. The mystery is well constructed with some humor and a satisfying conclusion. Koalas, puffins, and octopi complete the cast of characters. Illustrations are in watercolor.

566 *The Secret of Foghorn Island*. Ill. by author. Random House, hb and pap., 1988. ISBN 0-394-99614-3. SERIES: Step into Reading. SUBJECTS: Dinosaurs—Fiction; Mystery and detective stories. RL 3.2.

Dinosaurs Otto and Uncle Tooth save Auntie Hicks from Sid Rat, Weasel, and the magical Doctor Ocular in an adventure with sea witches and shipwrecks. Pastel comic drawings keep the tone light.

Hayward, Linda

567 *Hello, House!* Ill. by Lynn Munsinger. Random House, hb and pap., 1988. ISBN 0-394-98864-7. SERIES: Step into Reading. SUBJECTS: Folklore—Black Americans; Folklore—United States. RL 1.8.

Brer Rabbit outsmarts Brer Wolf again in a classic trickster tale. Pastel drawings with expressive main characters enhance this simple, effective retelling.

Hearn, Emily

568 *Ring around Duffy*. Ill. by Paul Frame. Garrard, 1974. ISBN 0-8116-6976-9. SERIES: Venture. SUBJECTS: Animals—Ducks—Fiction; Pollution—Fiction. RL 2.2.

An injured duckling, rescued by a family dog, is returned to the wild, but needs to be rescued again when he gets a soda can ring stuck around his bill. Pencil and turquoise wash drawings present animals best.

569 *TV Kangaroo*. Ill. by Tom Eaton. Garrard, 1975, o.p. SUBJECTS: Animals—Fiction; Weather—Fiction. RL 2.3.

No matter what weather the television kangaroo announces, some animals like it and others "avoid" it. Simple text and idea illustrated with light-hearted animal cartoons.

Heide, Florence

570 *Lost and Found*. Photos and drawings. Macmillan, 1975, o.p. SUBJECTS: Animals—Fiction; City and country life—Fiction; Water—Fiction. RL 1.7.

Although the language is pedestrian, the illustrations are varied and interesting, ranging from block printing to black and white or color photos to cartoons.

Heide, Florence P., and Heide, Roxanne

571 *A Monster Is Coming! A Monster Is Coming!* Ill. by Rachi Farrow. Watts, 1980, o.p. SUBJECTS: Monsters—Fiction; Television—Fiction. RL 2.4.

Neither her younger brother, Eddie, nor a monster can distract Alice from television. Pale lemon and lavender on a strong black and white checked floor contrast with the fuchsia, red, and gold monster.

Heide, Florence, and Van Clief, Sylvia Worth

572 *Hats and Bears*. Drawings. Macmillan, 1975, o.p. SUBJECTS: Animals—Bears—Fiction; Hats—Fiction. RL 1.8.

Short stories and verse touch on familiar things to children. Chapters have colorful humorous watercolor drawings by different illustrators. Writing is unimaginative.

Heilbroner, Joan

573 *The Happy Birthday Present*. Ill. by Mary Chalmers. Harper & Row, 1962. ISBN 0-06-022271-9. SERIES: I Can Read. SUBJECTS: Birthdays—Fiction; Siblings—Fiction. RL 1.6.

Peter takes his little brother, Davy, shopping for Mother's birthday. With limited resources they end up with an imaginative birthday tree. Very realistic dialogue, childlike misconceptions, and soft pencil drawings add to the appeal.

574 *Robert the Rose Horse*. Ill. by P. D. Eastman. Random House, 1962. ISBN 0-394-90025-1. SERIES: I Can Read It All By Myself. SUBJECTS: Allergies—Fiction; Animals—Horses—Fiction; Humorous stories. RL 1.7.

Robert's allergies cause him to end several careers prematurely, but when his big sneeze captures some bank robbers, he finally finds his calling. Cartoon sketches fit the humor.

575 *This Is the House Where Jack Lives*. Ill. by Aliki. Harper & Row, 1962. ISBN 0-06-022286-7. SERIES: I Can Read. SUBJECTS: Cumulative tales. RL 1.7.

The very best of modern cumulative tales includes an assortment of apartment dwellers, from the maid and window-washer to a boy walking a dog and Jack taking an exuberant bath on an upper floor. Drawings are fun in gray and fuchsia.

576 *Tom the TV Cat: A Step Two Book*. Ill. by Sal Murdocca. Random House, hb and pap., 1984. ISBN 0-394-96708-9. SERIES: Step into Reading. SUBJECTS: Animals—Cats—Fiction; Self-esteem—Fiction; Television—Fiction. RL 1.6.

Tom the cat tests some television roles by imitating the song man, the strong man, superman, and a ball man—with disastrous results. Murdocca's cartoons underline the humor of Tom's antics.

Henderson, Kathy

577 *Dairy Cows*. Photos. Childrens, 1988. ISBN 0-516-01152-9. SERIES: New True. SUBJECTS: Animals—Cows; Farm and country life. RL 2.6.

Seven brief chapters give information on the anatomy and digestive system of cows and on dairy farming. Glossary and index are appended. Excellent color photos accent the information.

Henriod, Lorraine

578 *Marie Curie*. Ill. by Fermin Rocker. Putnam, 1970, o.p. SERIES: See and Read. SUBJECTS: Biographies; Careers; Science. RL 2.3.

In simple terms, without neglecting the hardships or hazards, the story of Marie Curie's amazing accomplishments in science is told. Ink drawings have a pale blue wash.

Henwood, Chris

579 *Frogs*. Photos by Barrie Watts. Franklin Watts, 1988. ISBN 0-531-10643-8. SERIES: Keeping Minibeasts. SUBJECTS: Animals—Frogs and toads; Pets. RL 3.2.

Background information about frogs is geared for the catching, caring, and feeding of frogs as pets. Exceptional color photos give additional information about their habitat and handling.

580 *Spiders*. Photos by Barrie Watts. Franklin Watts, 1988. ISBN 0-531-10642-X. SERIES: Keeping Minibeasts. SUBJECTS: Animals—Spiders; Pets. RL 4.0.

The handling and feeding of spiders of different sizes are described and illustrated with excellent color photos. Information on webs and the exaggerated danger to man from spiders is given.

Hillert, Margaret

581 *Circus Fun*. Ill. by Elaine Raphael. Modern Curriculum, 1969, o.p. SUBJECTS: Circuses—Fiction. RL 1.2.

Fifty words are used to tell about the circus. Watercolors focus on clowns, lions, and elephants.

582 *Come Play with Me*. Ill. by Kinuko Craft. Follett, 1975, o.p. SERIES: Just Beginning-To-Read. SUBJECTS: Poetry. RL 1.3.

Simple poems about familiar things, composed of 75 pre-primer words, are illustrated with imaginative watercolors in a fairy tale atmosphere.

583 *Happy Birthday, Dear Dragon.* Ill. by Carl Kock. Modern Curriculum, hb and pap., 1977. ISBN 0-8136-5021-6. SERIES: Just Beginning-To-Read. SUBJECTS: Concepts—Color—Fiction; Holidays—Valentine's Day—Fiction; Mythical creatures—Fiction. RL 1.1.

A child and a baby dragon celebrate Valentine's Day by focusing on red things familiar to children: a cardinal, a fire truck, a stop light, school, apples, and a valentine. Drawings are simple.

584 *Little Puff.* Ill. by Sid Jordan. Modern Curriculum, hb and pap., 1973. ISBN 0-8136-5014-3. SUBJECTS: Trains—Fiction. RL 1.1.

Sixty words are used to tell the slight story of a train that is not wanted in town or at the zoo, only on the tracks with children as passengers. Drawings have color and pattern reminiscent of a mosaic.

585 *Play Ball.* Ill. by Dick Martin. Follett, hb and pap., 1978. ISBN 0-8136-5034-8. SERIES: Just Beginning-To-Read. SUBJECTS: Play—Fiction; Toys—Fiction. RL 1.2.

Interest and humor are generated with 58 words as two boys look for balls and equipment to play various games. There are unexpected and magical qualities to their play. Pale tans and yellows predominate in clever illustrations.

586 *Run to the Rainbow.* Ill. by Barbara Corey. Modern Curriculum, hb and pap., 1981. ISBN 0-695-41354-6. SERIES: Beginning-To-Read. SUBJECTS: Rainbows; Science. RL 1.2.

The text, even though a bit choppy, introduces some interesting, commonplace ways to produce rainbows. Watercolor illustrations are a bit busy to locate the "rainbows."

587 *Snow Baby.* Ill. by Liz Dauber. Follett, hb and pap., 1969. ISBN 0-8136-5065-8.

SERIES: Just Beginning-To-Read. SUBJECTS: Seasons—Winter—Fiction; Weather—Snow—Fiction. RL 1.4.

Children's play in the snow leads to a surprise find in this pre-primer with a 50-word vocabulary. Full color drawings fill the pages.

588 *What Is It?* Ill. by Kinuko Craft. Modern Curriculum, hb and pap., 1978. ISBN 0-8136-5056-9. SERIES: Just Beginning-To-Read My Stories in Verse. SUBJECTS: Imagination—Fiction; Stories in rhyme. RL 1.2.

Two elflike children follow a string through an imaginary land. The rhymed text uses 55 simple words. Illustrations are stilted pastels.

589 *Who Goes to School?* Ill. by Nan Brooks. Modern Curriculum, hb and pap., 1981. ISBN 0-8136-5075-5. SERIES: Just Beginning-To-Read. SUBJECTS: Animals—Cats; Animals—Dogs; School stories. RL 1.3.

Circus, television commercial, and police dogs go to school, as do children. A vocabulary of 65 words is used to give very basic information about school. Folk-style illustrations add appeal.

590 *The Witch Who Went for a Walk.* Ill. by Krystyna Stasiak. Follett, hb and pap., 1982. ISBN 0-695-41549-2. SERIES: Just Beginning-To-Read. SUBJECTS: Holidays—Halloween—Fiction; Witches—Fiction. RL 1.1.

Sixty-seven words are used to show the witch's fear of children dressed for Halloween. Some scary elements such as owls, caves, bats, and trees are shown with wide eyes in dark colors.

Hiscock, Bruce

591 *The Big Rock.* Ill. by author. Atheneum, 1988. ISBN 0-689-31402-7. SUBJECTS: Geology; Science. RL Off Spache scale.

The geological history of the Adirondacks is presented in an interesting and understandable way by following the movement of one rock. The watercolor illustrations complement the text well.

Hoban, Brom

592 *Jason and the Bees*. Ill. by author. Harper & Row, 1980. ISBN 0-06-022382-0. SERIES: Nature I Can Read. SUBJECTS: Animals—Bees; Nature. RL 2.0.
It takes 20,000 bees to collect a pound of nectar, which makes a pound of honey. Jason, who originally throws rocks at hives, learns from a neighbor how to care for the bees safely. Pen and wash drawings are a bit stilted.

Hoban, Julia

593 *Quick Chick*. Ill. by Lillian Hoban. Dutton, 1989. ISBN 0-525-44490-4. SUBJECTS: Animals—Chickens—Fiction. RL 2.8.
The littlest slow-learning chick is renamed after escaping from a cat. Friendly barnyard animals are in soft pastels.

Hoban, Lillian

594 *Arthur's Christmas Cookies*. Ill. by author. Harper & Row, 1972, pap., 1984. ISBN 0-06-022368-5. SERIES: I Can Read. SUBJECTS: Animals—Chimpanzees—Fiction; Bakers and baking—Fiction; Holidays—Christmas—Fiction. RL 2.5.
Arthur again turns defeat into triumph when his Bake E-Z Christmas cookies are rock-hard. Pencil and wash drawings complement this story of childhood mishaps featuring a loving chimp family.

595 *Arthur's Funny Money*. Ill. by author. Harper & Row, 1980; pap., 1984. ISBN 0-06-022344-8. SERIES: I Can Read. SUBJECTS: Animals—Chimpanzees—Fiction; Mathematics—Fiction; Siblings—Fiction. RL 2.6.
Violet finds out Arthur does not know numbers as well as he says when they go into the bike-washing business. Realistic characterization is underlined by soft pencil drawings with a four-color wash.

596 *Arthur's Great Big Valentine*. Ill. by author. Harper & Row, 1988. ISBN 0-06-022407-X. SERIES: I Can Read. SUBJECTS: Animals—Chimpanzees—Fiction; Friendship—Fiction; Holidays—Valentine's Day—Fiction. RL 2.8.
Arthur makes up with his friends by sending an unusual valentine. The pain and humor of childhood are shown throughout the book. Illustrations are of chimpanzee children.

597 *Arthur's Honey Bear*. Ill. by author. Harper & Row, 1974; pap., 1982. ISBN 0-06-022370-7. SERIES: I Can Read. SUBJECTS: Animals—Chimpanzees—Fiction; Growing-up—Fiction; Siblings—Fiction. RL 2.3.
Arthur becomes his Honey Bear's *uncle* when he reluctantly trades his beloved toy to Violet and regrets it. The sadness and joy of growing up are celebrated here.

598 *Arthur's Loose Tooth*. Ill. by author. Harper & Row, 1985; pap., 1987. ISBN 0-06-022354-5. SERIES: I Can Read. SUBJECTS: Animals—Chimpanzees—Fiction; Baby-sitting—Fiction; Human body—Teeth—Fiction. RL 2.7.
A cozy book has excellent dialogue, good relationships, and gentle humor. Arthur the chimp's loose tooth does not keep him from enjoying s'mores and taffy apples. Expressive chimps have child fears and childlike misbehaviors.

599 *Arthur's Pen Pal*. Ill. by author. Harper & Row, 1976; pap., 1982. ISBN 0-06-022372-3. SERIES: I Can Read. SUBJECTS: Animals—Chimpanzees—Fiction; Baby-sitting—Fiction; Siblings—Fiction. RL 2.7.
Arthur decides he does not want to trade families with his pen pal after all, despite the irritations of baby-sitting for a younger sister. Good characterization and dialogue. Softly colored pencil drawings capture the feeling of everyday family life.

600 *Arthur's Prize Reader*. Ill. by author. Harper & Row, 1978; pap., 1984. ISBN 0-06-022380-4. SERIES: I Can Read. SUBJECTS: Animals—Chimpanzees—Fiction; Books and reading—Fiction; Siblings—Fiction. RL 2.4.
While trying to help her older brother, Arthur, with a Super Chimp Comic contest, Violet learns to read hard words. Dialogue

and pencil and wash drawings capture the flavor of childhood.

601 *The Case of the Two Masked Robbers*. Ill. by author. Harper & Row, 1986. ISBN 0-06-022299-9. SERIES: I Can Read. SUBJECTS: Animals—Raccoons—Fiction; Animals—Turtles—Fiction; Mystery and detective stories. RL 2.6.
Raccoons Arabella and Albert, seeking the turtle-egg robber, have some noctural adventures and find a way to safeguard the eggs. The nighttime fears are most effectively portrayed in pencil with dusky violet, tan, and green.

602 *Mr. Pig and Sonny Too*. Ill. by author. Harper & Row, 1977. ISBN 0-06-022341-3. SERIES: I Can Read. SUBJECTS: Animals—Pigs—Fiction; Friendship—Fiction. RL 2.9.
Mr. Pig's mishaps while skating, picnicking, and going to a wedding (his own) have amusing and loving resolutions. The pigs are drawn with lumpy detail in pastel greens and pale oranges dominating.

603 *Silly Tilly and the Easter Bunny*. Ill. by author. Harper & Row, 1986. ISBN 0-06-022393-6. SERIES: Early I Can Read. SUBJECTS: Animals—Moles—Fiction; Animals—Rabbits—Fiction; Holidays—Easter—Fiction. RL 2.3.
Silly Tilly nearly misses the Easter Bunny's visit by her forgetful behavior. Slight story has friendly pastel, lumpy animal watercolors.

604 *Stick-in-the-Mud Turtle*. Ill. by author. Greenwillow, 1977, o.p. SERIES: Read-alone. SUBJECTS: Animals—Turtles—Fiction. RL 3.0.
Fred, his wife, and their ten turtle children live simply and well until another turtle family moves into their pond. Pastel sketches with dominant green underline their contentment—shattered and then regained.

605 *Turtle Spring*. Ill. by author. Greenwillow, 1978, o.p. SERIES: Read-alone. SUBJECTS: Animals—Turtles—Fiction; Seasons—Spring—Fiction. RL 2.5.
Turtle gossip and spring newborns flavor a gentle seasonal tale with interesting char-acter sketches. Spring green, yellow, and brown show the animals on the pond with their new babies.

Hoban, Lillian, and Hoban, Phoebe

606 *Laziest Robot in Zone One*. Ill. by Lillian Hoban. Harper & Row, 1983; pap., 1985. ISBN 0-06-022352-9. SERIES: I Can Read. SUBJECTS: Robots—Fiction; Science Fiction. RL 3.6.
Robots Sola and Sol's search for Big Rover leads them to rescue Power Puss and get a lot of help with their household chores. Interesting differences from and similarities to life familiar to modern children are illustrated in lavender, orange, gray, and fuchsia watercolor sketches in this science fiction story.

607 *Ready—Set—Robot*. Ill. by Lillian Hoban. Harper & Row, 1982; pap., 1985. ISBN 0-06-022346-4. SERIES: I Can Read. SUBJECTS: Humorous stories; Robots—Fiction; Science fiction. RL 3.0.
Space and robot humor evolves from a messy robot's involvement in a space race, which he wins only with his robot dog's help. Interesting ideas about life for robots are illustrated in pastels.

Hoban, Russell

608 *Ace Dragon Ltd*. Ill. by Quentin Blake. Jonathan Cape, 1980, o.p. SUBJECTS: Mythical creatures—Fiction. RL 2.2.
John's astute observation earns him a day of high adventure with a dragon named Ace in Wellingtons. This playful and imaginative tale has some amusing twists of plot. Lively pen sketches have light orange and gray washes.

609 *Bargain for Frances*. Ill. by Lillian Hoban. Harper & Row, 1970; pap., 1978. ISBN 0-06-02230-8. SERIES: I Can Read. SUBJECTS: Animals—Badgers—Fiction; Friendship—Fiction. RL 2.5.
Frances finds that carefully avoiding her friend's tricks is not as much fun as being friends. Fairly sophisticated ideas are presented in a reassuring, simple manner. Soft pencil drawings maintain that tone.

Hoban, Russell (cont.)

610 *Tom and the Two Handles*. Ill. by Lillian Hoban. Harper & Row, 1965; pap., 1984. ISBN 0-06-022431-2. SERIES: I Can Read. SUBJECTS: Fathers—Fiction; Friendship—Fiction. RL 2.0.

After Tom has a fight with his best friend, his father tells him about a jug having two handles. In other words, Tom can choose to pick up his friendship by the same handle next time, or choose the other. In ink and wash drawings Lillian Hoban's illustrations of the children capture the essence of the spat.

Hoff, Syd

611 *Albert the Albatross*. Ill. by author. Harper & Row, 1961. ISBN 0-06-022446-0. SERIES: Early I Can Read. SUBJECTS: Animals—Albatrosses—Fiction. RL 2.3.

While lost from his ship, Albert encounters a parrot, a cuckoo, a woodpecker, and a weathervane bird. When he roosts on a hat belonging to a lady off on a cruise, he finds his ship again. Plain cartoons follow Albert's adventures.

612 *Barney's Horse*. Ill. by author. Harper & Row, 1987. ISBN 0-06-022450-9. SERIES: Early I Can Read. SUBJECTS: Animals—Horses—Fiction; City and town life—Fiction. RL 2.5.

Barney the peddler's horse runs away—once. Warm view of city life is illustrated with cartoon drawings.

613 *Chester*. Ill. by author. Harper & Row, 1961; pap., 1986. ISBN 0-06-022456-8. SERIES: I Can Read. SUBJECTS: Animals—Horses—Fiction. RL 1.9.

The horse Chester's search for loving leads him to a farm, a market, a park, a carousel, and a firehouse. Simple cartoon drawings and predicaments evoke gentle humor.

614 *Danny and the Dinosaur*. Ill. by author. Harper & Row, 1958; pap., 1978. ISBN 0-06-022466-5. SERIES: I Can Read. SUBJECTS: Dinosaurs—Fiction. RL 2.6.

A dinosaur takes a day off from the museum to frolic with Danny. This imaginative tale is very appealing to children. Flat drawings have humor in the episodes, from the dinosaur's large size to its delighted expression.

615 *Happy Birthday, Henrietta!* Ill. by author. Garrard, 1983. ISBN 0-8116-4423-5. SERIES: Imagination. SUBJECTS: Animals—Chickens—Fiction; Birthdays—Fiction. RL 1.7.

Besides being treated to flowers, a movie, and popcorn in town, Henrietta has yet another birthday surprise in store. Watercolors make the cartoon animals appear warm.

616 *Henrietta Goes to the Fair*. Ill. by author. Garrard, 1979. ISBN 0-8116-4416-2. SERIES: Imagination. SUBJECTS: Animals—Chickens—Fiction; Fairs—Fiction; Farm and country life—Fiction. RL 2.2.

Henrietta accidentally wins a blue ribbon at the fair, but her real concern is for Winthrop the pig's feelings. Simple watercolors focus on the animals.

617 *Henrietta, the Early Bird*. Ill. by author. Garrard, 1978. ISBN 0-8116-4410-3. SERIES: Imagination. SUBJECTS: Animals—Chickens—Fiction; Farm and country life—Fiction. RL 2.1.

Henrietta mistakenly tries to arouse the barnyard and town in the middle of the night. Comic watercolors are simple and expressive.

618 *Henrietta's Fourth of July*. Ill. by author. Garrard, 1981. ISBN 0-8116-4422-7. SERIES: Imagination. SUBJECTS: Animals—Chickens—Fiction; Farm and country life—Fiction; Holidays—Fourth of July—Fiction. RL 2.0.

Henrietta carries the flag when the farm animals participate in the Fourth of July festivities. Cartoon drawings add humor.

619 *Horse in Harry's Room*. Ill. by author. Harper & Row, 1970; pap., 1985. ISBN 0-06-022483-5. SERIES: Early I Can Read. SUBJECTS: Animals—Horses—Fiction; Imagination—Fiction. RL 2.2.

Even after a trip to the country to see real horses, Harry knows that his imaginary horse will stay in his room as long as Harry wants. Typical Hoff cartoons have either turquoise or brown wash.

620 *Ida the Bareback Rider*. Ill. by author. Putnam, 1972, o.p. SERIES: See and

Read. SUBJECTS: Circuses—Fiction. RL 2.9.

Ida the circus bareback rider wants all the applause until a fire teaches her that teamwork is more important. A sampling of circus acts with a fairly didactic story is illustrated with typical Hoff cartoons in yellow, pink, and orange washes.

621 *Jeffrey at Camp.* Ill. by author. Putnam, 1968, o.p. SUBJECTS: Camps and Camping—Fiction. RL 3.2.

Jeffrey's moaning from overeating scares a bear away from camp, and changes Jeffrey's eating habits permanently. Cartoon drawings have yellow highlights.

622 *Julius.* Ill. by author. Harper & Row, 1959; pap., 1988. ISBN 0-06-022491-6. SERIES: I Can Read. SUBJECTS: Animals—Gorillas—Fiction; Circuses—Fiction. RL 2.2.

A circus gorilla gets lost when he tries to find the people he has just scared away. Simple sketches are typical of Hoff.

623 *Mrs. Brice's Mice.* Ill. by author. Harper & Row, 1988. ISBN 0-06-022452-5. SERIES: Early I Can Read. SUBJECTS: Animals—Mice—Fiction. RL 2.2.

Mrs. Brice fed her 25 mice the finest cheese, and washed and dried behind their ears so they were always clean. However, one mouse is always the nonconformist in Mrs. Brice and the mice's collective activities. Cartoon illustrations underline the humor.

624 *Sammy the Seal.* Ill. by author. Harper & Row, 1959; pap., 1980. ISBN 0-06-022526-2. SERIES: I Can Read. SUBJECTS: Animals—Seals—Fiction. RL 2.1.

Despite success in learning how to read at school, Sammy the seal discovers that at the zoo he can swim and have a tasty diet more easily than in his city explorations. Cartoon illustrations are appropriate for the slight tale.

625 *Soft Skull Sam.* Ill. by author. Harcourt Brace, 1981, o.p. SERIES: Let Me Read. SUBJECTS: Sports—Soccer—Fiction. RL 2.5.

Sam's afraid of hitting the ball with his head in soccer, but he discovers it doesn't hurt.

Didactic story is illustrated with Hoff's cartoons that have gray and green washes.

626 *Thunderhoof.* Ill. by author. Harper & Row, 1971. ISBN 0-06-022560-2. SERIES: Early I Can Read. SUBJECTS: Animals—Horses—Fiction; Cowboys—Fiction; Pets—Wild animals—Fiction. RL 2.8.

Wild Thunderhoof throws every comer from his saddle, but after escaping to the range, he misses the brushing and currying, so he returns to the ranch more docile. Illustrations are very simple.

627 *A Walk Past Ellen's House.* Ill. by author. McGraw-Hill, 1972, o.p. SUBJECTS: Behavior—Shyness—Fiction; Friendship—Fiction. RL 2.4.

Harvey overcomes his shyness only when he forgets himself to help someone else. Comic drawings have brown and blue wash.

628 *Walpole.* Ill. by author. Harper & Row, 1977. ISBN 0-06-022544-0. SERIES: Early I Can Read. SUBJECTS: Animals—Walruses—Fiction. RL 2.7.

Big, strong Walpole does not want to be leader of the walrus pack; he is busy caring for orphan walruses. Although the language is simple, there are some nice touches and real warmth. Illustrations in brown and blue match the quality of the text.

629 *Who Will Be My Friends?* Ill. by author. Harper & Row, 1960; pap., 1985. ISBN 0-06-022556-4. SERIES: Early I Can Read. SUBJECTS: Friendship—Fiction; Moving, household—Fiction. RL 1.7.

Freddy's ability to play baseball gives him an entry into a new neighborhood. This simple story is illustrated with typically simple Hoff pencil drawings, alternating sepia with four colors.

630 *Wilfred the Lion.* Ill. by author. Putnam, 1970, o.p. SUBJECTS: Animals—Lions—Fiction; Behavior—Bravery—Fiction; Friendship—Fiction. RL 2.7.

Wilfred's attempts to act as brave as his favorite animal, the lion, help him to be less fearful in the playground, but he ends up lonely—until his mother helps him become a boy again. Typical Hoff cartoons have pale blue and tan washes.

Hogan, Paula Z.

631 *The Beaver.* Ill. by Yoshi Miyake. Rain-tree, 1979. ISBN 0-8172-1502-6. SUBJECTS: Animals—Beavers; Nature. RL 3.0.
Information about beavers is skeletal. Basic watercolors add little.

632 *The Honeybee.* Ill. by Geri K. Strigenz. Raintree, 1979. ISBN 0-8172-1256-6. SERIES: Life Cycles. SUBJECTS: Animals—Bees; Nature. RL 2.7.
A glossary is appended to an outline of the life of a honeybee hive. Full page paintings show bee behavior.

Hogrogian, Nonny

633 *Billy Goat and His Well-Fed Friends.* Ill. by author. Harper & Row, 1972. ISBN 0-06-022565-3. SERIES: I Can Read. SUBJECTS: Animals—Goats—Fiction. RL 2.5.
Together Billy Goat and four friends escape being some farmers' dinner, and they scare wolves away from their new house in the woods. In cadence and result, the tale is reminiscent of the "Musicians of Bremen." Pale pastel pencil drawings are very appealing.

Holding, James

634 *The Robber of Featherbed Lane.* Ill. by author. Putnam, 1970, o.p. SERIES: See and Read. SUBJECTS: Mystery and detective stories. RL 2.7.
An imaginative cumulation of lost items includes a diamond ring, a banana cake, a monkey, a small child, and a kitten. Ink sketches are in yellow and avocado.

Holl, Adelaide

635 *Bedtime for Bears.* Ill. by Cyndy Szekeres. Garrard, hb and pap., 1973. ISBN 0-8116-6727-8. SERIES: Venture. SUBJECTS: Animals—Bears—Fiction; Seasons—Fall—Fiction. RL 2.2.
Full of curiosity, Small Bear succumbs to sleep only after finding the other animals too busy preparing for winter to have time to play. Pencil drawings with a pale blue wash give the animals a very appealing mien.

636 *George the Gentle Giant.* Ill. by Frank Daniel. Golden, 1962, o.p. SERIES: Read It Yourself. SUBJECTS: Friendship—Fiction; Giants—Fiction. RL 2.5.
George the Giant tries unsuccessfully with a picnic and singing to make friends with the village children. When his tears make a pool, friendly contact is made. Plain colored drawings have little imaginative detail.

637 *If We Could Make Wishes.* Ill. by Judy Pelikan. Garrard, 1977. ISBN 0-8116-4401-4. SERIES: Imagination. SUBJECTS: Imagination—Fiction. RL 3.1.
Two children play with dragons, ghosts, mermaids, and giants–in their imaginations! They are content with being themselves in real life. Message and pastel watercolors are a bit stilted.

638 *The Long Birthday.* Ill. by Ethel Gold. Garrard, 1974. ISBN 0-8116-6974-2. SERIES: Venture. SUBJECTS: Birthdays—Fiction. RL 2.2.
Jody finds a butterfly chrysalis, earns money to buy some seeds, and makes a card for her mother's birthday after giving away or losing her precious three dimes. Drawings in kelly green and pencil are static.

639 *Small Bear and the Secret Surprise.* Ill. by Tien. Garrard, 1978. ISBN 0-8116-4455-3. SERIES: Small Bear Adventures. SUBJECTS: Friendship—Fiction; Siblings—Fiction. RL 2.1.
Small Bear's "secret surprise" is a new baby sister, who wanders off while under his care, climbs a tree and will not come down. This quiet, gentle adventure is suitably illustrated with soft ink drawings with a turquoise wash.

640 *Small Bear Builds a Playhouse.* Ill. by Cyndy Szekeres. Garrard, 1978. ISBN 0-8116-4454-5. SERIES: Small Bear Adventures. SUBJECTS: Animals—Bears—Fiction; Behavior—Sharing—Fiction; Friendship—Fiction. RL 2.3.
Small Bear does not enjoy his new playhouse much until he invites his friends to share it. Pencil drawings of animals have a green wash.

641 *Small Bear's Birthday Party.* Ill. by Leigh Grant. Garrard, 1977. ISBN 0-8116-4453-7. SERIES: Small Bear

Adventures. SUBJECTS: Animals—Bears—Fiction; Birthdays—Fiction. RL 2.4.
When Small Bear's friends are too busy to play, his feelings are hurt, but the party they are planning for him changes his feelings. Patterned ink drawings with a pale turquoise wash suit the gentleness of the story.

642 *Small Bear's Name Hunt.* Ill. by Pat Bargielski. Garrard, 1977. ISBN 0-8116-4451-0. SERIES: Small Bear Adventures. SUBJECTS: Animals—Bears—Fiction. RL 1.8.
Small Bear's gentle encounters with other animals convince him that his own name is most appropriate. Bargielski's use of cool green detracts from the warmth of her drawings.

643 *Sylvester: The Mouse with the Musical Ear.* Ill. by N. M. Bodecker. Golden, 1973, o.p. SERIES: Read It Yourself. SUBJECTS: Animals—Mice—Fiction; City and town life—Fiction; Farm and country life—Fiction. RL 2.8.
When development encroaches on the pastoral music of his fields, Sylvester finds a home that suits his musical ear—a guitar! In delightful progression, a town-city mouse story becomes a tall tale, well underscored by delicate line drawings.

644 *Too Fat to Fly.* Ill. by Bill Morrison. Garrard, hb and pap., 1973. ISBN 0-8116-6731-6. SERIES: Venture. SUBJECTS: Animals—Elephants—Fiction; Self-esteem—Fiction. RL 2.7.
Marco's attempts to imitate Lark, Butterfly, and Fish are disastrous, but he is just right for being an elephant. Illustrations are adequate.

645 *Wake Up, Small Bear.* Ill. by Pat Bargielski. Garrard, 1977. ISBN 0-8116-4450-2. SERIES: Small Bear Adventures. SUBJECTS: Animals—Bears—Fiction; Seasons—Spring—Fiction. RL 2.0.
Joyfully Small Bear greets the spring after his winter nap, as he searches for his friend, Binky. Fuzzy ink animals have an apple green backdrop.

Holland, Marion

646 *Big Ball of String.* Ill. by author. Beginner, 1958. ISBN 0-394-90005-7.

SUBJECTS: Imagination—Fiction; Stories in rhyme. RL 2.2.
A boy's adventures while adding to his ball of string and using it when he is confined to bed are highly creative. Red and blue colored pencil highlights the drawings.

Hood, Flora

647 *One Luminaria for Antonio.* Ill. by Ann Kirn. Putnam, 1966, o.p. SERIES: See and Read. SUBJECTS: Holidays—Christmas—Fiction; Mexico—Fiction. RL 3.5.
Antonio gets a candle for a luminaria and an accompanying blessing despite his poverty and a temptation he has trouble resisting. Earth-tone textured sand paintings have an authentic flavor.

Hopkins, Lee B., ed.

648 *More Surprises.* Ill. by Megan Lloyd. Harper & Row, 1987. ISBN 0-06-022605-6. SERIES: I Can Read. SUBJECTS: Poetry. RL 2.8.
Poems by poets such as Aileen Fisher and Charlotte Zolotow deal with seasons, books, and nonsense. Faintly textured soft pastels give variety and humor.

Hornblow, Leonora, and Hornblow, Arthur

649 *Insects Do the Strangest Things.* Ill. by Michael K. Frith. Random House, 1968. ISBN 0-394-90072-3. SERIES: Step-Up. SUBJECTS: Animals—Insects; Nature; Science. RL 2.8.
The 17 insects shown are illustrated in four color. They range from caddis fly to flea and walking stick to termite.

650 *Reptiles Do the Strangest Things.* Ill. by Michael K. Frith. Random House, 1970. ISBN 0-394-90074-X. SERIES: Step-Up. SUBJECTS: Animals—Reptiles and amphibians; Nature; Science. RL 3.3.
Among the 25 reptiles introduced is the brontosaurus; however, the information is out of date. The wonder and variety of reptiles is stressed. Good watercolors dominate each double page spread.

Huber, M. B.

651 *It Happened One Day*. Harper & Row, 1976, o.p. SERIES: Wonder-Story. SUBJECTS: Fables; Folklore. RL 2.5.
The 11 folktales come from England, Finland, France, Germany, East Africa, and India, plus two of Aesop's fables. Tales retold, ranging from "Drakestail" to "Jack and the Beanstalk," are somewhat stilted. Pastel washes with textured gray sketches are varied and appealing.

Hudlow, Jean

652 *Eric Plants a Garden*. Ill. by author. Whitman, 1979, o.p. SUBJECTS: Gardening. RL 2.6.
In a photoessay a young boy is shown preparing the soil and planting, tending, and harvesting his vegetable garden. Serial photos, close-ups, some in color, show the progress from planning the garden to carving a jack-o'-lantern.

Hurd, Edith T.

653 *Come and Have Fun*. Ill. by Clement Hurd. Harper & Row, 1962. ISBN 0-06-022681-1. SERIES: Early I Can Read. SUBJECTS: Animals—Cats—Fiction; Animals—Mice—Fiction. RL 1.4.
A simple story deals with a cat chasing a mouse, incorporating some nice twists of language and cozy sketches that focus on the two animals.

654 *Johnny Lion's Bad Day*. Ill. by Clement Hurd. Harper & Row, 1970. ISBN 0-06-022708-7. SERIES: I Can Read. SUBJECTS: Animals—Lions—Fiction; Illness—Fiction; Parent and child—Fiction. RL 1.8.
Johnny Lion's cold miseries are accentuated by bad dreams and comforted by loving parents. Ink sketches with textured soft coloring convey a small child's feelings.

655 *Johnny Lion's Book*. Ill. by Clement Hurd. Harper & Row, 1965; pap., 1985. ISBN 0-06-022706-0. SERIES: I Can Read. SUBJECTS: Animals—Lions—Fiction; Behavior—Obedient—Fiction; Books and reading—Fiction. RL 1.8.

Johnny Lion is reading his first book. The story teaches him about some of the consequences of not minding his parents. Text and pencil illustrations are gently reassuring.

656 *Johnny Lion's Rubber Boots*. Ill. by Clement Hurd. Harper & Row, 1972. ISBN 0-06-022710-9. SERIES: I Can Read. SUBJECTS: Animals—Lions—Fiction; Imagination—Fiction. RL 2.3.
After a rainy day's play inside, Johnny gets to play outside in his new rubber boots. Delightful friendly lion sketches warm the small adventures of Johnny's imaginative day.

657 *Last One Home Is a Green Pig*. Ill. by Clement Hurd. Harper & Row, 1959. ISBN 0-06-022716-8. SERIES: I Can Read. SUBJECTS: Animals—Ducks—Fiction; Animals—Monkeys—Fiction. RL 1.8.
Duck and Monkey have a great race, hitching rides on everything from a bicycle and a horse to a submarine and a fire engine. They even vow to race again the next day. The language is simple, but with the rhythm of a cumulative tale. Sketchy action drawings have a green wash.

658 *Look for a Bird*. Ill. by Clement Hurd. Harper & Row, 1977. ISBN 0-06-022719-2. SERIES: Science I Can Read. SUBJECTS: Animals—Birds; Nature; Science. RL 2.6.
Robins, blue jays, hummingbirds, pigeons, cardinals, and crows are some of the birds that appear on double spreads, half text and half watercolor illustrations. Tips for identifying each are included.

659 *Mother Kangaroo*. Ill. by Clement Hurd. Little, Brown, 1976, o.p. SERIES: Mother Animal. SUBJECTS: Animals—Kangaroos; Growing-up; Nature. RL 3.1.
The growth of one "joey" is described in an intriguing fashion. Exceptional shaded block prints rivet one's attention.

660 *No Funny Business*. Ill. by Clement Hurd. Harper & Row, 1962. ISBN 0-06-022726-5. SERIES: I Can Read. SUBJECTS: Animals—Cats—Fiction; Dreams—Fiction; Picnics—Fiction. RL 1.6.
When the family goes on a picnic, their cat, Carl, is left at home. However, he has imagi-

nary picnic adventures in his dreams. Carl's expressive, mischievous eyes are the focal point of ink and two-tone wash drawings.

661 *Sandpipers.* Ill. by Lucienne Bloch. Crowell, 1961, o.p. SERIES: Let's-Read-and-Find-Out Science. SUBJECTS: Animals—Sandpipers; Nature. RL 2.4.
In rhythmic language, the life cycle of sandpipers is lovingly recounted. Exceptional block prints in a variety of perspectives are in khaki, gray, and blue.

662 *Stop Stop.* Ill. by Clement Hurd. Harper & Row, 1961. ISBN 0-06-022746-X. SERIES: I Can Read. SUBJECTS: Babysitting—Fiction; Humorous stories. RL 2.1.
Suzie's favorite baby-sitter Miss Mugs has an exaggerated passion for cleanliness, until the elephant at the zoo gives her a shower. Comic ink sketches add to the fun.

663 *White Horse.* Ill. by Tony Chen. Harper & Row, 1970. ISBN 0-06-022748-6. SUBJECTS: Emotions—Loneliness—Fiction; Imagination—Fiction. RL 1.9.
A lonely boy, Jimmie Lee, on a class trip to the zoo, takes a magical trip on a white horse in his imagination. Evocative story has four-color drawings that focus on the boy and an unusually textured white horse.

Hutchins, Pat

664 *The Best Train Set Ever.* Ill. by author. Greenwillow, 1978. ISBN 0-688-84086-8. SERIES: Read-alone. SUBJECTS: Birthdays—Fiction; Family life—Fiction; Holidays—Halloween—Fiction. RL 2.8.
Very satisfying stories are told of Peter's birthday wish coming true, little Maria creating a prize-winning Halloween costume, and a family laid low by measles saving their Christmas celebration for July. The family is drawn in avocado, pumpkin, cocoa, and lemon.

665 *The Tale of Thomas Mead.* Ill. by author. Greenwillow, 1980. ISBN 0-688-84282-8. SERIES: Read-alone. SUBJECTS: Books and reading—Fiction; Stories in rhyme. RL 3.1.

Thomas discovers that not knowing how to read gets him in lots of awkward situations. The rhyming of this exaggerated story is reminiscent of Maurice Sendak's *Pierre* (Harper & Row, 1962). Pastel paintings complement text well.

I

Iritani, Chika A.

666 *I Know an Animal Doctor.* Ill. by Haris Petie. Putnam, 1970, o.p. SERIES: Community Helpers. SUBJECTS: Careers; Community helpers. RL 2.3.
A boy gets a special tour of the animal hospital when his dog, Happy, nurses a sore paw. Factual but imaginative text is illustrated with pencil drawings.

J

Jacobs, Francine

667 *Supersaurus.* Ill. by D. D. Tyler. Putnam, 1982. ISBN 0-399-61150-9. SERIES: See and Read. SUBJECTS: Dinosaurs; Science. RL 3.6.
The true story of "Dinosaur Jim" Jensen's discovery of Supersaurus is heralded. Unusual dot-shaped pencil drawings are especially effective in showing fossils in the matrix as they are uncovered.

Jacobs, Leland B.

668 *April Fool!* Ill. by Lou Cunette. Garrard, 1973. ISBN 0-8116-6728-6. SERIES: Venture. SUBJECTS: Holidays—April Fool's Day. RL 2.6.
A series of standard April Fool's jokes played on Nancy gives her an idea on how to enjoy this holiday. Well written and illustrated with pencil and pale blue wash.

669 *Hello, Pleasant Places!* Ill. by Kelly Oechsli. Garrard, 1972. ISBN 0-8116-

Jacobs, Leland B. (cont.)

6951-3. SUBJECTS: Animals—Fiction; Poetry; Zoos—Fiction. RL 1.9.
Inventive poetic wordplay is grouped by settings: city, park, zoo, shore, woods, and country. Includes average ink drawings with an apple green or orange wash.

670 *Hello, Year!* Ill. by Frank Aloise. Garrard, 1972. ISBN 0-8116-6954-8. SERIES: Venture. SUBJECTS: Holidays—Fiction; Poetry; Seasons—Fiction. RL 2.4.
Poets such as Maurice Sendak and Aileen Fisher celebrate sensory experiences around various holidays. Bright orange and fuchsia highlight small ink sketches.

671 *I Don't, I Do.* Ill. by Frank Carlings. Garrard, hb and pap., 1971. ISBN 0-8116-6705-7. SERIES: Venture. SUBJECTS: Animals—Fiction; Poetry. RL 2.5.
In this poem, children *don't* want to be fish, penguins, or camels, but they *do* want to play, row, or eat ice cream. Mediocre ink drawings have flat apple green highlights.

672 *Playtime in the City.* Ill. by Kelly Oechsli. Garrard, hb and pap., 1971. ISBN 0-8116-6700-6. SERIES: Venture. SUBJECTS: City and town life; Poetry. RL 1.9.
Poems about swinging, playing games, blowing soap bubbles, and pretending are written by children's poets such as Aileen Fisher. Line drawings have turquoise highlights.

673 *Poems about Fur and Feather Friends.* Ill. by Frank Aloise. Garrard, hb and pap., 1971. ISBN 0-8116-6713-8. SERIES: Venture. SUBJECTS: Animals; Pets; Poetry. RL 2.1.
Simple verse about pets, birds, and farm animals is written by such poets as John Ciardi and Lois Lenski. Line drawings have chartreuse highlights.

674 *Poetry for Autumn.* Ill. by Stina Nagel. Garrard, 1968, o.p. SUBJECTS: Holidays—Fiction; Poetry; Seasons—Fall—Fiction. RL 3.6.
Robert Frost and David McCord are some of the poets who write about animals, voters, fall holidays, and books in simple poems. Ink sketches show tiny children and animals.

675 *Poetry for Chuckles and Grins.* Ill. by Tomie dePaola. Garrard, 1968. ISBN 0-8116-4101-5. SERIES: Poetry. SUBJECTS: Humorous stories; Poetry. RL 2.7.
Mary O'Neill opens this good anthology of humorous verse by such poets as Ogden Nash and Aileen Fisher. Broadly outlined humorous sketches have gold and pink coloring.

676 *Poetry for Space Enthusiasts.* Ill. by Frank Aloise. Garrard, 1971, o.p. SUBJECTS: Imagination—Fiction; Poetry; Space travel—Fiction. RL 3.7.
Planes, zeppelins, bubbles, planets, clouds, stars, and witches are the stuff dreams are made of. This collection of poems is illustrated with ink sketches highlighted in sky blue.

677 *Teeny-Tiny.* Ill. by Marilyn Lucey. Garrard, 1976. ISBN 0-8116-6070-2. SERIES: Easy Venture. SUBJECTS: Imagination—Fiction; Stories in rhyme. RL 2.7.
An enchanting adventure of teeny-tiny children in a teeny-tiny toy store is told in rhythmic rhyme. Bright watercolor pictures focus on the children's play.

Jameson, Cynthia

678 *Winter Hut.* Ill. by Ray Cruz. Coward, McCann, 1973, o.p. SUBJECTS: Folklore—Russia; Russia—Fiction. RL 2.8.
In this retelling of a Russian folktale, only by working together can the animals scare off Wolf and Bear from the shelter Bull has had to build alone. Ink drawings with beige focus on close-ups of the animals.

Janice

679 *Little Bear Learns to Read the Cookbook.* Ill. by Mariana. Lothrop, 1969, o.p. SUBJECTS: Animals—Bears—Fiction; Books and reading—Fiction; Cookery—Fiction. RL 2.3.
Little Bear learns to read so she can bake a chocolate cake. Of course she relates the alphabet to food, as do her animal friends.

Pencil drawings and washes showcase the animals.

Jaspersohn, William

680 *How the Forest Grew.* Ill. by Chuck Eckart. Greenwillow, 1980, o.p. SERIES: Read-alone. SUBJECTS: Nature; Plants—Trees; Science. RL 3.1.
The life cycle of a forest and its dependent wildlife is related in rich detail. The framed ink drawings have the same wealth of detail.

Jennings, Terry

681 *Time.* Ill. by David Anstey. Gloucester, 1988. ISBN 0-531-17112-4. SERIES: Junior Science. SUBJECTS: Concepts—Time; Science; Science experiments. RL 2.4.
Activities and experiments with water and candle clocks and a sundial are simply illustrated in bright watercolors.

Johnson, Crockett

682 *Picture for Harold's Room.* Ill. by author. Harper & Row, 1960; pap., 1985. ISBN 0-06-023006-1. SERIES: I Can Read. SUBJECTS: Imagination—Fiction. RL 2.1.
With a magic crayon, Harold travels the world, changing size and perspective with a stroke of the crayon. Very spare drawings of a boy show his artistic creations with a purple line.

Johnson, Jean

683 *Librarians A to Z.* Photos. Walker, 1988. ISBN 0-8027-6842-3. SERIES: Community Helpers. SUBJECTS: Alphabet; Books and reading; Community helpers. RL 3.9.
An alphabet presents various aspects of librarianship, from cataloging, programming, videos, weeding, and zigzag books. Excellent close-up black and white photos show librarianship as an active, current, and vital profession.

Johnson, Mildred

684 *Wait, Skates!* Ill. by Tom Dunnington. Childrens, hb and pap., 1983. ISBN 0-516-02039-0. SERIES: Rookie Readers. SUBJECTS: Sports—Roller skating—Fiction. RL 2.1.
With a 30-word vocabulary, a boy is shown learning how to roller skate. Action and humor are captured well in the bright colored drawings.

Johnson, Sylvia A.

685 *Elephants around the World.* Orig. French by Anne-Marie Pajot, trans. by Dyan Hammarberg. Photos by Guy Dhuit, Jean-Louis Nou, and Rapho; drawings by L'Enc Matte. Carolrhoda, 1977. ISBN 0-87614-075-4. SERIES: Animal Friends. SUBJECTS: Animals—Elephants; Nature. RL 2.9.
Although Frank's introduction to elephants is in the zoo, most of the information in this book is from their natural habitat. Appendix suggests elephants are now successfully protected from human hunters, which is *not* now true. Colored and black and white photos are combined with some drawings.

686 *Lions of Africa.* Orig. French by Anne-Marie Pajot, trans. by Dyan Hammarberg. Photos by Guy Dhuit, Klaus Paysan, and Rapho; drawings by L'Enc Matte. Carolrhoda, 1977. ISBN 0-87614-081-9. SERIES: Animal Friends. SUBJECTS: Animals—Lions; Nature. RL 3.8.
Uncle David shows Luke and Ted his movies of African lions, while they and the reader learn of the lions' habits vicariously. Excellent black and white photos alternate with color photos.

687 *Penney and Pete the Lambs.* Orig. French by Anne-Marie Pajot, trans. by Dyan Hammarberg. Photos by Antoinette Barrere, drawings by L'Enc Matte. Carolrhoda, 1976. ISBN 0-87614-067-3. SERIES: Animal Friends. SUBJECTS: Animals—Sheep; Nature; Pets. RL 3.4.
Information about sheep is imparted from the point of view of two children. Additional details are included in an appendix. Some drawings appear among the black and white photos.

Johnston, Tony

688 *The Adventures of Mole and Troll*. Ill. by
Wallace Tripp. Putnam, 1972, o.p.
SUBJECTS: Animals—Moles—Fiction;
Friendship—Fiction; Trolls—Fiction.
RL 2.8.
The friendship of neighbors Mole and Troll
survives a day at the beach, shoelaces that
constantly come untied, and attempts to live
like the other. Outstanding ink and wash
drawings by Tripp add to the humor and
appeal.

689 *Farmer Mack Measures His Pig*. Ill. by
Megan Lloyd. Harper & Row, 1986.
ISBN 0-06-023018-5. SUBJECTS: Animals—
Pigs—Fiction; Farm and country life—
Fiction; Humorous stories. RL 2.7.
Farmer Mack and Farmer Tubb compete to
determine whose pig is fatter and the better
jumper. Slapstick humor is delightful. Color-
ful comic drawings add to the spirited humor.

690 *Night Noises and Other Mole and Troll
Stories*. Ill. by Cyndy Szekeres. Putnam,
1977, o.p. SUBJECTS: Animals—Moles—
Fiction; Friendship—Fiction; Trolls—
Fiction. RL 3.1.
Troll is Mole's rain-or-shine friend. He sneezes
a tooth out after Mole's helpful schemes, such
as slamming a door, fail. Chapters about this
special friendship are illustrated with pencil-
drawn friendly looking critters.

691 *Odd Jobs*. Ill. by Tomie dePaola.
Putnam, 1977, o.p. SERIES: See and
Read. SUBJECTS: Humorous stories.
RL 2.9.
Washing an uncooperative dog, Bouncer (not
once but four times!), subbing in dance class,
and balloon-sitting are some of the jobs under-
taken by a sometimes successful Odd Jobs.
Pencil drawings are gloriously appropriate.

692 *Odd Jobs and Friends*. Ill. by Tomie
dePaola. Putnam, 1982. ISBN 0-399-
61204-1. SERIES: See and Read.
SUBJECTS: Friendship—Fiction;
Humorous stories. RL 3.0.
Odd Jobs takes on some odd tasks—protecting
an arm cast from a romantic scribbler, teaching Annie how to blow bubble-gum bubbles,
and keeping a new kid company until he finds

a friend. Warm, expressive pencil drawings
are of multiethnic friends.

Jordan, Helene J.

693 *How a Seed Grows*. Ill. by Joseph Low.
Crowell, 1960; pap., 1972. ISBN 0-690-
40645-2. SERIES: Let's-Read-and-Find-
Out. SUBJECTS: Nature; Plants—Seeds,
roots, and bulbs; Science experiments.
RL 2.4.
The author suggests planting ten bean seeds
and digging up one each day to understand
the way in which a seed begins to develop.
Sketches are accurate and visually interesting.

Judson, Clara I.

694 *Christopher Columbus*. Ill. by Polly
Jackson. Follett, 1960, o.p. SERIES:
Beginning to Read. SUBJECTS:
Biographies. RL 2.0.
In 368 basic vocabulary words, the outline of
Columbus's dream and the suspense of
whether he would achieve it before his crew
mutinied are well portrayed. Full color draw-
ings are a bit dated.

Justus, May

695 *Surprise for Perky Pup*. Ill. by Mimi
Korach. Garrard, hb and pap., 1971.
ISBN 0-8116-6704-9. SERIES: Venture.
SUBJECTS: Animals—Dogs—Fiction.
RL 2.1.
When Perky Pup is hit over the head, his
howling alarms all the dogs until they find
the source of the blow. Delightful simple
drawings are in emerald green, royal blue,
and cocoa.

K

Kantrowitz, Mildred

696 *Willy Bear*. Ill. by Nancy W. Parker.
Parents Magazine Press, 1976, o.p.;
Four Winds, pap., 1980. ISBN 0-02-

749790-9. SUBJECTS: School stories; Toys—Teddy bears—Fiction. RL 2.1.

A small boy eases his anxiety about his first day at school by talking to his faithful teddy bear. Neat pastel drawings have an appropriate simplicity and comfort.

Kay, Eleanor

697 *Let's Find Out about the Hospital.* Ill. by William Brooks. Watts, 1971, o.p. SERIES: Let's Find Out About. SUBJECTS: Hospitals. RL 3.2.

Information about hospital equipment, procedures, and personnel is geared to reassuring young patients. Despite date of publication this is still a useful book. Ink drawings with green highlights are appropriate.

Kaye, Marilyn

698 *Will You Cross Me?* Ill. by Ned Delaney. Harper & Row, 1985. ISBN 0-06-023103-3. SERIES: Early I Can Read. SUBJECTS: City and town life—Fiction; Friendship—Fiction. RL 2.1.

Two friends need frequent help to cross a city street to play together. Comic details of animals and newspapers add to the picture of the busy neighborhood.

Keller, Beverly

699 *Beetle Bush.* Ill. by Marc Simont. Coward, McCann, 1975, o.p. SUBJECTS: Self-esteem—Fiction. RL 2.7.

Arabella becomes an ex-failure when her garden produces snails, moles, beetles, and one overlooked melon. This story is sensitively told and illustrated sympathetically in colored pencil.

700 *Don't Throw Another One, Dover.* Ill. by Jacqueline Chwast. Coward, McCann, 1975, o.p. SERIES: Break-of-Day. SUBJECTS: Emotions—Anger—Fiction; Grandparents—Fiction; Sibling rivalry—Fiction. RL 2.7.

To his surprise, Dover is drawn into the daily activities of his grandmother's simple lifestyle. He is visiting her while his mother is having a baby; Grandma gets his attention by throwing her own "tantrum," since Dover has thrown some of his own while with his mother. Pencil drawings have a burnt orange wash.

701 *When Mother Got the Flu.* Ill. by Maxie Chambliss. Coward, McCann, 1984. ISBN 0-698-30743-7. SERIES: Break-of-Day. SUBJECTS: Humorous stories; Illness—Fiction. RL 3.0.

Despite his best intentions not to bother his mother, who has the flu, a small boy breaks the knob on the television set, gets bubble gum all over the cat, melts crayons on the television, and falls into a well while chasing the cat. Black and white illustrations alternate with two colors, thus exaggerating the mess.

Keller, Holly

702 *Geraldine's Big Snow.* Ill. by author. Greenwillow, 1988. ISBN 0-688-07514-2. SUBJECTS: Animals—Pigs—Fiction; Weather—Snow—Fiction. RL 2.7.

During Geraldine's impatient wait for the first snow she meets neighbors preparing for a blizzard. The story is simply told and joyfully illustrated in bright watercolors.

Kelley, Emily

703 *Happy New Year.* Ill. by Priscilla Kiedrowski. Carolrhoda, 1984. ISBN 0-87614-269-2. SERIES: On My Own. SUBJECTS: Holidays—New Year's Day. RL 2.8.

New Year's customs in seven countries, some jokes, food, songs, and games are described. Colored pencil drawings give some of the details of the various cultures.

Kennedy, Richard

704 *Contests at Cowlick.* Ill. by Marc Simont. Little, Brown, 1975, o.p. SUBJECTS: Humorous stories; Tall tales; Western stories. RL 3.3

A small boy single-handedly rounds up an entire outlaw gang of 15 by trickery in this most satisfying book. Colored pencil drawings add humor and action.

Kent, Jack

705 *The Biggest Shadow in the Zoo*. Ill. by author. Parents Magazine Press, 1981. ISBN 0-8193-1048-4. SUBJECTS: Animals—Elephants—Fiction; Shadows—Fiction; Zoos—Fiction. RL 2.4.
Goober the elephant is upset when he thinks his faithful shadow has drowned in the zoo moat. Crayon coloring of comic drawings is most fitting.

706 *Hoddy Doddy*. Ill. by author. Greenwillow, 1979, o.p. SERIES: Read-alone. SUBJECTS: Folklore—Denmark; Humorous stories; Nonsense. RL 2.8.
Three Danish tales of fools are retold, one about the Norse lobster sailors, another about marking the watery hiding place of the village clock, and the final one about the human winner of a cuckoo contest. Illustrations are well-suited to the simple retellings.

707 *Socks for Supper*. Ill. by author. Parents Magazine Press, 1978; Crown, pap., 1988. ISBN 0-8193-0965-6. SUBJECTS: Farm and country life—Fiction; Humorous stories. RL 3.0.
A poor farmer and his wife unravel his sweater to knit socks to trade for milk in order to make butter and cheese. The ending has a nice twist, with Kent's excellent full color drawings spicing the simple tale.

708 *Wizard of Wallaby Wallow*. Ill. by author. Parents Magazine Press, 1971, o.p. SUBJECTS: Animals—Mice—Fiction; Magic—Fiction; Self-esteem—Fiction. RL 3.1.
When discontented Mouse acquired one of the Wizard's unlabeled bottles containing a magic spell, he decides he likes being a mouse best. Comic illustrations underline the gentle humor.

Kessel, Joyce K.

709 *St. Patrick's Day*. Ill. by Cathy Gilchrist. Carolrhoda, 1982. ISBN 0-87614-193-9. SERIES: On My Own. SUBJECTS: Holidays—St. Patrick's Day; Ireland. RL 2.5.
The holiday celebrating Patrick's unifying and bringing Christianity to the tribes of Ireland 1,600 years ago is outlined. Ink drawings with green accents and borders underline the seriousness of this religious holiday.

Kessler, Ethel, and Kessler, Leonard

710 *The Big Fight*. Ill. by Pat Paris. Garrard, 1981. ISBN 0-8116-7550-5. SERIES: Begin to Read with Duck and Pig. SUBJECTS: Animals—Ducks—Fiction; Animals—Pigs—Fiction; Friendship—Fiction. RL 1.6.
Pig and Duck both make an effort to make up after they have a name-calling fight. Comic drawings add good characterization.

711 *Grandpa, Witch, and the Magic Doobelator*. Ill. by authors. Macmillan, 1981, o.p. SERIES: Ready-to-Read. SUBJECTS: Humorous stories; Magic—Fiction; Witches—Fiction. RL 2.5.
When Wanda and Willy learn magic tricks for Halloween, they find that Grandpa Witch's magic sometimes has unexpected results. Ink and wash drawings feature pet cats and a fabulous fantasy machine—the Doobelator.

712 *Our Tooth Story: A Tale of Twenty Teeth*. Ill. by authors. Dodd, Mead, 1972, o.p. SUBJECTS: Doctors and nurses; Human body—Teeth. RL 2.6.
A story for kindergartners about teeth gives simple facts from a child's perspective, as well as tips for good dental hygiene. Bold childlike line drawings extend the text.

713 *Pig's Orange House*. Ill. by Pat Paris. Garrard, 1981. ISBN 0-8116-7553-X. SERIES: Begin to Read with Duck and Pig. SUBJECTS: Animals—Fiction; Concepts—Color—Fiction; Humorous stories. RL 2.0.
When Pig's friends help him paint his house, it ends up with a most unusual effect. Full color comic drawings are appropriate for the fun.

714 *The Sweeneys from 9D*. Ill. by Leonard Kessler. Macmillan, 1985. ISBN 0-02-750230-9. SERIES: Ready-to-Read. SUBJECTS: Friendship—Fiction; Latchkey children—Fiction; Moving, household—Fiction. RL 2.2.
Tommy's nervous stomach disappears after his first full day in a new school and a new

apartment. Ink sketches have orange, gray, and beige washes.

715 *What's Inside the Box?* Ill. by Leonard Kessler. Dodd, Mead, 1976, o.p. SUBJECTS: Animals—Fiction; Concepts—Fiction; Mystery and detective stories. RL 2.7.

Seven animals find a box in the woods and scatter fearfully at each new noise or clue to its contents. Simple suspense and humor are effective, especially when matched with Kessler's three-color comic drawings.

Kessler, Leonard

716 *Are We Lost, Daddy?* Ill. by author. Grosset & Dunlap, 1967, o.p. SUBJECTS: Family life—Fiction; Humorous stories. RL 2.0.

After taking a circuitous back route, a family succeeds in finding Big Valley. However, they find it after they get a map. The humor and aggravations are in a childlike view.

717 *The Big Mile Race.* Ill. by author. Greenwillow, 1983. ISBN 0-688-01421-6. SERIES: Read-alone. SUBJECTS: Animals—Fiction; Sports—Running—Fiction. RL 2.2.

Animals with individual characteristics learn about running, and practice for the big race. The dialogue is lively, but the strength of the story is in the support and encouragement the animals provide for each other. Kessler's sketches add humor and action.

718 *Do You Have Any Carrots?* Ill. by Lori Pierson. Garrard, 1979. ISBN 0-8116-6074-5. SUBJECTS: Animals—Fiction; Animals—Rabbits—Fiction; Farm and country life—Fiction. RL 1.7.

Cuddly bunnies find out that none of the barnyard or woodland animals likes carrots as much as they do. Sunny yellow and apple greens set off a variety of animals in this slight story.

719 *The Forgetful Pirate.* Ill. by author. Garrard, 1974. ISBN 0-8116-6972-6. SERIES: Venture. SUBJECTS: Animals—Parrots—Fiction; Pirates—Fiction. RL 2.9.

The cider-drinking pirate is so forgetful that only his parrot can lead the crew to gold. Simple watercolors illustrate this thin tale.

720 *Hey Diddle Diddle.* Ill. by author. Garrard, 1980. ISBN 0-8116-7403-7. SERIES: Young Mother Goose. SUBJECTS: Mother Goose—Fiction; Nonsense; Stories in rhyme. RL 3.4.

Inventive rhyming wordplay nonsense is illustrated with cartoon drawings of animals.

721 *Hickory Dickory Dock.* Ill. by Doug Cushman. Garrard, 1980. ISBN 0-8116-7400-2. SERIES: Young Mother Goose. SUBJECTS: Concepts—Time—Fiction; Mother Goose—Fiction; Stories in rhyme. RL 1.3.

The hours of the day are celebrated with nonsense rhymes as the clock strikes each hour. Colored ink drawings focus on a cat and a mouse.

722 *Kick, Pass and Run.* Ill. by author. Harper & Row, 1966; pap., 1978. ISBN 0-06-023160-2. SERIES: Sports I Can Read. SUBJECTS: Animals—Fiction; Sports—Football—Fiction. RL 2.2.

Exceptionally well presented facts about football from the point of view of animals who find a football, watch the game being played, and then try to play themselves. Very simple drawings with rust and green capture the humor and action.

723 *Mixed-Up Mother Goose.* Ill. by Diane Dawson. Garrard, 1980. ISBN 0-8116-7404-5. SERIES: Young Mother Goose. SUBJECTS: Mother Goose—Fiction; Stories in rhyme. RL 2.9.

After a collision in which she hurts her head, Mother Goose thinks Little Bo Peep herds goats, and Little Miss Muffet is eating pink ice cream. Humor is illustrated with pastel drawings in this rhyming story.

724 *The Mother Goose Game.* Ill. by Pat Paris. Garrard, 1980. ISBN 0-8116-7402-9. SERIES: Young Mother Goose. SUBJECTS: Mother Goose—Fiction; Stories in rhyme. RL 2.1.

Mother Goose makes friends with Mole, Hen, Pig, Cat, Goat, Cow, Frog, Dog, Fox, Bird, Ant, Duck, and Mouse, who introduce themselves

Kessler, Leonard (cont.)

in rhyme. Comic animal drawings suit this simple text.

725 *Old Turtle's Riddle and Joke Book.* Ill. by author. Greenwillow, 1986. ISBN 0-688-05954-6. SERIES: Read-alone. SUBJECTS: Jokes and riddles. RL 2.3.
Standard riddles familiar to many adults, but new to children, are illustrated with apple green and pumpkin cartoons that exaggerate the humor.

726 *Old Turtle's Soccer Team.* Ill. by author. Greenwillow, 1988. ISBN 0-688-07158-9. SERIES: Read-alone. SUBJECTS: Animals—Fiction; Sports—Soccer—Fiction. RL 2.4.
The no-name animals have *much* to learn about soccer, and about cooperation, before they become a team. Colorful comic animal drawings add to the excellent simple dialogue, interesting characterization, and humorous wordplay.

727 *Old Turtle's Winter Games.* Ill. by author. Greenwillow, 1983. ISBN 0-688-02310-X. SERIES: Read-alone. SUBJECTS: Animals—Fiction; Sports—Winter—Fiction. RL 2.1.
The animals help each other—out of the snowbank after a ski jump, and down the hill when there are not enough sleds. With imaginative humor beginning readers are introduced to Olympic events. Four-color comic illustrations are simple, yet expressive.

728 *On Your Mark, Get Set, Go!* Ill. by author. Harper & Row, 1972. ISBN 0-06-023153-X. SERIES: Sports I Can Read. SUBJECTS: Animals—Fiction; Sports—Olympics—Fiction. RL 2.4.
In the animal Olympics, everyone can do something and everybody learns something. Exceptionally imaginative presentation of information and values is illustrated with comic ink drawings colored in three tones.

729 *The Pirate's Adventure on Spooky Island.* Ill. by author. Garrard, 1979. ISBN 0-8116-4414-6. SERIES: Imagination. SUBJECTS: Animals—Parrots—Fiction; Pirates—Fiction. RL 2.2.
An inept pirate, Captain Ben, needs his parrot's help to capture Bad Bart. Lively drawings by Kessler add to the fun.

730 *The Worst Team Ever.* Ill. by author. Greenwillow, 1985. ISBN 0-688-04235-X. SERIES: Read-alone. SUBJECTS: Animals Fiction; Sports—Baseball—Fiction. RL 2.7.
Melvin Moose, Bobo Bullfrog, and Pickles Frog improve at swampball with Old Turtle's encouragement and discipline. Clever humor lightens the lesson, as do the two-tone comic drawings.

Kim, Joy

731 *Come On Up!* Ill. by Paul Harvey. Troll, hb and pap., 1981. ISBN 0-89375-511-7. SERIES: Giant First-Start. SUBJECTS: Animals—Cats—Fiction; Animals—Dogs—Fiction. RL 1.2.
A small cat is afraid to climb a tree—until a dog comes along. Unfortunately the author puts the dog in the tree as well as the cat at the end. Bright comic illustrations show a rotund, timid yellow kitten and her raggedy playmate.

732 *Rainbows and Frogs: A Story about Colors.* Ill. by Paul Harvey. Troll, hb and pap., 1981. ISBN 0-89375-505-2. SUBJECTS: Concepts—Color. RL 1.2.
Using a 35-word vocabulary, Kim asks the reader what color he or she likes and what feelings each color generates. Rich, rainbow-colored close-ups are humorous.

King, P. E.

733 *Down on the Funny Farm: A Step Two Book.* Ill. by Alastair Graham. Random House, hb and pap., 1986. ISBN 0-394-97460-3. SERIES: Step into Reading. SUBJECTS: Farm and country life—Fiction; Humorous stories. RL 2.3.
As soon as the farmer trains his animals properly, the old owner shows up to confuse them all again. This well-paced story has an open ending. Full color comic illustrations suit the text.

Kirk, Ruth

734 *Desert Life.* Ill. by author and Louis Kirk. Natural History, 1970, o.p.

SUBJECTS: Deserts; Nature; Science.
RL 3.7.
Kirk describes the birds, mammals, reptiles, insects, weather, and plants of the desert. Colored close-up photos are compelling.

Kirkpatrick, Rena K.

735 *Look at Magnets.* Ill. by Ann Knight. Raintree, 1985. ISBN 0-8172-2354-1. SERIES: Look at Science. SUBJECTS: Magnets; Science; Science experiments. RL 3.4.
Simple tests to see the power of magnets, and how to make electromagnets and a compass are shown in an elementary fashion. Children doing the experiments are in brightly colored clothing on a white background.

736 *Look at Rainbow Colors.* Ill. by Anna Barnard. Raintree, 1985. ISBN 0-8172-2356-8. SERIES: Look at Science. SUBJECTS: Concepts—Color; Rainbows; Science. RL 2.9.
Ordinary sources of rainbows and some exploration of how colors change are introduced. Bright drawings show flowers and animals.

Klasky, Charles

737 *Rugs Have Naps (But Never Take Them).* Ill. by Mike Venezia. Childrens, hb and pap., 1984. ISBN 0-516-03571-1. SERIES: Easy Reading. SUBJECTS: English language—Homonyms. RL 2.9.
Twenty-four homonyms are in this book, including ones about knots and fillings in their double meanings. Illustrations are in watercolor cartoon format.

Klein, Howard

738 *My Best Friends Are Dinosaurs.* Ill. by Windrow. David McKay, 1965, o.p. SUBJECTS: Dinosaurs—Fiction; Stories in rhyme. RL 3.3.
A boy's affinity for dinosaurs is conveyed in simple verse. Ink drawings of dinosaurs are paralleled by the boy's imaginative play.

Klein, Monica

739 *Backyard Basketball Superstar.* Ill. by Nola Langner. Pantheon, 1981. ISBN 0-394-94521-2. SERIES: I Am Reading. SUBJECTS: Sex roles—Fiction; Sports—Basketball—Fiction. RL 2.6.
After some mental adjustments, the Flyers, the neighborhood basketball team, vote unanimously to have Melanie join the all-male team. Excellent pencil drawings lighten the message.

Knight, David

740 *Let's Find Out about Earth.* Ill. by Linda Chen. Watts, 1975, o.p. SUBJECTS: Astronomy; Science; Seasons. RL 3.0.
The topics of the seasons, gravity, the world, the oceans, and planetary travel are introduced by a good science author. Illustrations are brightly colored.

741 *Let's Find Out about Sound.* Ill. by Ulrick Schramm. Watts, 1974, o.p. SUBJECTS: Science; Sound. RL 3.4.
The variety of sources, kinds, and transmitters of sound to the human ear are introduced. Line drawings help convey the well-organized and carefully presented information.

Knowlton, Jack

742 *Geography from A to Z: A Picture Glossary.* Ill. by Harriett Barton. Crowell, 1988. ISBN 0-690-04618-9. SUBJECTS: Geography. RL 3.5.
Zones, palisade, key, and crevasse are some of the geographic terms defined and illustrated here. Large paintings are in flat primary colors. Very appealing, informative, and readable.

Kohn, Berniece

743 *Echoes.* Ill. by Albert Pucci. Coward, McCann, 1965, o.p. SUBJECTS: Science; Sound. RL 3.2.
The scientific applications for sonar properties are touched on by a scientist and science writer. The text is still useful despite dated prints and an old copyright.

Komaiko, Leah

744 *Earl's Too Cool for Me.* Ill. by Laura Cornell. Harper & Row, 1988. ISBN 0-06-023282-X. SUBJECTS: Fantasy; Friendship—Fiction. RL 2.9.

A boy imagines that Earl has accomplished exotic feats. After making Earl's acquaintance, the boy discovers that Earl is more ordinary than he had imagined. So begins a real cool friendship. Rhythmic text has appropriately exaggerated watercolor comic illustrations.

Kotzwinkle, William

745 *Up the Alley with Jack and Joe.* Ill. by Joe Servello. Macmillan, 1974, o.p. SERIES: Ready-to-Read. SUBJECTS: City and town life—Fiction; Imagination—Fiction. RL 3.0.

Three boys and an old dog spend a Saturday full of adventure just "up the alley." The story captures the spirit of childhood. Servello's two-tone ink drawings add flavor to the characters and suspense to the adventures.

Kowalczyk, Carolyn

746 *Purple Is Part of a Rainbow.* Ill. by Gene Sharp. Childrens, hb and pap., 1985. ISBN 0-516-02068-4. SERIES: Rookie Readers. SUBJECTS: Stories in rhyme. RL 2.2.

A simple vocabulary is used to present interesting ideas about the parts that make up a whole of familiar things, such as a rainbow. Rhyming couplets are accompanied by vivid, sprightly drawings.

Krasilovsky, Phyllis

747 *The Man Who Cooked for Himself.* Ill. by Mamoru Funai. Parents Magazine Press, 1981. ISBN 0-8193-1075-1. SERIES: Read Aloud and Easy Reading. SUBJECTS: Food—Fiction; Sex roles—Fiction. RL 3.1.

A lazy man living on the edge of a wood discovers he can be self-sufficient in feeding himself and his cat. The colorful pictures have a fuzzy appearance from poor reproduction.

748 *The Man Who Entered a Contest.* Ill. by Yuri Salzman. Doubleday, 1980, o.p. SERIES: Reading On My Own. SUBJECTS: Bakers and baking—Fiction; Contests—Fiction; Humorous stories. RL 2.5.

A man who had one last cake left from his old stove gets help from his cat to win a new stove in a contest for the most unusual cake. Two-color line drawings are original and effective in design and humor.

749 *The Man Who Tried to Save Time.* Ill. by Marcia Sewell. Doubleday, 1979, o.p. SERIES: Reading On My Own. SUBJECTS: Behavior—Efficient—Fiction; Concepts—Time—Fiction. RL 2.4.

A man's orderly life with his cat is disrupted by his efforts to save time by doing everything ahead of time. For example, he sleeps in his clothes, on top of the covers, and eats peculiarly. Three-color washes on ink have a folksy flavor.

Kraske, Robert

750 *Daredevils Do Amazing Things.* Ill. by Ivan Powell. Random House, 1978, o.p. SERIES: Step-Up. SUBJECTS: Adventure stories; Biographies. RL 2.7.

True stories about Blondin (a Niagara Falls tightrope walker), Houdini, Annie Oakley, a deep-sea fight with a 24-foot octopus, and Evel Knievel's skycycle jump over Snake River Canyon are extremely well told. Ink sketches are appropriate.

Kraus, Robert

751 *Trouble with Spider.* Ill. by author. Harper & Row, 1962. ISBN 0-06-023276-5. SUBJECTS: Animals—Flies—Fiction; Animals—Spiders—Fiction; Friendship—Fiction. RL 2.7.

Fly overcomes his suspicion of Spider when Spider needs help. Good dialogue and excellent ink and wash drawings have a marvelous sense of scale and provide selective detail.

Krensky, Stephen

752 *Lionel-at-Large.* Ill. by Susanna Natti. Dial, 1986. ISBN 0-8037-0241-8. SERIES:

Easy-to-Read. SUBJECTS: Family life—
Fiction; Growing-up—Fiction. RL 2.3.
Lionel finds his "vegetable shelf" (when deprived of dessert), and survives his first
sleepover and a shot at the doctor's office.
Familiar fears are overcome in the five humorous chapters on family life. Full color illustrations keep the tone light.

753 *Snow and Ice.* Ill. by John Hayes.
Scholastic, 1989. ISBN 0-590-41449-6.
SERIES: Science Is Fun. SUBJECTS:
Science; Science experiments;
Seasons—Winter. RL 3.1.
Besides basic information and simple experi-
ments about snow and ice, including icicles,
simple directions for making a snow fort are
included. Humorous line drawings have a
royal blue wash.

Krinsley, Jeanette

754 *The Cow Went over the Mountain.* Ill. by
Feodor Rojankovsky. Golden, 1963, o.p.
SUBJECTS: Animals—Fiction; Wordplay.
RL 2.0.
Five animals conclude after exploring the
next mountain that conditions are best right
at home. The language is playful and the full
color drawings show friendly animals.

Kroll, Steven

755 *The Goat Parade.* Ill. by Tim Kirk.
Parents Magazine Press, 1983. ISBN 0-
8193-1100-6. SUBJECTS: Humorous
stories; Parades—Fiction; Stories in
rhyme. RL 2.3.
Sam leads the goat parade into school—with
memorable results. Lively, rhythmic, zany
humor is illustrated with full color cartoon
drawings.

Kumin, Maxine W.

756 *Paul Bunyan.* Ill. by Dirk Gringhuis.
Putnam, 1966, o.p. SERIES: See and
Read Beginning to Read. SUBJECTS:
Folklore—United States; Tall tales.
RL 2.5.
Paul's antics account for the sun in the
morning, the tides in the Bay of Fundy, a
pancake griddle large enough to skate on, and

the formation of the Rocky Mountains. Tall-
tale humor shown in pencil with a blue wash.

Kumin, Maxine W., and Sexton, Anne

757 *Eggs of Things.* Ill. by Leonard Shortall.
Putnam, 1963, o.p. SERIES: See and
Read Beginning to Read. SUBJECTS:
Animals—Frogs and toads; Nature;
Seasons—Spring. RL 2.3.
Skippy and Buzz raise tadpoles secretly in a
third-floor bathtub. Cowboy, a dog, and
Skippy's sister, Pest, add to their difficulties in
parenting. This creative presentation about
spring eggs is well-illustrated by Shortall's ink
with two-tone wash drawings.

Kunhardt, Edith

758 *Danny's Birthday.* Ill. by author.
Greenwillow, 1986. ISBN 0-688-06177-X.
SUBJECTS: Animals—Alligators—Fiction;
Birthdays—Fiction. RL 2.2.
A slight story of the repeated viewing of a
fifth birthday party videotape has short
choppy sentences and dull language. Colorful animals attend the party—and save the
text.

Kuskin, Karla

759 *Something Sleeping in the Hall.* Ill. by
author. Harper & Row, 1985. ISBN 0-06-
023634-5. SERIES: I Can Read. SUBJECTS:
Animals—Fiction; Poetry. RL 2.4.
Gently humorous rhymed wordplay involves
familiar animals and events. Tiny, fuzzy colored pencil drawings are equally warm and
imaginative.

Kwitz, Mary D.

760 *Little Chick's Breakfast.* Ill. by Bruce
Degen. Harper & Row, 1983. ISBN 0-06-
023675-2. SERIES: Early I Can Read.
SUBJECTS: Animals—Chickens—Fiction;
Farm and country life—Fiction. RL 2.5.
Little Chick sees the whole barnyard awaken
and get breakfast before she gets hers. Colored pencil illustrations are rich in design
and detail.

Kwitz, Mary D. (cont.)

761 *Little Chick's Story.* Ill. by Cyndy Szekeres. Harper & Row, 1978. ISBN 0-06-023666-3. SERIES: Early I Can Read. SUBJECTS: Animals—Chickens—Fiction; Growing-up—Fiction. RL 2.7.
Broody Hen's bedtime story about Little Chick's future is comforting to both. Blue and cocoa highlight complementary pencil drawings.

L

LaFarge, Phyllis

762 *Joanna Runs Away.* Ill. by Trina Schart Hyman. Holt, Rinehart, 1973, o.p. SUBJECTS: Behavior—Running away—Fiction; City and town life—Fiction; Emotions—Loneliness—Fiction. RL 2.5.
A lonely girl who loves animals, especially an old vegetable cart horse, stows aboard the cart, and finds on her triumphant return that she does have friends. Hyman's pencil drawings are rich in detail and feeling.

Landshoff, Ursula

763 *Cats Are Good Company.* Ill. by author. Harper & Row, 1983. ISBN 0-06-023677-9. SERIES: I Can Read. SUBJECTS: Animals—Cats; Pet care; Pets—Cats. RL 2.3.
Care of cats, cat characteristics, and the benefits of owning a cat are given in a fascinating and humorous text. Childlike sketches match the tone perfectly.

764 *Okay, Good Dog.* Ill. by author. Harper & Row, 1978. ISBN 0-06-023673-6. SERIES: I Can Read. SUBJECTS: Animals—Dogs; Pet Care; Pets—Dogs. RL 2.2.
Loving training directions include housebreaking and teaching the dog to sit, come, heel, stay, and lie down. Whimsical pencil drawings keep the tone light.

Langner, Nola

765 *Dusty.* Ill. by author. Coward, McCann, 1976, o.p. SERIES: Break-of-Day.

SUBJECTS: Animals—Cats—Fiction. RL 2.5.
A girl's patience in gaining a stray cat's trust leads to a friendship that warms her even after Dusty no longer appears. This affecting story is illustrated with unsentimental soft pencil drawings.

Lapp, Eleanor J.

766 *The Mice Came in Early This Year.* Ill. by David Cunningham. Whitman, 1976, o.p. SUBJECTS: Grandparents—Fiction; Seasons—Fall—Fiction. RL 3.0.
A boy helps his grandfather prepare for winter by digging up potatoes, chopping wood, picking apples and hazelnuts, and watching a neighbor pull in his boat. Wonderful watercolors capture the atmosphere of homely seasonal preparations.

Larrick, Nancy, ed.

767 *More Poetry for Holidays.* Ill. by Harold Berson. Garrard, 1973. ISBN 0-8116-4116-3. SERIES: Poetry. SUBJECTS: Poetry. RL 2.9.
Poetry about holidays, including Jewish ones, is presented chronologically with brief notes appended. One holiday included is Children's Book Week. Fanciful ink sketches enliven the space and enrich the mental images.

768 *Poetry for Holidays.* Ill. by Kelly Oechsli. Garrard, 1966. ISBN 0-8116-4100-7. SERIES: Poetry. SUBJECTS: Poetry. RL 3.3.
John Ciardi, Aileen Fisher, and Henry Longfellow are among the noted poets celebrating ten holidays. This good selection has somewhat stilted tiny drawings.

Latham, Jean L.

769 *What Tabbit the Rabbit Found.* Ill. by Bill Dugan. Garrard, 1974. ISBN 0-8116-6052-4. SERIES: Easy Venture. SUBJECTS: Animals—Rabbits—Fiction. RL 1.6.
Using primer vocabulary, a small rabbit finds everything except the blue ball he was looking for. Childlike drawings are appropriate.

Lauber, Patricia

770 *Clarence and the Burglar.* Adapted by F. N. Monjo. Ill. by Paul Galdone. Coward, McCann, 1973, o.p. SERIES: Break-of-Day. SUBJECTS: Animals— Dogs—Fiction; Humorous stories; Pets—Fiction. RL 2.5.

Adapted from a chapter in *Clarence the TV Dog* (Coward, McCann, 1955). Clarence, the friendliest of dogs, overwhelms a burglar by untying the burglar's shoes when he refuses to play. Fun to read, with lively ink and wash pictures.

771 *Clarence and the Cat.* Ill. by Paul Galdone. Coward, McCann, 1977, o.p. SERIES: Break-of-Day. SUBJECTS: Animals—Cats—Fiction; Animals— Dogs—Fiction; Humorous stories. RL 2.2.

Clarence the dog is an incredibly generous host to a visiting cat, even sharing his food and toys, his favorite chair—and his canine friends. Cat is not so bossy after their visit! Galdone captures Clarence's irrepressible friendliness and Cat's hauteur perfectly.

772 *Snakes Are Hunters.* Ill. by Holly Keller. Crowell, 1988. ISBN 0-690-04630-8. SERIES: Let's-Read-and-Find-Out Science. SUBJECTS: Animals—Snakes; Nature. RL 3.6.

This clear, factual presentation about snakes of all sizes and kinds offers information on the life cycles and physical characteristics of snakes, and methods of hunting and feeding them. The spare cartoons present a nonmenacing animal that is sure to engage the interest of children.

Lawrence, James

773 *Binky Brothers and the Fearless Four.* Ill. by Leonard Kessler. Harper & Row, 1970; pap., 1983. ISBN 0-06-023761-9. SERIES: I Can Read. SUBJECTS: Clubs— Fiction; Mystery and detective stories. RL 2.0.

For a price, younger brother Dinky helps find out who wrecked the Fearless Four's snow fort. Dialogue is good in text illustrated simply with flat orange, turquoise, and black.

774 *Binky Brothers, Detectives.* Ill. by Leonard Kessler. Harper & Row, 1968; pap., 1978. ISBN 0-06-023759-7. SERIES: I Can Read. SUBJECTS: Clubs—Fiction; Mystery and detective stories; Siblings—Fiction. RL 2.4.

Dinky thinks he has the solution to the mystery—but has to be rescued by his younger brother, Binky, who demands full partnership in the detective business. Very simple ink drawings have orange and cocoa washes.

Lawrence, Judith

775 *Goat for Carlo.* Ill. by Liz Dauber. Garrard, hb and pap., 1971. ISBN 0-8116-6709-X. SERIES: Venture. SUBJECTS: Animals—Goats—Fiction; Mexico—Fiction. RL 2.0.

Carlo's new goat produces a surprise bonus. Red serapes, sashes, and skirts highlight the setting of this simple tale.

Lazarus, Keo F.

776 *Billy Goat in the Chili Patch.* Ill. by Carol Rogers. University of Chicago Press, 1975, o.p. SUBJECTS: Folklore—Mexico; Mexico—Fiction. RL 3.3.

A burro, a dog, a cock, and an ant try to help Pepito get a billy goat out of his chili patch. They discover that sometimes little and wise is better than big and strong. Simple earth-tone paintings enchance the Mexican flavor.

Leech, Jay, and Spencer, Zane

777 *Bright Fawn and Me.* Ill. by Glo Coalson. Crowell, 1979. ISBN 0-690-03937-9. SUBJECTS: Native Americans—Cheyennes—Fiction; Sibling rivalry—Fiction. RL 2.6.

A young girl caring for her toddler sister explores a trading fair. As the toddler draws a lot of attention, the older sister experiences a wide range of emotions. Earth-tone drawings give a feeling of the Native American culture and of relationships.

Lerner, Sharon

778 *Big Bird Says: A Game to Read and Play Featuring Jim Henson's Sesame Street*

Lerner, Sharon (cont.)

Muppets. Ill. by Joe Mathieu. Random House, hb and pap., 1985. ISBN 0-394-97499-9. SERIES: Step into Reading. SUBJECTS: Games—Fiction; Puppets—Fiction; Stories in rhyme. RL 2.5.
Rhymed exercise directions for stretching high and low include some wonderful nonsense. Cartoon drawings show familiar "Sesame Street" characters.

779 *Follow the Monsters.* Ill. by Tom Cooke. Random House, hb and pap., 1985. ISBN 0-394-97126-4. SERIES: Step into Reading. SUBJECTS: Concepts—Space—Fiction; Puppets—Fiction; Stories in rhyme. RL 2.4.
The monsters' destination is of course Sesame Street; they demonstrate a dozen spatial terms en route there. Drawings of Henson muppets in this rhyming story are in pastel colors.

LeSieg, Theo

780 *Come Over to My House.* Ill. by Richard Erdoes. Beginner, 1966. ISBN 0-394-90044-8. SERIES: I Can Read It All By Myself. SUBJECTS: Cultural diversity; Houses; Stories in rhyme. RL 2.3.
After skimming the world celebrating its diversity of housing, the tour concludes that despite the differences, houses are alike when friends are invited in. Indifferent comic illustrations keep the tone light in this rhyming story.

781 *Eye Book.* Ill. by Roy McKie. Random House, 1968. ISBN 0-394-91094-X. SERIES: Bright and Early. SUBJECTS: Human body—Eyes—Fiction; Stories in rhyme. RL 1.8.
Eyes that see blue, red, a bird and a bed, trees and clocks, bees and socks, are celebrated. Lively, simply outlined cartoons are in primary color watercolors.

782 *In a People House.* Ill. by Roy McKie. Random House, 1972. ISBN 0-394-92395-2. SERIES: Bright and Early. SUBJECTS: Houses; Stories in rhyme. RL 3.4.
A lively, rhyming catalog of household objects is illustrated with full color line drawings.

783 *Maybe You Should Fly a Jet! Maybe You Should Be a Vet!* Ill. by Michael J. Smollin. Beginner, hb and pap., 1980. ISBN 0-394-9444-8. SERIES: I Can Read It All By Myself. SUBJECTS: Careers; Stories in rhyme. RL 3.8.
Lively suggestions of career options range from teaching and preaching to being a turkey farmer. Cartoon sketches show mostly males.

784 *Please Try to Remember the First of Octember.* Ill. by Art Cumings. Beginner, 1977, o.p. SERIES: I Can Read It All By Myself. SUBJECTS: Nonsense; Stories in rhyme. RL 2.3.
In this rhyming story, wonderful, magical things come true by wishing on the first of October. Pastel drawings are more static than those in LeSieg's other books.

785 *Ten Apples Up on Top.* Ill. by Roy McKie. Beginner, 1961, o.p. SERIES: I Can Read It All by Myself. SUBJECTS: Humorous stories; Stories in rhyme. RL 1.3.
Toe-tapping rhythm, outrageous bragging, and a marvelous chase draw the reader into this story. Simple, expressive line drawings are accented with red and yellow.

786 *The Tooth Book.* Ill. by Roy McKie. Random House, 1981. ISBN 0-394-94825-4. SERIES: Bright and Early. SUBJECTS: Human body—Teeth—Fiction; Humorous stories; Stories in rhyme. RL 3.2.
Creative, humorous uses of teeth are detailed using rhyming text; the closing admonishes the readers to remember, no matter what, that the dentist is their teeth's best friend. Comic illustrations are lively and appropriate.

787 *Wacky Wednesday.* Ill. by George Booth. Beginner, 1974. ISBN 0-394-92912-8. SERIES: I Can Read It All By Myself. SUBJECTS: Concepts—Numbers; Puzzles; Stories in rhyme. RL 2.1.
Comic visual and rhyming puzzles intrigue the reader as well as delight the eye, as the reader is invited to identify all the errors in the pictures.

788 *Would You Rather Be a Bullfrog?* Ill. by Roy McKie. Random House, 1975. ISBN

0-394-93128-9. SERIES: Bright and Early. SUBJECTS: Humorous stories; Nonsense; Stories in rhyme. RL 3.0.
Rhymed couplets ask readers what outrageous animals or things they would like to be, from hammers or nails to minnows or whales. Humor is accentuated with McKie's usual comic drawings, with strong simple lines and bold colors.

Levinson, Nancy S.

789 *Clara and the Bookwagon.* Ill. by Carolyn Croll. Harper & Row, 1988. ISBN 0-06-023838-0. SERIES: I Can Read. SUBJECTS: Books and reading—Fiction; Farm and country life—Fiction; Libraries—Fiction. RL 2.2.
Though Clara works hard in the family farm, her father will not help her learn to read—until the bookwagon librarian changes his attitude. Simple colored pencil drawings add to this moving story of a child's determination to read.

Lewis, Thomas P.

790 *The Blue Rocket Fun Show: Or Friends Forever.* Ill. by Ib Ohlsson. Macmillan, 1986. ISBN 0-02-758810-6. SERIES: Ready-to-Read. SUBJECTS: Amusement parks—Fiction; Friendship—Fiction; Science fiction. RL 2.2.
Leslie and Niki's summer friendship is not interrupted by surprise revelations about Niki's origin at summer's end. Well-constructed story has imaginative details and two-tone pencil highlights.

791 *Clipper Ship.* Ill. by Joan Sandin. Harper & Row, 1978. ISBN 0-06-023809-7. SERIES: I Can Read History. SUBJECTS: Historical fiction; Sex roles—Fiction; Ships—Fiction. RL 2.8.
Based on true-life stories of captains' wives who took over responsibility for ships, this book details one such passage to the California gold fields via the treacherous Cape Horn. Absorbing adventure shown in gray and beige with a touch of turquoise.

792 *Hill of Fire.* Ill. by Joan Sandin. Harper & Row, 1971; pap., 1983. ISBN 0-06-023804-6. SERIES: I Can Read History. SUBJECTS: Geology; Historical fiction; Mexico. RL 2.1.
The true story of the 1943 eruption of Parícutin in a Mexican farmer's field is told from the point of view of his son, Pablo. Authentic ink drawings feature earth tones.

793 *Mr. Sniff and the Motel Mystery.* Ill. by Beth L. Weiner. Harper & Row, 1984. ISBN 0-06-023825-9. SERIES: I Can Read. SUBJECTS: Animals—Dogs—Fiction; Mystery and detective stories. RL 2.4.
Mr. Sniff identifies the perpetuator of motel mischief as someone without hay fever, who knows where to find lipstick, chews bubble gum, and is not afraid of crabs or jellyfish. Challenging puzzle has a compassionate conclusion and illustrations in turquoise, pumpkin, and avocado.

Lexau, Joan M.

794 *The Dog Food Caper.* Ill. by Marylin Hafner. Dial, 1985; pap., 1987. ISBN 0-8037-0108-X. SERIES: Easy-to-Read. SUBJECTS: Mystery and detective stories; Witches—Fiction. RL 2.2.
Willy gets help from a neighborhood witch, Miss Happ, when dog food is found all over Mr. Spring's house, for whom Willy is dog-sitting. Colored pencil drawings enhance the characterization.

795 *Don't Be My Valentine.* Ill. by Syd Hoff. Harper & Row, 1985; pap., 1988. ISBN 0-06-023873-9. SERIES: I Can Read. SUBJECTS: Friendship—Fiction; Holidays—Valentine's Day—Fiction; School stories. RL 2.8.
Even after Albert helps them make up, Sam and Amy Lou are bugging each other on Valentine's Day at school. Realistic relationships with typical Hoff comic drawings in strong colors.

796 *Finders Keepers, Losers Weepers.* Ill. by Tomie dePaola. Lippincott, 1976, o.p. SUBJECTS: Siblings—Fiction. RL 2.3.
Max tries to cover for his sister Amanda, but he has some hardships along the way. Stylized drawings have gold, blue, and avocado coloring.

Lexau, Joan M. (cont.)

797 *I Hate Red Rover.* Ill. by Gail Owens.
Dutton, 1979. ISBN 0-525-32527-1.
SERIES: Fat Cat. SUBJECTS: Emotions—
Fear—Fiction; Grandparents—Fiction;
Self-esteem—Fiction. RL 1.8.
Jill's weakness at playing Red Rover at school
is strengthened by her desire to help Grandpa
adjust to his new dentures—neither like being
laughed at. Expressive pencil drawings have
a pale red wash.

798 *Miss Happ in the Poison Ivy Case.* Ill. by
Marylin Hafner. Dial, 1983, o.p. SERIES:
Easy-to-Read. SUBJECTS: Mystery and
detective stories; Witches—Fiction.
RL 2.0.
When the magical peanut butter and grape
seed concoction of Miss Happ, a neighbor,
does not cure his sister's poison ivy, Willy
Nilly discovers the cure himself. Expressive,
action-filled drawings are brightened with
shades of orange and turquoise.

799 *The Rooftop Mystery.* Ill. by Syd Hoff.
Harper & Row, 1968. ISBN 0-06-023865-
8. SERIES: I Can Read. SUBJECTS: Moving,
household—Fiction; Siblings—Fiction;
Toys—Dolls and dollhouses—Fiction.
RL 2.3.
When Sam loses his sister's doll, for which he
was responsible during a move, his detective
work saves his skin. Flat comic drawings are
a bit dull.

800 *T for Tommy.* Ill. by Janet Compere.
Garrard, hb and pap., 1971. ISBN 0-
8116-6719-7. SERIES: Venture. SUBJECTS:
Storytelling. RL 1.9.
Another version of a familiar tell-and-draw
story with primary school-level vocabulary.
Very basic ink illustrations.

801 *That's Just Fine and Who-O-O Did It?*
Ill. by Dora Leder. Garrard, hb and
pap., 1971. ISBN 0-685-00127-X. SERIES:
Venture. SUBJECTS: Fairies—Fiction;
Magic—Fiction. RL 2.0.
A story of a magic pot and a boy's adventures
with a fairy girl are retold by Lexau. No
background for the tales is given. Ink drawings
show intriguing ash colored folk creations.

Lillegard, Dee

802 *I Can Be a Baker.* Photos and drawings.
Childrens, hb and pap., 1986. ISBN 0-
516-01892-2. SERIES: I Can Be. SUBJECTS:
Careers; Food. RL 3.0.
A picture glossary and an index accompany
information about machine- and hand-
baking, emphasizing the necessary speed and
teamwork. Excellent color photos and a few
drawings amplify the text.

803 *Where Is It?* Ill. by Gene Sharp.
Childrens, hb and pap., 1984. ISBN 0-
516-42065-8. SERIES: Rookie Readers.
SUBJECTS: Lost and found possessions—
Fiction. RL 1.1.
A small boy messes up his room looking for
his red cap. He finds it in an unexpected way.
Cheery full color illustrations.

Little, Emily

804 *David and the Giant.* Ill. by Hans
Wilhelm. Random House, hb and pap.,
1987. ISBN 0-394-98867-1. SERIES: Step
into Reading. SUBJECTS: Bible stories.
RL 1.8.
This very simplified version of the story of
David and Goliath stays close to the Old
Testament but omits any encounter with
King Saul. The pencil and watercolor pic-
tures are cartoon style and upbeat.

Littledale, Freya

805 *The Snow Child.* Ill. by Barbara
Lavallee. Scholastic, 1989. ISBN 0-590-
05398-1. SUBJECTS: Folklore—Russia;
Russia—Fiction. RL 2.7.
A childless couple make a snow child who
teaches the villagers how to make snow sculp-
tures, but the snow child disappears with the
spring thaw. This tale of renewal has the
lavenders, blues, and whites of fantasy.

Lobel, Anita

806 *The Straw Maid.* Ill. by author.
Greenwillow, 1983. ISBN 0-688-00330-3.
SUBJECTS: Folklore. RL 2.4.
A girl escapes from three robbers by dressing
a straw figure in her clothes, and dressing

herself in feathers stuck on with honey. This original folktale has a satisfying ending. Delicate ink drawings and patterns emphasize the folk flavor.

Lobel, Arnold

807 *Days with Frog and Toad*. Ill. by author. Harper & Row, 1978; pap., 1984. ISBN 0-06-023964-6. SERIES: I Can Read. SUBJECTS: Animals—Frogs and toads; Friendship—Fiction. RL 2.3.
Procrastination, kite-flying frustration, scary-story shivers, a too-big birthday hat, and two close friends, Frog and Toad, sitting alone together are the themes of the five chapters. Green and brown soft pencil drawings are reassuring and warm, like the friendship.

808 *Frog and Toad All Year*. Ill. by author. Harper & Row, 1976; pap., 1984. ISBN 0-06-023951-4. SERIES: I Can Read. SUBJECTS: Animals—Frogs and toads— Fiction; Friendship—Fiction. RL 2.4.
Toad needs Frog's encouragement to go sledding; they search together for spring and share chocolate ice cream cones and a late Christmas. Story and earth-tone drawings have humor and compassion.

809 *Frog and Toad Are Friends*. Ill. by author. Harper & Row, 1970; pap., 1979. ISBN 0-06-023958-1. SERIES: I Can Read. SUBJECTS: Animals—Frogs and toads—Fiction; Friendship—Fiction. RL 2.4.
Frog and Toad, as usual, support and encourage each other, in searching for spring and a lost button, and in waiting for a letter. Drawings focus closely on the two friends.

810 *Frog and Toad Together*. Ill. by author. Harper & Row, 1972; pap., 1979. ISBN 0-06-023960-3. SERIES: I Can Read. SUBJECTS: Animals—Frogs and toads— Fiction; Friendship—Fiction. RL 2.7.
Toad can do nothing without his list and he finds that helping frightened seeds is *very* hard work. With Frog's assistance everything becomes easier. The author's splendid illustrations help show the ways in which friends overcome irritations and frustrations.

811 *Grasshopper on the Road*. Ill. by author. Harper & Row, 1978; pap., 1986. ISBN 0-06-023962-X. SERIES: I Can Read. SUBJECTS: Animals—Grasshoppers— Fiction. RL 2.4.
Lobel writes powerfully about the joys of embracing new experiences in six small tales about Grasshopper. Grasshopper meets some small critters so involved in one narrow activity that they will not risk traveling with him. Rhythmic, imaginative language is accompanied by sympathetic drawings typical of Lobel.

812 *Lucille*. Ill. by author. Harper & Row, 1964; pap., 1986. ISBN 0-06-023966-2. SERIES: I Can Read. SUBJECTS: Animals— Horses—Fiction; Self-esteem—Fiction. RL 2.2.
Lucille considers herself dull and dirty as a workhorse, but chooses that role after she dresses up and tries to act like a lady. The lively drawings add humor and keep the tone light.

813 *Mouse Soup*. Ill. by author. Harper & Row, 1977; pap., 1983. ISBN 0-06-023968-9. SERIES: I Can Read. SUBJECTS: Animals—Mice—Fiction; Humorous stories. RL 2.4.
A mouse's tales of bees, thorns, stones, and mud help him escape from being the weasel's soup. Imaginative and varied ideas have excellent illustrations, highlighted by the picture of bee stings on the weasel's head.

814 *Mouse Tales*. Ill. by author. Harper & Row, 1972; pap., 1978. ISBN 0-06-023942-5. SERIES: I Can Read. SUBJECTS: Animals—Mice—Fiction; Friendship— Fiction. RL 2.4.
Seven simple tales of friendship and kindness deal with a child mouse afraid of a cloud that looks like a cat, and a wishing well that grants every wish after being given a pillow to cushion the impact of pennies being dropped in. Some drawings are small, some open and flowing.

815 *Owl at Home*. Ill. by author. Harper & Row, 1975; pap., 1982. ISBN 0-06-023949-2. SERIES: I Can Read. SUBJECTS: Animals—Owls—Fiction; Emotions— Fear—Fiction. RL 2.2.

Lobel, Arnold (cont.)

Owl has Winter for an unwelcome guest, strange bumps under his blanket, and some comforting tear-water tea. Humor warms Owl's apprehensions, as do the soft pencil drawings.

816 *Small Pig.* Ill. by author. Harper & Row, 1969; pap., 1988. ISBN 0-06-023932-8. SERIES: I Can Read. SUBJECTS: Animals—Pigs—Fiction; Farm and country life—Fiction; Humorous stories. RL 2.7.

When the farmer's wife cleans up Small Pig's beloved mud puddle, he goes in search of a new place to wallow—and chooses unwisely. Very effective story has expressive four-color drawings.

817 *Uncle Elephant.* Ill. by author. Harper & Row, 1981; pap., 1986. ISBN 0-06-023980-8. SERIES: I Can Read. SUBJECTS: Animals—Elephants—Fiction; Emotions—Loneliness—Fiction; Illness—Fiction. RL 2.3.

An old elephant helps a small, sick, lonely elephant while away the time. They share peanuts, have supper by moonlight, and trumpet in the dawn. Rose and pale green washes embellish the wrinkly pair's adventures.

Long, Ruthanna

818 *Tiny Bear Goes to the Fair.* Ill. by Joan Allen. Golden, 1969. ISBN 0-307-61156-6. SERIES: Beginning Readers. SUBJECTS: Animals—Bears—Fiction; Kites and kite flying—Fiction; Stories in rhyme. RL 2.2.

Precise, neat watercolors complement this rhyming story of Tiny Bear's adventure with a kite at the fair.

Lopshire, Robert

819 *How to Make Snop Snappers and Other Fine Things.* Ill. by author. Greenwillow, 1977, o.p. SERIES: Read-alone. SUBJECTS: Imagination; Toys. RL 2.7.

A tantalizing table of contents shows toys to be created, from an airboat and a sock puppet to a Ballimp (balloon-turned-blimp). Excep-

tionally imaginative ideas, directions, and wordplay. The comic illustrations are humorous, yet precise.

820 *I Am Better Than You!* Ill. by author. Harper & Row, 1968. ISBN 0-06-023997-2. SERIES: I Can Read. SUBJECTS: Animals—Lizards—Fiction; Behavior—Bragging—Fiction. RL 1.7.

In this story about two lizards, Sam tries to outdo Pete in *everything*, but oversells his abilities; perhaps he will make a new friend. Lovely lizard activities like zapping flies and changing colors are illustrated in avocado green.

821 *I Want to Be Somebody New!* Ill. by author. Beginner, 1986. ISBN 0-394-97616-9. SERIES: I Can Read It All By Myself. SUBJECTS: Animals—Fiction; Self-esteem—Fiction; Stories in rhyme. RL 2.0.

The disadvantages of being an elephant, a giraffe, or a mouse become apparent when a zoo animal uses its magic to try different shapes. Light tone is conveyed by rhyme and comic drawings.

Lorian, Nicole

822 *A Birthday Present for Mama: A Step Two Book.* Ill. by J. P. Miller. Random House, hb and pap., 1984. ISBN 0-394-96755-0. SERIES: Step into Reading. SUBJECTS: Animals—Rabbits—Fiction; Birthdays—Fiction; Mothers—Fiction. RL 2.7.

Little Rabbit seeks help in finding a birthday present for his mother from a sheep, a frog, a cat, a fox, and a squirrel—but a hug is enough! Spring colors brighten friendly cartoon drawings.

Low, Joseph

823 *Benny Rabbit and the Owl.* Ill. by author. Greenwillow, 1978, o.p. SERIES: Read-alone. SUBJECTS: Animals—Rabbits—Fiction; Emotions—Fear—Fiction. RL 2.4.

Father Rabbit has an ingenious way to allay Benny's fear of an owl in his closet. Imaginative, reassuring story has expressive ink and wash drawings.

824 *Mad Wet Hen and Other Riddles.* Ill. by author. Greenwillow, 1977, o.p. SERIES: Read-alone. SUBJECTS: Jokes and riddles; Wordplay. RL 2.7.

People, pigs, elephants, peacocks, and umbrellas are the focus of these refreshingly original riddles. Pen and wash drawings spark the imagination.

Lowery, Barbara

825 *Mammals.* Ill. by Michael Charlton. Watts, 1976, o.p. SERIES: Easy-read fact. SUBJECTS: Animals; Nature; Science. RL 2.9.

Good descriptions of mammal characteristics and behavior are accompanied by two-tone pencil illustrations and an index.

Lowery, Janette S.

826 *Six Silver Spoons.* Ill. by Robert Quackenbush. Harper & Row, 1971. ISBN 0-06-024037-7. SERIES: I Can Read History. SUBJECTS: Historical Fiction; United States—Revolution—Fiction. RL 2.0.

Some of the fear of the Redcoats' presence in Boston and the battle at Lexington are conveyed from a young girl's perspective. Pencil drawings with two-tone washes portray the spirit of the times.

Lowery, Linda

827 *Martin Luther King Day.* Ill. by Hetty Mitchell. Carolrhoda, 1987. ISBN 0-87614-299-4. SERIES: On My Own. SUBJECTS: Biographies; Black Americans; Holidays—Martin Luther King, Jr., Day. RL 2.6.

Lowery focuses on the injustices children can understand in talking about Martin Luther King, Jr.,'s concerns. Black pencil drawings alternate with colored ones to show scenes and people important to the civil rights movement.

Luttrell, Ida

828 *Lonesome Lester.* Ill. by Megan Lloyd. Harper & Row, 1984. ISBN 0-06-024030-

X. SUBJECTS: Animals—Prairie dogs—Fiction; Solitude—Fiction. RL 2.9.

Prairie dog Lester finds that ants, his superclean Aunt Martha, and a crying lost baby rabbit do not make good company— you cannot be just plain peaceful with company around. Soft colored drawings, particularly of frowning Aunt Martha, are especially effective.

829 *One Day at School.* Ill. by Jared D. Lee. Harcourt Brace, 1984, o.p. SERIES: Let Me Read. SUBJECTS: Humorous stories; School stories. RL 2.9.

Arnold B. Lipton finds he is in charge of the third grade—composed of his teachers—one topsy-turvy day. Some ideas intriguing to children are broached, but the theme falls apart in places. Wavy comic cartoons with red accents add to the humor.

830 *Tillie and Mert.* Ill. by Doug Cushman. Harper & Row, 1985. ISBN 0-06-024028-8. SERIES: I Can Read. SUBJECTS: Animals—Skunks—Fiction; Friendship—Fiction. RL 2.6.

The strong friendship of two skunks, Tillie and Mert, survives bad judgment in their small business and Tillie's success in fortune telling. Good characterization and cozy watercolors complement the theme well.

M

Maass, Robert

831 *Fire Fighters.* Photos by author. Scholastic, 1989. ISBN 0-590-41459-3. SUBJECTS: Fire fighting. RL 2.7.

This photoessay looks at a fire station on a quiet day and follows fire fighters doing maintenance work and relaxing while on call. When an alarm sounds, readers follow the fire fighters to the scene of a fire. Clear color photos and text explain what fire fighting is all about.

McArthur, Nancy

832 *Megan Gets a Dollhouse.* Ill. by Megan Lloyd. Scholastic, pap., 1988. ISBN 0-

McArthur, Nancy (cont.)

590-40831-3. SERIES: Hello Reader. SUBJECTS: Self-esteem—Fiction; Toys— Dolls and dollhouses—Fiction. RL 2.7. Megan's cousin Sharon has a beautiful but fragile dollhouse and Megan would like one of her own. When Mom and Dad say such a dollhouse is too expensive, Megan uses a lot of ingenuity to create her own from a cardboard box and odds and ends. Lively, humorous illustrations are in vibrant colors.

833 *Pickled Peppers*. Ill. by Denise Brunkus. Scholastic, pap., 1988. ISBN 0-590- 40997-2. SERIES: Hello Reader. SUBJECTS: Behavior—Responsible—Fiction; Pet care—Fiction; Pets—Birds—Fiction. RL 2.4.
Suzie wants to keep her aunt's dog, Pud, but she did not take good care of the dog when he visited and now her Mom and Dad say no. To prove that she is responsible, Suzie pet-sits for her neighbors' tongue-twister-reciting parakeet. The humorous story is illustrated with comic drawings with green accents.

McCauley, Jane

834 *Animals in Summer*. Photos. National Geographic, 1988. ISBN 0-87044-738-6. SERIES: Books for Young Readers. SUBJECTS: Animals; Seasons—Summer. RL 2.7.
A potpourri of impressive color photos has "animals" and "summer" as loose themes with the text serving mostly as captions. The book excites readers and interests them in nature rather than providing information or answering questions on nature. A brief bibliography is included.

835 *Let's Explore a River*. Ill. by Joseph H. Bailey. National Geographic, 1988. ISBN 0-87044-741-6. SERIES: Books for Young Explorers. SUBJECTS: Nature. RL 2.8.
A Florida park manager and his three children take a canoe trip on a river. Readers see the great diversity of nature through large color photos and a clear simple text. A two-page addendum suggests ways for parents to make such a trip with their children. A bibliography is included.

McClintock, Mike

836 *A Fly Went By*. Ill. by Fritz Siebel. Beginner, 1958. ISBN 0-394-90003-8. SERIES: I Can Read It All By Myself. SUBJECTS: Cumulative tales; Stories in rhyme. RL 1.5.
As he relaxes next to a lake, a little boy watches one animal after another race by. Each animal thinks it is being chased by the animal behind it. The charcoal and wash illustrations reflect the fast pace and the humor of the rhyming text.

837 *What Have I Got?* Ill. by Leonard Kessler. Harper & Row, 1961. ISBN 0-06- 024141-1. SERIES: Early I Can Read. SUBJECTS: Imagination—Fiction; Stories in rhyme. RL 1.7.
A little boy tells in rhyme about all the things he could do with what he has in his pockets. At times forced or awkward, the text is brief, easy to read, and helped by the simple line drawings with color accents.

McClung, Robert M.

838 *Horseshoe Crab*. Ill. by author. Morrow, 1967, o.p. SUBJECTS: Animals— Horseshoe crabs. RL 3.3.
Not really a crab but an ancient form of sea life, the horseshoe crab goes through many years of molting its shells before it becomes an adult. Watercolor pictures aid a carefully prepared text in describing this curious animal and its life cycle.

839 *Ladybug*. Ill. by author. Morrow, 1966, o.p. SUBJECTS: Animals—Ladybugs. RL 3.4.
The ladybug is one of the farmer's most valued insects. This book about its life cycle and habits makes fascinating reading. The illustrations are done in watercolors, and although the portraits of insects are good, larvae and eggs do not always seem to be drawn to the same scale.

McCrady, Lady

840 *The Perfect Ride*. Ill. by Dennis Kendrick. Parents Magazine Press, 1981. ISBN 0-8193-1052-2. SUBJECTS:

Amusement parks—Fiction; Animals—Dogs—Fiction. RL 2.4.
The Dog family spends Saturday at Play Land amusement park. With only four tickets left, they decide to take a boat ride to the "Bermuda Triangle." Scary and full of surprises, the ride is the perfect end to their day. The marker drawings show stodgy dogs finally enjoying themselves.

McCully, Emily A.

841 *The Grandma Mix-Up.* Ill. by author. Harper & Row, 1988. ISBN 0-06-024201-9. SERIES: I Can Read. SUBJECTS: Baby-sitting—Fiction; Grandparents—Fiction. RL 2.3.
Pip's parents have asked their respective mothers to baby-sit Pip and so the child is stuck with both. Grandma Nan is too strict and Grandma Sal is too easygoing until Pip asks them to do things Pip's way. A delightful portrait of a child of indeterminate sex is illustrated in ink and wash.

McDaniel, Becky B.

842 *Katie Can.* Ill. by Lois Axeman. Childrens, hb and pap., 1987. ISBN 0-516-02082-X. SERIES: Rookie Readers. SUBJECTS: Asian Americans—Fiction; Sibling rivalry—Fiction. RL 2.3.
Katie's older brother and sister seem to watch her only when she *cannot* do something. Finally they do see her do just what she said she could—teach the dog to catch the ball. Brightly colored ink and paint pictures capture the frustrations of a young child in this very short book.

843 *Katie Couldn't.* Ill. by Lois Axeman. Childrens, hb and pap., 1985. ISBN 0-516-02069-2. SERIES: Rookie Readers. SUBJECTS: Asian Americans—Fiction; Growing-up—Fiction; Siblings—Fiction. RL 2.2.
Katie watches her older brother and sister do many things she is not big enough to do. Then Daddy comes home and picks up Katie but not the others because they are too big. The very brief text and colorful paintings capture the frustration of being youngest in a warm Asian-American family.

844 *Katie Did It.* Ill. by Lois Axeman. Childrens, hb and pap., 1983. ISBN 0-516-02043-9. SERIES: Rookie Readers. SUBJECTS: Asian Americans—Fiction; Behavior—Fiction; Siblings—Fiction. RL 1.6.
The youngest child in a close-knit Asian-American family, Katie is always being blamed for things. Tired of hearing her sister and brother say Katie did it, she responds that she did it when mother asks who gave her flowers. Attractive, colorful pictures accompany a brief text.

McGovern, Ann

845 *Little Wolf.* Ill. by Nola Langner. Abelard-Schuman, 1965, o.p. SUBJECTS: Native Americans—Fiction; Self-esteem—Fiction. RL 1.9.
Little Wolf is often ridiculed by his tribe because he cannot kill an animal. He is wise in the lore of the forest, a knowledge that he uses to save the chief's son from poisoning and gain the tribe's respect. Sepia-colored drawings are lovely and restrained, complementing the fine story.

McInnes, John

846 *The Chocolate Chip Mystery.* Ill. by Paul Frame. Garrard, 1972. ISBN 0-8116-6964-5. SERIES: Venture. SUBJECTS: Business enterprises—Fiction; City and town life—Fiction; Mystery and detective stories. RL 1.8.
Forced to move, Max opens his ice cream store in a building that everyone thinks is haunted. His customers do not come and his chocolate chip ice cream starts disappearing. Max's young helper Peppino solves the mystery of the missing ice cream and finds a way to bring customers in. Realistic sketches.

847 *Goodnight Painted Pony.* Ill. by David Stone. Garrard, hb and pap., 1971. ISBN 0-8116-6707-3. SERIES: Venture. SUBJECTS: Animals—Fiction; Arts and crafts—Fiction; Fantasy. RL 1.4.
A class of schoolchildren paints pictures of pets and hangs the pictures on the walls. That night the animals leave their pictures and play school themselves. Illustrated with sim-

McInnes, John (cont.)

ple yet fanciful color drawings of animals and children, this is a rather slight fantasy.

848 *Have You Ever Seen a Monster?* Ill. by Tom Eaton. Garrard, 1974. ISBN 0-8116-6054-0. SERIES: Easy Venture. SUBJECTS: Monsters—Fiction. RL 2.1.

On every other page there are questions about things that a monster might do that are then answered with fantastic things that the narrator claims to have seen them do. Predictable refrains build the confidence of children struggling with reading. Illustrated with energetic cartoonlike artwork.

849 *How Pedro Got His Name.* Ill. by Edward Malsberg. Garrard, 1974. ISBN 0-8116-6064-8. SERIES: Venture. SUBJECTS: City and town life—Fiction; Pets—Dogs—Fiction. RL 1.5.

To earn enough money to buy a puppy, Tony works for a shoemaker. Once he has the money saved he gets sick and his physician, Dr. Pedro, promises he will buy the dog for Tony. The story has a Hispanic setting and is illustrated with full color realistic paintings.

850 *Leo Lion Paints It Red.* Ill. by Tom Eaton. Garrard, 1974. ISBN 0-8116-6060-5. SERIES: Easy Venture. SUBJECTS: Animals, zoo—Fiction; Humorous stories; Zoos—Fiction. RL 1.7.

When a little girl gives him red paint, clever Leo the Lion starts making signs for himself and the other zoo animals. Children respond to the signs by giving the animals what they want. Simple, colorful pictures illustrate this silly but engaging story.

851 *On with the Circus!* Ill. by William Hutchinson. Garrard, hb and pap., 1973. ISBN 0-8116-6722-7. SERIES: Venture. SUBJECTS: Circuses—Fiction. RL 2.1.

Judy gets a chance to be a part of the circus when the littlest clown gets sick. No one knows who she is when she is dressed in Bingo's clothes and she has a wonderful time. The realistic color illustrations recreate the old Big Top ambience.

McIntyre, Ida M.

852 *Unicorn Magic.* Ill. by Don Hedin. Garrard, 1972. ISBN 0-8116-6965-3. SERIES: Venture. SUBJECTS: Magic—Fiction; Mythical creatures—Fiction. RL 2.1.

A unicorn tells a tale of sorcery, a beautiful princess made from straw, and a prince seeking a bride. It is the unicorn's magic that saves the princess from being returned to straw by the sorcerer. The lack of unicorn stories has made this book popular despite the undistinguished illustrations.

McKie, Roy, and Eastman, Philip D.

853 *Snow.* Ill. by Roy McKie. Beginner, 1962. ISBN 0-394-90027-8. SERIES: I Can Read It All By Myself. SUBJECTS: Stories in rhyme; Weather—Snow—Fiction. RL 1.5.

Two children and their dog explore all the things that are fun to do with snow. Bold, lively pictures in blue, red, and yellow with heavy outlining and a rhyming text have the children sledding, making snow angels, and doing snow-related activities.

McKissack, Patricia

854 *The Apache.* Photos. Childrens, hb and pap., 1984. ISBN 0-516-01925-2. SERIES: New True. SUBJECTS: Native Americans—Apaches. RL 3.0.

The text begins with the Apaches' Canadian origins, and then discusses their descendants (for example, Navajo, Chiricahua, and Jicarilla), ways of life, religious beliefs, great leaders, and wars. Well written, the text is illustrated with color photographs.

855 *The Maya.* Photos. Childrens, hb and pap., 1985. ISBN 0-516-01270-3. SERIES: New True. SUBJECTS: Native Americans—Mayas. RL 3.7.

A great deal of information on Mayan history and culture is presented in an interesting text that might provoke youngsters to want to read more. As in other books in the New True series, this is illustrated with good full color photographs and has a glossary and an index.

856 *Monkey-Monkey's Trick*. Ill. by Paul Meisel. Random House, 1988. ISBN 0-394-99173-7. SERIES: Step into Reading. SUBJECTS: Animals—Hyenas—Fiction; Animals—Monkeys—Fiction; Folklore—Africa. RL 2.1.

Monkey-Monkey is pleased when a strange creature offers to help him build his house in exchange for food. Then, tricked out of the food, Monkey-Monkey finds a clever way to get what he needs. A funny retelling of an African tale. Illustrated with colorful, childlike, and humorous paintings.

857 *Our Martin Luther King Book*. Ill. by Helen Endres. Child's World, 1986. ISBN 0-89565-342-7. SERIES: A Special Day. SUBJECTS: Biographies; Black Americans; Holidays—Martin Luther King, Jr., Day. RL 2.8.

A class of young children learns from their teacher about Martin Luther King, Jr., and his commitment to equal rights for black Americans. The children role-play segregation, sing "We Shall Overcome," and have a party in King's honor. Illustrated with full color paintings and photos.

858 *Who Is Coming?* Ill. by Clovis Martin. Childrens, hb and pap., 1986. ISBN 0-516-02073-0. SERIES: Rookie Readers. SUBJECTS: Africa—Fiction; Animals—Fiction; Animals—Monkeys—Fiction. RL 1.3.

Little monkey runs up, down, in, out, and always *away* from the large African animals until an illustration shows a tiger. Little monkey does not run away then because, as everyone knows, there are no tigers in Africa. The simple, repetitive text has sketchy but colorful pictures.

859 *Who Is Who?* Ill. by Elizabeth Allen. Childrens, hb and pap., 1983. ISBN 0-516-02042-0. SERIES: Rookie Readers. SUBJECTS: English language—Synonyms and antonyms; Siblings—Twins—Fiction. RL 1.1.

The clues to help tell twins Bobby and Johnny apart are in their preferences for opposites. One likes up, the other down; one front, the other back, and so on. The very brief text and colorful illustrations of two lively black boys

in a variety of situations comprise a clever way to introduce opposites.

McKissack, Patricia, and McKissack, Fredrick

860 *Bugs!* Ill. by Clovis Martin. Childrens, 1988. ISBN 0-516-02088-9. SERIES: Rookie Readers. SUBJECTS: Animals—Insects—Fiction; Concepts—Numbers—Fiction. RL 1.7.

Two exuberant children explore the countryside and happily discover all kinds of fanciful bugs and show the numbers 1 to 5. The McKissacks and Martin successfully combine forces in their use of a very brief text and attractive watercolor pictures to tell their story.

861 *Constance Stumbles*. Ill. by Tom Dunnington. Childrens, hb and pap., 1988. ISBN 0-516-02086-2. SERIES: Rookie Readers. SUBJECTS: Bicycles and bicycling—Fiction. RL 2.5.

Prone to accidents, Constance nevertheless determines to learn to ride her bicycle. A very brief text relies on full color pictures of an ebullient black child and a watchful owl to capture children's interest.

862 *Messy Bessey*. Ill. by Richard Hackney. Childrens, 1987. ISBN 0-516-02083-8. SERIES: Rookie Readers. SUBJECTS: Behavior—Fiction; Cleanliness—Fiction; Stories in rhyme. RL 2.5.

Bessey's room and her clothes are a terrible mess. Finally she cleans herself and her room, stuffing most things into her closet. Attractive and colorful pictures help the very brief rhyming text tell the story.

McLenighan, Valjean

863 *One Whole Doughnut, One Doughnut Hole*. Ill. by Steven Roger Cole. Childrens, hb and pap., 1982. ISBN 0-516-02031-5. SERIES: Rookie Readers. SUBJECTS: English language—Homonyms. RL 2.7.

Pairs of humorous captioned pictures show the different meanings of words that sound the same. The series and format would indi-

McLenighan, Valjean (cont.)

cate that this is meant for a child just beginning to read, but the subject might be more fun for older children. The illustrations are colorful and comical.

864 *Stop-Go, Fast-Slow.* Ill. by Margrit Fiddle. Childrens, hb and pap., 1982. ISBN 0-516-03617-3. SERIES: Rookie Readers. SUBJECTS: English language—Synonyms and antonyms. RL 2.5.

A very brief, rhyming text and comical full color pictures successfully explain opposites such as left/right, day/night, and in/out.

McNamara, Louise G., and Litchfield, Ada B.

865 *Your Busy Brain.* Ill. by Ruth Hartshorn. Little, Brown, 1973, o.p. SERIES: All about you. SUBJECTS: Human body—Brain; Science. RL 3.1.

Using simple language and good, clear diagrams and pictures, the authors explain the many bodily functions that the human brain and nervous system control.

866 *Your Living Bones.* Ill. by Patricia Grant Porter. Little, Brown, 1973, o.p. SERIES: All about you. SUBJECTS: Human body—Skeleton; Science. RL 3.4.

A lively text discusses the function and growth of bones and encourages children to feel their own bones and pay attention to how they move. The pictures of children and bones are realistic.

McNulty, Faith

867 *The Elephant Who Couldn't Forget.* Ill. by Marc Simont. Harper & Row, 1980. ISBN 0-06-024146-2. SERIES: I Can Read. SUBJECTS: Animals—Elephants—Fiction; Memory and memorization—Fiction; Sibling rivalry—Fiction. RL 2.4.

Congo, the youngest elephant in his family, prides himself on his extraordinary memory and tries hard not to forget anything. Unfortunately he remembers things better left forgotten. Filled with good information, this story has lovely pencil and wash illustrations.

868 *Woodchuck.* Ill. by Joan Sandin. Harper & Row, 1974. ISBN 0-06-024167-5. SERIES: Science I Can Read. SUBJECTS: Animals—Groundhogs; Animals—Woodchucks. RL 1.7.

Readers first meet the woodchuck when she is hibernating, then observe her meeting a male, giving birth to and raising young, and finally being alone again. There is no romanticizing here, just an honest view of animal life. Realistic and detailed pencil and wash drawings.

McPhail, David M.

869 *Lorenzo.* Ill. by author. Doubleday, 1984, o.p. SUBJECTS: Animals—Fiction; Art and artists—Fiction; Houses—Fiction. RL 2.2.

Tired of his life as an itinerant painter, Lorenzo moves into a deserted house in a hollow tree and paints while making friends with the woodland animals. Illustrated with appealing ink sketches that have red and brown washes.

870 *Snow Lion.* Ill. by author. Parents Magazine Press, 1982; Crown, pap., 1987. ISBN 0-8193-1098-0. SERIES: Read Aloud and Easy Reading. SUBJECTS: Animals—Lions—Fiction; Weather—Fiction; Weather—Snow—Fiction. RL 2.4.

Tired of the torrid jungle weather, Lion climbs into the mountains and discovers snow. When no one believes his story of the fluffy cold stuff, lion takes the disbelievers into the mountains, where they have a wonderful time. Expressive, semirealistic pictures are lively and fun.

MacQuitty, Miranda, ed.

871 *Side by Side.* Photos. Putnam, 1988. ISBN 0-399-21582-4. SUBJECTS: Animals; Plants; Symbiosis. RL 2.7.

Symbiosis and parasitism, examples of how animals or plants live "side by side," are explained with excellent color photographs captioned with explanatory text showing animals and plants from around the world. An addendum offers more in-depth information on the animals and plants mentioned in the text.

McRae, Rodney

872 *The Trouble with Heathrow*. Ill. by
author. Childrens, 1987. ISBN 0-516-
08974-9. SERIES: Sunshine Books.
SUBJECTS: Humorous stories; Pets—
Dogs—Fiction. RL 2.4.
Heathrow, a big, lovable Afghan hound, is
always into mischief and never seems to learn
a lesson. The brief text is dominated by
vibrant and expressive paintings of the playful dog.

Madsen, Ross M.

873 *Perrywinkle and the Book of Magic
Spells*. Ill. by Dirk Zimmer. Dial, 1986;
pap., 1988. ISBN 0-8037-0243-4. SERIES:
Easy-to-Read. SUBJECTS: Humorous
stories; Magic—Fiction. RL 2.3.
Perrywinkle practices spells from the wizard's books and creates havoc for everyone.
His pet bird and his new friend Andromeda
try to help him control his "spelling." The
budding wizard's frustrations at mastering
magic are apparent in the lively pencil and
wash pictures.

Maestro, Betsy

874 *Ferryboat*. Ill. by Giulio Maestro. Crowell, 1986. ISBN 0-690-04520-4. SUBJECTS:
Boats and boating. RL 2.6.
Attractive watercolor paintings and a simple
text tell the story of a river crossing on the
modern ferryboat *Selden III* in Connecticut.
Readers learn how cars are loaded and how
captain and crew manage the boat. The brief
text gives a good sense of what it is like to
take a ferryboat trip.

Maestro, Giulio

875 *Leopard and the Noisy Monkeys*. Ill. by
author. Greenwillow, 1979, o.p. SERIES:
Read-alone. SUBJECTS: Animals—Fiction;
Humorous stories; Sleep—Fiction.
RL 2.4.
Escaping from the noise of the 20 monkeys he
has allowed to use his treehouse, Leopard
goes to Crocodile's house, and Crocodile goes
to Aardvark's to escape Leopard, Aardvark to
Hippo's, Hippo to Leopard's. Amusing illus-

trations and story are silly enough to please
young readers.

876 *Leopard Is Sick*. Ill. by author.
Greenwillow, 1978, o.p. SERIES: Read-
alone. SUBJECTS: Animals—Fiction;
Humorous stories; Illness—Fiction.
RL 2.4.
Bored with being sick but ordered by his
doctor to rest, Leopard feels better only when
his three friends disguise themselves as doctors to cheer him up. Simple yet interesting
paintings with gray outlining and details fit
well with the funny story.

Mallett, Anne

877 *Here Comes Tagalong*. Ill. by Steven Kellogg. Parents Magazine Press, 1971, o.p.
SUBJECTS: Emotions—Loneliness—Fiction; Humorous stories; Siblings—Fiction. RL 2.1.
Steve does not know any children his own age
so he tags along after his older brother and
his friends. Finally old enough to go around
the block, he makes his own friends and his
younger brother becomes Tagalong. Spirited
pictures catch the humor as well as Steve's
initial loneliness.

Malone, Mary

878 *Annie Sullivan*. Ill. by Lydia Rosier.
Putnam, 1971, o.p. SERIES: See and
Read Beginning to Read Biography.
SUBJECTS: Biographies; Physically and
mentally impaired. RL 2.4.
Annie Sullivan's life story is told in a con-
cise and straightforward way beginning with
her childhood poverty and going through
her years as "Teacher" to Helen Keller. No
dates are provided, although World War I
is mentioned. Illustrated with realistic ink
drawings.

Mantinband, Gerda B.

879 *Bing Bong Bang and Fiddle Dee Dee*. Ill.
by Anne Rockwell. Doubleday, 1979,
o.p. SERIES: Reading On My Own.
SUBJECTS: Farm and country life—
Fiction; Marriage—Fiction; Music—
Fiction. RL 2.3.

Mantinband, Gerda B. (cont.)

To his wife's dismay, an old man buys a fiddle and tries to play it. She starts banging on pots to stop his squeaking and their music drives the animals from their farm. An affectionate reconciliation ends this story of marital discord. Simple, childlike drawings accompany the humorous story.

Manushkin, Fran

880 *Buster Loves Buttons!* Ill. by Dirk Zimmer. Harper & Row, 1985. ISBN 0-06-024108-X. SERIES: I Can Read. SUBJECTS: Behavior—Greedy—Fiction; Collecting and collectors—Fiction; Pets—Dogs—Fiction. RL 2.6.

Buster is a compulsive collector of buttons, even cutting them off people's clothing, until he is given his comeuppance by Kippy and her dog. Full color humorous drawings effectively extend and make more exciting this occasionally plodding story.

881 *Hocus and Pocus at the Circus.* Ill. by Geoffrey Hayes. Harper & Row, 1983. ISBN 0-06-024092-X. SERIES: I Can Read. SUBJECTS: Circuses—Fiction; Holidays—Halloween—Fiction; Witches—Fiction. RL 3.0.

Intent on creating chaos, Hocus takes her little witch sister Pocus to the circus on Halloween night. Pocus uses her talent to thwart Hocus's spells in this slight but enjoyable story. The comic-style drawings are in full color with characters round and toylike rather than realistic.

882 *The Perfect Christmas Picture.* Ill. by Karen A. Weinhaus. Harper & Row, 1980; pap., 1987. ISBN 0-06-024069-5. SERIES: I Can Read. SUBJECTS: Family life—Fiction; Photography—Fiction. RL 2.9.

All year Mr. Green has tried with no success to take a perfect Christmas picture of his six children. His frustrations and the children's antics will have readers laughing. The spare, humorous ink and wash drawings work very well with the story.

Margolis, Richard J.

883 *Big Bear, Spare That Tree.* Ill. by Jack Kent. Greenwillow, 1980, o.p. SERIES: Read-alone. SUBJECTS: Animals—Bears—Fiction; Animals—Blue Jays—Fiction. RL 2.6.

Trying to save her soon-to-hatch eggs, a blue jay screams for Bear to stop chopping down her tree. He ignores her until he sees that the eggs are hatching and then he must really come to the rescue. The conflict is handled well and Kent's humorous drawings keep the story light.

884 *Homer the Hunter.* Ill. by Leonard Kessler. Macmillan, 1972, o.p. SERIES: Ready-to-Read. SUBJECTS: Animals—Fiction; Humorous stories; Hunting—Fiction. RL 2.4.

Rabbit, Squirrel, and Crow initially fool Homer, a terrible hunter, into believing they are ghosts haunting him. Finally Homer decides to share in the fun and pretends that he is a ghost too. Comical sketches in gray, brown, and red complement the story.

885 *Wish Again, Big Bear.* Ill. by Robert Lopshire. Macmillan, 1972, o.p.; pap., 1974. ISBN 0-02-044480-X. SERIES: Ready-to-Read. SUBJECTS: Animals—Bears—Fiction; Animals—Fish—Fiction; Wishes—Fiction. RL 2.2.

To save himself from being eaten, Fish tells Big Bear he is magic and will grant him three wishes. Fish saves himself and Bear gets what he wished for—a friend. The humor in Fish's trickery and Bear's gullibility acts as a perfect complement to Lopshire's comic ink drawings.

Markham, Marion M.

886 *The Halloween Candy Mystery.* Ill. by Emily A. McCully. Houghton Mifflin, 1982. ISBN 0-395-32437-8. SUBJECTS: Holidays—Halloween—Fiction; Mystery and detective stories; Siblings—Twins—Fiction. RL 2.5.

Dressed in their panda costumes and ready to go trick-or-treating, twin sisters Mickey and

Kate get involved in reporting a robbery and in helping to find the missing robber. Longer than most first readers, this is entertaining and has good black and white drawings.

Marshall, Edward

887 *Four on the Shore*. Ill. by James Marshall. Dial, 1985; pap., 1987. ISBN 0-8037-0142-X. SERIES: Easy-to-Read. SUBJECTS: Humorous stories; Siblings—Fiction; Storytelling—Fiction. RL 2.5.
Three children, Lolly, Spider, and Sam, share stories around a fire hoping to frighten Spider's little brother Willie into going home. Drawn in ink with colorful washes, the pictures are simple yet comical, adding to the already delightful humor of the stories.

888 *Fox All Week*. Ill. by James Marshall. Dial, 1984; pap., 1987. ISBN 0-8037-0066-0. SERIES: Easy-to-Read. SUBJECTS: Animals—Foxes—Fiction; Friendship—Fiction; Humorous stories. RL 2.3.
From Monday morning to Sunday evening, Fox, his friends, and his family face situations that are sure to stir memories in adults and be very funny to children. The book is illustrated with humorous full color ink and watercolor paintings.

889 *Fox and His Friends*. Ill. by James Marshall. Dial, hb and pap., 1982. ISBN 0-8037-2669-4. SERIES: Easy-to-Read. SUBJECTS: Animals—Foxes—Fiction; Baby-sitting—Fiction; Humorous stories. RL 2.2.
In each of three stories, Fox cannot seem to get away with anything. In two stories he is stuck taking care of his spunky little sister Louise and in the third his conscience gets the better of him. Each story is very funny, the third hilarious, especially with the deadpan, comic illustrations.

890 *Fox at School*. Ill. by James Marshall. Dial, hb and pap., 1983. ISBN 0-8037-2675-9. SERIES: Easy-to-Read. SUBJECTS: Animals—Foxes—Fiction; Humorous stories; School stories. RL 2.8.
Always wanting the easy way out, egocentric Fox is surprised that it takes hard work to act in the class play or control the class. Children are sure to identify with the imperfect but lovable Fox. Illustrated with comic ink drawings with coral and green tints.

891 *Fox in Love*. Ill. by James Marshall. Dial, hb and pap., 1982. ISBN 0-8037-2433-0. SERIES: Easy-to-Read. SUBJECTS: Animals—Foxes—Fiction; Humorous stories; Romance—Fiction. RL 2.3.
Forced to take his little sister Louise to the park, Fox is surprised to meet Raisin, a lovely white fox, and is soon swooning over her as well as Millie, Rose, and Lola. Fun to read, this book has whimsical ink cartoon drawings with orange and green washes.

892 *Fox on Wheels*. Ill. by James Marshall. Dial, hb and pap., 1983. ISBN 0-8037-0002-4. SERIES: Easy-to-Read. SUBJECTS: Animals—Foxes—Fiction; Baby-sitting—Fiction; Bicycles and bicycling—Fiction. RL 2.2.
In three stories with surprise endings, Fox gets into more trouble than he bargained for—especially when he baby-sits for his little sister Louise or goes biking through the park. Illustrations are ink line drawings with color overlays in a whimsical style.

893 *Three by the Sea*. Ill. by James Marshall. Dial, hb and pap., 1981. ISBN 0-8037-8687-5. SERIES: Easy-to-Read. SUBJECTS: Friendship—Fiction; Storytelling—Fiction. RL 2.4.
After a filling picnic lunch at the beach, Lolly decides to share a story from her reader with Spider and Sam. Bored, they try to create their own stories. Sure to appeal to children and adults, this book is illustrated with humorous ink and pencil drawings.

894 *Troll Country*. Ill. by James Marshall. Dial, 1980, o.s.i.; pap., 1980. ISBN 0-8037-6210-0. SERIES: Easy-to-Read. SUBJECTS: Fantasy; Humorous stories; Trolls—Fiction. RL 2.3.
After hearing her mother's story of her encounter with a troll, Elsie Fay is sure she will know exactly how to handle one. Droll ink drawings with colored pencil accents in gray, green, and rust are perfect for this entertaining story.

Marshall, James

895 *Fox on the Job.* Ill. by author. Dial, 1988. ISBN 0-8037-0351-1. SERIES: Easy-to-Read. SUBJECTS: Animals—Foxes—Fiction; Humorous stories. RL 2.1.

To impress the girls, Fox shows off on his bike and ends up demolishing it. When Mom refuses to buy him a new one, Fox goes through several jobs before he finds one just right for his special talents. Story and artwork continue to be as witty and satisfying as in the earlier Fox stories.

896 *Three up a Tree.* Ill. by author. Dial, 1986. ISBN 0-8037-0329-5. SERIES: Easy-to-Read. SUBJECTS: Friendship—Fiction; Storytelling—Fiction; Treehouses—Fiction. RL 2.1.

To get into Spider and Sam's treehouse, Lolly promises to tell a story. Soon the other two are trying to outdo Lolly with their storytelling. The colorful, often silly illustrations and stories are sure to evoke appreciative smiles.

Martin, Claire

897 *I Can Be a Weather Forecaster.* Photos. Childrens, hb and pap., 1987. ISBN 0-516-01908-2. SERIES: I Can Be. SUBJECTS: Careers; Weather. RL 3.4.

Weather forecasting is presented as an interesting and demanding profession with much more involved than what is seen on a television weather report. Illustrated with color photographs and simple drawings, the text mentions weather satellites, stations, computers, and other forecasting tools.

Martin, C.L.G.

898 *Day of Darkness, Night of Light.* Ill. by Victoria M. Williams. Dillon, 1988. ISBN 0-87518-357-3. SERIES: It Really Happened! SUBJECTS: Fire fighting—Fiction; Historical fiction. RL 2.8.

Fire breaks out threatening to destroy Menominee, Michigan, in October 1871. After getting his mother and sisters to safety, Daniel and his grandfather help battle the blaze and save their town. Based on an actual event, this suspenseful story is effectively illustrated in pencil.

Martin, Louise

899 *Bird Eating Spiders.* Photos. Rourke, 1988. ISBN 0-86592-966-1. SERIES: Spiders Discovery Library. SUBJECTS: Animals—Spiders. RL 2.7.

This book gives basic facts on large spiders such as the tarantula that can and do eat birds and provides information on their homes, appearance, webs, young, and their relationship to humans. Though attractive, the photos are not well matched to the text.

900 *Black Widow Spider.* Photos. Rourke, 1988. ISBN 0-86592-965-3. SERIES: Spiders Discovery Library. SUBJECTS: Animals—Spiders. RL 2.5.

There is good but limited information here on the black widow spider. Nothing is provided on the life cycle of the spider although something is given about its appearance, prey, venom, and danger to humans. Poor editing has reversed two pages and photos are not well matched to the text.

901 *Elephants.* Photos. Rourke, 1988. ISBN 0-86592-988-X. SERIES: Wildlife in Danger. SUBJECTS: Animals—Elephants; Animals—Endangered. RL 2.7.

A useful book for its facts about elephants and their habitat, it places emphasis on the threat to this species. The book is marred by mismatching of photos to the text. It includes a brief table of contents, glossary, and index.

902 *Funnel Web Spiders.* Photos. Rourke, 1988. ISBN 0-86592-962-9. SERIES: Spiders Discovery Library. SUBJECTS: Animals—Spiders. RL 2.5.

There is good information here about the deadly Australian funnel web spider. However, poor editing has left photos mismatched to the text and given an incorrect topic heading. Information on the spiders' burrows, senses, prey, bites, and defenses is included. Illustrated with color photos.

903 *Panda.* Photos. Rourke, 1988. ISBN 0-86592-996-3. SERIES: Wildlife in Danger. SUBJECTS: Animals—Endangered; Animals—Pandas. RL 2.6.

Martin provides interesting information to support her plea for the preservation of the panda, stressing threats to its existence such as poaching and loss of habitat. Some photographs are not matched correctly to the text but the information is good enough to compensate for that.

904 *Rhinoceros*. Photos. Rourke, 1988. ISBN 0-86592-997-1. SERIES: Wildlife in Danger. SUBJECTS: Animals— Endangered; Animals—Rhinoceroses. RL 2.3.

The threat of extinction is mentioned on nearly every page of this simply written and useful book. There is a good deal of information about rhinos: types, habitat, diet, poaching, protection, and horns. Color photos are not always matched to the text and captions could be more informative.

905 *Seals*. Photos. Rourke, 1988. ISBN 0-86592-999-8. SERIES: Wildlife in Danger. SUBJECTS: Animals—Endangered; Animals—Seals. RL 2.5.

Using only 18 pages of alternating text and photographs, Martin presents well-documented threats to the existence of seals without presenting much information on the various species of seals. The brief information could be useful for reports on endangered animals.

906 *Tarantulas*. Photos. Rourke, 1988. ISBN 0-86592-967-X. SERIES: Spiders Discovery Library. SUBJECTS: Animals— Spiders. RL 2.8.

The American tarantula, not the true tarantula of Europe, is the main subject in this small book. It includes information about their physical characteristics, prey, and predators, but few specifics about their habitats or life cycle. The color photos are good but often do not match the captions.

907 *Tigers*. Photos. Rourke, 1988. ISBN 0-86592-995-3. SERIES: Wildlife in Danger. SUBJECTS: Animals—Endangered; Animals—Tigers. RL 2.4.

The emphasis here is on the threat to Asian tigers through poaching and habitat destruction rather than on the general characteristics of the largest member of the cat family. Good information and attractive color photographs are provided.

908 *Trapdoor Spiders*. Photos. Rourke, 1988. ISBN 0-86592-963-7. SERIES: Spiders Discovery Library. SUBJECTS: Animals— Spiders. RL 2.2.

An excellent text describes the unusual burrow and some of the habits of the trapdoor spiders that are found all over the world. The scope of information is limited and a discussion of the spider's life cycle could have been included. The photos include two that have mismatched captions.

909 *Whales*. Photos. Rourke, 1988. ISBN 0-86592-988-2. SERIES: Wildlife in Danger. SUBJECTS: Animals—Endangered; Animals—Whales. RL 2.7.

Along with a brief history of whaling and mention of various types of whales, the 18 pages of alternating text and photographs include much on the status of whales as endangered animals. The color photographs are acceptable but are often not carefully chosen to match the text.

Martin, Patricia M.

910 *The Pumpkin Patch*. Ill. by Tom Hamil. Putnam, 1966, o.p. SUBJECTS: Holidays— Halloween—Fiction; School stories. RL 2.3.

Kate loves kindergarten and cannot wait for her class to go to the pumpkin patch so she can pick out her very own pumpkin. Once there she discovers that the perfect pumpkin already has an owner—a field mouse. Very sketchy drawings are busy and childlike and work well with this story.

911 *Thomas Alva Edison*. Ill. by Fermin Rocker. Putnam, 1971, o.p. SERIES: See and Read Beginning to Read Biography. SUBJECTS: Biographies; Inventors and inventions. RL 2.7.

Focusing on Edison's curiosity about all kinds of scientific ventures, this interesting text highlights his youthful adventures in school and at work and his adult scientific study. Pen and ink cross-hatchings are used to create the pictures of Edison and his work.

Martini, Teri

912 *Cowboys*. Photos. Childrens, 1981. ISBN 0-516-01611-3. SERIES: New True. SUBJECTS: Cowboys. RL 2.8.

Martini, Teri (cont.)

Rounding up and branding cattle, taking care of the ranch, being in a rodeo, and feeding cattle in winter are some of the parts of a cowboy's work that are presented in this short book with colorful photographs, a glossary, and an index.

913 *Indians*. Photos. Childrens, hb and pap., 1982. ISBN 0-516-01628-8. SERIES: New True. SUBJECTS: Native Americans. RL 3.1.

Rudimentary information is given on tribal culture and life-style, homes, hunting, and so forth, for the Native American tribes of the northwest, plains, southwest, and eastern woodlands. The simple language, color photos and archival drawings, glossary, and index make this text acceptable if not good.

Marzollo, Jean

914 *Amy Goes Fishing*. Ill. by Ann Schweninger. Dial, 1980, o.s.i. SERIES: Easy-to-Read. SUBJECTS: Fishing—Fiction; Parent and child—Fiction. RL 2.1.

On her first fishing trip with father, Amy remembers how boring her brother and sister thought fishing was. She is pleasantly surprised at how much she enjoys their day together. An understated text and quiet, soft-hued pictures blend to create an enjoyable, low-key story.

915 *Cannonball Chris*. Ill. by Blanche Sims. Random House, hb and pap., 1987. ISBN 0-394-98512-5. SERIES: Step into Reading. SUBJECTS: Emotions—Fear—Fiction; Parent and child—Fiction; Sports—Swimming—Fiction. RL 2.4.

Realizing that something is wrong, Chris's father convinces Chris to say what is bothering him—a fear of diving into deep water. His father helps Chris to face his fear, name it, and finally overcome it with his support. This very well done story has lively multiracial children drawn in pencil and wash.

916 *Red Sun Girl*. Ill. by Susan Meddaugh. Dial, 1983, o.s.i. SERIES: Easy-to-Read. SUBJECTS: Animals—Fiction; Magic—Fiction; Science fiction. RL 2.3.

Everyone on the planet is a human during Red Sun and an animal during Blue Sun except Kiri. Tired of being laughed at, she finds a way to get her own animal shape. This is an appealing, well-paced book that is divided into chapters. Simple, cartoon style pictures are drawn with colored pencil.

917 *Soccer Sam*. Ill. by Blanche Sims. Random House, hb and pap., 1987. ISBN 0-394-98406-4. SERIES: Step into Reading. SUBJECTS: Cultural diversity—Fiction; Mexicans—United States—Fiction; Sports—Soccer—Fiction. RL 2.7.

Although Sam's Mexican cousin Marco does not understand English, his prowess at soccer earns him friends. This well-done book about overcoming cultural differences has pencil and watercolor pictures.

Marzollo, Jean, and Marzollo, Claudio

918 *Blue Sun Ben*. Ill. by Susan Meddaugh. Dial, hb and pap., 1984. ISBN 0-8037-0063-6. SERIES: Easy-to-Read. SUBJECTS: Animals—Fiction; Magic—Fiction; Science fiction. RL 2.5.

On Ben's planet everyone is an animal during Blue Sun and a human during Red Sun. Caught by the evil Animal Singer while in his chipmunk shape, Ben manages to escape with the help of his cousin Kiri and the Fox Woman. Colored pencil drawings effectively delineate the exciting story.

919 *Jed and the Space Bandits*. Ill. by Peter Sis. Dial, 1987. ISBN 0-8037-0136-5. SERIES: Science Fiction Easy-to-Read. SUBJECTS: Science fiction. RL 2.8.

Since she is able to become invisible, Molly is not seen by the space bandits who kidnap her scientist parents. Jed, his cogs (telepathic half-dog, half-cat animals), and his robot Teddy Bear join Molly in an exciting rescue of her parents. The story is illustrated with good full color pictures.

920 *Jed's Junior Space Patrol*. Ill. by David S. Rose. Dial, 1982, o.s.i. SERIES: Easy-to-Read. SUBJECTS: Science fiction. RL 2.1.

Left alone while his space pilot parents work, Jed hears a call for help and rescues two cogs—telepathic half-dog, half-cat animals.

Taken from Jed, the little animals use telepathy to get him to rescue them again. This time they stay with him. The futuristic pictures are done in ink and washes.

921 *Robin of Bray*. Ill. by Diane Stanley. Dial, hb and pap., 1982. ISBN 0-8037-7332-3. SERIES: Easy-to-Read. SUBJECTS: Fairy tales; Magic—Fiction; Trolls—Fiction. RL 2.6.

In this creative and appealing fairy tale, Robin is stuck being a shepherd when he has talent enough to be a magician. After rescuing a princess from trolls, he discovers his true identity. Contains suitably fanciful pointillist ink drawings with washes.

922 *Ruthie's Rude Friends*. Ill. by Susan Meddaugh. Dial, 1984; pap., 1987. ISBN 0-8037-0116-0. SERIES: Easy-to-Read. SUBJECTS: Behavior—Manners—Fiction; Friendship—Fiction; Science fiction. RL 2.4.

Ruthie, newly arrived from Earth, is just as rude to the strange beings she meets as she believes they are to her until they rescue her from a terrible three-headed monster. Ink line drawings with vibrant colored pencil details carry and expand the successful science-fiction theme.

Massie, Diane R.

923 *The Komodo Dragon's Jewels*. Ill. by author. Macmillan, 1975, o.p. SERIES: Ready-to-Read. SUBJECTS: Animals—Lizards—Fiction; Humorous stories. RL 3.0.

The Komodo Dragon, a giant lizard, gets his chance to see the jewels shining from the mainland when he is mistaken for a passenger and is allowed aboard a tour boat. The fun found in the text is augmented by the outlandish ink and wash illustrations.

Matthias, Catherine

924 *I Can Be a Computer Operator*. Photos. Childrens, hb and pap., 1985. ISBN 0-516-01838-0. SERIES: I Can Be. SUBJECTS: Careers; Computers. RL 3.6.

This introduction to computer work is very superficial, with information frequently repeated. There are many colorful photographs, a glossary, an index, and a text that is more accessible to young readers than the readability scores indicate.

925 *I Can Be a Police Officer*. Photos. Childrens, hb and pap., 1984. ISBN 0-516-01840-X. SERIES: I Can Be. SUBJECTS: Careers; Police. RL 2.9.

Supported by full color photographs and drawings, this book gives an overview of police work in the United States and abroad. It also discusses the type of work done by American police officers and the educational requirements for entry into the force.

926 *I Love Cats*. Ill. by Tom Dunnington. Childrens, hb and pap., 1983. ISBN 0-516-02041-2. SERIES: Rookie Readers. SUBJECTS: Pets—Cats—Fiction; Stories in rhyme. RL 2.2.

A plump little boy admits that he likes all kinds of animals but he *loves* cats. Like other books in the Rookie Reader series, the text here is very brief. It relies on its rhyme and humorous pictures to interest readers.

927 *Out the Door*. Ill. by Eileen M. Neill. Childrens, hb and pap., 1982. ISBN 0-516-03560-6. SERIES: Rookie Readers. SUBJECTS: School stories. RL 1.7.

A forgetful little girl has to go back home for her lunchbox and then her umbrella as she tries to get to the school bus and a full day at school. The very brief text relies on the flat ink and wash pictures to carry the story.

928 *Over-Under*. Ill. by Gene Sharp. Childrens, hb and pap., 1984. ISBN 0-516-02048-X. SERIES: Rookie Readers. SUBJECTS: Concepts—Fiction; Playgrounds—Fiction. RL 1.7.

A young black child demonstrates on/off, in/out, over/under, around/between, inside/outside, above/below, and up/down using playground equipment. Cheerful ink and watercolor paintings illustrate the concepts mentioned in the very brief text.

929 *Too Many Balloons*. Ill. by Gene Sharp. Childrens, hb and pap., 1982. ISBN 0-516-03633-5. SERIES: Rookie Readers. SUBJECTS: Balloons—Fiction; Concepts—

Matthias, Catherine (cont.)

Numbers—Fiction; Zoos—Fiction.
RL 2.0.

Buying one balloon to correspond to the first animal she sees at the zoo, the little girl keeps buying balloons as she visits animals until she has 55 balloons and starts to float away. The brief and simple text has full color paintings with ink details.

May, Julian

930 *The Life Cycle of an Opossum.* Photos by Allan Roberts. Creative Education, 1973, o.p. SERIES: Life Cycle. SUBJECTS: Animals—Opossum. RL 3.0.

Facts about the opossum's rearing of its young, its eating habits, its enemies, and its relationship to humankind are accompanied by color photographs and a map showing the animal's territorial range. Also mentioned is the fact that the opossum has existed since the time of the dinosaurs and is a living fossil.

931 *Rockets.* Ill. by Bill Barss. Follett, 1967, o.p. SERIES: Beginning Science. SUBJECTS: Rocketry. RL 3.4.

Although written in the 1960s, the information on rocketry is basic enough not to have become dated. The author covers the history and development of rockets and the fuels used for them. The art is instructive rather than attractive and does seem dated.

932 *These Islands Are Alive.* Ill. by Rod Ruth. Hawthorne, 1971, o.p. SUBJECTS: Islands; Oceans and ocean life. RL 3.1.

Coral islands, such as the Florida Keys, grow continuously as offshore reefs, since reefs are formed as coral live and die. This book describes and explains some of the sea creatures found among the reefs. Illustrated with black and white realistic pencil and wash drawings with maps and diagrams.

Meddaugh, Susan

933 *Too Short Fred.* Ill. by author. Houghton Mifflin, 1978; pap., 1985. ISBN 0-395-27155-X. SUBJECTS: Animals—Cats—Fiction; Self-esteem—Fiction. RL 2.0.

Though he constantly complains of being short, Fred's size is usually no hindrance to having fun. Pencil and chalk drawings show an assortment of humanized cats illustrating the action in the text. Children will enjoy Fred and his friends in this well-written, well-illustrated piece.

Meeks, Esther

934 *The Dog That Took the Train.* Ill. by Ted Schroeder. Follett, 1972, o.p. SERIES: Beginning-to-Read. SUBJECTS: Animals—Dogs—Fiction; Lost, being—Fiction; Trains—Fiction. RL 2.1.

The conductor of a train tries to find the owner of a dog that has strayed onto the passenger line. The lively full color pictures add excitement to this book.

Mercer, Charles

935 *Roberto Clemente.* Ill. by George Loh. Putnam, 1974, o.p. SERIES: See and Read Beginning to Read Biography. SUBJECTS: Biographies; Black Americans. RL 3.0.

Hard work, determination, and a strong sense of honor help Roberto Clemente to become a great baseball player for the Pittsburgh Pirates and a great humanitarian. Coming from Puerto Rico he faces bigotry in the United States but overcomes it. Illustrated with realistic black, white, and yellow drawings.

Merriam, Eve

936 *The Birthday Cow.* Ill. by Guy Michel. Knopf, 1978, o.p. SUBJECTS: Nonsense; Poetry. RL 2.1.

This book contains fifteen nonsensical poems about silly things that children will be familiar with and enjoy, such as birthdays, Halloween, clowns, and cows. Illustrated with suitably whimsical multicolored drawings.

Meyers, Susan

937 *The Truth about Gorillas.* Ill. by John Hamberger. Dutton, 1980. ISBN 0-525-41564-5. SERIES: Smart Cat. SUBJECTS: Animals—Gorillas. RL 3.2.

Children reading this introduction to gorillas will find that it presents the gorilla's life in an interesting way. The book is well researched and well written, and encourages its readers to care about wildlife. The realistic illustrations are done with pencil and washes.

Michel, Anna

938 *Little Wild Chimpanzee.* Ill. by Peter Parnall and Virginia Parnall. Pantheon, 1978. ISBN 0-394-83716-3. SERIES: I Am Reading. SUBJECTS: Animals—Chimpanzees. RL 2.1.
The first five years of a chimpanzee's life are observed as he grows and interacts with his family and other animals. This carefully written story includes much factual information as well as lovely realistic drawings of chimpanzees and their environment.

939 *Little Wild Elephant.* Ill. by Peter Parnall and Virginia Parnall. Pantheon, 1979. ISBN 0-394-93884-4. SERIES: I Am Reading. SUBJECTS: Animals—Elephants. RL 2.6.
The first four years of Little Elephant's life, his relationships with family members, and his ability to care for himself are carefully examined. Soft, realistic pencil drawings complement and extend the text.

940 *Little Wild Lion Cub.* Ill. by Tony Chen. Pantheon, 1980, o.p. SERIES: I Am Reading. SUBJECTS: Animals—Growth and development; Animals—Lions. RL 2.4.
Readers follow Little Lion from birth until he is two years old—not yet grown up but no longer a cub. The place of a cub in a pride and a cub's relationship to its parents are seen in this informative and interesting story. Detailed, realistic watercolor paintings add to the appeal.

Miklowitz, Gloria

941 *Sad Song, Happy Song.* Ill. by Earl Thollander. Putnam, 1973, o.p. SERIES: See and Read. SUBJECTS: Animals—Alligators; Conservation. RL 2.7.
A baby alligator is captured and taken to a pet store, where he is sold. His life is frightening, and becomes hopeful only when he is returned to his natural environment. A well-

done look at the plight of wild animals kept as pets; it is illustrated with bold black paintings with some color washes.

Milburn, Constance

942 *The Seasons.* Ill. by Ann Baum. Bookwright, 1988. ISBN 0-531-18179-0. SERIES: Let's Look At. SUBJECTS: Seasons. RL 2.8.
Originally published in England, this book offers a clear explanation of why we have seasons and how they differ in various parts of the world. Illustrated with full color pictures, including one that shows the Earth's rotation around the sun and how this causes the seasons.

Miles, Miska

943 *Noisy Gander.* Ill. by Leslie Morrill. Dutton, 1978. ISBN 0-525-36026-3. SERIES: Unicorn Book. SUBJECTS: Animals—Geese—Fiction; Farm and country life—Fiction. RL 3.1.
The other animals mock the little gosling's father for his constant honking at animals until his vigilance—and honking—rids the barnyard of a coyote. The story, told simply and well, has realistic pencil drawings.

944 *Tree House Town.* Ill. by Emily A. McCully. Little, Brown, 1974, o.p. SUBJECTS: Conservation—Fiction. RL 2.7.
As children come into the forest to build tree houses, they drive out the animals. Night after night, as the tree houses multiply during the day, the animals leave for the other side of the forest. With its expressive ink and colored pencil drawings, this story could lead to discussion of conservation.

Milgrom, Harry

945 *Adventures with a Ball.* Ill. by the Strimbans. Dutton, 1965, o.p. SERIES: First Science Experiments. SUBJECTS: Science experiments. RL 2.5.
A variety of simple experiments entices children into discovering the properties of spheres. No elaborate equipment is necessary for these learning experiences. Illustrations

Milgrom, Harry (cont.)

have a flat geometric look to them and are in dark blue, orange, and black.

946 *Adventures with a Cardboard Tube.* Ill. by Tom Funk. Dutton, 1972. ISBN 0-525-25150-2. SERIES: First Science Experiments. SUBJECTS: Mathematics; Science experiments. RL 3.2.

The properties of cylinders are discussed and explored in a variety of experiments that are relatively easy and fun for younger children to perform. The simple pencil and wash drawings add to a child's understanding of how to do the experiments.

947 *Adventures with a Party Plate.* Ill. by George Wilde. Dutton, 1968, o.p. SERIES: First Science Experiments. SUBJECTS: Mathematics; Science experiments. RL 2.8.

Using a paper plate, children learn about circles; their radii, diameters, and circumferences; some aerodynamic principles; how a turbine works; and much, much more. Simple ink line drawings help to explain the experiments.

948 *Adventures with a Straw.* Ill. by Leonard Kessler. Dutton, 1967. ISBN 0-525-25229-0. SERIES: First Science Experiments. SUBJECTS: Science experiments. RL 2.7.

Nearly every page of this book has an activity that will help children discover the properties of cylinders. The many science experiments use straws and household materials. Though the simple ink line drawings with washes are somewhat dated, they are still effective with the text.

949 *Adventures with a String.* Ill. by Tom Funk. Dutton, 1965, o.p. SERIES: First Science Experiments. SUBJECTS: Science experiments. RL 2.8.

By using a piece of string and different household objects, children learn how string can make sounds and be used for a pulley or a pendulum, along with other interesting science facts. The book encourages children's experimentation and observation. The rather dated drawings are done in ink and wash.

Milios, Rita

950 *Bears, Bears, Everywhere.* Ill. by Tom Dunnington. Childrens, hb and pap., 1988. ISBN 0-516-02085-4. SERIES: Rookie Readers. SUBJECTS: Concepts—Numbers—Fiction; Stories in rhyme; Toys—Teddy bears—Fiction. RL 2.1.

A very brief rhyming text and soft watercolor pictures present bears in combinations from one to ten and in a variety of humorous situations. The vocabulary is very limited and the pictures play an important part in telling the story.

951 *I Am.* Ill. by Clovis Martin. Childrens, hb and pap., 1987. ISBN 0-516-42081-X. SERIES: Rookie Readers. SUBJECTS: English language—Synonyms and antonyms—Fiction; Stories in rhyme. RL 1.2.

Attractive full color pictures of children with different cultural backgrounds, some with physical impairments, accompany a brief rhyming text. Together they explain opposites like *up* and *down*, and compare and contrast words like *say* and *do*, and *one* and *many*.

Milton, Joyce

952 *Dinosaur Days.* Ill. by Richard Roe. Random House, hb and pap., 1985. ISBN 0-394-97023-3. SERIES: Step into Reading. SUBJECTS: Dinosaurs. RL 2.4.

Fans of dinosaurs will enjoy the brief but informative text. When a dinosaur is introduced, the pronunciation of its name is given along with a few important facts about it. The detailed drawings are in colored pencil.

953 *Secrets of the Mummies.* Ill. by Dolores Santoliquido. Random House, 1984. ISBN 0-394-96769-0. SERIES: Step-Up. SUBJECTS: Egypt, ancient; Mummies. RL 3.2.

An interesting and instructive narrative tells about mummies in general and those of ancient Egypt in particular. The description of the making of mummies is fascinating as are the sections on tombs and animal mummies. The lengthy text dominates well-chosen black and white photos.

Minarik, Else H.

954 *Cat and Dog.* Ill. by Fritz Siebel. Harper & Row, 1960. ISBN 0-06-024221-3. SERIES: Early I Can Read. SUBJECTS: Animals—Cats—Fiction; Animals—Dogs—Fiction; Pets—Fiction. RL 1.3.
The rivalry between a little girl's cat and dog creates havoc as they chase each other through the house and garden. Pencil drawings with some wash accents add to the fun of the story.

955 *Father Bear Comes Home.* Ill. by Maurice Sendak. Harper & Row, 1959; pap., 1978. ISBN 0-06-024231-0. SERIES: I Can Read. SUBJECTS: Animals—Bears—Fiction; Family life—Fiction; Mythical creatures—Fiction. RL 1.4.
Father Bear is finally home from ocean fishing and Little Bear and his family now share problems with hiccups, a picnic by the river, and fantasizing about a mermaid. This delightful story is a good portrayal of a nuclear family. Detailed drawings are of dignified turn-of-the-century bears.

956 *A Kiss for Little Bear.* Ill. by Maurice Sendak. Harper & Row, 1968; pap., 1984. ISBN 0-06-024299-X. SERIES: I Can Read. SUBJECTS: Animals—Bears—Fiction; Grandparents—Fiction. RL 2.0.
When Little Bear sends a picture to his grandmother via Hen, his grandmother sends back a kiss that is passed from animal to animal until it reaches Little Bear. The realistic drawings of animals, some in turn-of-the-century garb, are set in beautiful and detailed woodland areas.

957 *Little Bear.* Ill. by Maurice Sendak. Harper & Row, 1957; pap., 1978. ISBN 0-06-024241-8. SERIES: I Can Read. SUBJECTS: Animals—Bears—Fiction; Birthdays—Fiction; Family life—Fiction. RL 1.5.
This perennial favorite has childlike Little Bear in a variety of adventures, including a birthday party, that always lead him to a warm and loving family and friends. The detailed, realistic ink drawings show a happy bear cub, his friends, and his mother dressed in turn-of-the-century clothing.

958 *Little Bear's Friend.* Ill. by Maurice Sendak. Harper & Row, 1960; pap., 1984. ISBN 0-06-024256-6. SERIES: I Can Read. SUBJECTS: Animals—Bears—Fiction; Fantasy; Friendship—Fiction. RL 1.7.
Little Bear meets a little lost girl and in taking her home becomes her friend. During the summer he introduces her to Duck, Hen, Cat, and Owl and knows he will miss her when she goes home to attend school. Little Bear's story is illustrated with lovely, detailed drawings.

959 *Little Bear's Visit.* Ill. by Maurice Sendak. Harper & Row, 1961; pap., 1979. ISBN 0-06-024266-3. SERIES: I Can Read. SUBJECTS: Animals—Bears—Fiction; Grandparents—Fiction. RL 1.8.
Little Bear spends a lovely day with his grandparents. They eat, play, and tell stories—all to Little Bear's delight. The detailed realistic illustrations of bears dressed in turn-of-the-century clothing are part of what makes this book memorable.

960 *No Fighting, No Biting!* Ill. by Maurice Sendak. Harper & Row, 1958; pap., 1978. ISBN 0-06-024291-4. SERIES: I Can Read. SUBJECTS: Animals—Alligators—Fiction; Sibling rivalry—Fiction. RL 2.6.
Rosa and Willie pester Cousin Joan until she finally tells them stories about two little alligators who are so busy bickering that they are nearly eaten. The text is simple yet fascinating, especially with Sendak's detailed drawings setting the story at the turn of the century.

961 *Percy and the Five Houses.* Ill. by James Stevenson. Greenwillow, 1989. ISBN 0-688-08104-5. SUBJECTS: Animals—Beavers—Fiction; Houses—Fiction; Humorous stories. RL 1.7.
After Percy, a beaver, finds gold in the stream, he is invited by Ferd Fox to become a member of the House of the Month Club. Percy has fun playing with each fragile dwelling he receives, but finally decides home is the best house of all. Illustrated with zany, comic watercolors.

Mitchell, Barbara

962 *Cornstalks and Cannonballs.* Ill. by Karen Ritz. Carolrhoda, 1980. ISBN 0-

Mitchell, Barbara (cont.)

87614-121-1. SERIES: On My Own. SUBJECTS: United States—War of 1812. RL 2.5.

Besieged by English warships, the people of Lewes, Delaware, wait until the middle of the night and then, dressed like American soldiers, with cornstalks for guns, scare the English ships away. Based on an actual event, this story is illustrated with realistic blue ink drawings.

963 *Hush, Puppies.* Ill. by Cherie R. Wyman. Carolrhoda, 1983. ISBN 0-87614-201-3. SERIES: On My Own. SUBJECTS: Cookery—Fiction; United States—1783–1865—Fiction. RL 3.0.

Southern folk legends say that hush puppies were created by a clever slave cook to quiet the hounds at her master's fish fry. An entertaining and almost upbeat look at an unfortunate time, this book offers a good story as well as a recipe for hush puppies. Illustrated with ink drawings.

964 *Tomahawks and Trombones.* Ill. by George Overlie. Carolrhoda, 1982. ISBN 0-87614-191-2. SERIES: On My Own. SUBJECTS: Native Americans—Delaware; Religion; United States—French and Indian War. RL 2.6.

Waiting for the Delaware Indians to attack on Christmas day, the Moravians of Bethlehem, Pennsylvania, hide in their homes. Four men take their trombones and play them from a housetop—scaring away the Delaware. This interesting bit of U.S. history is illustrated with realistic paintings.

Mitgutsch, Ali

965 *From Gold to Money.* Ill. by author. Carolrhoda, 1985. ISBN 0-87614-230-7. SERIES: Start To Finish. SUBJECTS: Money. RL 3.0.

Starting with prehistoric times, Mitgutsch looks at the development of bartering, the use of gold, and then the minting of money. The text is clearly written with good examples and colorful, humorous illustrations that further a child's understanding of trade and money.

966 *From Idea to Toy.* Ill. by author. Carolrhoda, 1988. ISBN 0-87614-352-4. SERIES: Start to Finish. SUBJECTS: Toys—Teddy bears. RL 2.6.

From reading about the artist sketching live bears at the zoo to learning about the final "blowing in" of foam filling, children are presented with the rudiments of teddy bear creation. The simple, colorful paintings help to describe the process.

967 *From Picture to Picture Book.* Ill. by author. Carolrhoda, 1988. ISBN 0-87614-353-2. SERIES: Start to Finish. SUBJECTS: Books and reading; Publishing. RL 2.9.

One picture book is followed from an artist's idea and his interpretation of it in words and pictures through the steps leading to the book's sale in a bookstore. Simple yet colorful paintings help to explain the publishing process.

968 *From Tree to Table.* Ill. by author. Carolrhoda, 1981. ISBN 0-87614-165-3. SERIES: Start To Finish. SUBJECTS: Plants—Trees. RL 2.6.

Jolly, round-faced, and childlike characters mark, cut down, and plane trees and lumber. A carpenter constructs a table and chairs from the lumber while a forester plants new trees to complete the cycle. Very superficial information provides young readers with the basics of lumbering.

Mizumura, Kazue

969 *The Blue Whale.* Ill. by author. Crowell, 1971. ISBN 0-690-14994-8. SERIES: Let's-Read-and-Find-Out. SUBJECTS: Animals—Whales. RL 3.3.

The author compares blue whales to other animals in the way they move and develop. Information is also given on the whales' life cycle and their scarcity. Watercolor paintings sensitively illustrate the interesting text.

970 *Opossum.* Ill. by author. Crowell, 1974, o.p. SERIES: Let's-Read-and-Find-Out. SUBJECTS: Animals—Opossum. RL 2.9.

After seeing an opossum playing dead in the woods, a little boy goes home to find out everything he can about the animal. The interesting information is supported by well-done watercolor pictures in soft hues.

Moncure, Jane

971 *The Biggest Snowball*. Ill. by Joy Friedman. Childrens, 1988. ISBN 0-516-05745-6. SERIES: Magic Castle Readers. SUBJECTS: Animals—Bears—Fiction; Concepts—Size—Fiction; Weather—Snow—Fiction. RL 1.6.

In the library a little girl reads about Little Bear and her adventure with a snowball that grows from being tiny to very big. She and her friends build a snowbear and snowhouse and then watch them melt down to a tiny size. The pencil and wash paintings seem geared toward preschoolers.

972 *Butterfly Express*. Ill. by Linda Hohag. Childrens, 1988. ISBN 0-516-05746-4. SERIES: Magic Castle Readers. SUBJECTS: Animals—Butterflies and moths—Fiction. RL 1.9.

A little girl reads about another little girl's adventure—finding a caterpillar, watching it metamorphose, and finally seeing it become a butterfly. With snow on the ground, the little girl in the story's father finds a pilot to take the butterfly with him to California where it is warm. Watercolor illustrations seem geared toward preschoolers.

Monjo, F. N.

973 *Drinking Gourd*. Ill. by Fred Brenner. Harper & Row, 1970; pap., 1983. ISBN 0-06-024330-9. SERIES: I Can Read History. SUBJECTS: Historical fiction; Slavery—Fiction; Underground railroad—Fiction. RL 2.3.

Sent home from church for misbehaving, Tommy discovers a family of fugitive slaves. He becomes involved with helping his father get them to the next station on the family's journey to Canada and freedom. Realistic drawings add to the drama of the story.

974 *Indian Summer*. Ill. by Anita Lobel. Harper & Row, 1968. ISBN 0-06-024328-7. SERIES: I Can Read. SUBJECTS: Frontier and pioneer life—Fiction; Historical fiction; United States—Revolution—Fiction. RL 3.3.

With their father away fighting the British, four children and their mother have to fight off an attack by Indians. Detailed ink and wash pictures show an ingenious and brave woman and her family.

975 *The One Bad Thing about Father*. Ill. by Rocco Negri. Harper & Row, 1970; pap., 1987. ISBN 0-06-024334-1. SERIES: I Can Read. SUBJECTS: Family life—Fiction; Historical fiction; Presidents—United States—Fiction. RL 2.8.

Quentin's father, Theodore Roosevelt, could have been just about anything, but Quentin thinks that his father's being president makes life very difficult for the family. The entertaining yet informative text has detailed ink cross-hatchings with color overlays.

Montgomery, Elizabeth R.

976 *The Mystery of the Boy Next Door*. Ill. by Ethel Gold. Garrard, 1978. ISBN 0-8116-4309-3. SERIES: For Real. SUBJECTS: Friendship—Fiction; Physically and mentally impaired—Fiction. RL 2.0.

To the children the new boy on their street seems unfriendly and intent on ignoring them. They understand his behavior and renew their offers of friendship when they discover he is deaf. An attempt to further the acceptance of the impaired, this book has realistic ink and wash drawings.

Moon, Cliff

977 *Dairy Cows on the Farm*. Ill. by Anna Jupp. Bookwright, 1983, o.p. SERIES: Down on the Farm. SUBJECTS: Animals—Cows; Farm and country life. RL 2.5.

At a typical modern British dairy farm, calves are taken from cows so that milk can be used for humans. The text and full color pictures then take the reader to the milking area, where modern machinery is discussed and pictured, and finally to a local dairy where milk is bottled.

978 *Pigs on the Farm*. Ill. by Anna Jupp. Bookwright, 1983. ISBN 0-531-04696-6. SERIES: Down on the Farm. SUBJECTS: Animals—Pigs; Farm and country life. RL 2.6.

Children are introduced to pig farming in this British book. They are told in text and in full color realistic pictures how pigs are raised

Moon, Cliff (cont.)

and butchered, and how their meat is sold in markets. Throughout the book questions are occasionally asked so that children get involved in what they are reading.

979 *Poultry on the Farm.* Ill. by Bill Donohoe. Bookwright, 1983. ISBN 0-531-04697-4. SERIES: Down on the Farm. SUBJECTS: Animals—Poultry; Farm and country life. RL 2.2.

Both traditional and modern methods of raising poultry are discussed and shown in full color realistic pictures in this British book. Chickens, ducks, and turkeys are shown on farms and information is provided on hatcheries and the preparation of poultry for markets.

980 *Sheep on the Farm.* Ill. by Anna Jupp. Bookwright, 1983. ISBN 0-531-04698-2. SERIES: Down on the Farm. SUBJECTS: Animals—Sheep; Farm and country life. RL 2.7.

In this British book, sheep are shown wandering fields and hills under the protection of a shepherd and his dog. The way in which sheep are shorn and dipped as well as the products that come from their wool and meat are discussed and shown in full color realistic paintings.

Moore, Lilian

981 *Junk Day on Juniper Street and Other Easy-to-Read Stories.* Ill. by Arnold Lobel. Parents Magazine Press, 1969, o.p. SUBJECTS: Family life—Fiction; Farm and country life—Fiction. RL 2.3.

This is a collection of short stories with perfectly plausible happy endings. They are about families, neighbors, old married couples, a silly dog guarding a duckling, and a donkey who helps a boy find a silver mine. The gentle, whimsical stories have detailed and humorous ink drawings.

982 *Little Raccoon and the Outside World.* Ill. by Gioia Fiammenghi. McGraw-Hill, 1965, o.p. SUBJECTS: Animals—Fiction; Animals—Raccoons—Fiction; Behavior—Curiosity—Fiction. RL 1.7.

Little Raccoon is anxious to learn what really is in the outside world. With two little skunks

following him, he wanders away, discovers a house, and then decides that his own woodland home is preferable. This funny story has ink drawings with chartreuse accents.

983 *A Pickle for a Nickel.* Ill. by Susan Perl. Golden, 1961, o.p. SERIES: Read It Yourself. SUBJECTS: Animals—Parrots—Fiction; Humorous stories; Noise—Fiction. RL 2.2.

Mr. Bumble likes everything quiet—his house, his car, and even his parrot. While he is working, a neighbor boy talks to the parrot who, to Bumble's consternation, begins to squawk continuously. Detailed, comic illustrations in full color ink and wash add to the humor.

Mooser, Stephen

984 *Funnyman and the Penny Dodo.* Ill. by Tomie dePaola. Watts, 1984. ISBN 0-531-04393-2. SERIES: Easy-Read Story. SUBJECTS: Humorous stories; Jokes and riddles—Fiction; Mystery and detective stories. RL 3.1.

Detective Funnyman uses his jokes to find Putty Face Pete and reclaim valuable stolen stamps. Both the story and the jokes are enjoyable. Text is illustrated with humorous pencil drawings with beige and blue washes.

985 *Funnyman's First Case.* Ill. by Tomie dePaola. Watts, 1981, o.p. SERIES: Easy-Read Story. SUBJECTS: Humorous stories; Jokes and riddles—Fiction; Mystery and detective stories. RL 3.2.

Forever cracking jokes to his customers, Archie finds his job as a waiter is in jeopardy until he uses his talent to capture Big Red, a local thief. Though the jokes are old, children will enjoy them, the silly plot line, and the comical pencil drawings with pink and beige tones.

986 *The Ghost with the Halloween Hiccups.* Ill. by Tomie dePaola. Watts, 1977; Camelot, pap., 1981. ISBN 0-531-01316-2. SERIES: Easy-Read Story. SUBJECTS: Hiccups—Fiction; Holidays—Halloween—Fiction; Humorous stories. RL 3.1.

Mr. Penny's appearance in the Halloween play is a tradition that may be stopped by a bad case of hiccups. Almost scary full color pictures of Halloween creatures trying to cure him of the hiccups add to the fun.

Mooser, Stephen, and Oliver, Lin

987 *The Fat Cat.* Ill. by Susan Day. Warner, 1988. ISBN 1-55782-022-8. SERIES: Catch the Reading Bug. SUBJECTS: Animals—Cats—Fiction; Animals—Rats—Fiction; Humorous stories. RL 1.8.

Two stories, one with a fat cat and a hat and the other with a cat and a rat, rely on humorous ink and wash paintings to tell the stories. Meant as an introduction to reading alone, the texts use four sight words and ten words with "at" as their base.

988 *Tad and Dad.* Ill. by Susan Day. Warner, 1988. ISBN 1-55782-023-6. SERIES: Catch the Reading Bug. SUBJECTS: Animals—Bears—Fiction; Behavior—Fiction; Parent and child—Fiction. RL 1.4.

In two nearly wordless stories, a small bear and his father share adventures that need the ink and wash pictures to create their rather thin plots. Meant to facilitate reading for the very beginner, this book uses four sight words and eight words with "ad" as their base.

Morgan, Allen

989 *Christopher and the Elevator Closet.* Ill. by Franklin Hammond. Kids Can Press, 1981, o.p. SERIES: Kids-Can-Read. SUBJECTS: Fantasy; Weather—Rain—Fiction. RL 2.1.

On a rainy day Christopher goes into his closet and discovers elevator buttons. Pressing "up" takes him to a land of giants who grow clouds and create rain and thunder. Although the story is imaginative, the pencil drawings seem rather unskilled.

990 *Molly and Mr. Maloney.* Ill. by Maryann Kovalski. Kids Can Press, 1981, o.p. SERIES: Kids-Can-Read. SUBJECTS: Animals—Raccoons—Fiction; Fantasy; Friendship—Fiction. RL 2.1.

Molly's unexpected encounters with Mr. Maloney and his raccoon always mean excitement and adventure. She shares a giant sandwich with Mr. Maloney and is joined in a bubble bath by his very messy raccoon. This Cana-

dian book is illustrated with pencil and wash pictures.

Morley, Diana

991 *Marms in the Marmalade.* Ill. by Kathy Rogers. Carolrhoda, 1984. ISBN 0-87614-258-7. SERIES: On My Own. SUBJECTS: English language; Nonsense; Stories in rhyme. RL 3.3.

Poking fun at the illogical way that many English words are constructed, this rhyming book takes familiar words like *caterpillar* and gives logical though silly definitions for them. Children and adults will enjoy the nonsense and the attractive full color drawings.

Morris, Robert

992 *Dolphin.* Ill. by Mamoru Funai. Harper & Row, 1975; pap., 1983. ISBN 0-06-024342-2. SERIES: Science I Can Read. SUBJECTS: Animals—Dolphins; Conservation; Nature. RL 3.0.

Much can be learned about the bottle-nosed dolphin in a story of the birth and growth of a baby dolphin. Illustrated with realistic watercolor paintings, the book helps to promote a concern for nature and conservation.

993 *Seahorse.* Ill. by Arnold Lobel. Harper & Row, 1972. ISBN 0-06-024339-2. SERIES: Science I Can Read. SUBJECTS: Animals—Seahorses. RL 2.0.

A carefully worded and fascinating text with lovely, detailed pencil, ink, and wash drawings explains how seahorses live, travel, bear young, and hide from predators.

Moskin, Marietta

994 *Lysbet and the Fire Kittens.* Ill. by Margot Tomes. Coward, McCann, 1973, o.p. SERIES: Break-of-Day. SUBJECTS: Fire fighting—Fiction; Pets—Cats—Fiction; United States—Colonial period—Fiction. RL 3.3.

Left for a short time to care for the house and her cat Stuyver, who is about to have kittens, Lysbet builds a fire that accidentally sets the house ablaze while she is ice skating. After alerting her New Amsterdam neighbors, Lysbet rescues the cat and her new kittens. Ink drawings ably capture the 1662 setting.

Mueller, Virginia

995 *A Halloween Mask for Monster.* Ill. by Lynn Munsinger. Whitman, 1986. ISBN 0-8075-3134-0. SERIES: Just-for-Fun. SUBJECTS: Holidays—Halloween—Fiction; Monsters—Fiction. RL 2.7.
The little green monster tries on human and animal masks but finds them too scary. Finally he decides to go trick-or-treating as himself. The predictable repetition of phrases in the very brief story and the delightful color pictures make this just right for the beginning reader.

Muntean, Michaela

996 *The Old Man and the Afternoon Cat.* Ill. by Bari Weissman. Parents Magazine Press, 1982. ISBN 0-8193-1072-7. SERIES: Read Aloud and Easy Reading. SUBJECTS: Animals—Cats—Fiction; Old age—Fiction; Pets—Cats—Fiction. RL 2.6.
The lonely and grumpy old man looks forward to his afternoons at the park with a friendly cat. When the cat disappears, the old man begins a search that earns him friends, the cat, and a new outlook on life. This satisfying story has attractive full color illustrations.

Murdocca, Sal

997 *Take Me to the Moon!* Ill. by author. Lothrop, 1976, o.p. SERIES: Fun-to-Read. SUBJECTS: Fantasy; Kings and queens—Fiction. RL 2.3.
When the queen orders that she be taken to the moon, an astrologer, a carpenter, and a knight scramble to find a way to get her there, finally deciding on a dragon-propelled spaceship. Illustrated with humorous cartoon-type pictures in shades of blue and yellow.

998 *Tuttle's Shell.* Ill. by author. Lothrop, 1976, o.p. SERIES: Fun-to-Read. SUBJECTS: Animals—Turtles—Fiction. RL 2.4.
Louis the Rat steals Tuttle Turtle's shell while he is bathing. It takes the combined cunning of Tuttle and his friends to win it back. Comic pen and ink drawings with detailed cross-hatchings illustrate the silly but fun-to-read story.

Murphy, Jim

999 *Harold Thinks Big.* Ill. by Susanna Natti. Crown, 1980, o.p. SUBJECTS: Animals—Pigs—Fiction; Romance—Fiction; Sports—Football—Fiction. RL 1.9.
Smitten with Esther, a porcine cheerleader, Harold goes to lawyer Owl for advice. "Think big" is his suggestion and Harold does, with disastrous results. Comic line and wash illustrations complement this story of unrequited love that is sure to bring empathetic smiles to its readers.

Muschg, Hanna

1000 *Two Little Bears.* Trans. by Anthea Bell. Ill. by Kaethe Bhend-Zaugg. Bradbury, 1986. ISBN 0-02-767660-9. SUBJECTS: Animals—Bears—Fiction; Animals—Growth and development—Fiction. RL 2.3.
During the first year of their lives, two roly-poly bear cubs wrestle and play as they learn to fish, hunt for food, and hide from danger. This accurate fictionalized account of the growth of cubs is charming and has very detailed pen and ink pictures.

Myers, Bernice

1001 *Not at Home?* Ill. by author. Lothrop, 1981, o.p. SUBJECTS: Friendship—Fiction. RL 2.0.
When she arrives at Lorraine's to spend the night, the new baby-sitter tells Sally that Lorraine is not at home. Hurt, Sally rushes home vowing not to speak to Lorraine again. Later both girls discover that there was a mix-up. Illustrated with sketchy comic ink drawings.

Myrick, Mildred

1002 *Ants Are Fun.* Ill. by Arnold Lobel. Harper & Row, 1968. ISBN 0-06-024359-7. SERIES: I Can Read. SUBJECTS: Animals—Ants—Fiction; Friendship—Fiction; Moving, household—Fiction. RL 2.3.
From their treehouse observatories, two boys see a new neighbor who is their age carrying a

mysterious box. Later they learn it is an ant nest. Through the boys' curiosity, a great deal is discovered about ants. Charming pencil drawings with color washes add much to the story.

1003 *Secret Three.* Ill. by Arnold Lobel. Harper & Row, 1963; pap., 1982. ISBN 0-06-024356-2. SERIES: I Can Read. SUBJECTS: Clubs—Fiction; Codes and secret messages—Fiction; Friendship—Fiction. RL 2.4.

Finding a bottle on the beach with a secret message in it starts an exchange of coded messages and inspires the creation of the Secret Three Club. The codes, included in the detailed and attractive ink drawings with color washes, will be easily deciphered by readers.

N

Naden, Corinne

1004 *Let's Find Out about Frogs.* Ill. by Jerry Lang. Watts, 1972, o.p. SERIES: Let's Find Out About. SUBJECTS: Animals—Frogs and toads. RL 3.0.

The life cycle, physical characteristics, and general behavior of frogs are discussed in this brief, factual, and interesting book. The illustrations are carefully drawn in ink with some green accents.

Neasi, Barbara

1005 *Listen to Me.* Ill. by Gene Sharp. Childrens, hb and pap., 1986. ISBN 0-516-02072-2. SERIES: Rookie Readers. SUBJECTS: Grandparents—Fiction; Listening—Fiction. RL 2.7.

When the little boy feels neglected and not listened to, his grandma comes to the rescue. She spends time with him and carefully listens to everything the little boy says. Sketchy line drawings with full color washes help to tell this very short story.

1006 *Sweet Dreams.* Ill. by Clovis Martin. Childrens, hb and pap., 1987. ISBN 0-516-02084-6. SERIES: Rookie Readers. SUBJECTS: Dreams—Fiction; Stories in rhyme. RL 1.8.

A little girl looks forward to all the different kinds of dream stories she may encounter while sleeping. The dreams she imagines she might have and the entire text are illustrated with bright comic-style watercolor and ink pictures.

Newman, Alyse

1007 *It's Me, Claudia!* Ill. by author. Watts, 1981, o.p. SERIES: Easy-Read Story. SUBJECTS: Human body—Ears—Fiction; Self-esteem—Fiction. RL 2.1.

Thinking her large ears make her look like a mouse, Claudia tries different ways to hide them, finally settling on wearing a large hat. The hat acts as a barrier to friends and fun and Claudia finally gives it up. Ink and wash drawings show a little girl coming to terms with how she looks.

Newman, Nanette

1008 *That Dog!* Ill. by Marylin Hafner. Crowell, 1983. ISBN 0-690-04229-9. SUBJECTS: Death—Fiction; Pets—Dogs—Fiction. RL 2.3.

Ben and his dog Barnum are inseparable and when Barnum dies, Ben is sure he can never love another dog. With the support of loving family and friends, Ben finally does make room for a stray puppy. The gently humorous illustrations capture Ben and Barnum's very special relationship.

Newton, James R.

1009 *The March of the Lemmings.* Ill. by Charles Robinson. Crowell, 1976. ISBN 0-690-01085-0. SERIES: Let's-Read-and-Find-Out. SUBJECTS: Animals—Lemmings. RL 2.9.

When food and room are plentiful, the lemming population of northern Norway grows continuously until both food and room are scarce. Then many of the little animals leave their homes and head westward, toward the ocean. Good information and realistic pencil drawings make this a very useful book.

Nicklaus, Carol

1010 *Harry the Hider.* Ill. by author. Watts, 1979, o.p.; Avon, pap., 1980. ISBN 0-380-49189-3. SERIES: Easy-Read Story. SUBJECTS: Humorous stories; Pets—Cats—Fiction. RL 1.9.

Miranda thinks it is fruitless to try to enter her cat Harry in the circus—all he can do is hide. However, it is his camouflaging ability that not only wins him first prize but also intrigues the reader, who must look carefully at the ink line drawings to try to find the missing Harry.

Nixon, Hershell H., and Nixon, Joan L.

1011 *Oil and Gas: From Fossils to Fuels.* Ill. by Jean Day Zallinger. Harcourt Brace, 1977, o.p. SERIES: Let Me Read. SUBJECTS: Energy; Geology. RL 3.2.

The origins and nature of gas and oil deposits, oil exploration and recovery, uses of oil and gas, and the need for alternative energy sources are topics in this introduction to petroleum geology. The two-color illustrations are well done and sometimes more symbolic than literally accurate.

Nixon, Joan L.

1012 *Bigfoot Makes a Movie.* Ill. by Syd Hoff. Putnam, 1979, o.p.; Scholastic, pap., 1983. ISBN 0-590-32982-0. SUBJECTS: Fantasy; Humorous stories; Mythical creatures—Fiction. RL 2.6.

Young Bigfoot naively believes the film crew want to be his friends when they mistake him for an actor dressed as Bigfoot. The exaggerated cartoonlike illustrations are childlike and guarantee that the story is not taken seriously.

1013 *The Boy Who Could Find Anything.* Ill. by Syd Hoff. Harcourt Brace, 1978, o.p. SERIES: Let Me Read. SUBJECTS: Humorous stories; Lost and found possessions—Fiction. RL 2.0.

David accidentally finds one missing thing after another for his neighbors, who cannot get over how clever he is. At home he cannot seem to find anything and his mother laughs at his new reputation—the one jarring note in

the book. Illustrated with humorous, cartoonlike pictures.

1014 *Danger in Dinosaur Valley.* Ill. by Marc Simont. Putnam, 1978, o.p. SERIES: See and Read. SUBJECTS: Dinosaurs—Fiction; Science fiction; Sports—Baseball—Fiction. RL 2.5.

The climate is growing colder and the Diplodocus family must go south. Little Diplodocus, watching a baseball game on a Back Into Time tourist's television, learns to pitch rocks to help the family escape Tyrannosaurus Rex. Subject matter and humorous illustrations are sure to appeal to children.

1015 *Muffie Mouse and the Busy Birthday.* Ill. by Geoffrey Hayes. Seabury, 1978, o.p. SUBJECTS: Animals—Mice—Fiction; Birthdays—Fiction; Family life—Fiction. RL 2.6.

It is mother mouse's birthday and little Muffie decides to make it extra special. She concocts a very unusual birthday breakfast, teaches Tommy Mouse to share, and stops horrible cousin Harry from scaring her. The detailed drawings show a secure, well-loved, turn-of-the-century mouse.

1016 *The Mysterious Prowler.* Ill. by Berthe Amoss. Harcourt Brace, 1976, o.p. SERIES: Let Me Read. SUBJECTS: Behavior—Shyness—Fiction; Moving, household—Fiction; Mystery and detective stories. RL 2.2.

Spotting someone peeking in the window and later ringing his doorbell and vanishing, Jonathan decides to track down the mysterious prowler. He discovers it is his new neighbor, a boy too shy to stay and talk. The ink drawings add to the suspense created by Nixon's careful pacing.

1017 *The Thanksgiving Mystery.* Ill. by Jim Cummins. Whitman, 1980. ISBN 0-8075-7820-7. SERIES: First Read-Alone Mystery. SUBJECTS: Holidays—Thanksgiving—Fiction; Mystery and detective stories. RL 2.6.

Positive that she has seen a ghost, Susan, with Mark and Mrs. Pickett, devises a plan to trap it during their Thanksgiving holiday. This is a longer book than most readers are used to and may be just right for youngsters wanting a "long" book. Illustrated with prosaic ink and wash pictures.

1018 *The Valentine Mystery*. Ill. by Jim Cummins. Whitman, 1979. ISBN 0-8075-8450-9. SERIES: First Read-Alone Mystery. SUBJECTS: Holidays—Valentine's Day—Fiction; Mystery and detective stories. RL 2.8.
Susan's two-year-old brother's clue to the identity of the giver of her Valentine card adds to the mystery. Children reading the book will be trying to guess how to decipher the clue as well as the mystery. Illustrated with realistic ink and wash sketches.

Nobens, C. A.

1019 *The Happy Baker*. Ill. by author. Carolrhoda, 1979, o.p. SERIES: On My Own. SUBJECTS: Bakers and baking—Fiction; Food—Fiction. RL 2.4.
Having left his bakery and friends, Joseph travels the world sampling and refusing other countries' breads while relishing their soups. When he returns home, he reopens his bakery, adding soup to his menu. Illustrated with flat, humorous watercolor pictures in green and rust tones.

Norman, Gertrude

1020 *Johnny Appleseed*. Ill. by James Caraway. Putnam, 1960, o.p. SERIES: See and Read. SUBJECTS: Biographies; Legends. RL 1.8.
Although dated in format, this simple telling of the life of John Chapman, or Johnny Appleseed, is still good reading. It presents the man as nonviolent and as a friend to both settlers and Native Americans. The illustrations are realistic paintings in brown and green.

1021 *A Man Named Columbus*. Ill. by James Caraway. Putnam, 1960, o.p. SERIES: See and Read. SUBJECTS: Biographies; Explorers and exploration. RL 2.0.
A generally factual and interesting account of the life of Columbus, children will find this useful for school reports or to satisfy their curiosity about the great explorer. The illustrations are in blue and taupe and somewhat dated.

1022 *A Man Named Lincoln*. Ill. by Joseph Cellini. Putnam, 1960, o.p. SERIES: See and Read. SUBJECTS: Biographies; Presidents—United States. RL 2.0.
This is a well-written and useful book offering a simple, uncomplicated look at Lincoln's life. It includes some folklore, such as Lincoln's walking miles to return six cents, but generally remains factual. Brown-toned illustrations appear somewhat dated.

Numeroff, Laura J.

1023 *Amy for Short*. Ill. by author. Macmillan, 1976, o.p. SERIES: Ready to Read. SUBJECTS: Friendship—Fiction; Self-esteem—Fiction. RL 2.8.
Amy has no problem with being the tallest in her class but she worries that her friend Mark may not like her as much now that she is taller than he is. A good depiction of a child whose family and friends help her to accept and like herself. Illustrations are in coral and black pastels.

1024 *Beatrice Doesn't Want To*. Ill. by author. Watts, 1981, o.p. SERIES: Easy-Read Story. SUBJECTS: Books and reading—Fiction; Libraries—Fiction. RL 2.3.
Not liking books or reading, Beatrice resents her trips to the library until she hears the children's librarian read aloud. This upbeat look at nonreading children captures Beatrice's resistance to books and her reluctant capitulation. Illustrations are ink drawings and color washes.

1025 *Does Grandma Have an Elmo Elephant Jungle Kit?* Ill. by author. Greenwillow, 1980, o.p. SERIES: Read-Alone. SUBJECTS: Grandparents—Fiction. RL 2.8.
Though Donald is afraid there will be nothing to do at Grandma and Grandpa's house, the weekend is full of fun and Donald is anxious to visit again. This positive look at active, loving grandparents is well done and has appropriate, simple ink and wash drawings.

1026 *The Ugliest Sweater*. Ill. by author. Watts, 1980, o.p. SERIES: Easy-Read Story. SUBJECTS: Gifts and gift giving—Fiction. RL 2.3.

Numeroff, Laura J. (cont.)

Grandmother's intricately designed multicolored sweater seems ugly to Peter until his teacher says the student wearing red, white, and blue may bring in their special guest from France. Outlined in heavy ink with blue and red washes, the illustrations are bold and complement the story.

Nussbaum, Hedda

1027 *Animals Build Amazing Homes.* Ill. by Christopher Santoro. Random House, 1979. ISBN 0-394-83850-5. SERIES: Step-Up. SUBJECTS: Animals—Homes; Animals—Nests. RL 2.5.

The lengthy but very interesting text of this book includes looks at the nests and homes of bees, mice, the Darwin frog, the shipworm, the bubble fish, prairie dogs, and trap-door spiders. Two-color realistic pencil drawings frame the text in an attractive way.

1028 *Plants Do Amazing Things.* Ill. by Joe Mathieu. Random House, 1977. ISBN 0-394-93232-3. SERIES: Step-Up. SUBJECTS: Plants. RL 2.3.

In brief, entertaining, and informative chapters, many unusual plants and plant characteristics are described, including lichens, flytraps, cacti, and examples of symbiosis. The two-color illustrations are cartoonlike but appear to depict natural objects accurately.

O

O'Connor, Jane

1029 *Lulu and the Witch Baby.* Ill. by Emily A. McCully. Harper & Row, 1986. ISBN 0-06-024627-8. SERIES: I Can Read. SUBJECTS: Sibling rivalry—Fiction; Witches—Fiction. RL 3.2.

Witch Baby seems to get all the attention and Lulu Witch would like nothing better than for Baby to disappear. When Mama Witch flies off to the market, Lulu concocts a spell to do just that. Pencil and wash pictures show pointy-eared and disheveled but not menacing witches.

1030 *Lulu Goes to Witch School.* Ill. by Emily A. McCully. Harper & Row, 1987. ISBN 0-06-024629-4. SERIES: I Can Read. SUBJECTS: School stories; Witches—Fiction. RL 3.4.

Though Lulu Witch tries to be good-natured and friendly, Sandy Witch's meanness and constant besting of everyone annoy her. Lulu finally gets the best of Sandy. Fans of witch stories will enjoy Lulu's story and the full color humorous drawings accompanying it.

1031 *Sir Small and the Dragonfly.* Ill. by John O'Brien. Random House, 1988. ISBN 0-394-89625-4. SERIES: Step into Reading. SUBJECTS: Concepts—Size—Fiction; Fantasy; Knights and knighthood—Fiction. RL 2.1.

Smaller even than the very small people of Pee Wee, Sir Small is the only one brave enough to try to rescue Lady Teena from the dragonfly's cave. The fanciful color pictures have sketchy ink detailing and a need for more differentiation among the characters' faces.

1032 *The Teeny Tiny Woman.* Ill. by R. W. Alley. Random House, hb and pap., 1986. ISBN 0-394-98320-3. SERIES: Step into Reading. SUBJECTS: Folklore—England; Ghost stories. RL 2.3.

A well-known folktale frequently told to children, this version does not maintain the suspense as well as others. Its pacing is often awkward and the full color pictures are a little too "cute." Still, many young readers, having heard the story, will want to read this on their own.

Oda, Hidetomo

1033 *Insect Hibernation.* Trans. by Jun Amano. Ill. by Hidekazu Kubo. Raintree, hb and pap., 1986. ISBN 0-8172-2551-X. SERIES: Nature Close-Ups. SUBJECTS: Animals—Hibernation. RL 3.5.

A clear text and excellent color photos follow a variety of insects from fall to winter, when they hibernate hidden away in trees and earth, to spring when they emerge again. Detailed captions significantly supplement the text, which was originally published in Japan.

Oechsli, Kelly

1034 *Mice at Bat.* Ill. by author. Harper &
Row, 1986. ISBN 0-06-024624-3. SERIES:
I Can Read. SUBJECTS: Animals—
Mice—Fiction; Sports—Baseball—
Fiction. RL 2.9.

After the human crowd leaves the stadium,
two teams of mice, the Mighty Mites and the
Boomers, have an action-packed game of
their own. Multiethnic names and a knowledge of the sport provide broad appeal. Illustrations are ink drawings with orange- and
blue-toned washes.

Older, Jules

1035 *Don't Panic: A Book about Handling
Emergencies.* Ill. by J. Ellen Dolce.
Golden, 1986. SERIES: Learn about
Living. SUBJECTS: Emergencies; Safety.
RL 2.1.

A bee sting, a broken jar, burned fingers, a
nosebleed, and trying the high slide for the
first time all present problems for which
"Don't Panic!" is the first step to finding a
solution. The rather "preachy" text has full
color drawings of cute children at home,
school, and play.

Olson, Mary C., ed.

1036 *Big Ride for Little Bear.* Ill. by Joan Allen.
Golden, pap., 1987. ISBN 0-307-03679-0.
SERIES: Step Ahead Beginning Reader.
SUBJECTS: Animals—Bears—Fiction;
Sports—Sledding—Fiction. RL 1.4.

Little Bear has a new sled and only one
chance to use it before his "big nap." He and
his animal friends have one glorious ride
before Little Bear heads for his warm bed and
his long sleep. The watercolor pictures of
bundled-up animals seem more appropriate
to preschoolers than older children.

1037 *Elephant on Skates.* Ill. by Jerry Scott.
Golden, pap., 1987. ISBN 0-307-03676-6.
SERIES: Step Ahead Beginning Reader.
SUBJECTS: Animals—Elephants—
Fiction; Self-esteem—Fiction; Sports—
Roller Skating—Fiction. RL 2.0.

Everyone in her family tries to convince Edna
that elephants do not belong on roller skates.

Undaunted, she finally manages to get her
family to try roller skating too. The story is
fun as are the full color comic drawings of the
elephant family.

1038 *Fly, Max, Fly!* Ill. by Donald Leake.
Golden, 1976, o.p.; pap., 1987. ISBN 0-
307-03677-4. SERIES: Step Ahead
Beginning Reader. SUBJECTS:
Circuses—Fiction; Pets—Dogs—
Fiction. RL 1.5.

All the human members of the family are
trapeze artists and Max, their dog, longs to be
up flying with them. With the help of a clown,
the children of the family train Max to be a
part of their troupe. Children will enjoy the
story and the boldly colored pictures, each
with borders and stars.

1039 *The Magic Friend Maker.* Ill. by Renee
Graef. Golden, 1976; pap., 1987. ISBN
0-307-03682-0. SERIES: Step Ahead
Beginning Reader. SUBJECTS:
Friendship—Fiction. RL 1.6.

Kate meets Jill and becomes her friend after
admiring her beautiful rock. Jill and Kate
both think it is the magic of the rock that
made them friends. Somewhat superficial,
the story is illustrated with full color pictures. Difficult nouns are printed along with
rebus silhouettes of them.

1040 *Race Down the Mountain.* Ill. by
Giannini. Golden, 1976; pap., 1987.
ISBN 0-307-03675-8. SERIES: Step Ahead
Beginning Reader. SUBJECTS: Trains—
Fiction. RL 2.0.

As the little train travels down the mountain,
animals try to warn it that it has lost its
caboose. The train misunderstands them,
thinking they are urging it to race faster. Soft
full color watercolor paintings give a clear
view of the train and animals in this very
slight story.

1041 *This Room Is Mine!* Ill. by Gwen
Connelly. Golden, 1976, o.p.; pap.,
1987. ISBN 0-307-03681-2. SERIES: Step
Ahead Beginning Reader. SUBJECTS:
Sibling rivalry—Fiction. RL 1.6.

Mad at his older brother Bob, Dan decides to
divide their room in half, not realizing that
the door is on Bob's side. Bob ends the
dispute by including his little brother in a

Olson, Mary C., ed. (cont.)

ball game. The familiar family situation is illustrated with realistic full color pencil and wash drawings.

Oneal, Zibby

1042 *Maude and Walter.* Ill. by Maxie Chambliss. Lippincott, 1985. ISBN 0-397-32151-1. SUBJECTS: Siblings—Fiction. RL 1.8.

Walter is often too ready to tell his little sister Maude to go away. Maude is clever enough to get him to realize her importance as she helps him out in some situations and makes him jealous in others. Watercolor illustrations present Maude and Walter as rather ordinary children.

Orgel, Doris

1043 *Cindy's Snowdrops.* Ill. by Ati Forberg. Knopf, 1966, o.p. SUBJECTS: Gardening—Fiction; Plants—Flowers—Fiction; Plants—Seeds, roots and bulbs—Fiction. RL 2.5.

Cindy decides to plant snowdrop bulbs and carefully plans where to put them, hoping they will bloom in time for her March birthday. Impressionistic watercolor and ink pictures with blotted blackgrounds carry out the dreamy, expectant feeling of the story.

Orlowsky, Wallace, and Perera, Thomas B.

1044 *Who Will Wash the River?* Ill. by Richard Cuffari. Coward, McCann, 1970, o.p. SERIES: Science Is What and Why. SUBJECTS: Conservation; Pollution—Water. RL 3.0.

Since the last time Tommy and Sue visited the river, it has become terribly polluted with sewage and rubbish. The two then learn about the importance of water treatment plants in halting pollution. Though published a while ago this book is still valid. It is well written and has good realistic ink and wash drawings.

Osborne, Mary P.

1045 *Mo and His Friends.* Ill. by DyAnne DiSalvo-Ryan. Dial, 1989. ISBN 0-8037-

0504-2. SERIES: Easy-to-Read. SUBJECTS: Animals—Fiction; Friendship—Fiction. RL 2.1.

In four quiet stories set in the different seasons, the value and fun of friendship is seen through Sheriff Mo (a beaver), Peewee and Pearl (mice), Chicken Lucille, and the other Smith Pond characters. The pictures are in watercolor and pencil and reflect the gentle nature of the stories.

1046 *Mo to the Rescue.* Ill. by DyAnne DiSalvo-Ryan. Dial, 1985; pap., 1987. ISBN 0-8037-0182-9. SERIES: Easy-to-Read. SUBJECTS: Animals—Fiction; Friendship—Fiction; Sheriffs—Fiction. RL 2.0.

Kind-hearted sheriff Mo Beaver welcomes newcomers, cleverly breaks up fighting blue jays, sees monsters in the shadows, and finally gets away to just sit and read a book. The gentle, "folksy" story is illustrated with full color pencil sketches with watercolor washes.

Osinski, Alice

1047 *The Chippewa.* Photos. Childrens, hb and pap., 1987. ISBN 0-516-01230-4. SERIES: New True. SUBJECTS: Native Americans—Chippewas. RL 3.3.

Information about the Chippewa—history, hunting, farming, religious traditions, life today, and the effects of treaties on them—is provided in this brief book. There are good full color photographs as well as reproductions of historical prints accompanying the interesting text.

1048 *The Nez Perce.* Photos. Childrens, 1988. ISBN 0-516-01154-5. SERIES: New True. SUBJECTS: Native Americans—Nez Perce. RL 3.1.

The history of the Nez Perce whose unsuccessful flight to Canada is one of the tragic stories of the American West is flawed by its rather difficult language and its lack of clarity. However, the book does provide some good information about these Native Americans as well as attractive color photographs.

Overbeck, Cynthia

1049 *The Vegetable Book.* Ill. by Sharon Lerner. Lerner, 1975. ISBN 0-8225-0297-

6. SERIES: Early Nature Picture Book. SUBJECTS: Gardening; Vegetables. RL 2.8.

In a tour of a vegetable garden, this book comments on a dozen common edibles: how they are grown and used as food. The brightly colored illustrations are semirealistic.

P

Palmer, Helen M.

1050 *A Fish Out of Water*. Ill. by P. D. Eastman. Beginner, 1961. ISBN 0-394-90023-5. SERIES: I Can Read It All By Myself. SUBJECTS: Animals—Fish—Fiction; Humorous stories; Pets—Fish—Fiction. RL 1.9.

A little boy is warned that he must feed his new goldfish, Otto, no more than a spot of food, but he still feeds him the entire box. Otto grows and grows until the pet store owner, Mr. Carp, must use his magic to return him to goldfish size. Never having waned in popularity, this book remains a delight with its humorous yet simple drawings.

Papajani, Janet

1051 *Museums*. Photos. Childrens, 1983. ISBN 0-516-01682-2. SERIES: New True. SUBJECTS: Museums. RL 3.6.

From a discussion of the things Alexander the Great collected to a look at the Baseball Hall of Fame, museums of all kinds are mentioned. Young people are encouraged to visit and explore a variety of museums and the good color photographs of exhibits are an extra enticement to reading and visiting.

Pape, Donna L.

1052 *The Big White Thing*. Ill. by Bill Morrison. Garrard, 1975. ISBN 0-8116-6066-4. SERIES: Easy Venture. SUBJECTS: Animals—Raccoons—Fiction; Humorous stories. RL 1.5.

Not until a rainstorm fills it with water do the raccoons realize what the big white bathtub might be. Then they jump right in,

swimming and bathing. The pictures are a bit sweet but their comic portrayal of the woodland animals is appealingly done in colored pencil and wash.

1053 *The Book of Foolish Machinery*. Ill. by Fred Winkowski. Scholastic, 1988. ISBN 0-590-40907-7. SUBJECTS: Nonsense; Poetry. RL 2.9.

Nearly tongue twisters with their contortions of familiar words and with their silly rhymes, these poems about nonsensical machines and how they work are ideal for reading aloud by a confident young reader. The humorous, colorful illustrations are of complex machines.

1054 *Count on Leo Lion*. Ill. by Tom Eaton. Garrard, 1973, o.p. SERIES: Venture. SUBJECTS: Animals, zoo—Fiction; Concepts—Numbers—Fiction; Humorous stories. RL 1.5.

Asleep in his zoo cage, Leo Lion is awakened by two monkeys squabbling over how they should divide the peanuts they have. Deciding that they need to learn to count, Leo tries all kinds of ways to teach the monkeys their numbers. Illustrated with colorful and amusing drawings.

1055 *A Gerbil for a Friend*. Ill. by Diane Martin. Prentice-Hall, 1973, o.p. SUBJECTS: Pets—Gerbils. RL 2.3.

Mark already has a cage waiting for the little gerbil when she is finally old enough for him to take home. By following Mark's example, children will be able to provide a good home for a pet gerbil. Illustrated with expressive ink drawings.

1056 *Leo Lion Looks for Books*. Ill. by Tom Eaton. Garrard, 1972. ISBN 0-8116-6956-4. SERIES: Venture. SUBJECTS: Animals—Lions—Fiction; Books and reading—Fiction; Humorous stories. RL 2.0.

Leo likes reading but there is not much to read in the zoo. He leaves his cage and wanders through town, discovers a bookstore, and ends up in the library. When the zookeeper comes for him, Leo does not want to leave the books. Full color cartoon pictures show a dramatic lion who loves books.

Pape, Donna L. (cont.)

1057 *Mr. Mogg in the Log.* Ill. by Mimi
Korach. Garrard, 1972. ISBN 0-8116-
6961-0. SERIES: Venture. SUBJECTS:
Humorous stories. RL 2.3.
Trying to retrieve a quarter he has dropped,
Mr. Mogg gets stuck in a log. Mrs. Mogg and
their friend Mr. Jones try pulling him loose,
having a helicopter shake him free, and more
until they finally find a simple but sloppy
solution. Illustrated with colorful, sketchy
marker drawings.

1058 *Mrs. Twitter the Animal Sitter.* Ill. by
Dora Leder. Garrard, 1972. ISBN 0-
8116-6960-2. SERIES: Venture. SUBJECTS:
Animals—Fiction; Business
enterprises—Fiction; Pet care—Fiction.
RL 2.0.
Mrs. Twitter answers an ad for a sitter and
ends up taking care of a horse. She does
everything wrong until a child helps her.
Next she takes care of a seal and teaches it to
balance a ball on its nose. The very silly story
has realistic yet comical illustrations.

1059 *The Sleep-Leaping Kangaroo.* Ill. by
Tom Eaton. Garrard, hb and pap.,
1973. ISBN 0-8116-6723-5. SERIES:
Venture. SUBJECTS: Animals—
Kangaroos—Fiction; Sleep—Fiction.
RL 1.6.
Poor Kara Kangaroo sleep-leaps and ends up
in unusual places. She tries to stop the leaping
by wearing socks, putting a bell around her
neck, and even tying her tail to a tree. Finally
she does find a solution. This is a silly story
with colorful but rather pedestrian pictures.

1060 *Snowman for Sale.* Ill. by Raymond
Burns. Garrard, 1977. ISBN 0-8116-
4304-2. SERIES: For Real. SUBJECTS:
Birthdays—Fiction; Siblings—Fiction;
Weather—Snow—Fiction. RL 1.8.
To get enough money to buy mother a birthday present, Terry and Jerry build a huge
snowman to sell. Not allowed to help them,
their younger brother Todd makes little snow-
men, which sell while the big one does not.
The watercolor illustrations for this story are
rather bland.

1061 *Where Is My Little Joey?* Ill. by Tom
Eaton. Garrard, 1978. ISBN 0-8116-

4411-1. SERIES: Imagination. SUBJECTS:
Animals—Kangaroos—Fiction;
Humorous stories. RL 1.6.
After napping in a park, poor Kara Kangaroo
notices her little joey is gone. She searches
everywhere for him but is hampered by having her pouch used for all kinds of things
whenever she stops. The humorous story has
colorful, cartoonlike pictures.

Parish, Peggy

1062 *Amelia Bedelia.* Ill. by Fritz Siebel. Harper & Row, 1963; pap., 1983. ISBN 0-
06-024641-3. SUBJECTS: Humorous
stories. RL 2.1.
Amelia Bedelia is hired by the Rogers family
and left with a list of chores. Following their
instructions exactly, she "dusts" the furniture
with dusting powder, "dresses" the chicken in
clothes—and more! A perennial favorite, this
book is illustrated with delightful ink and
wash drawings.

1063 *Amelia Bedelia and the Baby.* Ill. by
Lynn Sweat. Greenwillow, 1981; Avon,
pap., 1982. ISBN 0-688-00316-8. SERIES:
Read-alone. SUBJECTS: Baby-sitting—
Fiction; Humorous stories. RL 2.0.
Mrs. Rogers insists that Amelia Bedelia take
care of the neighbor's baby. The child's
mother leaves detailed instructions for Amelia Bedelia to follow and to the baby's delight,
she follows them exactly. The ink and wash
pictures add to the fun.

1064 *Amelia Bedelia and the Surprise Shower.*
Ill. by Fritz Siebel. Harper & Row,
1966; pap., 1979. ISBN 0-06-024643-X.
SERIES: I Can Read. SUBJECTS:
Humorous stories. RL 2.1.
Not familiar with "showers," Amelia Bedelia
assumes she is to spray the bride-to-be with
water. In a story filled with her literal and
very funny interpretations of instructions,
Amelia Bedelia's antics will keep children
laughing. The book has humorous ink and
wash sketches.

1065 *Amelia Bedelia Goes Camping.* Ill. by
Lynn Sweat. Greenwillow, 1985; Avon,
pap., 1986. ISBN 0-688-04058-6. SERIES:
Read-alone. SUBJECTS: Camps and

camping—Fiction; Humorous stories. RL 1.9.

When Mr. Rogers says to hit the road, of course Amelia Bedelia takes a stick and hits the road. After creating her usual havoc on their camping trip, Amelia Bedelia again redeems herself with her cooking. This book is illustrated with spare ink drawings and washes.

1066 *Amelia Bedelia Helps Out*. Ill. by Lynn Sweat. Greenwillow, 1979; Avon, pap., 1982. ISBN 0-688-84231-3. SERIES: Read-alone. SUBJECTS: Humorous stories. RL 2.1.

When Miss Emma's gardener is ill, Amelia Bedelia and her niece offer to help. They create the usual problems because of Amelia Bedelia's literal interpretation of orders. Adding to the hilarity are the ink and wash pictures.

1067 *Amelia Bedelia's Family Album*. Ill. by Lynn Sweat. Greenwillow, 1988. ISBN 0-688-07677-7. SUBJECTS: Families—Fiction; Humorous stories. RL 2.5.

Mr. and Mrs. Rogers decide to have a party for their silly maid Amelia Bedelia and want to invite her family. When she shows them her family album, the Rogerses realize that her family is as unusual as Amelia Bedelia. A new format and full color pictures are used for this twenty-fifth anniversary book.

1068 *Be Ready at Eight*. Ill. by Leonard Kessler. Macmillan, 1979, o.p.; pap., 1987. ISBN 0-689-71163-8. SERIES: Ready-to-Read. SUBJECTS: Birthdays—Fiction; Memory and memorization—Fiction. RL 2.2.

Miss Molly cannot remember why she has a string tied around her finger although everybody in town is reminding her that they will see her at eight. Her forgetfulness turns her birthday party into a surprise. Simple line drawings with orange and green accents add to the fun.

1069 *The Cats' Burglar*. Ill. by Lynn Sweat. Greenwillow, 1983; Dell, pap., 1988. ISBN 0-688-01826-2. SERIES: Read-alone. SUBJECTS: Pets—Cats—Fiction; Robbers and outlaws—Fiction. RL 1.9.

Aunt Emma refuses to give up any of her nine cats. When a burglar breaks in, the cats gang up on the very allergic man. The independent Aunt Emma and the police know how lucky she is not to be hurt while the humorous drawings and antics of the cats keep the tone light.

1070 *Come Back, Amelia Bedelia*. Ill. by Wallace Tripp. Harper & Row, 1971; pap., 1978. ISBN 0-06-024688-5. SERIES: I Can Read. SUBJECTS: Humorous stories. RL 2.1.

After being fired by Mrs. Rogers for her latest literal interpretation of instructions, Amelia Bedelia starts looking for work with predictable and often hilarious results. The ink and wash drawings give Amelia Bedelia an innocence that adds to the story's humor and success.

1071 *Dinosaur Time*. Ill. by Arnold Lobel. Harper & Row, 1974; pap., 1983. ISBN 0-06-024654-5. SERIES: Early I Can Read. SUBJECTS: Dinosaurs. RL 2.1.

Eleven dinosaurs are introduced, giving the pronunciation of their names and facts about their size and life-style. The never waning popularity of dinosaurs and the attractive detailed drawings and brief text have made this a continual favorite.

1072 *Good Hunting, Blue Sky*. Rev. ed. Ill. by James Watts. Harper & Row, 1988. ISBN 0-06-024661-8. SERIES: I Can Read. SUBJECTS: Hunting—Fiction; Native Americans—Fiction. RL 2.4.

In a good revision of *Good Hunting, Little Indian* (Harper & Row, 1962), Blue Sky goes out hunting with bow and arrow and misses everything he aims for. Walking home he is chased by a boar and ends up riding it into his village, where his father kills it. This book is illustrated with attractive full color drawings.

1073 *Good Work, Amelia Bedelia*. Ill. by Lynn Sweat. Greenwillow, 1976; Avon, pap., 1982. ISBN 0-688-84022-1. SERIES: Read-alone. SUBJECTS: Humorous stories. RL 2.3.

Amelia Bedelia's well-known literal approach to following instructions gets her in more trouble as she patches a screen with cloth, serves cracked corn as a chicken dinner, and puts pieces of sponge in batter for a sponge cake. Ink and colored pencil drawings add to the humor.

Parish, Peggy (cont.)

1074 *Granny and the Desperadoes.* Ill. by
Steven Kellogg. Macmillan, 1970, o.p.
SUBJECTS: Humorous stories; Robbers
and outlaws—Fiction; Western stories.
RL 2.3.
The threat of Granny's shotgun, which does
not work, is the reason the robbers are helping Granny repair her house and capture
ducks. Kellogg's hilarious pencil sketches
guarantee fun.

1075 *Merry Christmas, Amelia Bedelia.* Ill. by
Lynn Sweat. Greenwillow, 1986; Avon,
pap., 1987. ISBN 0-688-06102-8. SERIES:
Read-alone. SUBJECTS: Holidays—
Christmas—Fiction; Humorous stories.
RL 2.4.
When Mrs. Rogers leaves to pick up Aunt
Myra, who is spending Christmas with the
Rogers family, Amelia Bedelia is left with a
list of instructions for trimming the tree, stuff-
ing stockings, and more, all of which she inter-
prets literally and humorously. Ink and wash
sketches support the zaniness of the story.

1076 *Mind Your Manners.* Ill. by Marylin
Hafner. Greenwillow, 1978. ISBN 0-688-
84157-0. SERIES: Read-alone. SUBJECTS:
Behavior—Manners. RL 2.3.
A humorous, light-handed approach to manners gives children the appropriate behavior
for 18 situations—from meeting new people to
chewing gum. The ink and wash illustrations
reinforce the importance of good manners.

1077 *Mr. Adams's Mistake.* Ill. by Gail
Owens. Macmillan, 1982. ISBN 0-02-
769800-9. SERIES: Ready-to-Read.
SUBJECTS: Animals—Chimpanzees—
Fiction; Humorous stories; School
stories. RL 2.1.
Mr. Adams, a nearsighted truant officer, mistakes a chimpanzee for a child and hurries it
off to school with riotous results. Realistic
full color drawings add to the humor in the
story.

1078 *No More Monsters for Me!* Ill. by Marc
Simont. Harper & Row, 1981; pap.,
1987. ISBN 0-06-024658-8. SERIES: I Can
Read. SUBJECTS: Monsters—Fiction;
Parent and child—Fiction; Pets—
Fiction. RL 2.5.
After arguing with her mother about having a
pet, Minn finds a gentle baby monster and
hides it in the basement. While there, it starts
to grow at an alarming rate. In the end, it is
taken back to its home and replaced by a more
ordinary pet. Humorous ink and wash pictures show a huge but still lovable monster.

1079 *Ootah's Lucky Day.* Ill. by Mamoru
Funai. Harper & Row, 1970. ISBN 0-06-
024645-6. SERIES: I Can Read. SUBJECTS:
Hunting—Fiction; Native Americans—
Eskimos—Fiction. RL 1.9.
With nothing to eat and no oil for a fire, little
Ootah, an Eskimo boy, takes his dogs and
goes hunting alone. Using all his training and
courage, Ootah surprises everyone by killing
a walrus, thus providing meat for all the
people in his village. Simple, realistic drawings illustrate the book.

1080 *Play Ball, Amelia Bedelia.* Ill. by
Wallace Tripp. Harper & Row, 1972;
pap., 1978. ISBN 0-06-024656-1. SERIES:
I Can Read. SUBJECTS: Humorous
stories. RL 2.5.
When the Grizzlies are short one player in
their game with the Tornadoes, Amelia
Bedelia volunteers to help out. Putting paper
tags on players, stealing bases, and carrying
boys "out" are typical of the good-natured
misunderstandings depicted in the ink and
wash line drawings.

1081 *Scruffy.* Ill. by Kelly Oechsli. Harper &
Row, 1988. ISBN 0-06-024660-X. SERIES:
I Can Read. SUBJECTS: Animal
shelters—Fiction; Birthdays—Fiction;
Pets—Cats—Fiction. RL 2.3.
For his birthday Todd gets a trip to the
animal shelter to pick out a kitten. While
there Todd chooses an older cat—Scruffy.
Information on shelters and responsible pet
ownership is provided. The sketchy ink and
wash pictures capture the concern and fun in
looking for a pet.

1082 *Teach Us, Amelia Bedelia.* Ill. by Lynn
Sweat. Greenwillow, 1977; Scholastic,
pap., 1987. ISBN 0-688-84069-8. SERIES:
Read-alone. SUBJECTS: Humorous
stories; School stories. RL 2.1.
Taking a message to the principal, Amelia
Bedelia is mistaken for the new teacher and

hurried into a classroom. She diligently follows a list of instructions, concocting her own hilarious way of teaching. Illustrated with funny ink, colored pencil, and wash pictures.

1083 *Too Many Rabbits*. Ill. by Leonard Kessler. MacMillan, 1974, o.p. SERIES: Ready-to-Read. SUBJECTS: Animals—Rabbits—Fiction; Pets—Rabbits—Fiction. RL 1.9.
When the rabbit she takes in has a litter, Miss Molly decides to keep them all until they start multiplying. Humorous line drawings and a simple text tell the story of a kindhearted woman who just cannot say no to stray animals.

1084 *Zed and the Monsters*. Ill. by Paul Galdone. Doubleday, 1979, o.p. SERIES: Reading On My Own. SUBJECTS: Monsters—Fiction; Tall tales. RL 2.2.
An offer of gold entices lazy Zed to match wits with and overcome four monsters. Humorous and good for storytelling, the story is illustrated with outlandishly funny ink and wash pictures.

Park, W. B.

1085 *The Costume Party*. Ill. by author. Little, Brown, 1983. ISBN 0-316-69077-5. SUBJECTS: Costumes—Fiction; Humorous stories; Parties—Fiction. RL 2.2.
All of her friends are annoyed at the antics of the rude stranger in the bear costume, so Shirley Cat takes charge, getting him to behave so that everyone can have fun. A good lesson in party behavior and a funny story, this has pencil sketches with fuchsia accents.

Parker, Philip

1086 *The Life Cycle of a Stickleback*. Ill. by Jackie Harland. Bookwright, 1988. ISBN 0-531-18190-1. SERIES: Life Cycles. SUBJECTS: Animals—Fish. RL 2.3.
Sticklebacks are notable in that they lay eggs in a nest and then the male guards the nest and looks after the hatchlings. The tiny three spined freshwater stickleback is seen in its habitat as readers learn about its breeding and diet. Full color paintings accurately depict the excellent text.

1087 *The Life Cycle of a Sunflower*. Ill. by Jackie Harland. Bookwright, 1988. ISBN 0-531-18191-X. SERIES: Life Cycles. SUBJECTS: Plants—Flowers. RL 2.2.
Using clear, carefully executed paintings that work very well with an excellent text, this book presents a good description of the growth of a sunflower from seed to maturity. Attention is also paid to clear instructions for growing a sunflower. A glossary, bibliography, and index are included.

Patent, Dorothy H.

1088 *All about Whales*. Photos. Holiday House, 1987. ISBN 0-8234-0644-X. SUBJECTS: Animals—Whales; Conservation. RL 2.7.
This book characterizes whales as mammals belonging to two groups (baleen and toothed) and discusses their growth, feeding, senses, and communication, and the efforts of humans to save them from extinction. An index is included. Black and white photos accompany an extensive text.

Patrick, Gloria

1089 *This Is*. Ill. by Joan Hanson. Carolrhoda, 1970. ISBN 0-87614-003-7. SUBJECTS: Stories in rhyme. RL 2.1.
Not so much a story as a collection of very brief rhyming phrases that accumulate into several short unrelated rhyming verses, the book is popular with many children just starting to read. The simple block print illustrations show a mouse, a house, and a boy.

Patterson, Lillie.

1090 *Haunted Houses on Halloween*. Ill. by Doug Cushman. Garrard, 1979. ISBN 0-8116-7253-0. SERIES: First Holiday. SUBJECTS: Folklore; Ghost stories; Holidays—Halloween—Fiction. RL 2.1.
The first of two stories of ghostly hauntings has a penniless youth bravely facing a skeletal apparition and earning a treasure. The second story has a hunter outwitting a dangerous witch. The ink and watercolor pictures reflect the plot, which is sure to attract young readers.

Payne, Elizabeth

1091 *Meet the North American Indians.* Ill. by Jack Davis. Random House, 1965. ISBN 0-394-90060-X. SERIES: Step-Up. SUBJECTS: Native Americans. RL 2.4.
Presented are five Native American tribes (Makah, Hopi, Creek, Penobscot, and Mandan) from different areas of the United States. There is discussion of each tribe's social life, rituals, and hunting and fishing before the time of Columbus. Realistic color illustrations are used.

1092 *Meet the Pilgrim Fathers.* Ill. by H. B. Vestal. Random House, 1966. ISBN 0-394-90063-4. SERIES: Step-Up. SUBJECTS: Holidays—Thanksgiving; Pilgrims; United States—Colonial period. RL 2.5.
The story of the Pilgrims begins when they flee to Holland for religious freedom. The detailed and interesting narrative follows the Pilgrims to America and through their first very difficult years in Plymouth and, of course, the thanksgiving celebration. This book is illustrated with textbooklike drawings.

Pearson, Susan

1093 *Molly Moves Out.* Ill. by Steven Kellogg. Dial, 1979. ISBN 0-8037-5802-2. SERIES: Easy-to-Read. SUBJECTS: Animals—Rabbits—Fiction; Friendship—Fiction; Siblings—Fiction. RL 2.3.
Tired of her little siblings taking her things and of their constant noise, Molly moves to her own house. There she makes a new friend and appreciates her family as visitors. The story and ebullient line drawings capture the chaos and love of this large and noisy rabbit family.

1094 *Monday I Was an Alligator.* Ill. by Sal Murdocca. Lippincott, 1979. ISBN 0-397-31830-8. SERIES: I-Like-To-Read. SUBJECTS: Humorous stories; Imagination—Fiction. RL 3.0.
Each day of the week a little girl imagines that she is a different animal terrorizing someone in her family. When she finally decides to be herself, everyone is relieved. Humorous ink sketches with some color capture the fun.

Penney, Richard L.

1095 *Penguins Are Coming!* Ill. by Tom Eaton. Harper & Row, 1969. ISBN 0-06-024693-6. SERIES: Science I Can Read. SUBJECTS: Animals—Penguins. RL 2.1.
A fascinating eyewitness account of life among the Adelie penguins in Antarctica is given. The book should be useful and interesting to children of all ages—not just beginning readers. It is illustrated with bold and lively ink drawings.

Perera, Thomas B., and Orlowsky, Wallace

1096 *Who Will Clean the Air?* Ill. by Richard Cuffari. Coward, McCann, 1971, o.p. SERIES: Science Is What and Why. SUBJECTS: Pollution—Air. RL 2.7.
Traveling home in their uncle's plane, Tony and Nan notice how dark the air is over their city. When their uncle explains some of the causes of air pollution, the two children try to work out ways to measure it, learning even more. Illustrated with simple, realistic ink and wash drawings.

Perkins, Al

1097 *The Ear Book.* Ill. by William O'Brien. Random House, 1968. ISBN 0-394-91199-7. SERIES: Bright and Early. SUBJECTS: Human body—Ears—Fiction; Stories in rhyme. RL 2.5.
A short, rhythmic text leads children not only to consider the many ways and things that ears hear but also offers children a chance for a successful beginning reading experience. Full color comic paintings of people and things are arranged on a white background.

1098 *Hand, Hand, Fingers, Thumb.* Ill. by Eric Gurney. Random House, 1969. ISBN 0-394-91076-1. SERIES: Bright and Early. SUBJECTS: Animals—Monkeys—Fiction; Stories in rhyme. RL 3.2.
A rhyming text introduces the reader to one monkey drumming, then more and more monkeys using their hands in a variety of ways. Finally millions of monkeys are drumming in this catchy nonstory that both readers and listeners enjoy. Illustrated with detailed line drawings and washes.

1099 *The Nose Book.* Ill. by Roy McKie. Random House, 1970. ISBN 0-394-90623-3. SERIES: Bright and Early. SUBJECTS: Human body—Nose—Fiction; Stories in rhyme. RL 1.9.

A brown dog explores the great variety of noses among animals and humans and notes the things noses are used for, such as holding up glasses and smelling food. The lively, rhyming text is matched to bright, bold paintings with black outlinings.

1100 *Tubby and the Lantern.* Ill. by Rowland Wilson. Beginner, 1971, o.p. SERIES: I Can Read It All By Myself. SUBJECTS: Adventure stories; Animals—Elephants—Fiction. RL 2.5.

Ah Mee, the son of a lantern maker, has Tubby, a small elephant, as his very special pet and friend. The two are lifted away by a huge lantern and carried out to sea and they have a great adventure. Illustrated with lively full color pictures.

Peters, Sharon

1101 *Animals at Night.* Ill. by Paul Harvey. Troll, 1983. ISBN 0-89375-903-1. SERIES: Now I Know. SUBJECTS: Animals—Nocturnal—Fiction. RL 2.0.

After being put to bed, the little bear looks out his window and wonders who is there. Very brief sentences and very simple, stylized paintings show a variety of nighttime animals hunting for food, calling to each other, or building new homes.

1102 *The Goofy Ghost.* Ill. by Tom Garcia. Troll, 1981. ISBN 0-89375-533-8. SERIES: Giant First-Start. SUBJECTS: Ghost stories; Haunted houses—Fiction. RL 2.2

A family of rather innocuous ghosts haunts a large old house. All the family members are competent ghosts except for the youngest, who is a klutz. When a mean old ghost tries to move in on the family, the bumbling little ghost scares him away. Illustrated with non-threatening pastel paintings.

1103 *Here Comes Jack Frost.* Ill. by Eulala Connor. Troll, hb and pap., 1981. ISBN 0-89375-513-3. SERIES: Giant First-Start. SUBJECTS: Fantasy; Seasons—Winter—Fiction. RL 1.7.

A short text with a very limited vocabulary works with rather sweet, colorful paintings to describe and illustrate an elflike Jack Frost painting winter windows. The text and illustrations are adequate to the subject.

1104 *Puppet Show.* Ill. by Alana Lee. Troll, hb and pap., 1980. ISBN 0-89375-385-8. SERIES: First-Start Easy Reader. SUBJECTS: Puppets—Fiction. RL 1.4.

Four children work together to make puppets and a stage and to put on a puppet show. The very brief story is good for children just beginning to read. The red and black illustrations are simple yet lively.

Petersen, David

1105 *Airplanes.* Photos. Childrens, hb and pap., 1981. ISBN 0-516-01606-7. SERIES: New True. SUBJECTS: Airplanes. RL 3.2.

Full color photographs of a variety of airplanes add interest to this brief look at aircraft from the time of the Wright brothers to that of the space shuttle. Also looked at are the way planes are used and the people who fly them.

1106 *Airports.* Photos. Childrens, 1981. ISBN 0-516-01607-5. SERIES: New True. SUBJECTS: Airports. RL 2.6.

The different parts and services of a modern airport are explored with full color photographs. There is also a glossary and an index. This book provides useful introductory information that may lead a child to read other books about aeronautics.

1107 *Helicopters.* Photos. Childrens, hb and pap., 1983. ISBN 0-516-01680-6. SERIES: New True. SUBJECTS: Helicopters. RL 3.3.

A brief history of the development of helicopters is followed by chapters that discuss the kinds of helicopters and their operation, mechanical parts, and safety requirements. There is a glossary and an index. The book is illustrated with full color photographs.

Petrie, Catherine

1108 *Hot Rod Harry*. Ill. by Paul Sharp. Childrens, hb and pap., 1982. ISBN 0-516-03493-6. SERIES: Rookie Readers. SUBJECTS: Bicycles and bicycling—Fiction. RL 1.8.

Hot Rod Harry is a terror on his bicycle because he cares about nothing but speed. The full color expressive pictures do more to tell the story than does the very brief text.

1109 *Joshua James Likes Trucks*. Ill. by Jerry Warshaw. Childrens, hb and pap., 1982. ISBN 0-516-03525-8. SERIES: Rookie Readers. SUBJECTS: Trucks—Fiction. RL 1.3.

At home and in town, Joshua James spots all types and sizes of trucks. A very limited vocabulary, brief text, and bright pictures with black outlining make this book attractive to children.

1110 *Sandbox Betty*. Ill. by Sharon Elzaurdia. Childrens, hb and pap., 1982. ISBN 0-516-03578-9. SERIES: Rookie Readers. SUBJECTS: Sand-castles—Fiction; Stories in rhyme. RL 2.4.

A very limited and repetitious text tells of Betty and her meticulously crafted and elaborate sandcastles. Simple, childlike colored drawings with black outlining are necessary to the telling of the story, since the text is so brief.

Petty, Kate

1111 *Dinosaurs*. Ill. by Richard Orr and Stephen Bennett. Watts, 1988. ISBN 0-531-17123-X. SERIES: Small World. SUBJECTS: Dinosaurs. RL 2.8.

Dinosaurs are colorfully painted in their surroundings as the illustrators perceive them to be in order to show a straightforward presentation of rather superficial information on dinosaurs. Several dinosaurs, early reptiles, and birds are described and their Latin names given.

1112 *Guinea Pigs*. Photos. Gloucester, 1989. ISBN 0-531-17131-0. SERIES: First Pets. SUBJECTS: Pets—Guinea pigs. RL 2.5.

More of an introduction to guinea pigs than a pet care book, this book offers good color photos and paintings, brief and rather casual information on care, and some background facts on guinea pigs. Children should find this an enticement to guinea pig ownership as well as interesting reading.

1113 *Whales*. Ill. by Norman Weaver. Watts, 1988. ISBN 0-531-17124-8. SERIES: Small World. SUBJECTS: Animals—Whales. RL 2.9.

A descriptive account of different kinds of whales, this book offers little in-depth information. Instead it introduces a variety of whales and gives brief facts on them and their behavior and habitat. Paintings are realistic and attractive.

Phillips, Joan

1114 *Lucky Bear*. Ill. by J. P. Miller. Random House, hb and pap., 1986. ISBN 0-394-97987-7. SERIES: Step into Reading. SUBJECTS: Toys—Teddy bears—Fiction. RL 1.8.

Named Lucky by the toymaker, a teddy bear falls out of a window and into a series of adventures that earn him a friend. A very brief text with large print is complemented by soft watercolor pictures.

1115 *My New Boy*. Ill. by Lynn Munsinger. Random House, hb and pap., 1986. ISBN 0-394-98277-0. SERIES: Step into Reading. SUBJECTS: Animals—Dogs—Fiction; Humorous stories; Pets—Dogs—Fiction. RL 1.7.

In this brief whimsical story a puppy teaches his boy tricks and takes care of him. Simple paintings with ink details effectively convey the humor and warmth of the story.

1116 *Tiger Is a Scaredy Cat*. Ill. by Norman Gorbaty. Random House, hb and pap., 1986. ISBN 0-394-98056-5. SERIES: Step into Reading. SUBJECTS: Animals—Cats—Fiction; Animals—Mice—Fiction; Emotions—Fear—Fiction. RL 1.8.

Tiger, a young cat, is afraid of dogs, trucks, the vacuum cleaner, the dark, and even mice. When a baby mouse is lost and needs help,

Tiger gathers his courage and returns the mouse to its home. Pictures are simple yet bold and colorful and work with the text to create an appealing book.

Phleger, Frederick B.

1117 *Red Tag Comes Back.* Ill. by Arnold Lobel. Harper & Row, 1961. ISBN 0-06-024706-1. SERIES: Science I Can Read. SUBJECTS: Animals—Fish. RL 1.9.
After explaining the purpose of tagging to a young boy, a naturalist tags a salmon just for him. The well-done book follows Red Tag the salmon's journey to the sea, her growth, and finally her return to the same area to spawn. Detailed ink and wash drawings realistically portray the life of the salmon.

Pickering, Robert

1118 *I Can Be an Archaeologist.* Photos. Childrens, hb and pap., 1987. ISBN 0-516-01909-0. SERIES: I Can Be. SUBJECTS: Careers. RL 3.3.
Study, persistence, painstaking care, and curiosity are the traits most important to becoming an archaeologist according to this brief look at the profession. The text and photographs have people doing all aspects of the work in the field and in museums.

Pitt, Valerie

1119 *Let's Find Out about Names.* Ill. by Patricia Grant Porter. Watts, 1971, o.p. SERIES: Let's Find Out About. SUBJECTS: Names. RL 2.2.
Surnames, Christian names, and meanings and origins of some names are clearly and entertainingly explained. This book might inspire children to start investigating the origins of their given names. Illustrated with representative black, fuchsia, and ocher sketches.

1120 *Let's Find Out about the Community.* Ill. by June Goldsborough. Watts, 1972, o.p. SERIES: Let's Find Out About. SUBJECTS: Communities; Community helpers. RL 3.0.
A clear and simple text and watercolor pictures together define what a community is made up of—libraries, schools, community helpers, citizens, and government. The community is then examined to see how the many parts work together to run smoothly.

Platt, Kin

1121 *Big Max.* Ill. by Robert Lopshire. Harper & Row, 1965; pap., 1978. ISBN 0-06-024751-7. SERIES: I Can Read Mystery. SUBJECTS: Humorous stories; Mystery and detective stories. RL 2.2.
Big Max, a diminutive detective, hurries via a hot-air umbrella to Pooka Pooka. Using his look-and-think method, Big Max finds a missing elephant. A clever text and comic-style illustrations have made this a perennial favorite.

1122 *Big Max and the Mystery of the Missing Moose.* Ill. by Robert Lopshire. Harper & Row, 1977; pap., 1983. ISBN 0-06-024757-6. SERIES: I Can Read Mystery. SUBJECTS: Humorous stories; Mystery and detective stories. RL 2.3.
Traveling by hot-air umbrella, Big Max heads for the zoo and begins his search for Marvin the missing moose. By trial and error and with plenty of humor, Max finds Marvin in Moose Land with his family. Comical pencil and wash drawings suit the text well.

Podendorf, Illa

1123 *Energy.* Photos. Childrens, 1982. ISBN 0-516-01625-3. SERIES: New True. SUBJECTS: Energy. RL 2.9.
Very simple language is used to provide basic information on a variety of energy sources from food for humans to wind for electricity. The emphasis is on the forms and uses of energy most noticeable in a child's environment with little on technology. Illustrated with color photographs.

1124 *Spiders.* Photos. Childrens, hb and pap., 1982. ISBN 0-516-01653-9. SERIES: New True. SUBJECTS: Animals—Spiders. RL 3.1.
Children will learn to distinguish spiders from insects and to appreciate the way the spiders weave their webs and help humans by eating harmful insects. The text is clear and

Podendorf, Illa (cont.)

easy to understand. The color photographs attest to the great many sizes, shapes, and kinds of spiders that exist.

1125 *Trees.* Photos. Childrens, hb and pap., 1982. ISBN 0-516-01657-1. SERIES: New True. SUBJECTS: Plants—Trees. RL 2.5.
The parts of trees, the way they grow, the different varieties, their uses, and the need to protect them from damage are clearly and concisely described. The text is accompanied by suitable full color photographs, a glossary, and an index.

Pollock, Penny

1126 *Ants Don't Get Sunday Off.* Ill. by Lorinda B. Cauley. Putnam, 1978, o.p. SERIES: See and Read. SUBJECTS: Animals—Ants—Fiction. RL 3.0.
Anya, an old ant, is tired of constantly taking care of the nursery yet she is the first to try to rescue the eggs from flooding. Caught in the water, she is carried away on a great adventure. Facts about ants are interspersed in the text, which is complemented by clever ink and chalk pictures.

1127 *The Slug Who Thought He Was a Snail.* Ill. by Lorinda B. Cauley. Putnam, 1980, o.p. SERIES: See and Read. SUBJECTS: Animals—Slugs—Fiction; Animals—Snails—Fiction; Self-esteem—Fiction. RL 3.1.
A forceful snail convinces Sam Slug that he is a snail who has lost his house and must find a new one. Sam does exactly as the snail tells him until he meets another slug who assures him he is fine as he is. Detailed pictures are slightly comical while the text provides accurate information on slugs.

1128 *The Spit Bug Who Couldn't Spit.* Ill. by Lorinda B. Cauley. Putnam, 1982. ISBN 0-399-61152-5. SERIES: See and Read. SUBJECTS: Animals—Insects—Fiction. RL 2.9.
Ezra, a newly hatched spittlebug, has little success making spit until he grows and matures, but each step in the process is difficult for the timid little bug. Factual information about spittlebugs is included at the end of this story, which has humorous colored pencil drawings.

Pomerantz, Charlotte

1129 *Buffy and Albert.* Ill. by Yossi Abolafia. Greenwillow, 1982, o.p. SERIES: Read-alone. SUBJECTS: Animals—Cats—Fiction; Grandparents—Fiction; Old age—Fiction. RL 2.2.
The two children's grandfather complains about having to take care of his two old cats. When their grandfather has an accident and is bedridden, the younger child lovingly shows him that the cats cannot help being old anymore than he can. The ink drawings with pastel accents are perfect for the story.

Porte, Barbara Ann

1130 *Harry in Trouble.* Ill. by Yossi Abolafia. Greenwillow, 1989. ISBN 0-688-07633-5. SUBJECTS: Behavior—Responsible—Fiction; Humorous stories; Lost and found possessions—Fiction. RL 1.9.
Harry is on his third library card: the first his dog ate, the second his father put in the wash, and the third he can't find. Now he has to face the librarian and tell her what he's done. Harry's humorous first person account is accompanied by warm and lively watercolor paintings.

1131 *Harry's Dog.* Ill. by Yossi Abolafia. Greenwillow, 1984; Scholastic, pap., 1986. ISBN 0-688-02556-0. SERIES: Read-alone. SUBJECTS: Allergies—Fiction; Families, single parent—Fiction; Pets—Dogs—Fiction. RL 2.3.
Knowing his father is allergic to dogs, Harry nonetheless accepts one. He tells outlandish stories to explain her presence and to convince his father to allow him to keep her. Aunt Rose finds the perfect solution to Harry's dilemma. Illustrated in soft colors with gentle humor.

1132 *Harry's Mom.* Ill. by Yossi Abolafia. Greenwillow, 1985. ISBN 0-688-04818-8. SERIES: Read-alone. SUBJECTS: Families, single parent—Fiction; Parent and child—Fiction. RL 2.3.

When the dictionary says an orphan is someone with one parent, Harry rushes home to his father for comfort. His dad assures him that, even though his mother is dead, he is not an orphan. Harry also gets to hear more about his sports reporter mom. Ink and pencil drawings and text are excellent.

1133 *Harry's Visit*. Ill. by Yossi Abolafia. Greenwillow, 1983. ISBN 0-688-01208-6. SERIES: Read-alone. SUBJECTS: Behavior—Shyness—Fiction. RL 2.4.

When his father's friends invite him to spend the day, Harry inaccurately predicts that he will have a terrible time. The reluctance of this shy and very polite only child to venture beyond his territory is capably portrayed. Simple pastel colored pictures help tell the story.

Porter, Wesley

1134 *About Monkeys in Trees*. Ill. by Dominique Churchill. Watts, 1979, o.p. SUBJECTS: Animals—Monkeys—Fiction; Folklore—Africa. RL 2.6.

This reworking of an African folktale tells how sly tortoise borrows money from monkey and, when the time comes to repay it, convinces monkey that she has thrown it away. This folktale explains why monkeys stay in trees (to search for the lost money). Illustrations are simple, uninspiring, but colorful paintings.

1135 *The Magic Kettle*. Ill. by Lynn Sweat. Watts, 1979, o.p. SUBJECTS: Folklore—Japan. RL 2.8.

An old man finds a kettle, polishes it, and sees it transformed into a wild little animal. Once it is back in its kettle form, the old man sells it to a merchant who gets wealthy by holding shows where the kettle changes into its animal form. Expressively illustrated in bright colors and ink.

Posell, Elsa

1136 *Cats*. Photos. Childrens, hb and pap., 1983. ISBN 0-516-01671-7. SERIES: New True. SUBJECTS: Animals—Cats; Pets—Cats. RL 2.2.

Good basic information on well-known wild and domestic cats is given in a clear text. The book is divided into chapters with full color photographs of the animals and includes a glossary and an index. Some general information on pet care is also provided.

1137 *Dogs*. Photos. Childrens, hb and pap., 1981. ISBN 0-516-01614-8. SERIES: New True. SUBJECTS: Animals—Dogs; Pets—Dogs. RL 2.2.

Types of dogs, such as sport and working, specific breeds, and pointers for their care and training are accompanied by full color photographs. The text is carefully and clearly written and an index and glossary are included.

1138 *Elephants*. Photos. Childrens, 1982. ISBN 0-516-01621-0. SERIES: New True. SUBJECTS: Animals—Elephants. RL 2.5.

A simple text describes types of elephants, their diet, and their lives in the wild and as captives of man. It is supplemented by color photos of elephants in the wild, at zoos, and at work. Although nothing here is in depth, the information is adequate for most young children.

1139 *Whales and Other Sea Mammals*. Photos. Childrens, hb and pap., 1982. ISBN 0-516-01663-6. SERIES: New True. SUBJECTS: Animals—Whales. RL 2.9.

This informative look at whales includes material on their origins and physiology, their many kinds, and the possibility of their extinction from whale hunting. Short chapters are accompanied by excellent color photos and a few drawings; also included is an index and a glossary.

Poulin, Stephane

1140 *Can You Catch Josephine?* Ill. by author. Tundra, 1987. ISBN 0-88776-198-4. SUBJECTS: Humorous stories; Pets—Cats—Fiction; School stories. RL 1.9.

When Daniel's cat Josephine sneaks into his backpack and into his school, she creates havoc as Daniel and others try to catch her. Set in Montreal, the detailed and colorful paintings show an old-fashioned school staffed by modern multiracial teachers and students.

Poulin, Stephane (cont.)

1141 *Could You Stop Josephine?* Ill. by
author. Tundra, 1988. ISBN 0-88776-
216-6. SUBJECTS: Farm and country
life—Fiction; Humorous stories; Pets—
Cats—Fiction. RL 1.8.

Thinking they have left Daniel's cat Josephine
safely home in Montreal, Daniel and his father
drive out to the country to visit cousins. When
they arrive, the spunky Siamese who has been
hiding in the car gets loose and leads them on a
merry chase. Illustrated with vibrant pictures
of the Quebec countryside in summer.

1142 *Have You Seen Josephine?* Ill. by
author. Tundra, 1988. ISBN 0-88776-
180-1. SUBJECTS: City and town life—
Fiction; Pets—Cats—Fiction. RL 1.7.

Daniel decides to follow his cat Josephine to
see where she goes every Saturday. He chases
her through his Montreal neighborhood and
finally to a neighbor's for a special Saturday
cat party. The colorful paintings and black
and white sketches offer readers a chance to
view Canadian culture.

Power, Barbara

1143 *I Wish Laura's Mommy Was My
Mommy.* Ill. by Marylin Hafner.
Lippincott, 1979. ISBN 0-397-31859-6.
SERIES: I-Like-To-Read. SUBJECTS:
Family life—Fiction; Humorous stories;
Mothers, working—Fiction. RL 2.8.

It is not until Laura's mommy agrees to baby-
sit for Jennifer and her two little brothers
that Laura has to wash dishes and make her
own bed. A good job is done showing how
much work is involved in caring for children.
Pencil drawings, often humorous, are a good
match for the text.

Prager, Annabelle

1144 *The Spooky Halloween Party.* Ill. by
Tomie dePaola. Pantheon, 1981. ISBN 0-
394-94370-8. SERIES: I Am Reading.
SUBJECTS: Holidays—Halloween—
Fiction; Humorous stories; Parties—
Fiction. RL 2.6.

Albert is sure he will not be frightened at
Nicky's spooky Halloween party. Once there,
he is surprised that he cannot identify any of
the children until he realizes he is at the
wrong party. Suitably scary black and white
illustrations and the delightful story will be
enjoyed by youngsters.

1145 *The Surprise Party.* Ill. by Tomie
dePaola. Random House, hb and pap.,
1988. ISBN 0-394-99596-1. SERIES: Step
into Reading. SUBJECTS: Birthdays—
Fiction; Friendship—Fiction; Parties—
Fiction. RL 2.1.

A little boy convinces his best friend to plan a
"surprise" party for his birthday. Fortunately
the best friend is wise enough to really make
it a surprise. The full color pictures of multiracial children add to the warmth and humor of
the story.

Prall, Jo

1146 *My Sister's Special.* Photos by Linda
Gray. Childrens, 1985. ISBN 0-516-
03862-1. SERIES: Real-life Photo
Stories. SUBJECTS: Physically and
mentally impaired. RL 2.2.

Angie cannot walk, talk, or use her arms and
hands very well because she is brain dam-
aged. However, she goes to school in a wheel-
chair and communicates with symbols. Black
and white photos of a smiling child and
loving family are accompanied by a proud
brother's description of his special sister.

Prather, Ray

1147 *Double Dog Dare.* Ill. by author.
Macmillan, 1975, o.p. SERIES: Ready-
to-Read. SUBJECTS: Dares—Fiction;
Friendship—Fiction. RL 2.2.

Finding a quarter leads Eddie and Rudy, two
young black friends, on a series of "daring" adventures through town. Illustrated with pencil
drawings with green and brown washes.

Prelutsky, Jack

1148 *It's Christmas.* Ill. by Marylin Hafner.
Greenwillow, 1981; Scholastic, pap.,
1986. ISBN 0-688-00440-7. SERIES: Read-
alone. SUBJECTS: Holidays—
Christmas—Fiction; Poetry. RL 2.9.

A dozen whimsical poems reflect a child's view of the celebration of Christmas at home and in school. The illustrations of vivacious families of various races capture the humor and warmth of these holiday poems.

1149 *It's Halloween.* Ill. by Marylin Hafner. Greenwillow, 1977; Scholastic, pap., 1986. ISBN 0-688-84102-3. SERIES: Read-alone. SUBJECTS: Holidays—Halloween—Fiction; Poetry. RL 2.9.

Excitement, fun, and a little bit of fear—necessary ingredients for a memorable Halloween night—are in these 13 poems and in the ink and wash pictures that accompany them. The poems are great fun for reading aloud and alone.

1150 *It's Thanksgiving.* Ill. by Marylin Hafner. Greenwillow, 1982; Scholastic, pap., 1987. ISBN 0-688-00442-3. SERIES: Read-alone. SUBJECTS: Holidays—Thanksgiving; Poetry. RL 3.8.

Twelve warm and witty poems about all aspects of Thanksgiving—from football to leftover turkey—are fun for children to read aloud or alone. The ink line drawings with orange and brown washes add to the reader's enjoyment.

1151 *Rainy Rainy Saturday.* Ill. by Marylin Hafner. Greenwillow, 1980. ISBN 0-688-84252-6. SERIES: Read-alone. SUBJECTS: Poetry; Weather—Rain. RL 2.5.

In 14 delightful poems, children's views of the fun, boredom, or disappointment caused by rainy Saturdays are presented in rhythmic and thoughtful verses. The pencil and wash comic drawings complement the poetry.

1152 *What I Did Last Summer.* Ill. by Yossi Abolafia. Greenwillow, 1984. ISBN 0-688-01755-X. SERIES: Read-alone. SUBJECTS: Poetry; Seasons—Summer—Fiction. RL 2.6.

In 13 poems a little boy remembers his summer: going on a picnic, having a nasty cousin visit, being sick, being hot, and so on. His memories are humorous now that he is back at school even though some of the actual events were not so funny when they were taking place. The softly colored drawings capture the emotions—especially the humor—of the delightful poetry.

Prescott, Ernest

1153 *Flying Creatures.* Ill. by Reginald Davis. Watts, 1976, o.p. SERIES: Easy-Read Wildlife. SUBJECTS: Animals, flying. RL 2.9.

Nine flying or gliding mammals, reptiles, amphibians, and fish from all over the world are discussed briefly. Each section deals with an individual animal, its habitat, and its method of flying in an interesting and informative way. Illustrated with full color realistic paintings.

1154 *Slow Creatures.* Ill. by Reginald Davis. Watts, 1976, o.p. SERIES: Easy-Read Wildlife. SUBJECTS: Animals. RL 2.8.

Noted for their slow speed, 11 animals—from the Galapagos tortoise to the South Pacific cuscus—are introduced and their life-styles discussed. Each article is interesting and informative and illustrated with realistic full color paintings.

Pringle, Laurence

1155 *Twist, Wiggle, and Squirm: A Book about Earthworms.* Ill. by Peter Parnall. Crowell, 1973. ISBN 0-690-84155-8. SERIES: Let's Read and Find Out. SUBJECTS: Animals—Earthworms. RL 3.3.

From why earthworms are found on sidewalks after a heavy rainfall to details of how and where they live and what they eat, this presents an interesting look at an important form of animal life. The illustrations are detailed, realistic pen and ink drawings.

1156 *Water Plants.* Ill. by Kazue Mizumura. Crowell, 1975. ISBN 0-690-00738-8. SERIES: Let's-Read-and-Find-Out Science. SUBJECTS: Plants; Pond life. RL 3.0.

One animal after another feeds and is fed upon in this story of the food chain of a freshwater pond. Readers learn a great deal about the plants of the pond as they follow the animals. Well written and very interesting, it is illustrated with realistic watercolor paintings.

Putnam, Polly

1157 *Mystery of Sara Beth*. Ill. by Judith
       Friedman. Follett, hb and pap., 1981.
       ISBN 0-8136-5116-6. SUBJECTS: Mystery
       and detective stories; School stories;
       Siblings—Twins—Fiction. RL 2.2.

Sara Beth, the new girl, is decidedly unfriendly in spite of her classmates' attempts
to welcome her. Only Becky guesses that Sara
Beth is really a twin coming on different days
because she and her sister share a winter
coat. The multiracial class is realistically
portrayed in ink and colored washes.

Q

Quackenbush, Robert

1158 *Animal Cracks*. Ill. by author. Lothrop,
       1975, o.p. SERIES: Fun-to-Read.
       SUBJECTS: Fables; Humorous stories.
       RL 2.8.

Seven short, humorous stories about animals
present situations explaining well-known sayings such as "his bark is worse than his bite."
All are illustrated with boldly outlined gold
and black pencil sketches and are fun to read.

1159 *Calling Doctor Quack*. Ill. by author.
       Lothrop, 1978, o.p. SERIES: Fun-to-
       Read. SUBJECTS: Animals—Fiction;
       Doctors and nurses—Fiction;
       Pollution—Water—Fiction. RL 3.7.

Dr. Quack, a duck, is besieged by patients
blaming their sudden illnesses on the bad-
tempered Mr. Snapping Turtle. The poor
animal is sick and disagreeable because the
pond has become polluted and trash has
lodged in his shell. Good pictures illustrate an
amusing, pointed tale.

1160 *Detective Mole*. Ill. by author. Lothrop,
       1976. ISBN 0-688-51726-9. SERIES: Fun-
       to-Read. SUBJECTS: Animals—Moles—
       Fiction; Mystery and detective stories.
       RL 2.9.

Almost as soon as he finishes detective school,
Mole begins solving mysteries. The five entertaining stories here involve the animals in
Mole's community and are accompanied by
bold pencil drawings.

1161 *Detective Mole and the Circus Mystery*.
       Ill. by author. Lothrop, 1980, o.p.
       SERIES: Fun-to-Read. SUBJECTS:
       Animals—Moles—Fiction; Circuses—
       Fiction; Mystery and detective stories.
       RL 3.0.

Melba the tatooed cow disappears from the
circus the day of her marriage to Boris the
bull. Mole masterfully pieces together the
clues and finds Melba in time for her wedding. The illustrations, in full color with blue
outlining, are as imaginative as the story.

1162 *Detective Mole and the Seashore
       Mystery*. Ill. by author. Lothrop, 1976,
       o.p. SERIES: Fun-to-Read. SUBJECTS:
       Animals—Moles—Fiction; Mystery and
       detective stories. RL 3.8.

Called to Land's End Island to find Captain
Bill's stolen pearl, Mole carefully listens for
clues and discovers the culprit—a giant clam.
Humorous heavy line drawings add to the
seaside flavor and to the fun of the story.

1163 *Detective Mole and the Secret Clues*. Ill.
       by author. Lothrop, 1977, o.p. SERIES:
       Fun-to-Read. SUBJECTS: Animals—
       Moles—Fiction; Mystery and detective
       stories. RL 3.3.

A mysterious stranger hands Mole a small
green pea as he sets off to help the Chicken
family claim their Uncle Ebenezer's mansion.
Clues are easy enough for children to work
out in order to solve the mystery. Animal
characters are drawn in heavy blue and black
pencil.

1164 *Detective Mole and the Tip-Top Mystery*.
       Ill. by author. Lothrop, 1978, o.p.
       SERIES: Fun-to-Read. SUBJECTS:
       Animals—Moles—Fiction; Mystery and
       detective stories. RL 3.3.

Down to their last guests, Mr. and Mrs. Goat
call in Mole to stop the strange occurrences
that are driving guests away from their mountain lodge. Humorous pencil drawings and a
bit of suspense make this an exciting mystery.

1165 *Henry Goes West*. Ill. by author.
       Parents Magazine Press, 1982; Crown,
       pap., 1988. ISBN 0-8193-1090-5. SERIES:
       Read Aloud and Easy Reading.
       SUBJECTS: Animals—Ducks—Fiction;

Humorous stories; Western stories. RL 2.5.

Henry, a duck, misses Clara and decides to join her on her guest ranch vacation out west. When he arrives everyone is gone. As he waits for their return, Henry accidentally creates one catastrophe after another. A very funny story with a nice ending, it is illustrated in full color.

1166 *Henry's Important Date.* Ill. by author. Parents Magazine Press, 1981. ISBN 0-8193-1068-9. SERIES: Read Aloud and Easy Reading. SUBJECTS: Animals—Ducks—Fiction; Birthdays—Fiction; Concepts—Time—Fiction. RL 2.2.

Henry, a duck, tries his best to get to Clara's birthday party on time—but he gets stuck in traffic, locks his keys in his car, and then gets on a bus that breaks down. Poor Henry's awful day is funny but one that everyone can empathize with. Illustrated in full color with bold comic drawings.

1167 *Mr. Snow Bunting's Secret.* Ill. by author. Lothrop, 1978, o.p. SERIES: Fun-to-Read. SUBJECTS: Animals—Fiction; Holidays—Christmas—Fiction. RL 3.5.

Only able to stay until November, Mr. Snow Bunting, a bird, opens a gift-wrapping business for the Christmas season that makes Mr. Dog jealous and suspicious. When Dog accuses Snow Bunting of being a sorcerer, Dog learns Snow Bunting's secret and is embarrassed. Illustrated with humorous heavy line drawings in red and black.

1168 *Moose's Store.* Ill. by author. Lothrop, 1979, o.p. SERIES: Fun-to-Read. SUBJECTS: Animals—Fiction; Farm and country life—Fiction; Friendship—Fiction. RL 2.9.

When Beaver and the other animals decide to help Moose by transforming his friendly, old-fashioned store into a deli, Moose feels uncomfortable and out of place. Bold pencil drawings are a good complement to this tale of tradition versus modernization.

1169 *No Mouse for Me.* Ill. by author. Watts, 1981, o.p. SERIES: Easy-Read Story. SUBJECTS: Animals—Mice—Fiction;

Cumulative tales; Humorous stories. RL 2.1.

A little boy returns a mouse to the pet shop demanding his money back. He claims that a mouse would attract a cat that would attract a dog and on and on until a catastrophe would occur and, anyway, he would rather have a snake. Outrageously silly, this is illustrated with bold drawings.

1170 *Pete Pack Rat.* Ill. by author. Lothrop, 1976, o.p. SERIES: Fun-to-Read. SUBJECTS: Animals—Fiction; Robbers and outlaws—Fiction; Western stories. RL 3.3.

Pete Pack Rat repeatedly outwits the notorious outlaw Gizzard Coyote in this old west style story with desert animals as characters. Illustrated with heavy line drawings, the book has humor and suspense that should appeal to young readers.

1171 *Pete Pack Rat and the Gila Monster Gang.* Ill. by author. Lothrop, 1978, o.p. SERIES: Fun-to-Read. SUBJECTS: Animals—Fiction; Robbers and outlaws—Fiction; Western stories. RL 3.1.

The Gila Monster Gang not only robs the Pebble Junction Bank but also kidnaps Sheriff Sally Gopher. Only Pete Pack Rat is clever enough to rescue Sally and capture the gang. The delightful old west story has bold black and purple drawings.

1172 *Sheriff Sally Gopher and the Haunted Dance Hall.* Ill. by author. Lothrop, 1977, o.p. SERIES: Fun-to-Read. SUBJECTS: Animals—Fiction; Ghost stories; Western stories. RL 3.2.

In spite of warnings that the old dance hall is haunted, Sheriff Sally Gopher tries to get it ready for a grand performance by dancer Lola Field Mouse. Suspense and humor combine in this story of an almost haunted hall. Illustrations are black and maroon pencil drawings.

Quin-Harkin, Janet

1173 *Helpful Hattie.* Ill. by Susanna Natti. Harcourt Brace, 1983, o.p.; pap., 1983. ISBN 0-15-233757-1. SERIES: Let Me Read. SUBJECTS: Birthdays—Fiction; Haircutting—Fiction; Human Body—Teeth—Fiction. RL 2.0.

Quin-Harkin, Janet (cont.)

Hattie has lots of ideas and little patience, which sometimes leads to trouble. She frosts her birthday cake with catsup, cuts her own hair, and disrupts her class picture-taking with her lost tooth. A funny story illustrated with droll ink line drawings.

1174 *Magic Growing Powder.* Ill. by Art Cumings. Parents Magazine Press, 1980. ISBN 0-8193-1038-7. SUBJECTS: Fairy tales; Magic—Fiction; Self-esteem—Fiction. RL 2.3.

King Max hates being short and will do just about anything to be taller. He is ready to give away half his kingdom and his daughter to two tricksters for their growing powder. Princess Penny cleverly outwits the two tricksters and saves the kingdom. Illustrated with humorous full color pictures.

R

Rabinowitz, Sandy

1175 *How I Trained My Colt.* Ill. by author. Doubleday, 1980, o.p.; Scholastic, pap., 1983. ISBN 0-590-23513-2. SERIES: Reading On My Own. SUBJECTS: Animals—Horses—Training; Pets—Horses. RL 2.4.

On the day of Sunny's birth, the colt's training begins. Told in the first person, the story shows how much patience and care go into the training of a horse during its first year. As a story or a horse-training book, this is very well done. Good watercolor illustrations.

Radford, Ruby

1176 *Robert Fulton.* Ill. by Salem Tamer. Putnam, 1970, o.p. SERIES: See and Read Beginning to Read Biography. SUBJECTS: Art and artists; Biographies; Inventors and inventions. RL 2.4.

Trained as an artist and a craftsman, Robert Fulton invented many things, including a submarine called the *Nautilus,* before he gained fame with the steamboat. Although fictionalized conversations are added, a good

portrait of a brilliant man is still provided. Realistic ink drawings.

Rappaport, Doreen

1177 *The Boston Coffee Party.* Ill. by Emily A. McCully. Harper & Row, 1988. ISBN 0-06-024825-4. SERIES: I Can Read. SUBJECTS: Historical fiction; United States—Revolution—Fiction. RL 2.7.

When Thomas, a greedy merchant, locks away all his coffee until the price rises, the women of Boston decide to hold a coffee "party" and break into his warehouse. Based on an actual occurrence, this story could lead children to a discussion of ethics. Illustrated with ink and wash sketches.

Reidel, Marlene

1178 *From Egg to Bird.* Ill. by author. Carolrhoda, 1981. ISBN 0-87614-159-9. SERIES: Start To Finish. SUBJECTS: Animals—Birds; Animals—Reproduction. RL 2.5.

The process of rearing young birds, from nest-building to the time of the young birds' departure, is told very simply and nicely. Text is perfectly coordinated with the artwork, full-color paintings of birds raising their young. Paintings are somewhat stylized but clearly depict their subject.

Ricciuti, Edward R.

1179 *An Animal for Alan.* Ill. by Tom Eaton. Harper & Row, 1970. ISBN 0-06-024987-0. SERIES: Science I Can Read. SUBJECTS: Pets; Pets—Wild animals. RL 2.5.

In trying to select the perfect pet, Alan slowly learns that most wild animals are not meant to be pets. Alan's father suggests that he might like a dog or a cat. The animals are realistically portrayed in ink and colored pencil drawings and the story has a good message for children.

1180 *Catch a Whale by the Tail.* Ill. by Geoffrey Moss. Harper & Row, 1969. ISBN 0-06-024989-7. SERIES: Science I Can Read. SUBJECTS: Animals—Whales. RL 2.9.

Hoping to find a way to get Robert, a Beluga whale, to sing or whistle, his curator heads to the far north to find a mate for him. Readers are taken on a whaling expedition and given good information on the Beluga whale. Illustrated with exuberant blue and brown sketches.

1181 *Donald and the Fish That Walked.* Ill. by Syd Hoff. Harper & Row, 1974. ISBN 0-06-024998-6. SERIES: Science I Can Read. SUBJECTS: Animals—Fish; Conservation. RL 2.3.

Donald thinks the walking catfish that begin to appear in his neighborhood are fun. Then Mr. Walter explains that they were brought from Asia and are driving out other fish. A thought-provoking look at a conservation problem, this story is illustrated in a cartoon style.

Rice, Eve

1182 *Mr. Brimble's Hobby and Other Stories.* Ill. by author. Greenwillow, 1975, o.p. SERIES: Read-alone. SUBJECTS: Family life—Fiction. RL 2.7.

What first seems to be a very traditional family is far more. All of its members are strong individuals who value themselves and each other and together create enjoyable stories of a loving family. The simple warmth of the ink and wash drawings are a perfect complement to the text.

1183 *Once in a Wood: Ten Fables from Aesop.* Ill. by author. Greenwillow, 1979, o.p. SERIES: Read-alone. SUBJECTS: Fables. RL 2.5.

The essence of Aesop is captured in Rice's adaptations of ten familiar fables. Each is carefully constructed with a final few lines devoted to a rhyming moral. The illustrations are very detailed, whimsical black and white drawings.

1184 *Papa's Lemonade and Other Stories.* Ill. by author. Greenwillow, 1976, o.p. SERIES: Read-alone. SUBJECTS: Animals—Dogs—Fiction; Family life—Fiction. RL 2.6.

Papa and Mama dog and their five pups share gentle yet whimsical adventures that include trying to find a substitute for a broken bank, going for a walk in the country, and making lemonade with oranges. Ink drawings of very humanized animals are given soft color washes.

Richardson, Joy

1185 *What Happens When You Breathe?* Ill. by Colin Maclean and Moira Maclean. Gareth Stevens, 1986. ISBN 1-55532-103-8. SERIES: What Happens When . . .? SUBJECTS: Human body—Respiration. RL 3.0.

A clear, easily understood text helps children learn how breathing works. Simple experiments simulate or measure the lung's activities and further clarify the respiration process. An index and a bibliography are included. Illustrated with colored diagrams and drawings.

1186 *What Happens When You Eat?* Ill. by Colin Maclean and Moira Maclean. Gareth Stevens, 1986. ISBN 1-55532-105-4. SERIES: What Happens When . . . ? SUBJECTS: Human body—Digestion. RL 2.7.

This explanation of digestion is clear and easily understood. Colored diagrams and drawings help show how food reaches the stomach and goes through the intestines. A bibliography and an index are included.

1187 *What Happens When You Listen?* Ill. by Colin Maclean and Moira Maclean. Gareth Stevens, 1986, o.p. SERIES: What Happens When . . . ? SUBJECTS: Human body—Ears; Senses—Hearing. RL 3.1.

A clear, straightforward text helps children understand how ears work. A number of simple experiments are also suggested. There is an index, a bibliography, and a list of nonbook sources for additional information. Colored diagrams and drawings aid in conveying the message.

1188 *What Happens When You Sleep?* Ill. by Colin Maclean and Moira Maclean. Gareth Stevens, 1986. ISBN 0-55532-111-9. SERIES: What Happens When . . . ? SUBJECTS: Human body—Sleep; Sleep. RL 2.5.

Richardson, Joy (cont.)

Basic information about how and why people sleep, dream, and wake up is conveyed in a simple writing style. A few experiments are suggested along with some questions to prod young readers. Included is a bibliography, a subject index, and an experiment and question index. Attractive full color pictures.

Richter, Alice, and Numeroff, Laura J.

1189 *You Can't Put Braces on Spaces*. Ill. by Laura J. Numeroff. Greenwillow, 1979, o.p. SERIES: Read-alone. SUBJECTS: Human body—Teeth—Fiction; Orthodontics—Fiction. RL 2.6.

A little boy can hardly wait for his teeth to grow in so that he can have braces like his brother and other older children. Good information on orthodontia is given as the older brother goes to have his braces put on. Boldly outlined pictures are flat and childlike but lively.

Rickard, Graham

1190 *Tractors*. Ill. by Clifford Meadway. Bookwright, 1988. ISBN 0-531-18256-8. SERIES: Let's Look At. SUBJECTS: Farm and Country Life; Tractors. RL 3.0.

After presenting a brief history of the tractor, the machine's many uses and types are then looked at. Rickard also includes a thoughtful section on some of the disadvantages of modern farming methods. Illustrated with realistic watercolor paintings. Includes a brief glossary.

Ridlon, Marci

1191 *A Frog Sandwich: Riddles and Jokes*. Ill. by Pat Dypold. Follett, 1973, o.p. SERIES: Beginning to Read. SUBJECTS: Jokes and riddles. RL 2.3.

The 33 riddles and jokes that are presented in this book are well known to older children and adults. However, these riddles and jokes will still be fun for the reader encountering them for the first time. They are illustrated with appropriately silly ink and wash pictures.

1192 *Kittens and More Kittens*. Ill. by Liz Dauber. Follett, 1967, o.p. SERIES: Beginning to Read. SUBJECTS: Animals—Cats—Fiction; Pets—Cats—Fiction. RL 1.7.

Finally old enough to own a pet, Jennifer Joan posts flyers in her neighborhood asking for a kitten and even gets into the newspaper. The inevitable donations of kittens occur and the little girl is fortunate to find someone to take them. Illustrated with colorful, attractive paintings.

Riehecky, Janet

1193 *Allosaurus*. Ill. by Llyn Hunter. Childrens, 1988. ISBN 0-516-06276-X. SERIES: Dinosaur Books. SUBJECTS: Animals—Prehistoric; Dinosaurs. RL 2.4.

A chatty, not altogether scientific approach to a discussion of the allosaurus, this book goes beyond descriptive passages and treats speculation on life-style as fact. Nonetheless, children will enjoy the bright, dramatic paintings and the detailed line drawings of the allosaurus.

1194 *Stegosaurus*. Ill. by Diana Magnuson. Childrens, 1988. ISBN 0-516-06269-7. SERIES: Dinosaur Books. SUBJECTS: Animals—Prehistoric; Dinosaurs. RL 2.8.

The stegosaurus is shown in a detailed drawing and his habits (which are speculative) and characteristics are discussed in a way often tending to anthropomorphize the animal. Though not always scientific in tone or presentation, the book has some useful information and dramatic pictures.

1195 *Tyrannosaurus*. Ill. by Diana Magnuson. Childrens, 1988. ISBN 0-516-06279-4. SERIES: Dinosaur Books. SUBJECTS: Animals—Prehistoric; Dinosaurs. RL 2.6.

What is known about the tyrannosaurus is mentioned in a brief text along with speculative ideas that some scientists hold. No in-depth information is here, merely a palatable introduction to the most popular of dinosaurs. The dramatic pictures are in watercolor.

Rinkoff, Barbara

1196 *Guess What Rocks Do.* Ill. by Leslie
      Morrill. Lothrop, 1975, o.p. SERIES:
      Guess What . . . SUBJECTS: Geology.
      RL 2.6.
An appreciation rather than a scientific look
at rocks is presented. The book shows the
many ways humans have used rocks—as
weapons, for building, and for grinding. The
illustrations give the reader a sense of time
passing with realistic figures drawn against
swaths of rust or olive.

1197 *Guess What Trees Do.* Ill. by Beatrice
      Darwin. Lothrop, 1974, o.p. SERIES:
      Guess What . . . SUBJECTS: Plants—
      Trees. RL 2.8.
An appreciation of the many things that trees
do for people rather than a botanical study of
trees, the text will remind readers that trees
provide oxygen, sap for maple syrup, wood
for furniture, and much more. The illustrations, which add little to the text, are in
turquoise, black, and olive.

1198 *No Pushing, No Ducking: Safety in the
      Water.* Ill. by Roy Doty. Lothrop, 1974,
      o.p. SUBJECTS: Boats and boating;
      Safety; Sports—Swimming. RL 2.3.
A girl surprises her show-offish friend Tom
with her knowledge of water safety and her
swimming skill. The book offers a humorous
but very effective approach to water safety—
swimming or boating—and includes a list of
water safety rules. It is nicely illustrated with
cartoonlike pictures.

1199 *Rutherford T. Finds 21B.* Ill. by Tomie
      dePaola. Putnam, 1970, o.p. SERIES:
      See and Read. SUBJECTS: Moving,
      household—Fiction; School stories.
      RL 2.2.
Rutherford bravely heads for school alone but
cannot find his room. New to the area, he asks
a succession of children for directions and all
of them end up helping him not only to find the
room but to feel less like a newcomer. Illustrated with simple taupe and blue pictures.

Robert, Adrian

1200 *The "Awful Mess" Mystery.* Ill. by Paul
      Harvey. Troll, hb and pap., 1985. ISBN

0-8167-0402-3. SERIES: Easy-to-Read
Mystery. SUBJECTS: Clubs—Fiction;
Mystery and detective stories. RL 2.5.
After Katie tries on her mother's new brace-
let, she loses it, creating an awful mess.
Katie's fellow club members help her retrace
her steps, and they finally find the bracelet.
The detecting in this story is complex enough
to interest young readers. Illustrated with
very simple, childlike pictures.

Robins, Joan

1201 *Addie Meets Max.* Ill. by Sue Truesdell.
      Harper & Row, 1985; pap., 1988. ISBN
      0-06-025064-X. SERIES: Early I Can
      Read. SUBJECTS: Friendship—Fiction;
      Moving, household—Fiction; Pets—
      Dogs—Fiction. RL 2.3.
Addie's new neighbor Max seems unfriendly
and so does his dog Ginger until Addie gets a
chance to know them. Lively watercolor paintings expressively illustrate this light but realistic story of a blossoming friendship.

1202 *Addie Runs Away.* Ill. by Sue Truesdell.
      Harper & Row, 1989. ISBN 0-06-
      025080-1. SERIES: Early I Can Read.
      SUBJECTS: Behavior—Running away—
      Fiction; Friendship—Fiction. RL 1.8.
Awakened by his dog Ginger, Max discovers
that his neighbor—and friend—Addie is running away from home rather than going to
camp. Max finally convinces her and himself
that camp is not so bad. Expressive watercolor pictures add a light touch to a story
about misunderstanding.

Robinson, Marileta

1203 *Mr. Goat's Bad Good Idea: Three
      Stories.* Ill. by Arthur Getz. Crowell,
      1977. ISBN 0-690-03864-X. SUBJECTS:
      Animals—Fiction; Native Americans—
      Navajos—Fiction. RL 2.2.
In the first of three entertaining stories set in
Navajo country, lazy Mr. Goat tries to get dirt
for his hogan from other animals. Instead of
less work, this cumulative tale shows he has
far more. The other two stories are quiet yet
fun. Illustrated with engaging ink and wash
pictures.

Robison, Nancy

1204 *Izoo.* Ill. by Edward Frascino. Lothrop, 1980, o.p. SERIES: Fun-to-Read. SUBJECTS: Science fiction; Zoos—Fiction. RL 2.3.

On their way to a space show, Max and Charlie are picked up by aliens and transported to their ice zoo; they escape just before they are to be cloned. Comical yet suitably sinister drawings add to the fun of this science fiction adventure.

1205 *The Mystery at Hilltop Camp.* Ill. by Ethel Gold. Garrard, 1979. ISBN 0-8116-6407-4. SERIES: Garrard Mystery. SUBJECTS: Camps and camping—Fiction; Mystery and detective stories. RL 2.6.

Equipped with her detective's magnifying glass, Patty is sure she can solve the mystery of the camp's missing milk. Although lacking real suspense, this is still a story that children will be comfortable reading. Illustrated with realistic pencil drawings in turquoise and chartreuse.

1206 *Space Hijack!* Ill. by Edward Frascino. Lothrop, 1979, o.p. SERIES: Fun-to-Read. SUBJECTS: Science fiction. RL 2.6.

While Mark and Ted are on their way to the moon with their prize-winning experiment, their ship is hijacked by an invisible alien who wants their atomic batteries. The two boys outwit the invisible man and finally return to Earth. Illustrated with comical ink and wash sketches.

1207 *UFO Kidnap!* Ill. by Edward Frascino. Lothrop, 1978, o.p. SERIES: Fun-to-Read. SUBJECTS: Science fiction; UFOs—Fiction. RL 1.8.

Roy and Barney are mistaken for interplanetary jewel thieves and are taken to another planet. When the stolen gem appears, Roy is designated the new ruler of the planet. In the end the boys use the gem's power to escape and get home. Illustrated with humorously weird comic line drawings.

Roche, P. K.

1208 *Webster and Arnold and the Giant Box.* Ill. by author. Dial, 1980. ISBN 0-8037-

9436-3. SERIES: Easy-to-Read. SUBJECTS: Animals—Mice—Fiction; Imagination—Fiction; Sibling rivalry—Fiction. RL 2.1.

Two little mouse brothers find a large box and let their imaginations run wild as they play at being cave dwellers, engineers on an African train, restaurant owners, and more. The story is nicely illustrated with soft pastel drawings outlined in ink.

Rockwell, Anne

1209 *A Bear, a Bobcat, and Three Ghosts.* Ill. by author. Macmillan, 1977. ISBN 0-02-777460-0. SERIES: Ready-to-Read. SUBJECTS: Ghost stories; Holidays—Halloween—Fiction. RL 2.5.

Three strange ghosts lead Timothy Todd, the miller and his wife, and Widow Wilson on a chase through the woods in search of three missing children. Flat, childlike ink drawings with washes of orange create a suitably "spooky" effect.

1210 *Big Bad Goat.* Ill. by author. Dutton, 1982. ISBN 0-525-45100-5. SERIES: Smart Cat. SUBJECTS: Animals—Fiction; Humorous stories. RL 2.3.

In this very brief story, Tommy goes from larger to larger animal trying to get one of them to help him get Big Bad Goat out of the flower garden. When all have refused, a bee stings Goat and Goat finally leaves. The simple ink and watercolor pictures are childlike and appealing.

1211 *Big Boss.* Ill. by author. Macmillan, 1975, o.p.; pap., 1985. ISBN 0-689-71125-5. SERIES: Ready-to-Read. SUBJECTS: Animals—Frogs and toads—Fiction; Animals—Tigers—Fiction; Folklore—China. RL 2.1.

A clever little frog outwits a huge tiger by claiming he is the Big Boss who eats tigers for dinner. Whimsical ink and watercolor pictures have a primitive look that fits this folk story well.

1212 *The Bump in the Night.* Ill. by author. Greenwillow, 1979, o.p. SERIES: Read-alone. SUBJECTS: Folklore—Spain; Ghost stories. RL 2.5.

Based on a Spanish folktale, the story has Toby, a boy who likes to fix things, agree to spend the night in a castle and face its ghost. His courage never wanes as the ghost, appearing in pieces, tests him. Flat, childlike ink drawings with yellow and brown are well suited to the story.

1213 *The Gollywhopper Egg.* Ill. by author. Macmillan, 1974, o.p.; pap., 1986. ISBN 0-689-71072-0. SERIES: Ready-to-Read. SUBJECTS: Tall tales. RL 2.9.
Timothy Todd sells a farmer a coconut telling him it is the egg of the Gollywhopper, a bird as big as a cow and as strong as a mule, which has unlimited talent. The simple, flat ink drawings have a primitive charm and humor that is perfect for the story.

1214 *Honk Honk!* Ill. by author. Dutton, 1980. ISBN 0-525-32120-0. SERIES: Smart Cat. SUBJECTS: Animals—Geese—Fiction; Farm and country life—Fiction. RL 2.5.
Gray Goose nips Billy Boy and the barnyard animals. After a chase the ornery goose flees to the pond, safe from everyone's anger. The brief text has flat, childlike pictures that are attractive and full of the story's vigor and humor.

1215 *No More Work.* Ill. by author. Greenwillow, 1976, o.p. SERIES: Read-alone. SUBJECTS: Animals—Monkeys—Fiction; Boats and boating—Fiction; Mythical creatures—Fiction. RL 2.4.
Trying to escape from hard work and boring food, the three little monkeys run away from their ship and land on an island with a dragon ready to eat them. Shipboard life has new appeal for the three as they head back. The very simple and childlike watercolor pictures are just right.

1216 *The Story Snail.* Ill. by author. Macmillan, 1974, o.p.; pap., 1987. ISBN 0-689-71164-6. SERIES: Ready-to-Read. SUBJECTS: Fantasy; Self-esteem—Fiction; Storytelling—Fiction. RL 2.5.
Though kind and good, John seems to have no special talent until he meets a very unusual silver snail who gives him 100 stories to tell. Tired of repeatedly telling them, John gains confidence as he searches for other tales. The

book has simple, childlike drawings with pastel washes.

1217 *Thump Thump Thump!* Ill. by author. Dutton, 1981. ISBN 0-525-41300-6. SERIES: Smart Cat. SUBJECTS: Folklore—United States; Monsters—Fiction. RL 2.5.
Using the simplest language, the familiar story of the "hairy toe"—a monster coming to reclaim his missing toe—is nicely paced and retold. Illustrations are childlike and not too scary.

1218 *Timothy Todd's Good Things Are Gone.* Ill. by author. Macmillan, 1978, o.p. SERIES: Ready-to-Read. SUBJECTS: Mystery and detective stories. RL 2.4.
Running from a thunderstorm, Timothy Todd takes refuge in an apparently deserted house and falls asleep. When he awakens, his pack full of goods is gone and he sets off to find it. The story is ably illustrated with Rockwell's easily recognizable, uncluttered ink and wash drawings.

1219 *Up a Tall Tree.* Ill. by Jim Arnosky. Doubleday, 1981, o.p. SERIES: Reading On My Own. SUBJECTS: Fantasy; Monsters—Fiction. RL 2.4.
Nick, the son of poor woodcutters, discovers a bottle with a little monster inside. After setting it free, Nick is rewarded with three berries that can turn any metal into gold. This gift makes his family rich. Ink and pencil drawings show an incongruously modern family of woodcutters.

1220 *Walking Shoes.* Ill. by author. Doubleday, 1980, o.p. SERIES: Reading On My Own. SUBJECTS: Fairy tales; Houses—Fiction. RL 1.8.
Lonely, neglected, and unwanted, the little house is granted magic walking shoes and uses them to go in search of people who will really love her. The simple story has childlike line drawings with red and green washes.

Rockwell, Anne, and Rockwell, Harlow

1221 *Blackout.* Ill. by authors. Macmillan, 1979, o.p. SERIES: Ready-to-Read. SUBJECTS: Blackouts, electric power

Rockwell, Anne, and Rockwell, Harlow (cont.)

    failures—Fiction; Emergencies—Fiction; Family life—Fiction. RL 2.3.
An ice storm and broken power lines mean Dan and his family must find ways to stay warm for three days with no heat and electricity. The story realistically presents a family doing its best during very difficult times. Illustrated with simple pictures that underscore the story's seriousness.

1222 *The Night We Slept Outside.* Ill. by Anne Rockwell. Macmillan, 1983; pap., 1986. ISBN 0-02-777450-3. SERIES: Ready-to-Read. SUBJECTS: Camps and camping—Fiction; Emotions—Fear—Fiction; Night—Fiction. RL 2.2.
Anxious to try out their new sleeping bags, two brothers spend the night on their deck and are frightened by the night noises and animals. Ink drawings with dark blue and gray watercolors capture the feeling of night outdoors while the story effectively shows children trying to combat fears.

1223 *Out to Sea.* Ill. by authors. Macmillan, 1980, o.p. SERIES: Ready-to-Read. SUBJECTS: Boats and boating—Fiction; Emergencies—Fiction. RL 2.4.
Two children playing in a boat are washed out to sea. Their desperate parents get the Coast Guard to try to rescue them in this suspenseful and realistic story. The simple yet effective ink drawings have aqua and gray washes.

Rockwell, Harlow

1224 *I Did It.* Ill. by author. Macmillan, 1974, o.p.; pap., 1987. ISBN 0-689-71126-3. SERIES: Ready-to-Read. SUBJECTS: Arts and crafts. RL 2.8.
Children explain how to create something they have enjoyed making: a paperbag mask, a bean mosaic, a papier-mâché fish, a paper airplane, invisible messages, and bread. Although no special safety precautions are given, the simple ink pictures show children working with adult supervision.

1225 *Look at This.* Ill. by author. Macmillan, 1978, o.p.; pap., 1987. ISBN 0-689-71165-4. SERIES: Ready-to-Read. SUBJECTS: Arts and crafts. RL 2.1.

Three children from different families explain how to make a dancing frog, applesauce, and a noisemaker. The instructions and the pictures accompanying them are clear and are easy for young children to follow.

Ronai, Lili

1226 *Corals.* Ill. by Arabelle Wheatley. Crowell, 1976. ISBN 0-690-00921-6. SERIES: Let's-Read-and-Find-Out. SUBJECTS: Oceans and ocean life. RL 3.4.
By means of an imaginary underwater journey through coral reefs and atolls and along the ocean floor, readers learn about corals and the ocean life around them. Simple ink and watercolor pictures are attractive and extend the information in the text.

Roop, Peter, and Roop, Connie

1227 *Keep the Lights Burning, Abbie.* Ill. by Peter E. Hanson. Carolrhoda, 1985. ISBN 0-87614-275-7. SERIES: On My Own. SUBJECTS: Behavior—Brave—Fiction; Historical fiction; Lighthouses—Fiction. RL 2.2.
For four weeks in 1856 a ferocious storm delays Abbie's father's return to their island lighthouse home. Young Abbie keeps the lights burning and tends to her ill mother until her father finally gets through to them. Excellent watercolors illustrate this understated tale of bravery.

Rosen, Ellsworth

1228 *Spiders Are Spinners.* Ill. by Teco Slagboom. Houghton, 1968, o.p. SUBJECTS: Animals—Spiders. RL 2.7.
Using a rhyming text, Rosen discusses a variety of spiders and webs without much attention to detail or specifics. The verse and carefully created pencil drawings act as an invitation to further reading about arachnids and should work well with children.

Rosenbloom, Joseph

1229 *Deputy Dan and the Bank Robbers.* Ill. by Tim Raglin. Random House, hb and pap., 1985. ISBN 0-394-97045-4.

SERIES: Step into Reading. SUBJECTS: Humorous stories; Robbers and outlaws—Fiction; Western stories. RL 2.7.

A literal-minded, persevering deputy, Dan accidentally uncovers clues to the identity of the notorious Scrambled Eggs Gang and captures them. Pen and wash pictures help to show the absurdity of this very funny story.

1230 *Deputy Dan Gets His Man.* Ill. by Tim Raglin. Random House, hb and pap., 1985. ISBN 0-394-97250-3. SERIES: Step into Reading. SUBJECTS: Humorous stories; Robbers and outlaws—Fiction; Western stories. RL 2.8.

Dan, an old west version of Amelia Bedelia who does everything exactly as instructed, catches the pearl thief Shootin' Sam and foils a train robbery. The story is accompanied by humorous full color ink and wash pictures.

1231 *The Funniest Dinosaur Book Ever!* Ill. by Hans Wilhelm. Sterling, 1987. ISBN 0-8069-6625-4. SUBJECTS: Dinosaurs—Fiction; Jokes and riddles. RL 2.1.

This collection of old jokes is bound to get laughs from young readers and groans from older siblings and adults who will be forced to hear them again. The jokes are arranged around and among funny and colorful pictures of dinosaurs that are in a variety of situations.

Rosenfeld, Sam

1232 *A Drop of Water.* Ill. by Helen Basilevsky. Harvey House, 1970, o.p. SERIES: Science Parade. SUBJECTS: Water; Weather. RL 2.1.

Opening and closing with illustrations of a drop of water slowly evaporating, this book shows the reader how condensation, cloud formation, and rain occur. The information given is slight but enough to satisfy superficial curiosity. Illustrated with simple black, gray, and gold pictures.

Rosenthal, Bert

1233 *Basketball.* Photos. Childrens, hb and pap., 1983. ISBN 0-516-01674-1. SERIES: New True. SUBJECTS: Sports—Basketball. RL 3.4.

This book explains the game, its rules and equipment, and the team composition. The differences among professional, college, and high school rules are also noted. Full color photographs of players of all ages, male and female, accompany the text.

Rosenthal, Mark

1234 *Bears.* Photos. Childrens, hb and pap., 1983. ISBN 0-516-01675-X. SERIES: New True. SUBJECTS: Animals—Bears. RL 2.6.

In brief chapters with short sentences, this volume presents a variety of bears, their habitats, and their habits. A glossary and an index are included. Illustrated with full color photographs.

Ross, Dave, and Wilson, Jeanne

1235 *Mr. Terwilliger's Secret.* Ill. by authors. Watts, 1981. ISBN 0-531-04191-3. SERIES: Easy-Read Story. SUBJECTS: Dinosaurs—Fiction; Fantasy. RL 2.4.

Mr. Terwilliger lets Margaret and Joel in on his secret: He has a real triceratops, Sara, in his basement. On the day the two children agree to feed Sara, she gets loose and does damage to the neighbors' yards. Sketchy childlike drawings fit this fantasy well.

Ross, Jan

1236 *Dogs Have Paws.* Ill. by Robert Masheris. Follett, 1982, o.p. SERIES: Beginning to Read. SUBJECTS: Families, single parent—Fiction; Pets—Dogs—Fiction. RL 2.3.

When his father reminds him to wash his hands or put on boots, a little boy enviously thinks of his dog's paws, which are not washed and do not wear boots. Then he realizes that having hands means he can do many things a dog cannot do. Good realistic pictures show a close-knit single-parent family.

Ross, Pat

1237 *M and M and the Bad News Babies.* Ill. by Marylin Hafner. Pantheon, hb and pap., 1983. ISBN 0-394-94532-8. SERIES: I Am Reading. SUBJECTS: Baby-

Ross, Pat (cont.)

sitting—Fiction; Friendship—Fiction; Siblings—Twins—Fiction. RL 2.4.
Trying to earn money for a new fish tank, two friends, Mimi and Mandy, agree to baby-sit for the twins, Richie and Benjie. The girls' spunk and ingenuity in the face of two very lively babies make this story a lot of fun. Pencil and wash pictures of the four further the humor.

1238 *M and M and the Big Bag.* Ill. by Marylin Hafner. Pantheon, 1981, o.p.; Penguin, pap., 1985. ISBN 0-14-031852-6. SERIES: I Am Reading. SUBJECTS: Friendship—Fiction; Shopping—Fiction. RL 2.8.
On their first solo trip to the grocery store, two friends, Mandy and Mimi, lose their shopping list and almost buy all the wrong things. Fortunately they find the list just in time. This delightful story has humorous pencil and wash pictures.

1239 *M and M and the Haunted House Game.* Ill. by Marylin Hafner. Pantheon, 1980, o.p.; Dell, pap., 1981. ISBN 0-440-45544-8. SERIES: I Am Reading. SUBJECTS: Emotions—Fear—Fiction; Friendship—Fiction; Games—Fiction. RL 2.8.
The haunted house game seems a perfect choice for a boring afternoon until two friends, Mimi and Mandy, accidentally scare themselves. A sense of fun—and near fear—in the characters' imaginative play is successfully created. The lively pictures add to the humor.

1240 *M and M and the Mummy Mess.* Ill. by Marylin Hafner. Viking Kestrel, 1985; pap., 1986. ISBN 0-670-80548-3. SUBJECTS: Friendship—Fiction; Mummies—Fiction; Museums—Fiction. RL 2.9.
Too early for the Egyptian mummy show, two friends, Mandy and Mimi, sneak into the exhibit area and become fascinated by the mummies and the museum before being caught by the director. The light, humorous illustrations are in gray-toned pencil and wash.

1241 *M and M and the Santa Secrets.* Ill. by Marylin Hafner. Viking Kestrel, 1985.

ISBN 0-670-80624-2. SUBJECTS: Friendship—Fiction; Holidays—Christmas—Fiction. RL 2.7.
Two best friends, Mimi and Mandy, do not know what to get each other for Christmas until each hears the other tell Santa what she wants most. The story realistically captures the joys and frustrations of best friends while the illustrations depict the girls in light-hearted pencil sketches.

1242 *M and M and the Superchild Afternoon.* Ill. by Marylin Hafner. Viking Kestrel, 1987. ISBN 0-670-81200-0. SUBJECTS: Dancing—Fiction; Friendship—Fiction; Sports—Gymnastics—Fiction. RL 2.9.
Unable to decide which Superchild activity to join, two friends, Mimi and Mandy, try each other's choices—ballet and gymnastics—and discover hidden talents. Pencil and wash pictures effectively complement the text.

1243 *Meet M and M.* Ill. by Marylin Hafner. Pantheon, 1980, o.p.; Penguin, pap., 1988. ISBN 0-14-032651-0. SERIES: I Am Reading. SUBJECTS: Behavior—Argumentative—Fiction; Friendship—Fiction. RL 2.5.
Two best friends, Mandy and Mimi, seem inseparable until one day they are crabby and fight. Slowly they overcome their anger and hurt and decide to renew their friendship. The pencil and wash drawings in gray and white capture the emotions of these two little girls.

1244 *Molly and the Slow Teeth.* Ill. by Jerry Milord. Lothrop, 1980, o.p. SUBJECTS: Human body—Teeth—Fiction; Tooth fairy—Fiction. RL 2.8.
Everyone in second grade but Molly has lost a tooth so she tries ways to fool her friends and the tooth fairy into believing that she is missing a tooth. Sketchy ink drawings with some color accents create pictures of less than pristine but very appealing children.

Rowland, Florence W.

1245 *Amish Boy.* Ill. by Dale Payson. Putnam, 1970, o.p. SERIES: See and Read. SUBJECTS: Amish—Fiction. RL 2.2.
When lightning hits and destroys a barn, other Amish families come to help Jonathan's

family build a new one. The text, a vehicle for information about the Amish, is readable but occasionally stilted, relying on the realistic pencil drawings to soften the tone.

1246 *Amish Wedding.* Ill. by Dale Payson. Putnam, 1971, o.p. SERIES: See and Read. SUBJECTS: Amish—Fiction; Marriage and wedding customs— Fiction. RL 2.7.

Young Jonathan Lapp's oldest sister, Rebecca, is about to be married and it is through Jonathan's eyes that the reader sees Amish courtship and wedding customs. A good introduction to the Amish, the story has realistic charcoal pencil and wash pictures.

Roy, Ron

1247 *Awful Thursday.* Ill. by Lillian Hoban. Pantheon, 1979, o.p. SERIES: I Am Reading. SUBJECTS: Behavior— Responsible—Fiction; Emotions— Fear—Fiction. RL 2.0.

Jack borrows a tape recorder from the school library. He puts it down, and a bus runs over it. Devastated, he cannot imagine how he can tell the librarian what happened and is afraid she will be very angry. Well written with some humorous moments, the story is illustrated with simple sketches.

1248 *Great Frog Swap.* Ill. by Victoria Chess. Pantheon, 1981, o.p. SUBJECTS: Animals—Frogs and toads—Fiction; Contests—Fiction. RL 2.5.

Harriet defeats the neighborhood boys' best-laid plans and shady efforts at winning the frog-jumping contest. The boys' machinations are a bit convoluted but fascinating as they try to win. Illustrations are in shades of gray.

1249 *A Thousand Pails of Water.* Ill. by Vo-Dinh Mai. Knopf, 1978, o.p. SUBJECTS: Animals—Whales—Fiction; Japan— Fiction; Parent and child—Fiction. RL 2.5.

Yukio does not like the fact that his father has to kill whales for a living when his friend's father can work in a market. Finding a whale stranded on the beach, Yukio tries to save it by pouring water over it. The quiet story has soft charcoal sketches that place it in Japan.

Royston, Angela

1250 *The Deer.* Ill. by Bernard Robinson. Warwick, 1988. ISBN 0-531-19038-2. SERIES: Animal Life Stories. SUBJECTS: Animals—Deer. RL 2.8.

The life of a red deer fawn is told as a work of fiction as he grows into adulthood in the English forest. A two page addendum gives more information about the deer. Illustrations are in full color and detailed with occasional black and white drawings. A very short glossary is included.

1251 *The Duck.* Ill. by Maurice Pledger and Bernard Robinson. Warwick, 1988. ISBN 0-531-19039-0. SERIES: Animal Life Stories. SUBJECTS: Animals—Ducks. RL 2.3.

Courtship and rearing of young by mallard ducks are presented in a factual look at a year in a duck's life. The text introduces some of the dangers of life, differentiates between drakes and ducks, and is illustrated with full color, detailed, and realistic paintings.

1252 *The Fox.* Ill. by Bernard Robinson. Warwick, 1988. ISBN 0-531-19040-4. SERIES: Animal Life Stories. SUBJECTS: Animals—Foxes. RL 2.5.

A young vixen leaves her mother and siblings to find her own habitat, mate, and raise her cubs in this realistic account of a red fox's life. Lovely, full color paintings illustrate the story along with black and white sketches. The glossary seems inadequate for the somewhat difficult text.

1253 *The Otter.* Ill. by Bernard Robinson. Warwick, 1988. ISBN 0-531-19041-2. SERIES: Animal Life Stories. SUBJECTS: Animals—Otters. RL 2.6.

The description of the life and habitat of a river otter is spare, nearly poetic, in this story that follows its travels along the river to the sea and back from fall to summer. The full color paintings and black and white drawings are realistic. Includes an addendum and short glossary.

1254 *The Penguin.* Ill. by Trevor Boyer. Warwick, 1988. ISBN 0-531-19042-0. SERIES: Animal Life Stories. SUBJECTS: Animals—Penguins. RL 3.1.

Royston, Angela (cont.)

The penguin's life on the ice and in the sea is described in a richly illustrated story about typical events in a year of a penguin—including the rearing of young. A two page section, "More about Penguins," defines some terms and clarifies differences among penguins. A glossary is included.

1255 *The Tiger.* Ill. by Graham Allen. Warwick, 1988. ISBN 0-531-19043-9. SERIES: Animal Life Stories. SUBJECTS: Animals—Tigers. RL 2.6.

A female tiger is observed as she seeks a mate, has a litter, and, over a two year period, raises and trains her cubs. Realistic full color paintings and black and white sketches ably depict this largest of the cat family. A two page addendum and short glossary are included.

Ruchlis, Hy

1256 *How a Rock Came to Be in a Fence on a Road near a Town.* Ill. by Mamoru Funai. Walker, 1973. ISBN 0-8027-6162-3. SUBJECTS: Geology. RL 2.4.

Formed from fossil sediments millions of years ago, a piece of gray limestone is now part of a fence. A clear, informative narrative follows the stone from its beginnings, through different geologic eras, to the stone fence. Illustrated with line drawings with aquamarine and gray washes.

Rudeen, Kenneth

1257 *Roberto Clemente.* Ill. by Frank Mullins. Crowell, 1974, o.p. SERIES: Crowell Biography. SUBJECTS: Biographies; Sports—Baseball. RL 2.9.

A member of the Baseball Hall of Fame, Clemente worked hard to be a professional player. The book looks back on his life in Puerto Rico, his triumphs with the Pittsburgh Pirates, and his tragic death on a humanitarian mission to Nicaragua. Illustrated with impressionistic drawings.

Ruthstrom, Dorotha

1258 *The Big Kite Contest.* Ill. by Lillian Hoban. Pantheon, 1980. ISBN 0-394-84430-0. SERIES: I Am Reading.

SUBJECTS: Kites and kite flying—Fiction; Siblings—Fiction. RL 2.9.

Stephen is practicing for the kite contest when he trips and tears his prize kite. Unable to earn enough money to replace it, he gives up. Stephen's little sister repairs the kite and wins the contest with her brother's help. Illustrated with warm, sketchy drawings.

Ryckman, John

1259 *Ginger's Upstairs Pet.* Ill. by Erica Merkling. Garrard, hb and pap., 1971. ISBN 0-8116-6717-0. SERIES: Venture. SUBJECTS: Animals—Giraffes—Fiction; Humorous stories; Pets—Fiction. RL 1.6.

All morning Ginger runs up and down the stairs asking her mother for food for her new pet. Sure that Ginger is eating everything herself, Mother goes upstairs and discovers a giraffe at Ginger's window. The ink drawings with green and orange accents help to maintain the reader's interest.

Ryder, Joanne

1260 *Fireflies.* Ill. by Don Bolognese. Harper & Row, 1977. ISBN 0-06-025153-0. SERIES: Science I Can Read. SUBJECTS: Animals—Fireflies. RL 2.6.

A simple text tells how, after spending nearly two years underground as a glowworm, the firefly goes in search of a mate, using his special yellow light as a signal to attract a female. Detailed ink and colored wash illustrations.

1261 *White Bear, Ice Bear.* Ill. by Michael Rothman. Morrow, 1989. ISBN 0-688-07174-0. SERIES: Just for a Day. SUBJECTS: Animals—Bears; Seasons—Winter; Weather—Snow. RL 2.1.

A boy wakes up to a snow-covered world and, as he looks out at it, he is transformed into a polar bear. For a day he is a bear—living on the ice, hunting for food, and surviving the cold. Wintry, blue-toned landscapes and a well-paced, poetic text make his transformation believable.

Ryder, Joanne, and Feinburg, Harold S.

1262 *Snail in the Woods.* Ill. by Jo Polseno. Harper & Row, 1979. ISBN 0-06-

825169-7. SERIES: Nature I Can Read. SUBJECTS: Animals—Snails. RL 2.9.

A tiny white-lipped snail hatches and begins to grow and explore its environment. It faces many dangers, survives them, and finally is old enough to lay its own eggs. The story provides good information about the snail's life cycle and is illustrated in watercolors.

Rylant, Cynthia

1263 *Henry and Mudge in Puddle Trouble: The Second Book of Their Adventures.* Ill. by Sucie Stevenson. Bradbury, 1987. ISBN 0-02-778002-3. SERIES: Henry and Mudge. SUBJECTS: Humorous stories; Pets—Dogs—Fiction; Seasons—Spring—Fiction. RL 2.2.

Henry and his big dog, Mudge, enjoy spring as they discover a beautiful blue flower and try not to pick it, play in a deep puddle, and become protectors of their neighbor's five new kittens. Full color washes with bold outlining make simple yet lively pictures for these gentle, funny stories.

1264 *Henry and Mudge in the Green Time.* Ill. by Sucie Stevenson. Bradbury, 1987. ISBN 0-02-778003-1. SERIES: Henry and Mudge. SUBJECTS: Pets—Dogs—Fiction; Seasons—Summer—Fiction. RL 2.0.

Henry shares a summer picnic with his lovable dog, Mudge, gives him a bath, and turns Mudge into a dragon in these delightful and imaginative adventures. Bright summery watercolors capture the warmth and liveliness of the devoted friends.

1265 *Henry and Mudge in the Sparkle Days.* Ill. by Sucie Stevenson. Bradbury, 1988. ISBN 0-02-778005-8. SERIES: Henry and Mudge. SUBJECTS: Holidays—Christmas—Fiction; Pets—Dogs—Fiction; Seasons—Winter—Fiction. RL 2.3.

After an almost interminable wait, snow finally falls and Henry and his big dog, Mudge, play in it, build forts, enjoy a special Christmas dinner, and share quiet and cozy moments at home or on special family walks.

The well-written stories capture the best parts of childhood winters helped by vibrant and colorful pictures.

1266 *Henry and Mudge under the Yellow Moon.* Ill. by Sucie Stevenson. Bradbury, 1987. ISBN 0-02-778004-X. SERIES: Henry and Mudge. SUBJECTS: Pets—Dogs—Fiction; Seasons—Fall—Fiction. RL 2.1.

With his dog, Mudge, beside him, Henry finds that fall is better than ever. The ghost stories are not as frightening, and Aunt Sally's dreaded visit is actually fun. One of a series, this book continues to maintain high-quality writing along with lively, warm, and childlike illustrations.

S

Sabin, Louis

1267 *Birthday Surprise.* Ill. by John Magine. Troll, hb and pap., 1981. ISBN 0-89375-527-3. SERIES: Giant First-Start. SUBJECTS: Animals—Skunks—Fiction; Birthdays—Fiction; Self-esteem—Fiction. RL 1.5.

Sammy, a skunk, is sure no one likes him or will remember his birthday. A huge box arrives with a birthday hat inside, and he feels more unhappy and goes to bed. Just then his many friends arrive to wish him a happy birthday. Pencil and marker drawings look hurried and too childlike.

Sadler, Marilyn

1268 *It's Not Easy Being a Bunny.* Ill. by Roger Bollen. Beginner, 1983. ISBN 0-394-96102-1. SERIES: I Can Read It All By Myself. SUBJECTS: Animals—Fiction; Animals—Rabbits—Fiction; Self-esteem—Fiction. RL 2.1.

Tired of eating cooked carrots, having long ears, and being in a large family, P. J. Funny-bunny tries being a variety of other animals. Finally he decides that being a bunny is just right. Full color comic-style pictures complement the brief, humorous story.

Sadler, Marilyn (cont.)

1269 *P. J. Funnybunny in the Great Tricycle Race.* Ill. by Roger Bollen. Western, 1988. ISBN 0-307-11745-6. SERIES: Golden Look-Look. SUBJECTS: Animals—Rabbits—Fiction; Bicycles and bicycling—Fiction; Humorous stories. RL 1.9.

Against all odds P. J. and his family decide that he will win the Great Turtle Creek Tricycle Race. He practices hard and, despite a spill, manages to win the race. The silly cartoon style pictures in bold colors should appeal to many children.

1270 *The Very Bad Bunny.* Ill. by Roger Bollen. Beginner, 1984. ISBN 0-394-96861-1. SERIES: I Can Read It All By Myself. SUBJECTS: Animals—Rabbits—Fiction; Behavior—Fiction. RL 2.5.

P. J.'s thoughtless behavior causes his family to think him a very bad bunny until cousin Binky arrives. Binky's intentionally nasty conduct leads them to change their opinion of P. J. Humorous, cartoonlike pictures in vibrant colors illustrate this very funny story.

Saintsing, David

1271 *The World of Butterflies.* Photos. Gareth Stevens, 1987. ISBN 0-55532-072-4. SERIES: Where Animals Live. SUBJECTS: Animals—Butterflies and moths. RL 3.3.

The different stages in the development of butterflies are presented along with a discussion of their enemies and the way butterflies protect themselves. The text, color photographs, and food-chain diagram are all well done and accessible to young readers.

1272 *The World of Owls.* Photos. Gareth Stevens, 1988. ISBN 1-55532-301-4. SERIES: Where Animals Live. SUBJECTS: Animals—Owls. RL 2.8.

The habitats, prey, anatomy, and life cycles of a variety of owls are carefully documented in color photos and clear text. Photos are arranged to reflect exactly what is being discussed in the text and arrows are used to match captions and photos. Excellent glossary clearly defines new terms. Adapted from

Jennifer Coldrey's *The Owl in the Tree* (Gareth Stevens, 1988).

Saltzberg, Barney

1273 *What to Say to Clara.* Ill. by author. Atheneum, 1984. ISBN 0-689-31041-2. SUBJECTS: Behavior—Shyness—Fiction; School stories; Self-esteem—Fiction. RL 2.2.

Otis wants to be his new classmate Clara's friend but cannot make up his mind how to do it. After much agonizing he decides to try the direct approach. He tries saying hello and it works! Ink line drawings shaded with dots illustrate this good story about overcoming shyness.

Sandin, Joan

1274 *The Long Way to a New Land.* Ill. by author. Harper & Row, 1981; pap., 1986. ISBN 0-06-025194-8. SERIES: I Can Read History. SUBJECTS: Emigration and immigration—Fiction; Sweden—Fiction; United States—Fiction. RL 2.7.

A Swedish farm family reluctantly decides to leave their drought-stricken land and emigrate to the United States. Their journey across the Atlantic is harrowing but ends with hope in the United States. The moving story has detailed, realistic drawings.

Saunders, Susan

1275 *Charles Rat's Picnic.* Ill. by Robert Byrd. Dutton, 1983. ISBN 0-525-44067-4. SUBJECTS: Animals—Armadillos—Fiction; Animals—Rats—Fiction; Picnics—Fiction. RL 2.0.

Charles Rat, intent on doing things just right, ends up very wet and without dinner when he takes Miranda Armadillo on a picnic. Illustrated with carefully drawn pictures of a nattily attired rat and armadillo.

Scarf, Maggi

1276 *Meet Benjamin Franklin.* Ill. by Harry Beckhoff. Random House, 1968, o.p. SERIES: Step-Up. SUBJECTS:

Biographies; Inventors and inventions; United States—Revolution. RL 2.4.
This biography of Benjamin Franklin is a complete history of his life. The writing is simple and clear with no fictionalized dialogue. Information on electricity is inaccurate, however, but it is a very small part of an otherwise good book. Illustrated with somewhat idealized colored drawings.

Schick, Alice, and Schick, Joel

1277 *Just This Once*. Ill. by Alice Schick. Lippincott, 1978. ISBN 0-397-31803-0. SERIES: I-Like-to-Read. SUBJECTS: Animals—Dogs—Fiction; Cave dwellers—Fiction; Historical fiction. RL 2.7.
Og, Glok, and their children are the only ones in their tribe not terrified by the friendly wolf. Again and again they say "just this once" as they pet and feed her. Ultimately they make her a part of their tribe and the first domesticated "dog." Realistic drawings of the prehistoric setting have a humorous look to them.

Schick, Eleanor

1278 *Home Alone*. Ill. by author. Dial, 1980. ISBN 0-8037-4255-X. SERIES: Easy-to-Read. SUBJECTS: Latchkey children—Fiction; Self-esteem—Fiction. RL 2.1.
On his first day home alone after school, Andy carefully follows the instructions his mother and father gave him as he passes the time waiting for them to come home. Carefully executed realistic colored pencil drawings illustrate this very common situation.

1279 *Joey on His Own*. Ill. by author. Dial, 1982. ISBN 0-8037-4302-5. SERIES: Easy-to-Read. SUBJECTS: Behavior—Responsible—Fiction; Shopping—Fiction. RL 2.3.
Joey's little sister is sick and he must go to the store for his mother. Walking past unsavory characters on the way, Joey finally makes it to the store and returns home with a new sense of responsibility. The sympathetic text has realistic colored pencil drawings.

1280 *Neighborhood Knight*. Ill. by author. Greenwillow, 1976, o.p. SERIES: Read-alone. SUBJECTS: Families, single parent—Fiction; Imagination—Fiction. RL 2.4.
Since his father, the "king," has been gone a long time, the little boy pretends he is a courageous knight defending his mother and sister and their apartment "castle." Sensitively written and drawn, the story shows a small child dealing in the best way he can with anger and frustration.

1281 *Rainy Sunday*. Ill. by author. Dial, 1981, o.s.i.; pap., 1981. ISBN 0-8037-7371-4. SERIES: Easy-to-Read. SUBJECTS: City and town life—Fiction; Family life—Fiction; Weather—Rain—Fiction. RL 2.1.
Everything in the city looks gray and feels cold when a little girl wakes up. As she shares a quiet day with her mother and father, the day brightens with their pleasure in one another's company. The colored pencil illustrations are spare and as clearly defined as the activities the small family shares.

1282 *Summer at the Sea*. Ill. by author. Greenwillow, 1979, o.p. SERIES: Read-alone. SUBJECTS: Seashore—Fiction; Vacation—Fiction. RL 2.5.
After an entire summer at the ocean spent meeting people, fishing, planting flowers, and enjoying almost every minute, it is hard for a little girl to return to her busy city life. The meticulous pencil and wash drawings are a perfect complement to the quiet text.

Schneider, Herman, and Schneider, Nina

1283 *Science Fun with a Flashlight*. Ill. by Harriet Sherman. McGraw-Hill, 1975, o.p. SUBJECTS: Science experiments; Shadows. RL 2.1.
A clever text shows children how to have a good time experimenting with light and shadows. By using a flashlight they can discover color in light, how the angle of light affects shadows, and how color and light are reflected. The pictures are delightful.

Schulman, Janet

1284 *The Big Hello*. Ill. by Lillian Hoban. Greenwillow, 1976; Dell, pap., 1980.

Schulman, Janet (cont.)

ISBN 0-688-80036-X. SERIES: Read-alone. SUBJECTS: Emotions—Fear—Fiction; Moving, household—Fiction; Toys—Dolls and dollhouses—Fiction. RL 1.8.

A little girl comforts her doll as they fly to their new home in California. Once there the doll is lost but fortunately found by a child certain to be the little girl's hoped-for new friend. Pencil drawings help readers to empathize with the child's fear of the unknown.

1285 *Camp Kee Wee's Secret Weapon.* Ill. by Marylin Hafner. Greenwillow, 1979, o.p. SERIES: Read-alone. SUBJECTS: Camps and camping—Fiction; Sports—Softball—Fiction. RL 2.2.

Forced to go to camp when she wants to stay home and play softball, Jill reluctantly goes but ends up loving it, especially when she becomes the pitcher on a softball team. Attractive colored pencil sketches of children are lively and fit Jill's varying moods.

1286 *The Great Big Dummy.* Ill. by Lillian Hoban. Greenwillow, 1979, o.p. SERIES: Read-alone. SUBJECTS: Emotions—Loneliness—Fiction; Friendship—Fiction; Imagination—Fiction. RL 2.1.

When her friends are too busy to play with her, Anna decides to create a "sister" out of her clothes and play with her until her friends are free to play. The story and appealing pencil and wash drawings successfully present a child who is both imaginative and independent.

1287 *Jack the Bum and the Halloween Handout.* Ill. by James Stevenson. Greenwillow, 1977; U.S. Committee for UNICEF, pap., 1977. ISBN 0-688-80057-2. SERIES: Read-alone. SUBJECTS: Holidays—Halloween—Fiction; Tramps—Fiction. RL 2.0.

Wanting a cup of coffee, Jack the bum tries trick-or-treating and even using the word *UNICEF* as he goes door to door. Finally he follows children into a UNICEF party where he is the winner of $5.00, which he donates to UNICEF. Illustrated with humorous pencil and wash drawings.

1288 *Jack the Bum and the Haunted House.* Ill. by James Stevenson. Greenwillow, 1977, o.p. SERIES: Read-alone. SUBJECTS: Haunted houses—Fiction; Robbers and outlaws—Fiction; Tramps—Fiction. RL 2.1.

With nowhere else to go during the cold weather, Jack takes up residence in a supposedly haunted house. Jack's determination to stay there results in his capturing a jewel thief. Humorous pencil and wash drawings show a kindly but resolute "tramp" resigned to his lot.

1289 *Jack the Bum and the UFO.* Ill. by James Stevenson. Greenwillow, 1978, o.p. SERIES: Read-alone. SUBJECTS: Tramps—Fiction; UFOs—Fiction. RL 2.0.

When the children beg Jack the bum to stop a land developer from turning their forest and pond into a parking lot, Jack cleverly convinces the developer that the area is a haven for UFOs. The text combines humor with concern for the environment. Illustrated with comic pencil and wash sketches.

1290 *Jenny and the Tennis Nut.* Ill. by Marylin Hafner. Greenwillow, 1978, o.p.; Dell, pap., 1981. ISBN 0-440-44211-7. SERIES: Read-alone. SUBJECTS: Self-esteem—Fiction; Sports—Gymnastics—Fiction; Sports—Tennis—Fiction. RL 2.5.

Insistent that Jenny be accomplished in at least one sport, her father tries to teach her his favorite—tennis—overlooking her obvious talent in gymnastics. Imaginative pencil drawings capture the enthusiasm that father and daughter give to their respective sports.

Schwartz, Alvin

1291 *All of Our Noses Are Here and Other Noodle Tales.* Ill. by Karen A. Weinhaus. Harper & Row, 1985; pap., 1987. ISBN 0-06-025288-X. SERIES: I Can Read. SUBJECTS: Folklore—United States; Humorous stories. RL 2.3.

Anyone reading these five stories about the Brown family is sure to end up laughing. The Browns are typical noodles doing absolutely ridiculous things in total seriousness. The colored pencil and wash drawings give these silly folktales from around the world a special zany look.

1292 *Busy Buzzing Bumblebees and Other Tongue Twisters.* Ill. by Kathie Abrams. Harper & Row, hb and pap., 1982. ISBN 0-06-025269-3. SERIES: I Can Read. SUBJECTS: Tongue twisters. RL 3.7.
Children and adults will have a good time with the 46 phrases that are guaranteed to twist and torment tongues. The brightly colored, blue-outlined pictures are clear and definitely add to the fun.

1293 *I Saw You in the Bathtub and Other Folk Rhymes.* Ill. by Syd Hoff. Harper & Row, 1989. ISBN 0-06-025298-7. SERIES: I Can Read. SUBJECTS: Folklore—United States; Humor; Poetry. RL 2.1.
Included here are rhymes and chants that children in the United States say or sing at play. Readers will be familiar with most of them and enjoy their familiarity. Hoff's comic ink and wash drawings are in his popular sketchy and very funny style and are attractive to children.

1294 *In a Dark, Dark Room and Other Scary Stories.* Ill. by Dirk Zimmer. Harper & Row, 1984; pap., 1985. ISBN 0-06-025274-X. SERIES: I Can Read. SUBJECTS: Folklore; Ghost stories; Scary stories. RL 2.0.
The seven short, scary stories and lyrics from spooky songs are perfect for young readers to learn and tell at camp or on Halloween. The detailed ink pictures have red and yellow accents that blend humor into somewhat scary pictures.

1295 *Ten Copycats in a Boat and Other Riddles.* Ill. by Marc Simont. Harper & Row, 1980; pap., 1985. ISBN 0-06-025238-3. SERIES: I Can Read. SUBJECTS: Jokes and riddles. RL 2.2.
Familiar yet still funny jokes and riddles get two pages each—one for the joke or riddle and the other for the answer. The ink, watercolor, and colored pencil drawings capably extend the silliness.

1296 *There Is a Carrot in My Ear and Other Noodle Tales.* Ill. by Karen A. Weinhaus. Harper & Row, 1982; pap., 1986. ISBN 0-06-025234-0. SERIES: I Can Read. SUBJECTS: Folklore—United States; Humorous stories. RL 2.5.
The Brown family are the noodles as they swim in a waterless pool, try to hatch a "mare's egg," or mistake long underwear for an intruder. The six stories offer children an opportunity to have fun with absolutely ridiculous characters and comic illustrations in red, yellow, and gray.

Scott, Geoffrey

1297 *Egyptian Boats.* Ill. by Nancy L. Carlson. Carolrhoda, 1981. ISBN 0-87614-138-6. SERIES: On My Own. SUBJECTS: Boats and boating; Egypt, ancient. RL 2.3.
A vocabulary builder, this informative history of Egyptian watercraft describes different types and sizes of boats, how they were used, and for what purposes. It provides a brief glance at the social structure of ancient Egypt. Illustrated with detailed, realistic ink drawings.

1298 *Labor Day.* Ill. by Cherie R. Wyman. Carolrhoda, 1982. ISBN 0-87614-178-5. SERIES: On My Own. SUBJECTS: Holidays—Labor Day. RL 3.1.
A brief look at the first Labor Day celebration shows the difficult working conditions in the 1880s when the Central Labor Union and the Knights of Labor held the first Labor Day parade. The book, illustrated with romanticized pictures of workers, encourages pride in the labor movement.

1299 *Memorial Day.* Ill. by Peter E. Hanson. Carolrhoda, 1983. ISBN 0-87614-219-6. SERIES: On My Own. SUBJECTS: Holidays—Memorial Day. RL 3.0.
The origin of Memorial Day is traced to just after the Civil War and the celebration by the northern states of Decoration Day. Carefully written and providing good historical information and context, this book is illustrated with semirealistic ink drawings of historical scenes.

Seixas, Judith S.

1300 *Alcohol: What It Is, What It Does.* Ill. by Tom Huffman. Greenwillow, 1977, o.p.; pap., 1981. ISBN 0-688-00462-8. SERIES: Read-alone. SUBJECTS: Drugs and drug abuse. RL 2.3.

Much of the 56 pages is devoted to the nature of alcohol and its effect on the body and mind of the average person. One section also deals with alcoholism from the perspective of the alcoholic's family and stresses not taking the blame for another's drinking. Illustrated with comic ink sketches.

1301 *Drugs: What They Are, What They Do.* Ill. by Tom Huffman. Greenwillow, 1987. ISBN 0-688-07400-6. SERIES: Read-alone. SUBJECTS: Drugs and drug abuse. RL 3.3.

How drugs affect a person's ability to think and act and the other dangers they present are discussed in this guide to psychoactive drugs. The book stresses that it is important for children not to try *any* drugs. It is effectively illustrated with comic drawings that add to the book's impact.

1302 *Junk Food: What It Is, What It Does.* Ill. by Tom Huffman. Greenwillow, 1984. ISBN 0-688-02560-9. SERIES: Read-alone. SUBJECTS: Food; Nutrition. RL 2.7.

A useful guide to nutrition, this book encourages children to compare "junk" food to foods that are lower in calories, are good to eat, and provide more nutrients for growth and development. Clever ink sketches with orange accents accompany the well-written text.

1303 *Vitamins: What They Are, What They Do.* Ill. by Tom Huffman. Greenwillow, 1986. ISBN 0-688-06066-8. SERIES: Read-alone. SUBJECTS: Nutrition; Vitamins. RL 3.3.

Children reading this book will learn what vitamins are, how they were discovered, why they are added to foods, who needs supplements, and more. A section on nutrition and an easy-to-use vitamin chart are also included. Two-color ink drawings of smiling fruit and vegetables highlight the text.

1304 *Water: What It Is, What It Does.* Ill. by Tom Huffman. Greenwillow, 1987. ISBN 0-688-06608-9. SERIES: Read-alone. SUBJECTS: Conservation; Pollution—Water; Water. RL 3.2.

Using simple, straightforward language, the author discusses water's properties, its uses, and the abuses it suffers. With five interesting experiments, the text offers a relatively thorough examination of the subject. Illustrated with funny line drawings.

Selsam, Millicent E.

1305 *Benny's Animals and How He Put Them in Order.* Ill. by Arnold Lobel. Harper & Row, 1966. ISBN 0-06-025273-1. SERIES: Science I Can Read. SUBJECTS: Animals—Classification. RL 1.9.

Benny's curiosity about how to classify his pictures of animals takes him, with his parents' encouragement, to the natural science museum. While there he learns about the way in which animals are classified. Sketchy ink and colored pencil drawings keep this story upbeat and entertaining.

1306 *Egg to Chick.* Rev. ed; photos. Ill. by Barbara Wolff. Harper & Row, 1970; pap., 1987. ISBN 0-06-025290-1. SERIES: Science I Can Read. SUBJECTS: Animals—Reproduction. RL 2.5.

The development of a chick embryo is examined from the day of conception until 21 days later when the chick hatches. Multicolored drawings alternate with black and white photographs to present an accurate portrayal of the growth of the embryo.

1307 *Greg's Microscope.* Ill. by Arnold Lobel. Harper & Row, 1963. ISBN 0-06-025296-0. SERIES: Science I Can Read. SUBJECTS: Microscopes. RL 2.2.

Soon after Greg's father gives him a microscope, the whole family becomes involved in using it to learn about the things around them. A well-done introduction to the microscope, the book has charming and informative pictures that help to explain the use of this instrument.

1308 *Let's Get Turtles.* Ill. by Arnold Lobel. Harper & Row, 1965. ISBN 0-06-025311-8. SERIES: Science I Can Read.

SUBJECTS: Animals—Turtles; Pets—Turtles. RL 1.7.
Two best friends, Billy and Jerry, agree to get the same kind of pet—a turtle. Once they have them they learn how to take care of them and what to feed them. The lively ink and wash drawings add to the appeal of the book.

1309 *More Potatoes!* Ill. by Ben Shecter. Harper & Row, 1972. ISBN 0-06-025324-X. SERIES: Science I Can Read. SUBJECTS: Farm and country life; Vegetables. RL 2.3.
Curious about how the grocery store gets potatoes, Sue asks questions that lead her class to a trip to a warehouse and a farm. Through the illustrations and the text, readers will quickly learn that vegetables do not just appear on the shelves of supermarkets.

1310 *Plenty of Fish.* Ill. by Erik Blegvad. Harper & Row, 1960. ISBN 0-06-025321-5. SERIES: Science I Can Read. SUBJECTS: Animals—Fish; Pets—Fish. RL 2.0.
Irrepressible Willy is determined to have goldfish but must be constantly reminded to stop and find out the proper way to care for them. Willy's father patiently explains the curious world of goldfish to him. Illustrated with ink drawings showing a middle-class British family.

1311 *Seeds and More Seeds.* Ill. by Tomi Ungerer. Harper & Row, 1959. ISBN 0-06-025395-9. SERIES: Science I Can Read. SUBJECTS: Plants—Seeds, roots, and bulbs. RL 1.7.
With his father's encouragement, Benny explores why seeds grow. He plants a variety of things and watches as seeds grow while other things do not. The sketchy ink drawings show a turn-of-the-century father and son in an opulent setting investigating seeds.

1312 *Strange Creatures That Really Lived.* Ill. by Jennifer Dewey. Scholastic, 1987. ISBN 0-590-40493-8. SUBJECTS: Animals—Prehistoric. RL 2.6.
Not all of the creatures described in Selsam's clear style and Dewey's colored pencil, sometimes too-fanciful, drawings are all that strange, but all are interesting. A useful chart on the last page lists the dinosaurs, ancient mammals, insects, and birds included in the book.

1313 *Terry and the Caterpillars.* Ill. by Arnold Lobel. Harper & Row, 1962. ISBN 0-06-025406-8. SERIES: Nature I Can Read. SUBJECTS: Animals—Butterflies and moths; Animals—Caterpillars. RL 1.9.
Terry finds three caterpillars and watches curiously as they eat, grow, spin cocoons, and months later become moths. The story is full of factual information and, with its detailed ink and wash pictures, continues to fascinate children.

1314 *Tony's Birds.* Ill. by Kurt Werth. Harper & Row, 1961. ISBN 0-06-025421-1. SERIES: Science I Can Read. SUBJECTS: Animals—Birds—Fiction. RL 1.7.
An evening walk with his father leads Tony to an interest in birds. The well-developed relationship between father and son is the foundation of a story that introduces children to the rudiments of bird watching. The spare ink and wash sketches still appeal and do not appear dated.

1315 *Up, Down and Around: The Force of Gravity.* Ill. by Kenneth Dewey. Doubleday, 1977, o.p. SERIES: Chicago Museum of Science and Industry. SUBJECTS: Gravity. RL 2.9.
A clearly written text accurately explains the fundamental concepts associated with gravity, using space travel and planetary systems as examples. Realistic but sketchy illustrations and diagrams do not add much to the text.

1316 *When an Animal Grows.* Ill. by John Kaufmann. Harper & Row, 1966. ISBN 0-06-025461-0. SERIES: Science I Can Read. SUBJECTS: Animals; Animals—Growth and development. RL 2.1.
Four baby animals, two mammals and two birds, are contrasted from birth to independent living. A gorilla is compared with a lamb while a sparrow is compared with a mallard on alternating pages using different colors of ink for the text. Illustrated with gray watercolor paintings.

Selsam, Millicent E., and Hunt, Joyce

1317 *A First Look at Animals with Horns*. Ill.
by Harriett Springer. Walker, 1989.
ISBN 0-8027-6872-5. SERIES: First Look
At. SUBJECTS: Animals—Horned. RL 2.3.
After identifying and defining "horns," animals with varying numbers of horns are then
distinguished from one another. Accurate
black and white pencil drawings accompany
the simple text and work with it to help
readers identify different varieties of animals
by their characteristics.

1318 *A First Look at Animals without
Backbones*. Ill. by Harriett Springer.
Walker, 1976. ISBN 0-8027-6269-7.
SERIES: First Look At. SUBJECTS:
Animals—Invertebrates. RL 2.7.
After differentiating between animals that
have and do not have backbones, the book
discusses a variety of invertebrates. Those
covered include arthropods, echinoderms,
mollusks, worms, coelenterates, sponges, and
protozoa. Illustrated with detailed pencil
drawings that help clarify the text.

1319 *A First Look at Bird Nests*. Ill. by
Harriett Springer. Walker, 1984. ISBN
0-8027-6565-3. SERIES: First Look At.
SUBJECTS: Animals—Nests. RL 2.8.
Basic information on the identification of
nests of specific birds is offered. Also, an
attempt is made to involve readers in identifying a nest, which is shown in detailed and
realistic pencil drawings. Well researched, the
book provides good information for school
assignments or the satisfaction of curiosity.

1320 *A First Look at Birds*. Ill. by Harriett
Springer. Walker, 1973. ISBN 0-8027-
6164-X. SERIES: First Look At.
SUBJECTS: Animals—Birds. RL 2.3.
Children can learn a great deal about birds
and their physical characteristics by reading
this clearly written and factually accurate
book. Intending to hone powers of observation, Selsam and Hunt ask readers to choose
the correct illustration from among detailed
pencil drawings.

1321 *A First Look at Caterpillars*. Ill. by
Harriett Springer. Walker, 1988. ISBN
0-8027-6702-8. SERIES: First Look At.

SUBJECTS: Animals—Butterflies and
moths; Animals—Caterpillars. RL 2.3.
Children reading this are encouraged to use
the information in the text to help them in
examining the pictures of caterpillars, butterflies, and moths, and detecting differences
among them. The book has detailed, realistic
pencil drawings with green accents.

1322 *A First Look at Dinosaurs*. Ill. by
Harriett Springer. Walker, 1982;
Scholastic, pap. ISBN 0-8027-6456-8.
SERIES: First Look At. SUBJECTS:
Dinosaurs; Geology. RL 2.7.
All kinds of dinosaurs are introduced and
compared in the text and in the many detailed pencil drawings. Children are encouraged to match information in the text to
pictures of dinosaurs. The book also includes
some information on continental drift.

1323 *A First Look at Horses*. Ill. by Harriett
Springer. Walker, 1981, o.p. SERIES:
First Look At. SUBJECTS: Animals—
Horses. RL 2.6.
After a brief introduction to equine anatomy,
several breeds of horses are mentioned and
compared. The book emphasizes the importance of recognizing observable external differences among and between the horses pictured in detailed pencil drawings. Horse fans
should enjoy this one.

1324 *A First Look at Insects*. Ill. by Harriett
Springer. Walker, 1974. ISBN 0-8027-
6182-8. SERIES: First Look At. SUBJECTS:
Animals—Insects. RL 2.8.
Like others in the First Look At series, this
book attempts to get readers to use the
information in the well-written text to test
their powers of observation. Here they are
asked to distinguish detailed pencil drawings
of particular insects from pictures of other
animals and insects.

1325 *A First Look at Leaves*. Ill. by Harriett
Springer. Walker, 1972. ISBN 0-8027-
6118-6. SERIES: First Look At. SUBJECTS:
Plants—Trees. RL 2.7.
Like others in the First Look At series, this
book asks the reader to scan the illustrations
on a page and match an object (a leaf) to a
description. It also presents useful information about leaves and their parts. Simple line

drawings are very clear and sufficiently accurate for leaf identification.

1326 *A First Look at Owls, Eagles, and Other Hunters of the Sky.* Ill. by Harriett Springer. Walker, 1986. ISBN 0-8027-6642-0. SERIES: First Look At. SUBJECTS: Animals—Birds of Prey. RL 3.3.
Owls, eagles, falcons, and other birds of prey are pictured in lovely, realistic drawings and are compared to facilitate identification. The book further challenges the reader to identify birds' pictures based on the facts presented in the text.

1327 *A First Look at Poisonous Snakes.* Ill. by Harriett Springer. Walker, 1987. ISBN 0-8027-6683-8. SERIES: First Look At. SUBJECTS: Animals—Snakes. RL 3.1.
Encouraging children to notice the distinguishing marks and behavior of poisonous snakes, the book compares the snakes by body shape, especially head, and by type of fangs. Cobras, vipers, pit vipers, and sea snakes are contrasted. Illustrated with very detailed pencil drawings.

1328 *A First Look at Sharks.* Ill. by Harriett Springer. Walker, 1979. ISBN 0-8027-6373-1. SERIES: First Look At. SUBJECTS: Animals—Sharks. RL 3.3.
Like other books in the First Look At series, this book presents its subject, sharks, in terms of classification characteristics. It encourages the reader to distinguish sharks from bony fishes and different sharks from one another. The black and white pencil drawings are detailed and realistic.

1329 *A First Look at Spiders.* Ill. by Harriett Springer. Walker, 1983, o.p. SERIES: First Look At. SUBJECTS: Animals—Spiders. RL 3.4.
Children are prompted to examine detailed black and white pencil drawings to learn what distinguishes a spider from an insect, one spider from another, and one web from another. Children reading this will increase their observational skills rather than gaining in-depth knowledge.

1330 *A First Look at the World of Plants.* Ill. by Harriett Springer. Walker, 1978. ISBN 0-8027-6299-9. SERIES: First Look At. SUBJECTS: Plants. RL 2.5.
This book gives its readers an opportunity to learn about plants in a variety of ways. It encourages children not only to read the text but to carefully examine the pencil and wash drawings for differences among fungi, gymnosperms, and other plants.

Serventy, Vincent

1331 *Kangaroo.* Photos. Raintree, 1985; Scholastic, pap., 1987. ISBN 0-8172-2418-1. SERIES: Animals in the Wild. SUBJECTS: Animals—Kangaroos. RL 2.5.
About five kinds of kangaroos are introduced in the brief text. Much of the book is devoted to following baby kangaroos from birth to the time that they are ready to leave the pouch. Good information is presented well, and the large full color photographs are delightful.

1332 *Koala.* Photos. Raintree, 1983; Scholastic, pap., 1987. ISBN 0-8172-2416-5. SERIES: Animals in the Wild. SUBJECTS: Animals—Koalas. RL 2.4.
A full color photograph dominates each page with the brief text below it acting like a caption. The information ranges from the koala's diet and habitat to its young, its enemies, and current attempts by Australia to protect it. This appealing book is an Australian production.

1333 *Turtle and Tortoise.* Photos. Raintree, 1985; Scholastic, pap., 1987. ISBN 0-8172-2403-3. SERIES: Animals in the Wild. SUBJECTS: Animals—Turtles. RL 2.9.
Good information and excellent full color photographs tell about the natural habitats (land, sea, and shore) and life cycle of turtles and tortoises. The photos dominate this book, and the text acts as captions.

Seuling, Barbara

1334 *Just Me.* Ill. by author. Harcourt Brace, 1982, o.p. SERIES: Let Me Read. SUBJECTS: Imagination—Fiction. RL 1.9.
Using odds and ends from around her home and a lot of imagination, a little girl tries being a horse, a dragon, and a robot but she always returns to being "just me." Ink and wash drawings are simple, uncluttered, and attractive.

Seuss, Dr.

1335 *Cat in the Hat*. Ill. by author. Random
House, 1957. ISBN 0-394-90001-4.
SERIES: I Can Read It All By Myself.
SUBJECTS: Humorous stories; Stories in
rhyme. RL 1.9.

With nothing to do on a cold, rainy day, two
children are roused from their lethargy by the
Cat in the Hat, who promises lots of good fun.
Seuss's cartoon drawings and rhymed text
always attract young readers and listeners.

1336 *Cat in the Hat Comes Back*. Ill. by
author. Beginner, 1958. ISBN 0-394-
90002-2. SERIES: I Can Read It All By
Myself. SUBJECTS: Humorous stories;
Stories in rhyme. RL 2.2.

While Mother is gone, the children are busily
working when the Cat in the Hat returns to create havoc and fun with his Little Cats A to Z.
Seuss's absurdly funny drawings and text
quickly capture the attention of young readers.

1337 *Foot Book*. Ill. by author. Random
House, 1968. ISBN 0-394-90937-2.
SERIES: Bright and Early. SUBJECTS:
Human body—Feet—Fiction; Stories
in rhyme. RL 2.5.

The many varieties of feet and the many
things they can do are amusingly described in
words and lively colorful pictures in this
humorous rhyming text with a total of 126
words.

1338 *Fox in Socks*. Ill. by author. Beginner,
1965. ISBN 0-394-90038-3. SERIES: I Can
Read It All By Myself. SUBJECTS:
Humorous stories; Stories in rhyme;
Tongue twisters. RL 3.6.

Children who are about to read these wild
tongue twisters are warned at the outset to
take them slowly. Children will sympathize
with poor Mr. Knox's attempts at tongue
twisters and will enjoy his final victory over
Fox. Typical zany Seuss creations illustrate
the text.

1339 *Great Day for Up!* Ill. by Quentin
Blake. Beginner, 1974. ISBN 0-394-
92913-6. SERIES: Bright and Early.
SUBJECTS: Stories in rhyme. RL 2.0.

This rousing, jubilant rhyme encourages
everyone to get "up" in the morning—except

for the narrator, who is sleeping in. The clever
illustrations are lively, funny, and perfect for
the rhyme.

1340 *Green Eggs and Ham*. Ill. by author.
Beginner, 1960. ISBN 0-394-90016-2.
SERIES: I Can Read It All By Myself.
SUBJECTS: Food—Fiction; Nonsense;
Stories in rhyme. RL 1.6.

Sam-I-am relentlessly pursues a furry top-
hatted creature trying every way he can think
of to get the creature to eat green eggs and
ham. The well-known, cleverly illustrated
creatures and the silly rhyming text are per-
petual favorites of young children.

1341 *Hop on Pop*. Ill. by author. Beginner,
1963. ISBN 0-394-90029-4. SERIES: I Can
Read It All By Myself. SUBJECTS:
Stories in rhyme. RL 2.0.

Introducing the very simplest of words, usually of one syllable, Seuss puts them into a
nonsensical rhyming format with humorous
results. His illustrations of outlandish
"things" entice children into trying to read.

1342 *I Am Not Going to Get Up Today!* Ill.
by James Stevenson. Beginner, 1987.
ISBN 0-394-99217-2. SERIES: I Can Read
It All By Myself. SUBJECTS: Humorous
stories; Sleep—Fiction; Stories in
rhyme. RL 2.1.

In a rhyming story, neighbors, police, newspapers, and television attempt to get a little
boy out of bed, but he refuses to get up.
Illustrations are done with full color wash
and ink sketches in an amusing comic style.

1343 *I Can Read with My Eyes Shut!* Ill. by
author. Beginner, 1978. ISBN 0-394-
93912-3. SERIES: I Can Read It All By
Myself. SUBJECTS: Books and reading—
Fiction; Stories in rhyme. RL 2.4.

The Cat in the Hat gives children countless
reasons for reading and learning while they
involve themselves in a rousing, rhyming text.
Seuss's typical free-form creatures are colorfully illustrated and will attract children.

1344 *Mister Brown Can Moo! Can You?* Ill.
by author. Random House, 1970. ISBN
0-394-90622-5. SERIES: Bright and
Early. SUBJECTS: Sound—Fiction;
Stories in rhyme. RL 2.7.

From the noises made by cows and owls to that of thunder, Mister Brown can imitate just about any sound. The humorous text and illustrations encourage children not only to try making the sounds themselves but also to decode new words.

1345 *Oh, Say Can You Say?* Ill. by author. Beginner, 1979. ISBN 0-394-94255-8. SERIES: I Can Read It All By Myself. SUBJECTS: Tongue twisters. RL 2.4.

The cover warns children that the tongue twisters inside are terrible to try to read and to try not to stumble over. The text is longer than others by Seuss and more challenging. His comic drawings of imaginative creatures will encourage children to try these creative phrases.

1346 *Oh, the Thinks You Can Think!* Ill. by author. Beginner, 1975. ISBN 0-394-93129-7. SERIES: I Can Read It All By Myself. SUBJECTS: Imagination— Fiction; Stories in rhyme. RL 1.6.

Children reading this will be encouraged to think imaginatively and to enjoy playing with words. Seuss creates outlandish word and picture combinations that should spur children to try making up some of their own. The illustrations are full color, cartoonlike, and fun.

1347 *One Fish Two Fish Red Fish Blue Fish.* Ill. by author. Beginner, 1960. ISBN 0-394-90013-8. SERIES: I Can Read It All By Myself. SUBJECTS: Humorous stories; Nonsense; Stories in rhyme. RL 1.8.

Aided by a delightfully nonsensical rhyming text, two children explore the world of funny creatures. Seuss's silly story introduces children to wordplay and to an enjoyment of language. The illustrations are extremely entertaining.

1348 *There's a Wocket in My Pocket!* Ill. by author. Beginner, 1974. ISBN 0-394-92920-9. SERIES: Bright and Early. SUBJECTS: Stories in rhyme. RL 2.3.

Zany Seuss creations rhyming with the names of familiar items and common household objects are sure to inspire children to try to make up their own rhyming words. Typical Seuss illustrations.

Shaffer, Ann

1349 *The Camel Express.* Ill. by Robin Cole. Dillon, 1989. ISBN 0-87518-400-6. SERIES: It Really Happened! SUBJECTS: Animals—Camels—Fiction; Historical fiction; Western stories. RL 3.0.

When the pony express rider is hurt, Grandpa and Mary Claire ride Carlos, a camel set free by the army, nearly 35 miles through storms and great danger to the next post. Loosely based on events of the times, the adventure is fast paced and nicely illustrated with pencil drawings.

Shannon, George

1350 *The Gang and Mrs. Higgins.* Ill. by Andrew Vines. Greenwillow, 1981. ISBN 0-688-84303-4. SERIES: Read-alone. SUBJECTS: Frontier and pioneer life— Fiction; Robbers and outlaws— Fiction; Western stories. RL 2.9.

The Andersons, the meanest gang in Kansas, try to rob kindly Mrs. Higgins of her gold. She tells them there is no gold, as she washes and washes clothes. They give up and leave, and she takes the gold out of the washtub. The humorous story is illustrated with comic, semirealistic pictures.

Shapiro, Irwin

1351 *Gretchen and the White Steed.* Ill. by Herman Vestal. Garrard, 1972. ISBN 0-8116-6962-9. SERIES: Venture. SUBJECTS: Adventure stories; Animals—Horses— Fiction; Frontier and pioneer life— Fiction. RL 2.4.

On the way to Texas with her big family, Gretchen is tied to their gentle mare when it wanders away with her. Lost on the prairie and surrounded by wild horses, the little girl is rescued by a wonderful white horse. Illustrated with detailed ink and wash drawings.

Shapp, Martha, and Shapp, Charles

1352 *Let's Find Out about Animals of Long Ago.* Ill. by Bette Davis. Watts, 1968, o.p. SERIES: Let's Find Out About.

Shapp, Martha, and Shapp, Charles (cont.)

SUBJECTS: Animals—Prehistoric;
Dinosaurs. RL 2.4.

After being introduced to several dinosaurs and other prehistoric animals, the reader learns how fossils are made and what scientists do with the fossils and the information from them. The realistic illustrations are done in pencil and ink.

1353 *Let's Find Out about Babies.* Ill. by
Jenny Williams. Watts, 1974, o.p.
SERIES: Let's Find Out About. SUBJECTS:
Animals—Reproduction. RL 2.4.

From egg and sperm to birth, the development of animal and human babies is discussed without great detail and in general terms. The authors stress the importance of loving, supportive families for babies. The book has realistic, full color pictures.

1354 *Let's Find Out about Houses.* Rev. ed.
Ill. by Tomie dePaola. Watts, 1975,
o.p. SERIES: Let's Find Out About.
SUBJECTS: Houses. RL 2.2.

Houses from around the world, the material used to construct them, and the reasons for their particular kind of construction are briefly surveyed in this attractive book with vibrant pencil and watercolor pictures.

1355 *Let's Find Out about Safety.* Ill. by
Carolyn Bentley. Watts, 1975, o.p.
SERIES: Let's Find Out About. SUBJECTS:
Safety. RL 2.1.

Children are given warnings about safety on the street, in playgrounds, at home, in a car, or during recreational activities. The book is very brief with alternating pages of text and full color paintings. Little information is provided, only a couple of warning sentences per page.

1356 *Let's Find Out about the Moon.* Ill. by
Brigitte Hartmann. Watts, 1975, o.p.
SERIES: Let's Find Out About. SUBJECTS:
Astronomy; Space travel. RL 2.9.

In this book children learn of discoveries about the moon, how the moon's rotation affects the earth, and what the men who landed on the moon found there. The text is interesting and illustrated with detailed and informative pencil drawings.

1357 *Let's Find Out about Trees (Arbor Day).*
Ill. by Allan Eitzen. Watts, 1970, o.p.
SERIES: Let's Find Out About. SUBJECTS:
Holidays—Arbor Day; Plants—Trees.
RL 2.1.

The emphasis here is on the importance of trees to everyday life with additional information—such as trees being the oldest and largest living things—briefly given. It does not include information on kinds of trees and their growth. Illustrated with spare pictures in gold, gray, and green.

Sharmat, Marjorie W.

1358 *Burton and Dudley.* Ill. by Barbara
Cooney. Holiday House, 1975, o.p.;
Avon, pap., 1977. ISBN 0-380-01732-6.
SUBJECTS: Friendship—Fiction;
Humorous stories; Walking—Fiction.
RL 1.8.

Dudley Possum has to prod his quiet friend Burton into taking a walk with him, but it is Burton who revels in the outdoors and only reluctantly comes home, determined to walk all over the world. The well-done pen and ink drawings are detailed and clever and reflect the story's humor.

1359 *Griselda's New Year.* Ill. by Normand
Chartier. Macmillan, 1979. ISBN 0-02-
782420-9. SERIES: Ready-to-Read.
SUBJECTS: Animals—Geese—Fiction;
Holidays—New Year's Day—Fiction;
Humorous stories. RL 2.1.

Oblivious to the problems she is creating for her friends, Griselda Goose pushes forward with her New Year's resolution to make someone happy. The funny story is illustrated with detailed ink and wash drawings of semi-realistic, humorous animals.

1360 *Little Devil Gets Sick.* Ill. by Marylin
Hafner. Doubleday, 1980, o.p. SERIES:
Reading On My Own. SUBJECTS:
Devils—Fiction; Fantasy; Illness—
Fiction. RL 2.2.

When Little Devil wakes up with a terrible cold, he tries everything (hot spider soup, warm fires, nasty spells) to get rid of it. Only when he does a good deed does it go away. Illustrated with comical colored pencil drawings that are sure to appeal to children.

1361 *Mitchell Is Moving.* Ill. by Jose Aruego and Ariane Dewey. Macmillan, 1978; pap., 1985. ISBN 0-02-782410-1. SERIES: Ready-to-Read. SUBJECTS: Dinosaurs—Fiction; Friendship—Fiction; Moving, household—Fiction. RL 2.4.

After 60 years of living in his house, dinosaur Mitchell decides to move. He has not counted on missing his good friend and neighbor Margo and is ecstatic when she follows and moves next to him. Simple, humorous drawings effectively illustrate this delightful story.

1362 *Mooch the Messy.* Ill. by Ben Shecter. Harper & Row, 1976. ISBN 0-06-025532-3. SERIES: I Can Read. SUBJECTS: Animals—Rats—Fiction; Parent and child—Fiction; Self-esteem—Fiction. RL 2.3.

When his father comes to visit his hole, Mooch, a rat, tries to make him more comfortable by cleaning up. Though he enjoys the time with his father, Mooch is happy to be alone and messy again. Simple pencil and wash drawings illustrate this humorous story about self-acceptance.

1363 *Nate the Great.* Ill. by Marc Simont. Coward, McCann, 1972; Dell, pap., 1977. ISBN 0-698-30444-6. SERIES: Break-of-Day. SUBJECTS: Mystery and detective stories. RL 1.8.

Pancake-eating child detective Nate the Great is involved in solving mysteries for his friends. Using a "Dragnet" style speech pattern, Nate tells about his sleuthing. Expressive pencil and wash pictures showing Nate in a trench coat and deer-stalker cap are a perfect match to the text.

1364 *Nate the Great and the Boring Beach Bag.* Ill. by Marc Simont. Coward, McCann, 1987. ISBN 0-698-20631-2. SERIES: Break-of-Day. SUBJECTS: Mystery and detective stories; Seashore—Fiction. RL 2.1.

Even while swimming in the ocean, Nate is asked to help solve a mystery. This time it is Oliver's beach bag that is missing. The watercolor paintings place the well-known children from this series and their pets at a crowded beach in the summer.

1365 *Nate the Great and the Fishy Prize.* Ill. by Marc Simont. Coward, McCann, 1985; Dell, pap., 1988. ISBN 0-698-20639-8. SERIES: Break-of-Day. SUBJECTS: Mystery and detective stories. RL 2.3.

Rosamond asks Nate to find her prize tuna fish can for the smartest pet contest. After diligent detecting, Nate and his dog Sludge find it. Illustrated with amusing pencil and watercolor pictures.

1366 *Nate the Great and the Lost List.* Ill. by Marc Simont. Coward, McCann, 1975; Dell, pap., 1981. ISBN 0-698-30593-0. SERIES: Break-of-Day. SUBJECTS: Mystery and detective stories. RL 2.0.

Taking a well-earned break from detecting, Nate reluctantly agrees to use his detective skills to help Claude find his missing grocery list. Short, choppy sentences are perfectly suited to reading aloud and the pencil and wash illustrations are expressive and humorous.

1367 *Nate the Great and the Missing Key.* Ill. by Marc Simont. Coward, McCann, 1981; Dell, pap., 1982. ISBN 0-698-30726-7. SERIES: Break-of-Day. SUBJECTS: Mystery and detective stories. RL 2.2.

Rosamond has put Annie's house key in a safe place leaving clues to its whereabouts in a poem. Annie turns to Nate for help and again he solves the case—just in time to go to Fang's birthday party. The pencil and wash drawings capture Nate and his friends perfectly.

1368 *Nate the Great and the Phony Clue.* Ill. by Marc Simont. Coward, McCann, 1977; Dell, pap., 1981. ISBN 0-698-30650-3. SERIES: Break-of-Day. SUBJECTS: Mystery and detective stories. RL 2.0.

A strange piece of paper with "vita" on it leads Nate on a challenging hunt for the rest of the message. Adults and children will have fun reading aloud this text reminiscent of "Dragnet's" Joe Friday dialogue. Pencil and wash drawings ably capture the tongue-in-cheek humor.

1369 *Nate the Great and the Snowy Trail.* Ill. by Marc Simont. Coward, McCann, hb and pap., 1982. ISBN 0-698-30738-0. SERIES: Break-of-Day. SUBJECTS: Mystery and detective stories. RL 1.9.

Sharmat, Marjorie W. (cont.)

Busy making a snow detective, Nate the Great and his dog are interrupted by Rosamund and her four cats. Rosamund wants Nate and his dog Sludge to find Nate's lost and very mysterious birthday present. Soft, humorous pencil and wash illustrations are delightful, as is the story.

1370 *Nate the Great and the Sticky Case.* Ill. by Marc Simont. Coward, McCann, 1978; Dell, pap., 1981. ISBN 0-698-30697-X. SERIES: Break-of-Day. SUBJECTS: Dinosaurs—Fiction; Mystery and detective stories. RL 2.0.

After Claude asks him to find his missing stegosaurus stamp, Nate the Great begins searching for clues. During the search Nate learns a lot about the stegosaurus and of course finds the missing stamp. The illustrations, done in ink and wash, capture perfectly the detective and his friends.

1371 *Nate the Great Goes Down in the Dumps.* Ill. by Marc Simont. Coward-McCann, 1989. ISBN 0-689-20636-3. SERIES: Break-of-Day. SUBJECTS: Humorous stories; Mystery and detective stories. RL 2.0.

When Rosamond cannot find her empty money box she turns to the inimitable Nate the Great for help. His search takes him to the garbage dump before he realizes just how to find the box. Lots of humor, a challenging mystery, and delightful pencil and wash pictures are sure to attract readers.

1372 *Nate the Great Goes Undercover.* Ill. by Marc Simont. Coward, McCann, 1974; Dell, pap., 1978. ISBN 0-698-30547-7. SERIES: Break-of-Day. SUBJECTS: Mystery and detective stories. RL 2.8.

Pesky Oliver insists that Nate find out who or what is getting into his garbage cans. Nate does a thorough job and uncovers the numerous culprits, including his own dog, Sludge. Charcoal, pencil, and wash pictures.

1373 *Nate the Great Stalks Stupidweed.* Ill. by Marc Simont. Coward, McCann, 1986; Dell, pap., 1989. ISBN 0-698-20626-6. SERIES: Break-of-Day. SUBJECTS: Mystery and detective stories. RL 2.7.

Oliver goes to Nate for help in finding his newly adopted and lost weed. With his usual panache Nate recovers it while providing great reading fun. Pencil and watercolor pictures of the familiar cast of characters add to the book's appeal.

1374 *Scarlet Monster Lives Here.* Reissued ed. Ill. by Dennis Kendrick. Harper & Row, 1988. ISBN 0-06-025527-7. SERIES: I Can Read. SUBJECTS: Monsters—Fiction; Moving, household—Fiction; Neighbors—Fiction. RL 2.8.

When Scarlet Monster moves into a new house, she tries hard to make it inviting to her new neighbors and cannot understand why none of them have come to meet her. The ink and wash drawings show a variety of gawky, nonthreatening monsters wanting to be liked by each other.

1375 *Sophie and Gussie.* Ill. by Lillian Hoban. Macmillan, 1973. ISBN 0-02-782310-5. SERIES: Ready-to-Read. SUBJECTS: Animals—Squirrels—Fiction; Friendship—Fiction. RL 2.7.

Sophie and Gussie's friendship survives misunderstandings and hurt feelings as the two squirrels visit each other, plan a party, and share special moments. The quiet story is illustrated with sketchy ink and wash drawings that are a delight.

1376 *The Story of Bentley Beaver.* Ill. by Lillian Hoban. Harper & Row, 1984. ISBN 0-06-025513-7. SERIES: I Can Read. SUBJECTS: Animals—Beavers—Fiction; Family life—Fiction; Old age—Fiction. RL 2.1.

From his birth to loving beaver parents to his quiet death, Bentley Beaver's journey through a long and happy life is gently and affectionately recalled. The sketchy, whimsical animal pictures add to the reader's appreciation of Bentley and his family.

1377 *The Trip and Other Sophie and Gussie Stories.* Ill. by Lillian Hoban. Macmillan, 1976, o.p. SERIES: Ready-to-Read. SUBJECTS: Animals—Squirrels—Fiction; Friendship—Fiction; Humorous stories. RL 2.1.

Although close friends Sophie and Gussie, two squirrels, sometimes disagree, they share a special friendship that sees them through occasional difficulties and their own foolish behavior. The sketchy, lighthearted drawings are in pen with gray, green, and yellow washes.

1378 *The Trolls of Twelfth Street.* Ill. by Ben Shecter. Coward, McCann, 1979, o.p. SERIES: Break-of-Day. SUBJECTS: Fantasy; Trolls—Fiction. RL 2.5.
Eldred Troll's curiosity leads the Troll family from their safe and comfortable home beneath the Brooklyn Bridge up to the streets of New York City. Mistaking human rudeness for Troll good behavior gets them into difficulty. The charcoal drawings have a rough and hurried but fanciful look.

1379 *Uncle Boris and Maude.* Ill. by Sammis McLean. Doubleday, 1979, o.p. SERIES: Reading On My Own. SUBJECTS: Animals—Moles—Fiction; Behavior—Bored—Fiction. RL 2.2.
Maude tries everything to rid Uncle Boris of his apparently incurable boredom until she becomes bored too. Then it is his turn to drag her out of the dumps. The illustrations, done with humorous ink and wash drawings, show two very pleasant moles.

1380 *Who's Afraid of Ernestine?* Ill. by Maxie Chambliss. Coward, McCann, 1986. ISBN 0-698-30746-1. SERIES: Break-of-Day. SUBJECTS: Emotions—Fear—Fiction. RL 2.3.
Afraid of Ernestine, Cecil imagines her as a vampire, a dragon lady, and a devil as he tries to escape her clutches. Finally the two children are forced to work together and Cecil discovers Ernestine is actually very nice. Illustrated with humorous ink and wash drawings.

Sharmat, Mitchell

1381 *Reddy Rattler and Easy Eagle.* Ill. by Marc Simont. Doubleday, 1979, o.p. SERIES: Reading On My Own. SUBJECTS: Animals—Eagles—Fiction; Animals—Snakes—Fiction; Self-esteem—Fiction. RL 2.1.
Depressed because nobody seems to like him, Reddy Rattler is helped by his good friend Easy Eagle to find a new career as part of a desert rock band. The expressive ink, wash,

and pencil drawings add humor and individualize the characters of the story.

Sharoff, Victor

1382 *The Heart of the Wood.* Ill. by Wallace Tripp. Coward, McCann, 1971, o.p. SERIES: Break-of-Day. SUBJECTS: Historical fiction; Religion—Fiction; Wood carving—Fiction. RL 2.9.
Isaac is torn between obeying the laws of Judaism and not carving animals and keeping his promise to carve a bowl with animals for the duke. The wood he finds enables him to obey the laws of his faith and keep his promise. Realistic ink and wash drawings place the story in medieval times.

Sharp, Paul

1383 *Paul the Pitcher.* Ill. by author. Childrens, hb and pap., 1984. ISBN 0-516-02064-1. SERIES: Rookie Readers. SUBJECTS: Sports—Baseball—Fiction; Stories in rhyme. RL 3.1.
Paul has great fun pitching, unless the batter gets a hit. He hopes that someday he will be a professional baseball player. The lively, rhyming text uses 38 words and has ink and wash action drawings.

Shaw, Evelyn

1384 *Alligator.* Ill. by Frances Zweifel. Harper & Row, 1972. ISBN 0-06-025557-9. SERIES: Science I Can Read. SUBJECTS: Animals—Alligators. RL 2.6.
A female alligator makes a nest, lays eggs, guards them, is nearly killed by hunters, and survives to care for her young. A straightforward, unsentimental account of an interesting animal's life, this book is illustrated with realistic colored pencil drawings.

1385 *Elephant Seal Island.* Ill. by Cherryl Pape. Harper & Row, 1978. ISBN 0-06-025604-4. SERIES: Science I Can Read. SUBJECTS: Animals—Seals, elephant. RL 2.7.
The behavior and life cycle of elephant seals are explored in this factual, descriptive look at a young bull's birth and growth. The well-done illustrations are detailed and realistic.

Shaw, Evelyn (cont.)

1386 *Fish Out of School.* Ill. by Ralph
Carpentier. Harper & Row, 1970. ISBN
0-06-025564-1. SERIES: Science I Can
Read. SUBJECTS: Animals—Fish. RL 2.0.
Focusing on the plight of one fish separated
from its school, the author uses a story format
to explain how fish live and the dangers they
face. Other fish are seen in the realistic
watercolor paintings and identified as the
little herring swims past them to join a new
school.

1387 *A Nest of Wood Ducks.* Ill. by Cherryl
Pape. Harper & Row, 1976. ISBN 0-06-
025592-7. SERIES: Nature I Can Read.
SUBJECTS: Animals—Ducks. RL 2.2.
Two wood ducks are followed from mating
season to the hatching and raising of their
ducklings. Solid factual information combines with clear, realistic full color pencil and
watercolor pictures to present an interesting
look at the wood duck.

1388 *Octopus.* Ill. by Ralph Carpentier.
Harper & Row, 1971. ISBN 0-06-
025559-5. SERIES: Science I Can Read.
SUBJECTS: Animals—Octopi; Oceans
and ocean life. RL 2.2.
The life cycle and behavior of this eight-
armed mollusk are discussed in such a way
that the octopus seems less threatening and
far more interesting than usually thought.
The realistic illustrations add to the reader's
knowledge and appreciation of the animal.

1389 *Sea Otters.* Ill. by Cherryl Pape. Harper
& Row, 1980. ISBN 0-06-025614-1.
SERIES: Nature I Can Read. SUBJECTS:
Animals—Otters, sea. RL 2.3.
Susan, a scientist, observes two sea otters,
Garbo and her pup, Bo. Through Susan's
eyes, children learn how this endangered
mammal survives the cold Pacific waters,
what it eats, and how Garbo trains Bo to be
independent. Excellent realistic watercolor
paintings.

Shecter, Ben

1390 *Hester the Jester.* Ill. by author. Harper
& Row, 1977. ISBN 0-06-025599-4.

SERIES: Early I Can Read. SUBJECTS:
Sex roles—Fiction. RL 1.7.
A little girl tries being a jester, a knight, and a
king and finally chooses just to be a little girl.
The author's seriocomic pictures with ink
cross-hatchings show a very self-confident
child who manages to convince adults that
she can be whatever she wishes.

Sheehan, Angela

1391 *The Duck.* Ill. by Maurice Pledger and
Bernard Robinson. Warwick, 1976, o.p.
SERIES: A First Look at Nature.
SUBJECTS: Animals—Ducks. RL 2.8.
This rather lengthy and detailed look at the
courtship of mallards and the raising of their
ducklings presents factual information in a
story format. The very realistic full color
paintings give a clear idea of what the mallard looks like. This book was first published
in England.

Sheehan, Cilla

1392 *The Colors That I Am.* Ill. by Glen
Elliott. Human Sciences, 1981. ISBN 0-
89885-047-9. SUBJECTS: Concepts—
Color; Emotions. RL 2.2.
Intent on getting children to express their
feelings, Sheehan chooses color as the vehicle for discussion. Emotions are related to
colors. Each color is given a full page of text,
the facing page contains an abstract painting. Conversational in tone, the text might
stimulate discussion among children regarding their feelings.

Shiefman, Vicky

1393 *M Is for Move.* Photos by Bill Miller.
Dutton, 1981. ISBN 0-525-34295-8.
SERIES: Smart Cat. SUBJECTS: English
language—Verbs. RL 1.7.
Schoolchildren are captured in lively black
and white photos as they demonstrate the
action of verbs. The children seem natural
rather than posed in the well-done pictures.
The arrangement of the text, which captions
the photos using first a letter and then a verb,
is not alphabetical.

Shortall, Leonard

1394 *Just-in-Time Joey.* Ill. by author. Morrow, 1973, o.p. SUBJECTS: Grandparents—Fiction; Plants—Trees—Fiction. RL 2.3.

The diseased elm trees on Joey's grandmother's street are being marked with big yellow circles of paint and then cut down. As a prank, one of the boys in the neighborhood sprays Joey's grandmother's healthy tree and Joey is just in time to save it. Illustrated with detailed ink drawings.

1395 *Steve's First Pony Ride.* Ill. by author. Morrow, 1966, o.p. SUBJECTS: Animals—Horses—Fiction; Behavior—Responsible—Fiction; Farm and country life—Fiction. RL 2.2.

Steve's neighbor Mr. Turner gets a horse and pony and allows the little boy to help him take care of them. When Steve discovers the horses missing one day, he finds them for Mr. Turner and earns the opportunity to ride the pony. The well-written story is illustrated with realistic paintings.

1396 *Tony's First Dive.* Ill. by author. Morrow, 1972, o.p. SUBJECTS: Emotions—Fear—Fiction; Self-esteem—Fiction; Sports—Swimming—Fiction. RL 2.6.

Seeing that Tony is afraid of the water, one of the lifeguards at the beach gives him special lessons. He teaches Tony not only to swim but also to dive with a mask and flippers. A good story of overcoming fear and gaining self-esteem, it is illustrated with attractive ink drawings.

Showers, Paul

1397 *A Baby Starts to Grow.* Ill. by Rosalind Fry. Crowell, 1969; pap., 1972. ISBN 0-690-11320-X. SERIES: Let's-Read-and-Find-Out. SUBJECTS: Human body—Reproduction. RL 2.9.

Drawings of siblings, mothers, and babies combine with an upbeat text to present a limited picture of how a baby develops from fertilized ovum to birth. This book does not contain information on human sexuality. Illustrations are semirealistic.

1398 *Drop of Blood.* Ill. by Don Madden. Crowell, 1967; pap., 1972. ISBN 0-690-24526-2. SERIES: Let's-Read-and-Find-Out. SUBJECTS: Human body—Blood. RL 3.1.

A little boy explains what blood is made of, tells how much people have, and suggests ways to use a flashlight to see blood in a hand, an ear, or a cheek. The rather limited amount of information is presented in an interesting way with lively pen, ink, and wash drawings.

1399 *Find Out by Touching.* Ill. by Robert Galster. Crowell, 1961. ISBN 0-690-29782-3. SERIES: Let's-Read-and-Find-Out. SUBJECTS: Senses—Touch. RL 1.8.

To reinforce the importance of touch, readers are encouraged to try using only that sense to identify objects randomly chosen from a bag. The orange, beige, and black colors in the illustrations have a rather dated look.

1400 *How Many Teeth.* Ill. by Paul Galdone. Crowell, hb and pap., 1962. ISBN 0-690-40716-5. SERIES: Let's-Read-and-Find-Out. SUBJECTS: Human body—Teeth. RL 2.1.

Through Sam and his family, facts about teeth are introduced in an occasionally rhyming text. The book explains how human teeth are lost and replaced, but both the text and the ink and wash pictures focus on how teeth are used rather than on their anatomy or function.

1401 *How You Talk.* Ill. by Robert Galster. Crowell, 1966; pap., 1975. ISBN 0-690-42136-2. SERIES: Let's-Read-and-Find-Out. SUBJECTS: Human body—Speech. RL 2.3.

Starting with how a baby first attempts to talk, this book presents a variety of activities to help children understand some of the elements of human speech. Although brief, the information is clearly and engagingly presented. Expressive pictures are in orange, turquoise, and black.

1402 *Listening Walk.* Ill. by Aliki. Crowell, 1961. ISBN 0-690-49663-X. SERIES: Let's-Read-and-Find-Out. SUBJECTS: Senses—Hearing; Sound. RL 2.0.

As a little boy, his father, and their dog stroll their neighborhood, the boy listens carefully

Showers, Paul (cont.)

to the many sounds around him and tries to identify them. The story may nudge children to pay closer attention to sounds. Illustrated with very simple ink drawings.

1403 *Look at Your Eyes*. Ill. by Paul Galdone. Crowell, 1962; pap., 1976. ISBN 0-690-50728-3. SERIES: Let's-Read-and-Find-Out. SUBJECTS: Human body—Eyes. RL 2.0.

By closely observing their own eyes, children reading the book will discover how their eyes are made, how the pupils change with light, and how some eyes seem to "smile" or be happy. Both text and pictures deal superficially with the human eye. Illustrated with ink and wash.

1404 *Me and My Family Tree*. Ill. by Don Madden. Crowell, 1978. ISBN 0-690-03887-9. SERIES: Let's-Read-and-Find-Out. SUBJECTS: Heredity. RL 2.2.

Parents, grandparents, and even great-great grandparents are seen as a part of a child's heritage in this overview of genetics. Gregor Mendel and his pioneering experiments in genetics are briefly mentioned and explained. The detailed Pentel drawings with orange and gold add appeal.

1405 *No Measles, No Mumps for Me*. Ill. by Harriett Barton. Crowell, 1980; pap., 1982. ISBN 0-690-04018-0. SERIES: Let's-Read-and-Find-Out. SUBJECTS: Diseases; Vaccination. RL 2.5.

A little boy tells how he will never have to get diseases like measles, mumps, and whooping cough because he has had the shots or drops that vaccinate him against them. The text and the simple, childlike pictures explain the way white cells act to fight bacteria and viruses.

1406 *Sleep Is for Everyone*. Ill. by Wendy Watson. Crowell, 1974. ISBN 0-690-01118-0. SERIES: Let's-Read-and-Find-Out. SUBJECTS: Human body—Sleep; Sleep. RL 2.2.

After a discussion of the ways a variety of animals sleep, the reader is led into a look at why humans need sleep and what happens when they are deprived of it. The pictures are detailed ink and wash sketches that complement the subject very well.

1407 *What Happens to a Hamburger*. Rev. ed. Ill. by Anne Rockwell. Crowell, hb and pap., 1985. ISBN 0-690-04427-5. SERIES: Let's-Read-and-Find-Out. SUBJECTS: Human body—Digestion. RL 3.2.

A simple, straightforward presentation is made of how digestion works. The book's diagrams and the simple observations that children are encouraged to make will help them to understand the digestive process. Attractive, full color illustrations supplement the text.

1408 *Where Does the Garbage Go?* Ill. by Loretta Lustig. Crowell, 1974. ISBN 0-690-00402-0. SERIES: Let's-Read-and-Find-Out. SUBJECTS: Conservation; Garbage and garbage disposal. RL 3.3.

Discovering that the United States produces a billion pounds of garbage a day, a little girl talks about ways to dispose of it, some successful, some not. She finally decides it is best to make less of it and to recycle what she can. Illustrated with comic-style pencil and wash drawings.

1409 *You Can't Make a Move without Your Muscles*. Ill. by Harriett Barton. Crowell, 1982. ISBN 0-690-04185-3. SERIES: Let's-Read-and-Find-Out. SUBJECTS: Human body—Muscles. RL 2.8.

As they learn about the kinds of muscles and their functions, children are encouraged to take part in activities that help them understand and feel how their muscles work. The text is illustrated with very simple childlike pictures, some in color.

1410 *Your Skin and Mine*. Ill. by Paul Galdone. Crowell, 1965; pap., 1985. ISBN 0-690-91127-0. SERIES: Let's-Read-and-Find-Out Science. SUBJECTS: Human body—Skin. RL 2.8.

A child tells how skin works to protect the body, what colors it can be, how sensitive it is to touch, and how easy it is to clean. The pen and ink sketches with beige, brown, and black accents are lively and attractive.

Showers, Paul, and Showers, Kay S.

1411 *Before You Were a Baby*. Ill. by Ingrid
Fetz. Crowell, 1968. ISBN 0-690-12882-
7. SERIES: Let's-Read-and-Find-Out
Science. SUBJECTS: Human body—
Reproduction. RL 2.5.
Accurate but not explicit information on human reproduction is provided through a brief
text and ink and colored pencil diagrams and
drawings. Many children reading this may be
inspired to seek more information from other
books or from their parents.

Shub, Elizabeth

1412 *Clever Kate*. Ill. by Anita Lobel.
Macmillan, 1973; pap., 1986. ISBN 0-02-
782490-X. SERIES: Ready-to-Read.
SUBJECTS: Folklore—Germany;
Humorous stories. RL 2.2.
The farmer's bride is a kindhearted simpleton
who lets peddlers steal their gold. Her foolish-
ness ultimately helps her husband to retrieve
it. A well-known humorous German folktale,
this version maintains the wit and charm of
the Grimms' original. The detailed ink and
wash drawings have a folk look.

1413 *Seeing Is Believing*. Ill. by Rachel
Isadora. Greenwillow, 1979, o.p.
SERIES: Read-alone. SUBJECTS:
Folklore—England; Folklore—Ireland.
RL 2.5.
In the first of two stories based on folklore,
Tom encounters a leprechaun who tricks him.
In the second Tom bravely makes his way
home in spite of troublesome Piskies. Care-
fully executed drawings using ink cross-
hatchings blend well with the two stories.

1414 *The White Stallion*. Ill. by Rachel
Isadora. Greenwillow, 1982; Bantam,
pap., 1984. ISBN 0-688-01211-6. SERIES:
Read-alone. SUBJECTS: Animals—
Horses—Fiction; Frontier and pioneer
life—Fiction; Western stories. RL 2.6.
Gretchen's grandmother tells her how her
great-great-grandmother Gretchen was rescued by a beautiful white stallion on her
family's journey west in 1845. A lovely and
exciting story, it is illustrated with remarkable ink drawings using cross-hatchings and
pointillism.

Silverman, Maida

1415 *Dinosaur Babies*. Ill. by Carol Inouye.
Simon & Schuster, 1988. ISBN 0-671-
65897-2. SUBJECTS: Animals—
Prehistoric; Dinosaurs. RL 3.0.
After a good introduction that attempts to
differentiate between facts and speculation,
Silverman presents theories about the behav-
ior and rearing of young of nine dinosaurs.
The text is easily understood and interesting.
Attractive detailed pictures do not always
interpret the text well.

Simon, Norma

1416 *Why Am I Different?* Ill. by Dora Leder.
Whitman, 1976. ISBN 0-8075-9074-6.
SERIES: Concept Books. SUBJECTS:
Families; Self-esteem. RL 2.1.
The many ways that children and their families can differ from each other are presented
from many children's perspectives, one per
page. The overriding theme of the book is that
it is okay to be different—everyone is. The full
page drawings are in black and yellow.

Simon, Seymour

1417 *The BASIC Book*. Ill. by Barbara
Emberley and Ed Emberley. Crowell,
hb and pap., 1985. ISBN 0-690-04473-9.
SERIES: Let's-Read-and-Find-Out.
SUBJECTS: Computer languages;
Computers; Computers—
Programming. RL 2.8.
By carefully following the instructions in this
book, children with access to a computer can
learn something about creating a program in
the BASIC computer language. Humorous
illustrations of multiethnic children and computer creatures illustrate the book.

1418 *Finding Out with Your Senses*. Ill. by
Emily A. McCully. McGraw-Hill, 1971,
o.p. SERIES: Let's-Try-It-Out. SUBJECTS:
Science experiments; Senses. RL 2.8.
A thoughtful text calls attention to many
things in daily life that are experienced
through the senses. Very simple experiments
also help readers to appreciate sight, touch,
hearing, taste, and smell. Well written, it has
attractive black, gray, and blue drawings.

Simon, Seymour (cont.)

1419 *How to Talk to Your Computer*. Ill. by Barbara Emberley and Ed Emberley. Crowell, hb and pap., 1985. ISBN 0-690-04450-X. SERIES: Let's-Read-and-Find-Out. SUBJECTS: Computer languages; Computers. RL 2.2.

Almost too simplistic in its approach to computers, this book serves as an introduction to two computer languages, BASIC and LOGO. Following an explanation of how important it is to tell the computer exactly what to do, children are given examples of programs. The humorous pictures help to clarify the text.

1420 *Meet the Computer*. Ill. by Barbara Emberley and Ed Emberley. Crowell, hb and pap., 1985. ISBN 0-690-04448-8. SERIES: Let's-Read-and-Find-Out. SUBJECTS: Computers. RL 2.5.

In this introduction to the computer, Simon explains in simple terms the main parts of a computer and what they do. The book includes a glossary of computer terms and jargon. Unfortunately definitions are not always clear. Humorous drawings of multiethnic children expand the text.

1421 *The Smallest Dinosaurs*. Ill. by Anthony Rao. Crown, 1982. ISBN 0-517-54425-3. SUBJECTS: Dinosaurs. RL 2.3.

Young readers are introduced to fossils and to seven kinds of small dinosaurs, ranging in size from about eight inches to that of a person. These dinosaurs may be the ancestors of present-day birds. Generally consistent with current scientific thought, the book is illustrated in three colors in a realistic way.

1422 *Soap Bubble Magic*. Ill. by Stella Ormai. Lothrop, 1985. ISBN 0-688-02685-0. SUBJECTS: Science experiments; Science experiments—Soap bubbles. RL 3.1.

The "magic" of bubbles is explained in easily understood terms. Children are encouraged to experiment with soap and water to understand how surface tension and soap film can entrap air in a bubble. The realistic, three-color drawings are lively and enticing.

1423 *Turtle Talk: A Beginner's Book of LOGO*. Ill. by Barbara Emberley and Ed Emberley. Crowell, hb and pap.,

1986. ISBN 0-690-04522-0. SERIES: Let's-Read-and-Find-Out. SUBJECTS: Computer Languages; Computers. RL 2.7.

An introduction to the LOGO programming language, this starts by briefly explaining that a cursor (a "turtle" in LOGO) can be manipulated to create graphic designs. It then presents several examples in LOGO accompanied by full color comic-style drawings using multiethnic children.

Sislowitz, Marcel

1424 *Look! How Your Eyes See*. Ill. by Jim Arnosky. Coward, McCann, 1977, o.p. SERIES: Science Is What and Why. SUBJECTS: Human body—Eyes. RL 2.5.

Detailed information is provided on the various parts of the eye with clear explanations of how each works. The section on eye care and visual problems suggests seeing an ophthalmologist for treatment. A page on eye care, a glossary, and a brief index are included. Amusing ink drawings help clarify text.

Sitomer, Mindel, and Sitomer, Harry

1425 *Circles*. Ill. by George Giusti. Crowell, 1971, o.p.; Harper & Row, pap., 1973. ISBN 0-690-00206-8. SERIES: Young Math. SUBJECTS: Mathematics. RL 2.7.

Exercises using compass, ruler, and paper introduce the young reader to some of the terminology (radius, diameter) of circles and to many of their properties. Diagrams show the concepts and present a number of attractive geometric designs based on the circle.

Skurzynski, Gloria

1426 *Honest Andrew*. Ill. by David Wiesner. Harcourt Brace, 1980, o.p. SERIES: Let Me Read. SUBJECTS: Animals—Otters—Fiction; Behavior—Honest—Fiction; Behavior—Manners—Fiction. RL 3.1.

Andrew, a young otter, tries hard to keep his word to his father and always tell the truth. Unfortunately, telling the truth can sometimes conflict with good manners and Andrew's honesty gets him into trouble. The humorous story is illustrated with skillful, realistic drawings.

Sleator, William

1427 *Once, Said Darlene*. Ill. by Steven Kellogg. Dutton, 1979. ISBN 0-525-36410-2. SERIES: Fat Cat. SUBJECTS: Behavior—Lying—Fiction; Fantasy; Friendship—Fiction. RL 1.8.
When Darlene tells fantastic stories about the adventures she used to have, none of her friends but Peter believe her. It is his belief that frees her to return to her magic kingdom. Children will empathize with Darlene while enjoying the fanciful illustrations, in ink and wash.

1428 *That's Silly*. Ill. by Lawrence DiFiori. Dutton, 1981. ISBN 0-525-40981-5. SERIES: Smart Cat. SUBJECTS: Fantasy; Imagination—Fiction; Magic—Fiction. RL 1.6.
More practical and analytical than Tom, Rachel thinks that his constant need to pretend is silly until the two children become involved with magic. Then imagination is essential to their survival. Pastel peach and gray washes with pencil and ink accents illustrate the story well.

Smath, Jerry

1429 *The Housekeeper's Dog*. Ill. by author. Parents Magazine Press, 1980; Crown, pap., 1987. ISBN 0-686-91531-3. SUBJECTS: Behavior—Manners—Fiction; Behavior—Selfish—Fiction; Pets—Dogs—Fiction. RL 2.2.
While the housekeeper is away on a brief vacation, her dog is at a dog-training school becoming a vain and arrogant semihuman. On her return she gets fed up with her dog's behavior and sends him away. He returns, happy to be just a dog again. The rollicking story is illustrated in full color.

Smith, Lucia

1430 *My Mom Got a Job*. Ill. by C. Christian Johanson. Holt, Rinehart, 1979, o.p. SUBJECTS: Family life—Fiction; Mothers, working—Fiction. RL 2.1.
A little girl recalls the special times she and her mother shared before she went back to work. Then she tells about the special things she does instead that have become just as important. A good look at the pros and cons of having a working mother. The detailed ink drawings have pink accents.

Smith, Susan M.

1431 *No One Should Have Six Cats*. Ill. by Judith Friedman. Follett, 1982, o.p. SERIES: Beginning to Read. SUBJECTS: Pets—Cats—Fiction. RL 2.1.
David rescues one homeless cat after another until his mother says no one should have six cats. While David worries about which cat to give up, Mom, as kindhearted as her son, picks up another stray. The story and humorous watercolor pictures depict a caring and responsible child.

Snow, Pegeen

1432 *Eat Your Peas, Louise!* Ill. by Mike Venezia. Childrens, hb and pap., 1985. ISBN 0-516-02067-6. SERIES: Rookie Readers. SUBJECTS: Food—Fiction; Stories in rhyme. RL 2.1.
Louise seems impervious to any attempts to convince her to eat her peas until her big brother finally says please. The rough, full color illustrations and brief rhyming text are vibrant and funny.

1433 *A Pet for Pat*. Ill. by Tom Dunnington. Childrens, hb and pap., 1984. ISBN 0-516-02049-8. SERIES: Rookie Readers. SUBJECTS: Pets—Dogs—Fiction; Stories in rhyme. RL 1.8.
Pat's parents take her to the pound to choose a dog. Back home with her new pet, Pat introduces it to her friend. The rhyming story is short, uses very few words, and depends on the realistic full color paintings to help in its telling.

Solomon, Chuck

1434 *Our Little League*. Photos by author. Crown, 1988. ISBN 0-517-56798-9. SUBJECTS: Sports—Baseball. RL 2.1.
The Little Mets, a little league baseball team from Brooklyn, practice batting and fielding, get pep talks, and play and win a game. Throughout the photo story the children (one

Solomon, Chuck (cont.)

girl is on the team) are encouraged to have fun. The color photographs are excellent and the text is good.

1435 *Our Soccer League.* Photos by author. Crown, 1988. ISBN 0-517-56956-6. SUBJECTS: Sports—Soccer. RL 2.0.

While Solomon's text is not meant to "teach" soccer, his photostory of a game played by elementary school children does show what fun the game can be. Further, it presents in clear color photos a multiracial melting pot of boys and girls having a good time.

Sorrells, Dorothy

1436 *The Little Shell Hunter.* Ill. by Carol Rogers. Steck-Vaughn, 1961, o.p. SUBJECTS: Shells. RL 2.6.

Realistic three-color pictures of shells in their habitats are matched to a very brief, informative text. The shell pictures are all labeled and the text includes something about the live inhabitants of the shells and how they live.

Spanjian, Beth

1437 *Baby Grizzly.* Ill. by John Butler. Childrens, 1988. ISBN 0-516-09062-3. SERIES: Little Reader. SUBJECTS: Animals—Bears. RL 2.8.

Two grizzly bear cubs share a summer day with their mother—fishing, playing, and learning to take care of themselves. The interesting story is short, has large print, and is illustrated with full color, realistic pictures. The text is followed by a page of facts about grizzlies.

1438 *Baby Raccoon.* Ill. by Eva Cellini. Childrens, 1988. ISBN 0-516-09063-1. SERIES: Little Reader. SUBJECTS: Animals—Raccoons. RL 2.7.

The text tells about a family of raccoons exploring their surroundings on a quiet summer night. The brief story is interesting, has large print, and is followed by a page of facts about raccoons. Realistic full color pictures.

1439 *Baby Wolf.* Ill. by Bob Travers. Childrens, 1988. ISBN 0-516-09064-X.

SERIES: Little Reader. SUBJECTS: Animals—Wolves. RL 2.8.

Baby Wolf is shown in the midst of his family practicing his hunting, playing, and learning from others. The brief text is followed by a page of facts about wolves and is illustrated with full color, realistic paintings.

Springstubb, Tricia

1440 *My Minnie Is a Jewel.* Ill. by Jim La Marche. Carolrhoda, 1980. ISBN 0-87614-131-9. SERIES: On My Own. SUBJECTS: Humorous stories; Marriage—Fiction. RL 1.8.

Minnie is forever distracted and her cooking suffers because of it. To her husband, Henry, everything she does is just right. Strangers bet a casket of jewels that Henry will not like or eat the huge and ugly cake she baked and of course they lose. This humorous story is illustrated with detailed ink sketches.

Srivastava, Jane J.

1441 *Averages.* Ill. by Aliki. Crowell, 1975, o.p. SERIES: Young Math. SUBJECTS: Mathematics. RL 2.8.

Clear, careful explanations paired with opportunities to try out concepts help children to gain an understanding of mean, mode, and arithmetic mean. Ink and pencil drawings aid in the communication of information.

Stadler, John

1442 *Cat at Bat.* Ill. by author. Dutton, 1988. ISBN 0-525-44416-5. SERIES: Easy Reader. SUBJECTS: Animals—Fiction; Stories in rhyme. RL 3.2.

Fourteen three-line, rhyming verses describe animals doing many different and very silly things. The humorous illustrations will help the beginning reader to decipher the nonsensical rhymes.

1443 *Hooray for Snail!* Ill. by author. Crowell, 1984; pap., 1985. ISBN 0-690-04413-5. SUBJECTS: Animals—Snails—Fiction; Sports—Baseball—Fiction. RL 3.6.

When Snail finally gets to bat, he hits the ball so hard it lands on the moon and bounces back. Snail barely makes it around the bases before the ball returns. Full color illustrations show comical animal teammates shouting encouragement to the tiny runner.

1444 *Snail Saves the Day.* Ill. by author. Crowell, 1985; pap., 1988. ISBN 0-690-04469-0. SUBJECTS: Animals—Fiction; Sports—Football—Fiction. RL 2.6.

When his team of small animals is pitted against a team of bears, hippos, and other large creatures, Snail oversleeps, making it to the stadium just in time to make a winning touchdown. Bright, comic illustrations and a very brief story make this appropriate for the beginning reader.

1445 *Three Cheers for Hippo!* Ill. by author. Crowell, 1987. ISBN 0-690-04668-5. SUBJECTS: Animals—Fiction; Humorous stories. RL 1.6.

Hippo, who is teaching Cat, Dog, and Pig to parachute, must quickly rescue them before they are eaten by alligators. The book's extremely brief text relies on humorous pencil, ink, and watercolor pictures to help tell the story.

Standiford, Natalie

1446 *The Best Little Monkeys in the World.* Ill. by Hilary Knight. Random House, hb and pap., 1987. ISBN 0-394-98616-4. SERIES: Step into Reading. SUBJECTS: Animals—Monkeys—Fiction; Baby-sitting—Fiction; Humorous stories. RL 2.4.

Marvin and Mary are two mischievous little monkeys whose baby-sitter is so wrapped up in her telephone conversations that she is oblivious to the mess they are creating. The colorful pencil and wash pictures are full of unexpected details and add to the humor in this funny story.

Stanek, Muriel

1447 *Left, Right, Left, Right!* Ill. by Lucy Hawkinson. Whitman, 1969, o.p. SERIES: Concept Books. SUBJECTS: Concepts—Left and right—Fiction; Self-esteem—Fiction. RL 2.1.

Katie gets confused between left and right, turns in the wrong direction during a parade, and is humiliated. Her grandmother gives her a ring for her right hand and that solves her problem. A sensitive look at a problem faced by many children, it is illustrated in black and white and in color.

Stanovich, Betty Jo

1448 *Hedgehog Adventures.* Ill. by Chris L. Demarest. Lothrop, 1983, o.p. SUBJECTS: Animals—Hedgehogs—Fiction; Animals—Woodchucks—Fiction. RL 2.7.

Exuberant Hedgehog takes his friend Woodchuck on three ill-fated adventures. Each time his spirits are revived by his kindly homebody friend Woodchuck. The gentle, expressive pencil drawings capture the pair's moods and the story's fun.

1449 *Hedgehog Surprises.* Ill. by Chris L. Demarest. Lothrop, 1984. ISBN 0-688-02691-5. SUBJECTS: Animals—Hedgehogs—Fiction; Animals—Woodchucks—Fiction; Birthdays—Fiction. RL 2.6.

Excitable Hedgehog is saved from worry and a disastrous case of nerves by his friend Woodchuck as he tries to give Bear a perfect birthday party. Expressive colored pencil drawings are as humorous as the very funny story.

Stevens, Bryna

1450 *Ben Franklin's Glass Armonica.* Ill. by Priscilla Kiedrowski. Carolrhoda, 1983. ISBN 0-87614-202-1. SERIES: On My Own. SUBJECTS: Biographies; Musical instruments; United States—History. RL 2.5.

Ben Franklin hears someone perform a concert on crystal glasses and is so fascinated by the sound that he creates an armonica—an instrument played by rubbing one's fingertips over glass bowls on rods. Even Mozart composed for the armonica. Illustrated with realistic pencil drawings.

Stevens, Carla

1451 *Anna, Grandpa, and the Big Storm.* Ill.
by Margot Tomes. Clarion, 1982;
Penguin, pap., 1986. ISBN 0-89919-066-
9. SUBJECTS: Emergencies—Fiction;
Grandparents—Fiction; Weather—
Snow—Fiction. RL 2.6.

Grandpa changes his mind about staying in
New York City after helping Anna and other
stranded passengers get back home during a
terrible blizzard in the late 1800s. The exciting story is illustrated with detailed realistic
pen and ink drawings.

1452 *Hooray for Pig!* Ill. by Rainey Bennett.
Seabury, 1974, o.p. SUBJECTS:
Animals—Pigs—Fiction; Emotions—
Fear—Fiction; Sports—Swimming—
Fiction. RL 1.8.

Afraid of the water, Pig does not even want to
try swimming until Otter patiently helps him
begin to overcome his fear. A good handling
of a common situation—it does not make
fears magically disappear but shows how
much work it takes. Illustrated with simple
line drawings with washes.

1453 *Pig and the Blue Flag.* Ill. by Rainey
Bennett. Seabury, 1977. ISBN 0-395-
28825-8. SUBJECTS: Animals—Fiction;
School stories; Self-esteem—Fiction.
RL 2.6.

Pig is so big and heavy that he never seems to
do anything right in gym. Then Otter suggests
they play Capture the Flag, and everyone is a
winner. Children will empathize with Pig and
be glad he finally succeeds. Illustrated with
pen and ink drawings with soft blue and
orange washes.

1454 *Sara and the Pinch.* Ill. by John
Wallner. Houghton Mifflin, 1980, o.p.
SUBJECTS: Behavior; School stories.
RL 2.3.

At school Sara is always determined to have
things her own way and can be quite pesky
when she does not. Reprimanded for pinching
and sent into the hall, Sara is comforted by
Mr. Zamatsky, the school custodian. Colored
pencil and wash pictures capture Sara's
feisty, independent nature.

1455 *Your First Pet and How to Take Care of
It.* Ill. by Lisl Weil. Macmillan, 1974.
ISBN 0-02-788200-4. SERIES: Ready-to-
Read. SUBJECTS: Pet care; Pets. RL 2.3.

Good advice on the care and training of eight
popular animals is offered to children about
to select a pet. Not the usual overview of a
subject found in most books for beginning
readers, this is a substantial 120 pages of
good information with help from sketchy ink
drawings.

Stevenson, James

1456 *Clams Can't Sing.* Ill. by author.
Greenwillow, 1980, o.p. SERIES: Read-
alone. SUBJECTS: Animals—Mollusks—
Fiction; Humorous stories; Seashore—
Fiction. RL 2.2.

The seashore animals confidently prepare for
their concert and just as confidently tell
Beatrice and Foster they are not in it because
clams cannot sing. The two surprise everyone
with a symphony for two clams. Hilarious
text and drawings might get children to try to
create their own music.

1457 *Fast Friends: Two Stories.* Ill. by
author. Greenwillow, 1979. ISBN 0-688-
84197-X. SERIES: Read-alone. SUBJECTS:
Animals—Fiction; Friendship—Fiction;
Self-esteem—Fiction. RL 2.1.

The first story has Murry, a turtle, and Fred, a
snail, get plenty of friends when they find a
skateboard. In the second story Clem Turtle
convinces Thomas Mouse to build a house to
attract friends. In both stories the humorous
characters come to accept themselves. Pictures are ink and wash.

1458 *Winston, Newton, Elton, and Ed.* Ill. by
author. Greenwillow, 1978, o.p. SERIES:
Read-alone. SUBJECTS: Animals—
Penguins—Fiction; Animals—
Walruses—Fiction; Sibling rivalry—
Fiction. RL 2.1.

In the first of two Antarctic stories, three little
walrus brothers are so intent on upstaging
each other that they lose their dinners. In the
second, Ed, a penguin, is marooned on an ice
floe, far from his friends. Deftly drawn humorous pictures accompany the two very funny
stories.

Stolz, Mary

1459 *Emmett's Pig*. Ill. by Garth Williams. Harper & Row, 1959. ISBN 0-06-025856-X. SERIES: I Can Read. SUBJECTS: Animals—Pigs—Fiction; Pets—Fiction. RL 1.8.
More than anything else, city dweller Emmett wants to see a real pig. For his birthday Emmett's parents take him to a farm and he is given his own piglet—to be raised by the farmer. Soft pencil and wash drawings complement this quiet story of a dream fulfilled.

Stone, Lynn

1460 *Eagles*. Photos. Rourke, 1989. ISBN 0-86592-321-3. SERIES: Bird Discovery Library. SUBJECTS: Animals—Eagles. RL 2.9.
Stone introduces several species of eagles and gives examples of their habitats, diet, nesting, and relationship to humans without dwelling on life cycles or any specifics. The color photographs are good. The brief book includes an index and glossary.

1461 *Endangered Animals*. Photos. Childrens, hb and pap., 1984. ISBN 0-516-01724-1. SERIES: New True. SUBJECTS: Animals—Endangered. RL 3.0.
Many of the world's endangered animals are discussed. Stone stresses the role played by humans as hunters, consumers, and farmers in destroying wildlife. Animals are shown in clear full color photographs.

1462 *Ostriches*. Photos. Rourke, 1989. ISBN 0-86592-323-X. SERIES: Bird Discovery Library. SUBJECTS: Animals—Ostriches. RL 2.4.
A simple, clear text and excellent photos describe an ostrich's habitat, appearance, nesting, diet, and its predators. The book is small with only 18 pages of alternating text and photos.

1463 *Owls*. Photos. Rourke, 1989. ISBN 0-86592-326-4. SERIES: Bird Discovery Library. SUBJECTS: Animals—Owls. RL 2.3.
Examples of several species and the characteristics, habitat, and prey of owls are presented in color photos and easily understood text. Although not a detailed study, this does provide good information in 18 pages of alternating text and photos.

1464 *Pelicans*. Photos. Rourke, 1989. ISBN 0-86592-322-1. SERIES: Bird Discovery Library. SUBJECTS: Animals—Pelicans. RL 2.5.
A generally informative text that offers facts on the different varieties of pelicans and their eating habits, nesting, and relationship to humans. Unfortunately the book is marred by the mismatching of photos and one wrong caption. Photos are generally good and in color.

1465 *Penguins*. Photos. Rourke, 1989. ISBN 0-86592-325-6. SERIES: Bird Discovery Library. SUBJECTS: Animals—Penguins. RL 2.5.
Although information about the penguin's life cycle is not included, this book is nevertheless a nice introduction to penguin types, habitats, diets, and predators. The color photos are quite good.

1466 *Vultures*. Photos by author. Rourke, 1989. ISBN 0-86592-324-8. SERIES: Bird Discovery Library. SUBJECTS: Animals—Vultures. RL 2.6.
An excellent text that gives an overview of the types of vultures, habitats, and diet. Explains why most vultures have no head feathers. Illustrated with color photos.

Stone, Rosetta (pseud.)

1467 *Because a Little Bug Went Ka-Choo!* Ill. by Michael Frith. Beginner, 1975. ISBN 0-394-93130-0. SERIES: I Can Read It All By Myself. SUBJECTS: Humorous stories; Stories in rhyme. RL 2.3.
A mere sneeze from a bug sets off a chain of events that results in a ship being airlifted into a circus parade. The silliness of this rhyming story is carried over into the zany full color pictures.

Storr, Catherine

1468 *David and Goliath*. Ill. by Chris Molan. Raintree, 1985. ISBN 0-8172-1995-1.

Storr, Catherine (cont.)

SERIES: People of the Bible. SUBJECTS: Bible stories. RL 2.4.

A brief text and many colorful romanticized paintings tell the story of the shepherd David and how he came to slay the giant Goliath and lead the Israelites to victory. Included is a map showing the sites mentioned in the Old Testament story.

1469 *Noah and His Ark.* Ill. by Jim Russell. Raintree, 1982. ISBN 0-8172-1975-7. SERIES: People of the Bible. SUBJECTS: Bible stories. RL 2.3.

The Old Testament story of Noah and the flood is retold in simple language with much dialogue. The detailed watercolor pictures set the story in biblical times. This might be useful for Sunday school classes as well as individual interest.

Sullivan, George

1470 *Willie Mays.* Ill. by David Brown. Putnam, 1973, o.p. SERIES: See and Read Beginning to Read Biography. SUBJECTS: Biographies; Black Americans; Sports—Baseball. RL 2.9.

The story of baseball great Willie Mays's beginnings and career is written very clearly and well. One of the leading home-run hitters of all time, Mays was also one of the first black athletes to integrate major-league baseball. Illustrated with black, white, and green line drawings.

Swayne, Dick, and Savage, Peter

1471 *I Am a Farmer.* Photos by Dick Swayne. Lippincott, 1978, o.p. SERIES: I-Like-To-Read. SUBJECTS: Careers; Farm and country life. RL 2.4.

First published in Britain, this book shows a young girl (the farmer) as she leads the reader around her farm and discusses animals and chores. The text is interesting and offers some insights into farm life. Photographs are in full color.

1472 *I Am a Fisherman.* Photos by Dick Swayne. Lippincott, 1978. ISBN 0-397-31778-6. SERIES: I-Like-To-Read. SUBJECTS: Careers; Fishing. RL 2.9.

A short but lively text shows a young boy on a fishing expedition with four seasoned sailors. The climax of this British story comes when the child catches a flounder almost as large as he is. Illustrated with good full color photographs.

T

Tangborn, Wendell V.

1473 *Glaciers.* Rev. ed. Ill. by Marc Simont. Crowell, hb and pap., 1988. ISBN 0-690-04684-7. SERIES: Let's-Read-and-Find-Out. SUBJECTS: Geology. RL 2.9.

Children will find this look at glaciers fascinating as they discover how they are made, how they move, and what happens to them as they travel. The pencil and watercolor illustrations make the book even more interesting and will add to a child's understanding of the information.

Taylor, Sydney

1474 *The Dog Who Came to Dinner.* Ill. by John Johnson. Follett, 1966, o.p. SERIES: Beginning to Read. SUBJECTS: Animals—Dogs—Fiction; Moving, household—Fiction. RL 2.2.

When a large dog comes into the Browns' home along with their new neighbors, each family assumes it belongs to the other. Both families are too polite to say anything when the dog misbehaves. The detailed illustrations are realistic yet humorous and are done in full color.

Terban, Marvin

1475 *In a Pickle and Other Funny Idioms.* Ill. by Giulio Maestro. Clarion, hb and pap., 1983. ISBN 0-89919-153-3. SUBJECTS: English language—Idioms. RL 3.1.

Every right-hand page of this book presents an idiom, its definition, an explanation for it, and its origin. Each left-hand page has a funny illustration of the idiom. Definitions and illustrations do a good job of clarifying idioms while being entertaining to readers.

Tether, Graham

1476 *The Hair Book.* Ill. by Roy McKie. Beginner, 1979, o.p. SERIES: Bright and Early. SUBJECTS: Animals—Fiction; Human body—Hair—Fiction; Stories in rhyme. RL 2.8.

A whimsical rhyming text points out all kinds of hair on people and animals. Animals such as baboons do many kinds of things with hair—wash it, comb it, set and dry it, and even cut it. Illustrated with comic-style drawings in full color.

Thaler, Mike

1477 *Hippo Lemonade.* Ill. by Maxie Chambliss. Harper & Row, 1986. ISBN 0-06-026162-5. SERIES: I Can Read. SUBJECTS: Animals—Hippopotami—Fiction; Humorous stories. RL 2.3.

Childlike Hippo wishes to be something else, sets up a lemonade stand in competition with Snake, gets scared telling spooky stories, and finally decides that being alone is all right but being with friends is better. Lively, humorous text and carefully drawn illustrations work well together.

1478 *It's Me, Hippo!* Ill. by Maxie Chambliss. Harper & Row, 1983. ISBN 0-06-026154-4. SERIES: I Can Read. SUBJECTS: Animals—Hippopotami—Fiction; Birthdays—Fiction; Humorous stories. RL 1.9.

Whether he is trying to build a house, is feeling left out when everyone else is sick, is trying to paint a picture, or thinks his friends have forgotten his birthday, Hippo should appeal to young readers with his slapstick humor. Illustrated with peach and green humorous drawings.

1479 *Pack 109.* Ill. by Normand Chartier. Dutton, 1988. ISBN 0-525-44393-2. SERIES: Easy Reader. SUBJECTS: Animals—Fiction; Humorous stories; Scouts and scouting—Fiction. RL 2.6.

The five scouts of Pack 109 are avid collectors of Merit Badges. In one of the stories in this book, the little woodland animals earn them even for unsuccessful attempts—cookies as hard as rocks are piled together to earn a rock-collecting badge. Good humor always reigns in these stories with delightful color illustrations.

1480 *There's a Hippopotamus under My Bed.* Ill. by Ray Cruz. Watts, 1977, o.p.; Avon, pap., 1978. ISBN 0-380-40238-6. SERIES: Easy-Read Story. SUBJECTS: Animals—Hippopotami—Fiction; Animals, zoo—Fiction; Humorous stories. RL 2.0.

Followed home by a hippopotamus, the little boy lets it into his house. Because of its size the hippo creates disaster wherever it moves until zoo keepers finally arrive to claim it. The imaginative and funny story is illustrated with humorous ink and wash paintings.

Thomas, Art

1481 *Fishing Is for Me.* Photos by author. Lerner, 1980. ISBN 0-8225-1096-0. SERIES: Sports for Me. SUBJECTS: Fishing. RL 3.1.

Kevin takes the reader on his fishing trips for bluegill, bass, and trout. He explains about the kinds of equipment and bait and about the fishing techniques that are used. He also gives instructions on how to cast, set a hook, and cook fish. Illustrated with black and white photographs.

Thompson, Brenda, and Giesen, Rosemary

1482 *Pirates.* Ill. by Simon Stern and Rosemary Giesen. Lerner, 1977, o.p. SERIES: First Fact. SUBJECTS: Pirates. RL 3.3.

The short text of this book briefly discusses pirates, the terrors of the sea, and provides information on some of the most famous pirates. Busy ink and watercolor pictures dominate the pages.

Thompson, Vivian

1483 *The Horse That Liked Sandwiches.* Ill. by Aliki. Putnam, 1962, o.p. SERIES: See and Read. SUBJECTS: Animals—Horses—Fiction; Humorous stories. RL 2.0.

Thompson, Vivian (cont.)

While Tony is taking an afternoon nap, his horse Mario goes off in search of sandwiches. Poor Tony is left to deal with the angry and hungry people Mario has deprived of lunch. This humorous story has comic-style ink and wash illustrations that are lively and fun though somewhat dated.

Thomson, Pat

1484 *Can You Hear Me, Grandad?* Ill. by Jez Alborough. Delacorte, hb and pap., 1988. ISBN 0-385-29599-5. SERIES: Share-A-Story. SUBJECTS: Grandparents—Fiction; Humorous stories; Zoos—Fiction. RL 2.0.
Silly Grandad feigns deafness, pretending to mis-hear everything his granddaughter tells him about a trip to the zoo. His twisting of her words and her reactions to it are hilarious. Meant to be read by an adult and child alternating pages, it is illustrated with expressive, humorous drawings and is delightful.

1485 *Good Girl Granny.* Ill. by Faith Jaques. Delacorte, 1987; Dell, pap., 1988. ISBN 0-385-29602-9. SERIES: Share-A-Story. SUBJECTS: Behavior—Fiction; Grandparents—Fiction; Humorous stories. RL 2.3.
In response to her grandchild's questions about her youth, Granny insists that in those days all children behaved well as she tells of one bit of mischief after another. Alternating pages for adult and child to read, good colorful illustrations, and great humor make this perfect for sharing.

1486 *My Friend Mr. Morris.* Ill. by Satoshi Kitamura. Delacorte, hb and pap., 1988. ISBN 0-385-29603-7. SERIES: Share-A-Story. SUBJECTS: Humorous stories; Nonsense; Shopping—Fiction. RL 2.1.
A little boy's neighbor, Mr. Morris, looks through catalogs and muses about what he might buy: socks for his bed (bed socks), a can of food as a pet (pet food), and other silly but delightful nonsense. To be read by children and adults together, it is illustrated with watercolors.

1487 *One of Those Days.* Ill. by Bob Wilson. Delacorte, hb and pap., 1986. ISBN 0-385-29601-0. SERIES: Share-A-Story. SUBJECTS: Emotions—Frustrations—Fiction; Humorous stories; Parent and child—Fiction. RL 2.3.
A little girl rushes home to tell Mom about her terrible day at school only to discover that her mother's day was far worse and far more humorous. Meant to be read alternately by adult and child, the book is delightfully silly and has colorful illustrations of people and settings.

1488 *Thank You for the Tadpole.* Ill. by Mary Rayner. Delacorte, hb and pap., 1988. ISBN 0-385-29604-5. SERIES: Share-A-Story. SUBJECTS: Birthdays—Fiction; Nonsense; Parent and child—Fiction. RL 1.8.
Having asked his dad for an idea for Becky's birthday present, a little boy seriously considers all the silly things his father suggests. Meant to be shared by an adult and child reading alternate pages, this delightful story shows colorful pictures of a house-husband father and his son.

1489 *The Treasure Sock.* Ill. by Tony Ross. Delacorte, hb and pap., 1987. ISBN 0-385-29600-2. SERIES: Share-A-Story. SUBJECTS: Clothing—Fiction; Humorous stories; Parent and child—Fiction. RL 2.4.
Holding up a very full sock, a little girl tells her mother about all the "treasures" she has found on her way home. Mother and daughter alternate pages and reactions to the frog, pig, key, rubber band, chewing gum, false teeth, perfume, and so on. Illustrated with outrageously funny pictures.

Tobias, Tobi

1490 *Maria Tallchief.* Ill. by Michael Hampshire. Crowell, 1970, o.p.; pap., 1972. ISBN 0-690-51830-7. SERIES: Crowell Biography. SUBJECTS: Biographies; Dancing; Native Americans—Osage. RL 2.7.
A member of the Osage tribe, Maria Tallchief begins dancing as a child, practices hard, has good teachers, and becomes a member of the Ballet Society of New York and a world-

renowned ballerina. Well written and interesting, it is illustrated with realistic sketches.

1491 *Marian Anderson.* Ill. by Symeon Shimin. Crowell, 1972. ISBN 0-690-51847-1. SERIES: Crowell Biography. SUBJECTS: Biographies; Black Americans; Music. RL 2.5.

One of the world's great singers, Marian Anderson fought poverty and prejudice to get recognition for her talent. This inspiring biography covers her life until her retirement. The illustrations are realistic, lovely, and often moving pencil and wash pictures.

Tompert, Ann

1492 *Little Otter Remembers and Other Stories.* Ill. by John Wallner. Crown, 1977, o.p. SUBJECTS: Animals—Otters—Fiction; Parent and child—Fiction. RL 2.1.

In three stories Little Otter tries hard to find something for his mother's birthday, attempts to remember where he put his pinecone, and wants to get his friends to a coasting party. With Mother Otter's support each story ends happily. Illustrated with detailed color pencil drawings.

Towne, Peter

1493 *George Washington Carver.* Ill. by Elizia Moon. Crowell, 1975, o.p. SERIES: Crowell Biography. SUBJECTS: Biographies; Black Americans; Science. RL 2.6.

Born into slavery, George Washington Carver fights hard against bigotry and hatred to get an education. Although his research at Tuskegee Institute wins him fame, Carver has a social mission as well. Well written and interesting, this is illustrated with charcoal drawings.

Tremain, Ruthven

1494 *Teapot, Switcheroo, and Other Silly Word Games.* Ill. by author. Greenwillow, 1979. ISBN 0-688-80210-9. SERIES: Read-alone. SUBJECTS: Wordplay. RL 2.5.

Spoonerisms, Pig Latin, Gotcha, palindromes, secret messages, and word scrambles are just some of the "games" that help children have fun with language. Ink and wash sketches are used to give hints to the answers, which can be found at the end of the book.

Trier, Carola S.

1495 *Exercise: What It Is, What It Does.* Ill. by Tom Huffman. Greenwillow, 1982. ISBN 0-688-00951-4. SERIES: Read-alone. SUBJECTS: Exercise; Physical fitness. RL 2.6.

With the silly commentary of an omnipresent cat, this volume takes children through an assortment of exercises meant to promote good posture and strengthen the body. The instructions and the exercises themselves invite participation. Humorous ink line drawings add to the fun.

Tripp, Valerie

1496 *The Penguins Paint.* Ill. by Sandra Cox Kalthoff. Childrens, 1987. ISBN 0-516-01567-2. SERIES: Just One More. SUBJECTS: Animals—Penguins—Fiction; Concepts—Color—Fiction; Stories in rhyme. RL 1.6.

A family of penguins wants color in its life and goes to the new paint store to try first blue, then green, then yellow, and finally red. When they are done they have a rainbow. The rhyming verse moves well and the color reinforcement is good.

Troughton, Joanna

1497 *How Rabbit Stole the Fire: A North American Indian Folk Tale.* Ill. by author. Peter Bedrick, 1986. ISBN 0-87226-040-2. SERIES: Folk-tales of the World. SUBJECTS: Folklore—Native Americans. RL 2.3.

Rabbit the mischief maker contrives a way to steal fire from the Sky People, entering their land with a special headdress that he sets ablaze. He runs back to his own land with the Sky People chasing him and passes the fire to animal after animal. Lavish illustrations capture the excitement of the tale.

V

Van Leeuwen, Jean

1498 *Amanda Pig and Her Big Brother Oliver.*
Ill. by Ann Schweninger. Dial, hb and
pap., 1982. ISBN 0-8037-0017-2. SERIES:
Easy-to-Read. SUBJECTS: Animals—
Pigs—Fiction; Family life—Fiction;
Sibling rivalry—Fiction. RL 1.8.
One of a series of books about a close-knit
family of pigs with very human personality
characteristics, this story takes Amanda and
Oliver through five everyday events common
to small children. The illustrations are soft
pastel colored.

1499 *More Tales of Amanda Pig.* Ill. by Ann
Schweninger. Dial, 1985; pap., 1988.
ISBN 0-8037-0224-8. SERIES: Easy-to-
Read. SUBJECTS: Animals—Pigs—
Fiction; Family life—Fiction. RL 1.7.
Amanda Pig; her brother Oliver; their good-
natured parents, Aunt, Uncle, and cousins;
and assorted stuffed animals share a variety
of adventures common to small children
everywhere. The illustrations are done in soft
watercolors and pencil that deftly capture a
loving family.

1500 *More Tales of Oliver Pig.* Ill. by Arnold
Lobel. Dial, hb and pap., 1981. ISBN 0-
8037-8714-6. SERIES: Easy-to-Read.
SUBJECTS: Animals—Pigs—Fiction;
Family life—Fiction; Siblings—Fiction.
RL 1.7.
From one spring to the next, Oliver shares
gentle everyday adventures with his family.
The stories are low key and quiet and present
situations common to young children. The
ink and wash illustrations capture the love,
warmth, and frustrations of a very human
family of pigs.

1501 *Oliver, Amanda, and Grandmother Pig.*
Ill. by Ann Schweninger. Dial, 1987.
ISBN 0-8037-0362-7. SERIES: Easy-to-
Read. SUBJECTS: Animals—Pigs—
Fiction; Family life—Fiction;
Grandparents—Fiction. RL 2.0.
Initially disturbed by Grandmother's inabil-
ity to bend over or read without her glasses,
Oliver and Amanda soon begin to cherish the
time they spend with her. A gem of a story of
intergenerational understanding and love, it
is supported by simple yet colorful pastel
drawings.

1502 *Tales of Amanda Pig.* Ill. by Ann
Schweninger. Dial, hb and pap., 1983.
ISBN 0-8037-8450-3. SERIES: Easy-to-
Read. SUBJECTS: Animals—Pigs—
Fiction; Emotions—Fear—Fiction;
Family life—Fiction. RL 1.8.
The pig family's youngest member, Amanda,
is the center of five gentle stories of everyday
life with which children can identify. She
faces fears, gains responsibility, and puts
Mother to sleep by telling her a bedtime
story. Pastel pictures add humor and warmth
to a lovely book.

1503 *Tales of Oliver Pig.* Ill. by Arnold Lobel.
Dial, hb and pap., 1979. ISBN 0-8037-
8736-7. SERIES: Easy-to-Read. SUBJECTS:
Animals—Pigs—Fiction; Family life—
Fiction; Sibling rivalry—Fiction.
RL 1.9.
Oliver is a part of a very loving family of
pigs. He bakes cookies on cold wet days and
does not always appreciate his little sister,
Amanda. The four short chapters about Oli-
ver's family are illustrated in ink and wash
pictures that bring them all to life.

Van Woerkom, Dorothy

1504 *Abu Ali: Three Tales of the Middle East.*
Ill. by Harold Berson. Macmillan,
1976, o.p. SERIES: Ready-to-Read.
SUBJECTS: Folklore—Turkey; Humorous
stories. RL 2.0.
Abu Ali, which is Van Woerkom's name for
the foolish Hodja of Turkish folklore, has
trouble keeping track of nine donkeys, gets
even with his friends who try to cheat him,
and gets his own comeuppance. The delightfully funny stories are illustrated with whimsical ink sketches in full color.

1505 *Becky and the Bear.* Ill. by Margot
Tomes. Putnam, 1975, o.p. SERIES: See
and Read. SUBJECTS: Animals—Bears—
Fiction; Behavior—Brave—Fiction;

United States—Colonial period—
Fiction. RL 2.4.
With only corn and berries to eat, Becky and Granny hope that Ned and father will be bringing back meat. Left alone briefly, Becky bravely and cleverly captures a bear. Based on a true story set in colonial Maine. The illustrations are done with ink, wash, and silhouettes.

1506 *The Friends of Abu Ali: Three More Tales of the Middle East.* Ill. by Harold Berson. Macmillan, 1978, o.p. SERIES: Ready-to-Read. SUBJECTS: Folklore—Turkey; Humorous stories. RL 2.1.
The three stories of Abu Ali and his friends are ridiculously silly, like those in the Hodja stories from Turkey, and are sure to have children smiling at the men's antics. Illustrated with ink line drawings and watercolor washes.

1507 *Harry and Shellburt.* Ill. by Erick Ingraham. Macmillan, 1977, o.p. SERIES: Ready-to-Read. SUBJECTS: Animals—Rabbits—Fiction; Animals—Turtles—Fiction; Friendship—Fiction. RL 1.8.
The title characters—Harry, a hare, and Shellburt, a tortoise—agree to rerun the race made famous by Aesop. Predictably, the tortoise wins but the two remain friends. The well-written and entertaining story has soft, detailed pencil drawings of realistic animals and settings.

1508 *Hidden Messages.* Ill. by Lynne Cherry. Crown, 1979. ISBN 0-517-53520-3. SUBJECTS: Animals—Communication; Science. RL 3.1.
The experiments of Benjamin Franklin and other scientists lead to the discovery of pheromones, the odors particular to a species that provide them with a variety of nonverbal messages. The interesting narrative and realistic paintings combine to provide a good introduction to an unusual subject.

1509 *Meat Pies and Sausages.* Ill. by Joseph Low. Greenwillow, 1976, o.p. SERIES: Read-alone. SUBJECTS: Animals—Foxes—Fiction; Animals—Wolves—Fiction; Folklore. RL 1.9.

Three stories based on Eastern European folklore pit Fox and Wolf against one another in their quest for food. Fox cleverly outwits Wolf, leading him into trouble with humans. The humorous stories are illustrated with ink and wash pictures with an Eastern European setting.

1510 *Old Devil Is Waiting: Three Folktales.* Ill. by Jan Brett. Harcourt Brace, hb and pap., 1985. ISBN 0-15-257766-1. SERIES: Let Me Read. SUBJECTS: Folklore; Humorous stories. RL 2.6.
In the first two tales devils try to get a clever glassblower and wicked landlord to go back with them to hell. In the third, the Old Devil himself is outwitted by a farmer's wife. The three humorous stories, based on folklore from around the world, are tied together by Old Devil and all are illustrated with detailed black and white pictures.

1511 *Sea Frog, City Frog.* Ill. by Jose Aruego and Ariane Dewey. Macmillan, 1975, o.p. SERIES: Ready-to-Read. SUBJECTS: Animals—Frogs and toads—Fiction; Folklore—Japan. RL 1.7.
In this Japanese folktale, two frogs meet at the top of a high hill on their respective journeys to see the city and the sea. They help each other to stand up and see where they are going. Their eyes point backward and each believes where he is going is just like where he comes from. Humorous ink and wash drawings.

1512 *Tit for Tat.* Ill. by Douglas Florian. Greenwillow, 1977, o.p. SERIES: Read-alone. SUBJECTS: Behavior—Greedy—Fiction; Folklore—Latvia. RL 1.9.
On a bitter winter night, a ragged stranger seeks shelter from a miser, who refuses him, and then from a kindly old woman, who helps him. Both are appropriately rewarded for their treatment of him. Based on a Latvian folktale, this is illustrated with stylized ink, wash, and pencil pictures.

Venezia, Mike

1513 *Van Gogh.* Ill. by author. Childrens, 1988. ISBN 0-516-02274-1. SERIES: Getting to Know the World's Greatest

Venezia, Mike (cont.)

Artists. SUBJECTS: Art and artists;
Biographies. RL 2.4.

A factual text presents an interesting picture of Van Gogh and his struggles as an artist. The reproductions of his work are carefully chosen to represent his genius. However, some adults may find that Venezia's use of cartoons belittles the life of Van Gogh, and therefore may be offended by the cartoons.

Victor, Joan B.

1514 *Shells Are Skeletons*. Ill. by author. Crowell, 1977. ISBN 0-690-01038-9. SERIES: Let's-Read-and-Find-Out. SUBJECTS: Animals—Mollusks; Shells. RL 2.7.

Carefully drawn pen-and-wash pictures of a variety of shells combine with the text to explain how shells and the mollusks they house grow, protect themselves, and eat.

Vinton, Iris

1515 *Look Out for Pirates*. Ill. by H. B. Vestal. Beginner, 1961. ISBN 0-394-90022-7. SERIES: I Can Read It All By Myself. SUBJECTS: Pirates—Fiction. RL 2.1.

Pursued by pirates, Captain Jim's ship capsizes and his trunk of gold washes overboard. His men dive and retrieve the gold and Captain Jim finds a way to outwit the pirates. Though the sailors' use of diving gear seems odd, the story is popular. Illustrated with realistic paintings.

Voigt, Cynthia

1516 *Stories about Rosie*. Ill. by Dennis Kendrick. Atheneum, 1986. ISBN 0-689-31296-2. SUBJECTS: Humorous stories; Pets—Dogs—Fiction. RL 2.0.

Rosie, a large, irrepressible spaniel, thinks Mommy, Daddy, Jessie, and Duff are meant to serve her. Rosie barks, runs, chases, and is always happy and excited in four humorous stories about her and her family. Color and ink sketches in a comic style capture Rosie's exuberance.

W

Waddell, Martin

1517 *The Tough Princess*. Ill. by Patrick Benson. Philomel, 1986. ISBN 0-399-21380-5. SUBJECTS: Fairy tales; Humorous stories; Sex roles—Fiction. RL 2.7.

The king and queen want their daughter to marry a prince who will take care of them. Instead Princess Rosamund heads off on her rickety bicycle to fight monsters and rescue princes. The role reversals are splendid in this modern, humorous fairy tale as are the comic illustrations of feisty Rosamund.

Wagner, Ken, and Olson, Mary C., eds.

1518 *The Lion Who Couldn't Say No*. Ill. by Don Page. Golden, 1976, o.p.; pap., 1987. ISBN 0-307-03680-4. SERIES: Step Ahead Beginning Reader. SUBJECTS: Animals—Lions—Fiction; Behavior—Generous—Fiction; Humorous stories. RL 1.9.

Leo the lion is so generous with the hair in his mane, allowing the birds to use it for nests, that he is soon almost bald. When nothing helps his hair grow back, the birds create a mane for him out of greenery. Comically illustrated in watercolors with attractive borders.

Wahl, Jan

1519 *Drakestail*. Ill. by Byron Barton. Greenwillow, 1978, o.p. SERIES: Read-alone. SUBJECTS: Animals—Ducks—Fiction; Folklore—France. RL 2.2.

On his way to get his money from the king, Drakestail is joined by four friends who shrink and hop into his gizzard. They reappear just in time to save him from disaster. A marvelous retelling of a French folktale, it is illustrated in green, gold, and orange with black outlining.

1520 *The Teeny, Tiny Witches*. Ill. by Margot Tomes. Putnam, 1979, o.p. SUBJECTS: Witches—Fiction. RL 3.4.

Too tiny to do much magic and always driven from their homes by animals, Ma, Pa, and Sam Witch finally find a little cottage with a friendly old mouse who welcomes them. The gentle and whimsical pen and ink drawings are carefully created with red and brown accents.

Wandro, Mark, and Blank, Joani

1521 *My Daddy Is a Nurse.* Ill. by Irene Trivas. Addison-Wesley, 1981. ISBN 0-317-56673-3. SUBJECTS: Careers; Sex roles. RL 2.9.
Ten fathers are seen in occupations usually associated with women, such as flight attendant, nurse, ballet dancer, preschool teacher, librarian, and telephone operator. The brief text is illustrated with black and white cartoon drawings.

Waters, John F.

1522 *Camels: Ships of the Desert.* Ill. by Reynold Ruffins. Crowell, 1974. ISBN 0-690-00395-1. SERIES: Let's-Read-and-Find-Out. SUBJECTS: Animals—Camels. RL 3.0.
By comparing the camel's physiology to that of humans, Waters is able to explain the camel's suitability for desert life. He also does away with myths surrounding the animal's hump while presenting a very interesting and factual book. Pencil and wash pictures are well done.

1523 *Hungry Sharks.* Ill. by Ann Dalton. Crowell, 1973. ISBN 0-690-01121-0. SERIES: Let's-Read-and-Find-Out. SUBJECTS: Animals—Sharks. RL 3.6.
The shark is a subject of perennial interest to children. Shark behavior and physiology is briefly explained without placing undue emphasis on its predatory nature. Expressive rather than realistic drawings suggest the shark, possibly making this book less attractive to many young readers.

1524 *A Jellyfish Is Not a Fish.* Ill. by Kazue Mizumura. Crowell, 1979. ISBN 0-690-03888-7. SERIES: Let's-Read-and-Find-Out. SUBJECTS: Animals—Jellyfish. RL 2.5.
Found all over the world, jellyfish come in all sizes. Some are harmless while others, such as the sea wasp of Australia, are poisonous and deadly. Children will find the text and realistic watercolor paintings attractive.

Watson, Jane W.

1525 *The First Americans: Tribes of North America.* Ill. by Troy Howell. Pantheon, 1980. ISBN 0-394-84194-8. SERIES: I Am Reading. SUBJECTS: Native Americans. RL 3.1.
A look at customs and life-styles among the Native Americans of the plains, eastern woodlands, far north, northwest coast, and the southwest places some emphasis on the role of children in these cultures. Black and white illustrations realistically depict the clothing, artifacts, and so on.

Watts, Barrie

1526 *Potato.* Photos. Ill. by Helen Senior. Silver Burdett, 1988. ISBN 0-382-09528-6. SERIES: Stopwatch. SUBJECTS: Plants; Vegetables. RL 2.3.
A straightforward, clearly written text takes the reader through the different stages of growth for the potato plant. The photographs, many of them cutaways of underground growth, and the line drawings work well with the text to explain the plant's life cycle.

Webster, Vera

1527 *Weather Experiments.* Photos. Childrens, 1982. ISBN 0-516-01662-8. SERIES: New True. SUBJECTS: Science experiments—Weather; Weather. RL 2.4.
Simple experiments, none dangerous or requiring adult supervision, help children to learn about air pressure, measuring rainfall, and determining the difference in temperature between sun and shade areas. Clearly explained, experiments are illustrated with diagrams and full color photos.

Weiss, Ellen

1528 *Millicent Maybe*. Ill. by author. Watts, 1979, o.p.; Avon, pap., 1980. ISBN 0-380-49197-4. SERIES: Easy-Read Story. SUBJECTS: Behavior—Decisive—Fiction; Humorous stories. RL 2.1.
Unable to make choices, Millicent fills her home with things she does not need. She buys a large number of parrots to make decisions for her. They lead her into more trouble and finally into taking responsibility for herself. This funny story is illustrated with humorous ink drawings with blue, yellow, and green.

Weiss, Leatie

1529 *Funny Feet!* Ill. by Ellen E. Weiss. Watts, 1978, o.p.; Avon, pap., 1984. ISBN 0-380-45856-X. SUBJECTS: Animals—Penguins—Fiction; Physically and mentally impaired—Fiction; Self-esteem—Fiction. RL 2.4.
Priscilla Penguin is supposed to wear corrective shoes and take ballet lessons because she is pigeon-toed. She loves ballet lessons but not her klunky shoes. At her recital someone takes her ballet slippers but Priscilla soars with her clodhoppers. Illustrated with comic sketches.

1530 *Heather's Feathers*. Ill. by Ellen E. Weiss. Watts, 1976, o.p.; Avon, pap., 1978. ISBN 0-380-40279-3. SERIES: Easy-Read Story. SUBJECTS: Animals—Birds—Fiction; Self-esteem—Fiction; Tooth fairy—Fiction. RL 2.1.
The only bird in her class, Heather is happy and popular until her classmates start losing their teeth. Heather feels left out when they talk of the Tooth Fairy but when she starts molting she feels like one of the crowd again. Well written, this is illustrated with soft yet playful paintings.

Weiss, Nicki

1531 *Menj*. Ill. by author. Greenwillow, 1981, o.p. SERIES: Read-alone. SUBJECTS: Animals—Frogs and toads—Fiction; Sibling rivalry—Fiction. RL 2.5.
To rile Francine, her older sister Norma uses the word *Menj* repeatedly and refuses to tell its meaning. Finally Francine wises up and ignores the teasing. This story about two frog sisters and the other similar stories are fun, recall the rivalry between children, and are delightfully illustrated with simple, homey pictures.

Wheeler, M. J.

1532 *Fox Tales*. Ill. by Dana Gustafson. Carolrhoda, 1984. ISBN 0-87614-255-2. SERIES: On My Own. SUBJECTS: Animals—Foxes—Fiction; Folklore—India. RL 2.0.
Based on folktales from India, these three stories have a fox outwitting a rascal of a farmer and a hungry tiger and being made foolish by his own ignorance. Well written and suitable for storytelling, the stories are illustrated with line drawings and watercolor pictures.

White, Laurence B.

1533 *Science Toys and Tricks*. Ill. by Marc Brown. Addison-Wesley, 1975; Lippincott, pap., 1980. ISBN 0-201-08659-X. SUBJECTS: Science experiments. RL 2.6.
Twenty-three very simple and enticing science activities or crafts introduce children to scientific principles without giving lengthy explanations. Pencil drawings are clear and should help children to duplicate the activities.

Wilkinson, Sylvia

1534 *I Can Be a Race Car Driver*. Photos. Childrens, hb and pap., 1986. ISBN 0-516-01898-1. SERIES: I Can Be. SUBJECTS: Careers; Sports—Car racing. RL 2.9.
Beginning with a picture dictionary, this survey of the world of car racing repeats dictionary entries in the margins as the words appear in the text. Facts on go-carts, cars, trucks, drivers, dangers, safety, and so on are included along with full color photos, a glossary, and an index.

Williams, John

1535 *The Life Cycle of a Swallow.* Ill. by Jackie Harland. Bookwright, 1989. ISBN 0-531-18258-4. SERIES: Life Cycles. SUBJECTS: Animals—Birds. RL 2.1.

Realistically illustrated with full color paintings, the book clearly describes the major events in the swallows' breeding season and its habits, habitat, and diet. The book also includes an invitation to observe other birds. A glossary, index, bibliography, and table of contents are included.

1536 *The Life Cycle of a Tree.* Ill. by Jackie Harland. Bookwright, 1989. ISBN 0-531-18259-2. SERIES: Life Cycles. SUBJECTS: Plants—Trees. RL 2.3.

A clear, simple text and accurate color paintings depict the stages in the development of a chestnut tree from buried nut to mature plant. With an emphasis on explanation in the text and pictures, this is an inviting science book with a glossary, bibliography, index, and table of contents.

Williamson, Stan

1537 *The No-Bark Dog.* Ill. by Tom O'Sullivan. Follett, hb and pap., 1962. ISBN 0-8136-5042-9. SERIES: Beginning to Read. SUBJECTS: Pets—Dogs—Fiction. RL 1.6.

Everyone keeps asking Timothy why his new dog does not bark. His mother and father tell him to be patient but Timothy worries. Illustrated with full color realistic paintings, this is a quiet story with a humorous and satisfying ending.

Wilson, Beth

1538 *Martin Luther King, Jr.* Ill. by Floyd Sowell. Putnam, 1971, o.p. SERIES: See and Read Beginning to Read Biography. SUBJECTS: Biographies; Black Americans. RL 2.5.

Opening with King's funeral in 1968, the text looks back on King's life and especially notes the Montgomery bus boycott, his winning the Nobel Peace Prize, and his "I have a dream" speech. The writing style is good, giving a sense of the times. Illustrated with very effective sketches.

Winnick, Karen

1539 *Sandro's Dolphin.* Ill. by author. Lothrop, 1980, o.p. SUBJECTS: Animals—Dolphins—Fiction; Fishing—Fiction. RL 2.5.

The mullet are becoming scarce and the fishermen in Sandro's village often come back with none at all. Young Sandro is befriended by a dolphin that seems to understand the village's problem and with other dolphins comes to the villagers' rescue. Illustrated with ink drawings with blue accents.

Wise, William

1540 *The Amazing Animals of North America.* Ill. by Joseph Sibal. Putnam, 1971, o.p. SERIES: See and Read Beginning to Read. SUBJECTS: Animals—Endangered; Conservation. RL 2.3.

Eighteen animals, some rare or endangered, are given at least one page each of text that offers general information on them and their habitats. The book stresses the importance of preserving the world's animal resources. Illustrated with detailed pencil sketches with blue accents.

1541 *Booker T. Washington.* Ill. by Paul Frame. Putnam, 1968, o.p. SERIES: See and Read Beginning to Read Biography. SUBJECTS: Biographies; Black Americans. RL 2.0.

Born into slavery, Booker T. Washington does whatever is necessary to earn an education. He then begins a lifelong career as a teacher and educator at Tuskegee Institute. Well written and factual, the book does not overlook the controversy surrounding Washington. Illustrated with sketches.

1542 *Monsters of the Middle Ages.* Ill. by Tomie dePaola. Putnam, 1971, o.p. SERIES: See and Read. SUBJECTS: Mythical creatures. RL 2.6.

The 14 fantastic creatures of medieval lore that are presented here are by no means all fearful monsters. They include a race of one-legged people, centaurs, unicorns, and giants,

Wise, William (cont.)

to mention a few. Entertainingly written, the book is fancifully illustrated in black line with red highlights.

1543 *The World of Giant Mammals.* Ill. by Lewis Zacks. Putnam, 1965, o.p. SERIES: See and Read Beginning to Read. SUBJECTS: Animals—Prehistoric. RL 1.7.

From the time of the dinosaurs to that of man, large animals of different eras are discussed. Although the text is usually objective and factual, one passage in the book does call an animal terrible for eating other animals. Illustrated with heavy black and gold pictures.

Wiseman, Bernard

1544 *Bobby and Boo.* Ill. by author. Holt, Rinehart, 1978, o.p. SUBJECTS: Humorous stories; Science fiction. RL 2.0.

Bobby is playing spaceman when Boo arrives in a flying saucer. The amazing visitor spends the day with Bobby. He eats lunch, does tricks, and plays ball while Mom and Dad think he is the new boy on the street. Illustrated with heavily outlined, comic pictures in yellow and gray.

1545 *Christmas with Morris and Boris.* Ill. by author. Little, Brown, 1983; Scholastic, pap., 1986. ISBN 0-316-94855-1. SERIES: Morris and Boris. SUBJECTS: Animals—Fiction; Friendship—Fiction; Holidays—Christmas—Fiction. RL 1.6.

Though infuriated by Morris's constant interruptions, Boris the bear still attempts to introduce the silly moose to Christmas and Santa Claus. Morris's misunderstandings and Boris's impatience are very funny, as are the heavily outlined brown, red, and green pictures.

1546 *Don't Make Fun!* Ill. by author. Houghton Mifflin, 1982. ISBN 0-395-32086-0. SUBJECTS: Animals—Pigs—Fiction; Behavior—Manners—Fiction. RL 2.6.

The way Bobby, a boar, constantly makes fun with words irritates his father, but when obnoxious, ill-mannered relatives arrive, his parents rely on Bobby's special wit to drive them away. Funny drawings and a humorous text have readers rooting for Bobby.

1547 *Halloween with Morris and Boris.* Ill. by author. Dodd, Mead, 1975, o.p.; Scholastic, pap., 1986. ISBN 0-590-41498-4. SERIES: Morris and Boris. SUBJECTS: Animals—Fiction; Friendship—Fiction; Holidays—Halloween—Fiction. RL 1.9.

Boris takes Morris on a Halloween adventure filled with costumes, trick-or-treating, a party, and their own brand of slapstick humor. Popular with many children, the silly but appealing characters and settings are illustrated in brown, orange, and blue.

1548 *Little New Kangaroo.* Ill. by Robert Lopshire. Macmillan, 1973, o.p. SERIES: Ready-to-Read. SUBJECTS: Animals—Kangaroos—Fiction; Stories in rhyme. RL 2.1.

Baby Kangaroo invites four other Australian animals—Koala, Wombat, Bandicoot, and Platypus—to join him for a ride in his mother's pouch. The rhyming text is often awkward but the unusual animals and the comic illustrations of a very doting mother with a very full pouch are fun.

1549 *The Lucky Runner.* Ill. by author. Garrard, 1979. ISBN 0-8116-4313-1. SERIES: For Real. SUBJECTS: Sports—Running—Fiction; Superstitions—Fiction. RL 2.0.

Buddy practices hard and is a good runner but he thinks he wins races because of his lucky socks. At the big track meet he accidentally puts on the wrong pair and still wins—reinforcing his coach's message about hard work, not luck, making winners. Illustrated in gray and coral.

1550 *Morris and Boris: Three Stories.* Ill. by author. Dodd, Mead, 1974, o.p.; Scholastic, pap., 1974. ISBN 0-590-09849-7. SUBJECTS: Animals—Fiction; Jokes and riddles—Fiction; Tongue twisters—Fiction. RL 2.2.

Serious, impatient Boris the bear tries to get the good-natured but very dense Morris the moose to try riddles, tongue twisters, and games. Children will laugh at the pair's antics and enjoy the comical green and brown illustrations.

1551 *Morris and Boris at the Circus.* Ill. by author. Harper & Row, 1988. ISBN 0-06-026478-0. SERIES: I Can Read. SUBJECTS: Animals—Bears—Fiction; Animals—Moose—Fiction; Circuses—Fiction. RL 1.5.

Ever-patient Boris the bear takes Morris the moose to the circus. When he sees no moose in the show, Morris joins in with predictably funny results. The text is illustrated in three colors with comical drawings.

1552 *Morris Goes to School.* Ill. by author. Harper & Row, 1970; pap., 1983. ISBN 0-06-026548-5. SERIES: I Can Read. SUBJECTS: Animals—Moose—Fiction; Humorous stories; School stories. RL 1.7.

After going to the wrong store and being unable to count his money, Morris the moose decides he needs to go to school. At school, he has a great time and learns enough to read store names and count his change. Children will enjoy the funny story and the humorous illustrations.

1553 *Morris Has a Birthday Party!* Ill. by author. Little, Brown, 1983. ISBN 0-316-94854-3. SUBJECTS: Animals—Bears—Fiction; Animals—Moose—Fiction; Birthdays—Fiction. RL 1.7.

Morris the moose knows nothing of birthdays until Boris the bear gives him a party. Morris's predictable misunderstandings of common words continue to plague poor, impatient Boris and entertain the reader. The comic-style illustrations are amusingly drawn in orange, green, and brown.

1554 *Morris Has a Cold.* Ill. by author. Dodd, Mead, 1978, o.p. SUBJECTS: Animals—Bears—Fiction; Animals—Moose—Fiction; Illness—Fiction. RL 1.9.

Boris the bear nearly loses his patience when he tries to help literal-minded Morris the moose get over a cold. Everything Boris suggests is misinterpreted by the moose in this very silly and very funny story. The cartoon-style pictures capture the two characters well.

1555 *Morris Tells Boris Mother Moose Stories and Rhymes.* Ill. by author. Dodd, Mead, 1979, o.p.; Scholastic, pap., 1980. ISBN 0-590-30999-4. SUBJECTS: Animals—Bears—Fiction; Animals—Moose—Fiction; Sleep—Fiction. RL 2.0.

Trying to help Boris the bear get to sleep, Morris the moose tells him Mother Moose stories. Boris's constant interruptions and his demands for changes in the stories are great fun for the reader. The two friends are comically illustrated in brown, black, and green.

1556 *Morris the Moose.* Rev. ed. Ill. by author. Harper & Row, 1989. ISBN 0-06-026475-6. SERIES: Early I Can Read. SUBJECTS: Animals—Moose—Fiction; Humorous stories. RL 1.7.

When Morris the Moose meets a cow, he tries to convince her that she is a moose, too. Unsuccessful he asks two other "moose"—a cow and a deer—who turn out to be as silly as he is. New, more colorful illustrations as well as a revised text make this more attractive than the original.

1557 *Quick Quackers.* Ill. by author. Garrard, 1979. ISBN 0-8116-6077-X. SERIES: Easy Venture. SUBJECTS: Animals—Ducks—Fiction; Animals—Parrots—Fiction; English language—Pronunciation—Fiction. RL 1.9.

Polly, a parrot, cannot pronounce *r* so her request for a "quacker" brings on a trio of ducks. After much frustration and many hijinks, the ducks finally decipher her request and provide crackers. The simple story is illustrated with full color humorous paintings.

Wittman, Sally

1558 *Pelly and Peak.* Ill. by author. Harper & Row, 1978. ISBN 0-06-026560-4. SERIES: I Can Read. SUBJECTS: Animals—Peacocks—Fiction; Animals—Pelicans—Fiction; Friendship—Fiction. RL 1.9.

Sharing April Fool's Day jokes and fishing together are just two of the special things that Pelly Pelican and Peak Peacock do to bring smiles to young readers. Ink, colored pencil, and paint are used to create the simple, almost childlike illustrations.

Wittman, Sally (cont.)

1559 *Plenty of Pelly and Peak.* Ill. by author. Harper & Row, 1980. ISBN 0-06-026564-7. SERIES: I Can Read. SUBJECTS: Animals—Peacocks—Fiction; Animals—Pelicans—Fiction; Friendship—Fiction. RL 2.2.

In four stories, Pelly Pelican and Peak Peacock try adopting an egg, learn the earth is round, help each other fly a kite, and lose a birthday—February 29th. The simple illustrations are done with ink, colored pencils, and paint and are appealing and humorous.

Wolcott, Patty

1560 *Beware of a Very Hungry Fox.* Ill. by Lucinda McQueen. Addison-Wesley, 1975. ISBN 0-201-14250-3. SERIES: First Read-By-Myself. SUBJECTS: Animals—Chipmunks—Fiction; Animals—Foxes—Fiction; Behavior—Brave—Fiction. RL 1.3.

Professing not to be afraid of a very hungry fox, the chipmunks change their minds when they see one and flee leaving the fox to eat crabapples. The very limited and repetitious text relies on the vibrant illustrations to create a sense of story.

1561 *The Cake Story.* Ill. by Lucinda McQueen. Addison-Wesley, 1974. ISBN 0-201-14244-9. SERIES: First Read-By-Myself. SUBJECTS: Animals—Fiction; Food—Fiction. RL 1.7.

Bear excitedly announces to the other animals that he has baked a cake. While he naps they eat the entire cake, but they make another to replace it. The ten words in this story are constantly repeated and rely on the expressive and colorful pictures to actually create the story.

1562 *The Forest Fire.* Ill. by Robert Binks. Addison-Wesley, 1974. ISBN 0-201-14247-3. SERIES: First Read-By-Myself. SUBJECTS: Animals—Fiction; Plants—Flowers—Fiction. RL 2.3.

Using a ten-word text and much repetition, a story is told through colorful illustrations more than words. In the story animals mistake flame-colored flowers for a forest fire. Although the words are not all easy or famil-

iar, the repetition may make them a part of a reading vocabulary.

1563 *I'm Going to New York to Visit the Queen.* Ill. by Blair Drawson. Addison-Wesley, 1974. ISBN 0-201-14248-1. SERIES: First Read-By-Myself. SUBJECTS: Boats and boating—Fiction; City and town life—Fiction. RL 1.4.

Two little girls walk through New York City on their way to visit the queen—the *Queen Elizabeth II* steamship. Full color pictures show well-known New York attractions and provide a brief tour of the ship. The ten-word text is repetitious and very dependent on the illustrations.

1564 *Pirates, Pirates Over the Salt, Salt Sea.* Ill. by Bill Morrison. Addison-Wesley, 1981. ISBN 0-317-56694-6. SERIES: First Read-By-Myself. SUBJECTS: Animals—Mice—Fiction; Animals—Whales—Fiction; Pirates—Fiction. RL 1.2.

The ten words of this text are rearranged and repeated throughout. The text is popular with beginning readers and the repetition helps to introduce new words. The story, told in detailed and colorful drawings, is of a small sailboat of mice that are rescued from pirates by a friendly whale.

1565 *Super Sam and the Salad Garden.* Ill. by Marc Brown. Addison-Wesley, 1975. ISBN 0-201-14253-8. SERIES: First Read-By-Myself. SUBJECTS: Animals—Dogs—Fiction; Gardening—Fiction. RL 1.2.

A boy and a girl plant a garden only to have it vandalized by other children. When Sam, a dog, is left in the yard, the next planting is safe and grows to be harvested. The ten-word text relies on the brightly colored pictures to tell the story.

Wolff, Barbara

1566 *Evening Gray, Morning Red: A Handbook of American Weather Wisdom.* Ill. by author. Macmillan, 1976, o.p. SERIES: Ready-to-Read. SUBJECTS: Folklore—Weather; Weather. RL 3.1.

A potpourri of weather rhymes and lore is given historical context and meanings are explained. This interesting book is illustrated with detailed ink and colored wash pictures.

Wong, Herbert, and Vessel, Matthew

1567 *My Ladybug.* Ill. by Marie N. Bohlen. Addison-Wesley, 1969, o.p. SERIES: Science Series for the Young. SUBJECTS: Animals—Ladybugs. RL 1.5.
The narrator of this investigation of ladybugs talks about what they look like, their diet, the different stages in their development, and how helpful they are to farmers. The illustrations are detailed and lovely, and demonstrate the many different varieties of ladybugs.

1568 *Plant Communities: Where Can Cattails Grow?* Ill. by Michael Eagle. Addison-Wesley, 1970, o.p. SERIES: Science Series for the Young. SUBJECTS: Plants. RL 1.7.
By following cattail seeds into different natural areas, readers learn about various kinds of habitats and the plant life they support. Ink drawings are sometimes so full of things that it is difficult to distinguish the plants being discussed.

Wood, Audrey

1569 *The Horrible Holidays.* Ill. by Rosekrans Hoffman. Dial, 1988. ISBN 0-8037-0544-1. SERIES: Easy-to-Read. SUBJECTS: Family life—Fiction; Holidays—Christmas—Fiction; Holidays—Thanksgiving—Fiction. RL 2.1.
Tormented by his horrible cousin Mert, Alf does not enjoy the holidays. Worse, when he tries to get even with her, he is the one punished. Funny and a very real view of just how horrible holidays can be (family fights, bickering children), this has humorous illustrations done in pencil and watercolors.

1570 *Three Sisters.* Ill. by Rosekrans Hoffman. Dial, 1986. ISBN 0-8037-0280-9. SERIES: Easy-to-Read. SUBJECTS: Animals—Pigs—Fiction; Humorous stories; Siblings—Fiction. RL 2.2.
Three exuberant porcine sisters unabashedly create their own version of French, anxiously await stardom for the dancing member of the trio, and finally confront Uncle George

about his smelly cigars. The softly colored pictures have confident pigs creating inoffensive mischief.

1571 *Tugford Wanted to Be Bad.* Ill. by author. Harcourt Brace, hb and pap., 1983. ISBN 0-15-291083-2. SERIES: Let Me Read. SUBJECTS: Animals—Mice—Fiction; Behavior—Fiction; Family life—Fiction. RL 2.8.
Inspired by movie outlaws, Tugford, a mouse, takes a can full of shiny coins and buries it. When his father says his money is missing, Tugford mistakenly confesses to stealing it and promises to reform. The lush 1940s setting in the illustrations is perfect for Tugford's misadventure.

Wright, Mildred W.

1572 *Henri Goes to the Mardi Gras.* Ill. by Syd Hoff. Putnam, 1970. SUBJECTS: Animals—Bears—Fiction; Holidays—Mardi Gras—Fiction; Humorous stories. RL 2.7.
Looking for honey, Henri the bear leaves the swamp for New Orleans during Mardi Gras. Everyone thinks he is in costume and treats him to all kinds of food until Henri slips away, surprised that no one was afraid of him. The cartoon-style pictures in brown and blue fit this story well.

Wyler, Rose

1573 *Science Fun with Mud and Dirt.* Ill. by Pat Stewart. Messner, 1986; pap., 1987. ISBN 0-671-55569-3. SERIES: Science Fun. SUBJECTS: Science experiments. RL 3.1.
From a brief narrative and easily performed experiments, children learn that the makeup of dirt determines what can be done with it and whether plants will grow in it. The realistic brown and rust drawings help to clarify the instructions and the narrative sections.

1574 *What Happens If . . . ? Science Experiments You Can Do by Yourself.* Ill. by Daniel Nevins. Walker, 1974. ISBN 0-8027-6167-4. SUBJECTS: Science experiments. RL 2.3.

Wyler, Rose (cont.)

A variety of simple experiments teach children about air pressure, chemical solutions, batteries, shadows, and the properties of ice cubes. The projects are interesting and the instructions easy to follow. The illustrations are sketchy but informative.

Wyler, Rose, and Ames, Gerald

1575 *Magic Secrets.* Ill. by Talivaldis Stubis. Harper & Row, 1967, o.p.; pap., 1978. ISBN 0-06-444007-9. SERIES: I Can Read. SUBJECTS: Magic. RL 2.3.

Twenty-six magic tricks, the ingredients for a successful magic show, are explained along with a warning never to tell how they are done. The lively illustrations are simple, multicolored with heavy ink outlining, and help children to understand and follow the instructions.

1576 *Prove It!* Ill. by Talivaldis Stubis. Harper & Row, 1963. ISBN 0-06-020051-0. SERIES: Science I Can Read. SUBJECTS: Science experiments. RL 2.1.

By trying these very simple experiments, children at home or in the classroom can have fun learning the properties of water, air, sound, and magnets. The illustrations are simple and help to explain the procedures.

1577 *Spooky Tricks.* Ill. by Talivaldis Stubis. Harper & Row, 1968. ISBN 0-06-026334-1. SERIES: I Can Read. SUBJECTS: Magic. RL 3.0.

For aspiring magicians this sequel to *Magic Secrets* (see above) has more easy-to-do tricks that will need some practice but should be within the capabilities of seven- and eight-year-olds. The simple, multicolored illustrations use a little ghost to help explain the tricks.

Y

Yolen, Jane

1578 *Commander Toad and the Big Black Hole.* Ill. by Bruce Degen. Coward, McCann, hb and pap., 1983. ISBN 0-698-30741-0. SERIES: Break-of-Day. SUBJECTS: Animals—Frogs and toads—Fiction; Humorous stories; Science fiction. RL 3.2.

What appears to be a black hole is actually an extraterrestrial toad whose long pink tongue has taken hold of Commander Toad's ship, *Star Warts*. The brave and bright commander ingeniously finds a way to free it. The story and the pencil drawings of the zany crew are delightfully funny.

1579 *Commander Toad and the Dis-Asteroid.* Ill. by Bruce Degen. Coward, McCann, hb and pap., 1985. ISBN 0-698-30744-5. SERIES: Break-of-Day. SUBJECTS: Animals—Frogs and toads—Fiction; Humorous stories; Science fiction. RL 3.0.

Heroic Commander Toad leads his crew on a rescue mission after receiving a cryptic message about bad beans. The droll, mock science fiction story is accompanied by carefully drawn, comic illustrations.

1580 *Commander Toad and the Intergalactic Spy.* Ill. by Bruce Degen. Coward, McCann, hb and pap., 1986. ISBN 0-698-20623-1. SERIES: Break-of-Day. SUBJECTS: Animals—Frogs and toads—Fiction; Humorous stories; Science fiction. RL 3.5.

The crew of the spaceship *Star Warts* is sent to the planet Eden to pick up Space Fleet's most famous spy (0007 1/2), a master of disguise who happens to be Commander Toad's cousin. The commander has great difficulty finding him in this funny spoof illustrated with pencil drawings.

1581 *Commander Toad and the Planet of the Grapes.* Ill. by Bruce Degen. Coward, McCann, hb and pap., 1982. ISBN 0-698-30736-4. SERIES: Break-of-Day. SUBJECTS: Animals—Frogs and toads—Fiction; Humorous stories; Science fiction. RL 2.8.

In a hilarious parody of "Star Trek," Commander Toad takes his bored and tired crew to a planet where purple grapes mysteriously engulf them. Good old Doc Peeper finds a way to free them all. The carefully drawn illustrations are done in pencil and have a zany humor of their own.

1582 *Commander Toad and the Space Pirates.* Ill. by Bruce Degen. Coward, McCann, hb and pap., 1987. ISBN 0-698-30749-6. SERIES: Break-of-Day. SUBJECTS: Animals—Frogs and toads—Fiction; Pirates—Fiction; Science fiction. RL 3.0.

After a long journey taking them where no spaceship has ever gone before, the crew of the *Star Warts* is tired and bored. They are caught off guard by a shipload of pirate salamanders who try to take over the ship. A terrific parody of "Star Trek," this farce is illustrated in pencil.

1583 *The Giants' Farm.* Ill. by Tomie dePaola. Seabury, 1977, o.p. SUBJECTS: Farm and country life—Fiction; Giants—Fiction; Humorous stories. RL 2.7.

Five giants, very different in size and temperament, decide to build a farm and live together on it. In five chapters the work and fun they share help them to care about each other and become a family. Muted pencil drawings are well matched to the story. A recipe for candy is also included.

1584 *The Giants Go Camping.* Ill. by Tomie dePaola. Seabury, 1979, o.p. SUBJECTS: Camps and camping—Fiction; Giants—Fiction; Humorous stories. RL 2.0.

The five friendly giants of Fe-Fi-Fo Farm decide to go camping together and have a much better time than any of them expected. Huge Grizzle adopts a bear as his dog; they fish, play, and do not want to go home. The delightful story is illustrated with amusing multicolored drawings.

1585 *Sleeping Ugly.* Ill. by Diane Stanley. Coward, McCann, pap., 1981. ISBN 0-698-30721-6. SERIES: Break-of-Day. SUBJECTS: Behavior—Manners—Fiction; Fairy tales; Humorous stories. RL 2.5.

A wise fairy is forced to put herself and kindly Plain Jane under a sleeping spell to stop the nasty antics of Princess Miserella. Years later a prince, wise to the ways of princesses, finds them and kisses the first two, but lets the "lying princess sleep." Delightful, humorous text and illustrations.

1586 *Spider Jane on the Move.* Ill. by Stefen Bernath. Coward, McCann, 1980, o.p. SERIES: Break-of-Day. SUBJECTS: Animals—Spiders—Fiction; Moving, household—Fiction. RL 2.8.

Argumentative Spider Jane is helped by her ever-faithful friend Bluebottle Burt to make a new web, have a party, and finally relax. The pictures are slightly humorous and appropriate to the story.

York, Carol B.

1587 *The Midnight Ghost.* Ill. by Charles Robinson. Coward, McCann, 1973, o.p. SERIES: Break-of-Day. SUBJECTS: Humorous stories; Mystery and detective stories. RL 2.8.

With his new detective kit, Andrew determines to solve the mystery of a ghost that appears around midnight and leaves clues and gifts. Realistic pencil drawings capture the humor and suspense of the story.

Z

Zarins, Joyce A.

1588 *Toasted Bagels.* Ill. by author. Coward, McCann, 1988. ISBN 0-698-30571-X. SERIES: Break-of-Day. SUBJECTS: Animals—Fiction; Bakers and baking—Fiction; Friendship—Fiction. RL 2.7.

Pleased at how his bagels have turned out, P. C. invites his animal friends for a special treat. Instead of attending a party, they all battle a fire in the bakery. The gentle and satisfying story is illustrated with cartoonlike ink and watercolor and black and white pictures.

Zemach, Harve, and Zemach, Kaethe

1589 *The Princess and Froggie.* Ill. by Margot Zemach. Farrar, Straus, 1975. ISBN 0-374-36116-9. SUBJECTS: Animals—Frogs and toads—Fiction; Fantasy; Humorous stories. RL 1.7.

Zemach, Harve, and Zemach, Kaethe (cont.)

In each of three stories, when things seem to be going poorly for the little princess, Froggie appears to save the day and earn himself a lollipop. The princess appears as a rather disheveled and very likable child and Froggie as comic and appealing in the lively pictures.

Ziefert, Harriet

1590 *Andy Toots His Horn*. Ill. by Sanford Hoffman. Viking Kestrel, hb and pap., 1988. ISBN 0-670-82035-0. SERIES: Hello Reading! SUBJECTS: Family life—Fiction; Noise—Fiction. RL 1.8.

Andy gets out his horn and starts making noise until other family members complain. Frustrated, he leaves and toots his horn outside until his family misses him. The very brief text has large print and is illustrated with humorous, childlike paintings in full color.

1591 *Cat Games*. Ill. by Claire Schumacher. Viking Kestrel, hb and pap., 1988. ISBN 0-670-82031-8. SERIES: Hello Reading! SUBJECTS: Animals—Cats—Fiction; Games—Fiction. RL 1.9.

Pat and Matt, two cats, play a game of hide-and-seek in a tree in Chapter 1. In Chapter 2 they chase each other until a friendly dog intrudes on their game. The text is very brief and repetitive, is in large type, and is easy enough for beginners. Simple but engaging color pictures.

1592 *A Clean House for Mole and Mouse*. Ill. by David Prebenna. Viking Kestrel, hb and pap., 1988. ISBN 0-670-82032-6. SERIES: Hello Reading! SUBJECTS: Animals—Mice—Fiction; Animals—Moles—Fiction; Cleanliness—Fiction. RL 2.3.

Mole and Mouse work hard to clean their home and then, not wanting to dirty it, go outside to shower, nap, and eat. The very brief and humorous story has large print and is illustrated with comical pencil and wash pictures in full color.

1593 *A Dozen Dogs: A Read-and-Count Story*. Ill. by Carol Nicklaus. Random House, hb and pap., 1985. ISBN 0-394-96935-9.

SERIES: Step into Reading. SUBJECTS: Animals—Dogs—Fiction; Concepts—Numbers—Fiction. RL 2.1.

The story starts with a dozen dogs cavorting on the beach, but their number changes as they swim, dive, fish, or play. Children will want to count them as they read the simple text. The illustrations are done in full color and tell more of a story than does the very brief text.

1594 *Harry Takes a Bath*. Ill. by Mavis Smith. Viking Kestrel, hb and pap., 1987. ISBN 0-670-81721-X. SERIES: Hello Reading! SUBJECTS: Animals—Hippopotami—Fiction; Bathing—Fiction. RL 2.6.

Hippopotamus Harry gathers his things and heads for the bathroom for a good cleanup and some fun. Afterward the bathroom is a mess and Harry cleans it up. The very limited vocabulary and large type with clearly drawn, colorful illustrations are good for a child just starting to read.

1595 *Jason's Bus Ride*. Ill. by Simms Taback. Viking Kestrel, hb and pap., 1987. ISBN 0-670-81718-X. SERIES: Hello Reading! SUBJECTS: Buses—Fiction; Emergencies—Fiction. RL 1.7.

Jason gets on the bus expecting an uneventful ride. Instead he becomes a hero when he is the only one able to get a dog to move out of the path of the bus. The bold, full color pictures are marvelous, offering a variety of perspectives of the bus and its riders.

1596 *Mike and Tony: Best Friends*. Ill. by Catherine Siracusa. Viking Kestrel, hb and pap., 1987. ISBN 0-670-81719-8. SERIES: Hello Reading! SUBJECTS: Friendship—Fiction. RL 2.2.

Mike and Tony do everything together—walk to school, ride bikes, play on the same team. They even spend Friday night at one or the other's home until they have a fight that takes some effort to settle. The vibrant full color pictures are a good match to the story of a common situation.

1597 *A New House for Mole and Mouse*. Ill. by David Prebenna. Viking Kestrel, hb and pap., 1987. ISBN 0-670-81720-1. SERIES: Hello Reading! SUBJECTS:

Animals—Mice—Fiction; Animals—Moles—Fiction; Moving, household—Fiction. RL 2.4.

Mouse and Mole move into a new house and excitedly try everything out. Pastel pictures of the two friendly little animals and their very cozy home accompany the short but interesting story.

1598 *Nicky Upstairs and Down.* Ill. by Richard Brown. Viking Kestrel, hb and pap., 1987. ISBN 0-670-81717-1. SERIES: Hello Reading! SUBJECTS: Animals—Cats—Fiction; Pets—Cats—Fiction. RL 2.1.

Nicky, a kitten, and his mother are pets in a household with an upstairs and a downstairs. Nicky runs from floor to floor when his mother calls until he decides he wants to stay in the middle. The pictures to this very brief story are bright and childlike; the cats have expressive faces.

1599 *Say Good Night!* Ill. by Catherine Siracusa. Viking Kestrel, hb and pap., 1988. ISBN 0-670-81722-8. SERIES: Hello Reading! SUBJECTS: Morning—Fiction; Night—Fiction; Sleep—Fiction. RL 1.5.

A little girl has to be convinced that night and morning are "good." Her parents oblige, and she goes to sleep and gets up happily. The very short text is accompanied by simple, colorful, and attractive pictures.

1600 *So Hungry!* Ill. by Carol Nicklaus. Random House, hb and pap., 1987. ISBN 0-394-99127-3. SERIES: Step into Reading. SUBJECTS: Animals—Lions—Fiction; Food—Fiction. RL 2.7.

Hungry and unable to find cookies, Kate and Lewis, lions, decide to make great big sandwiches and race to finish them. With a very limited and repetitive but not necessarily easy vocabulary, the bold, full color cartoonlike illustrations carry the story.

1601 *So Sick!* Ill. by Carol Nicklaus. Random House, hb and pap., 1985. ISBN 0-394-97580-4. SERIES: Step into Reading. SUBJECTS: Animals—Lions—Fiction; Illness—Fiction. RL 2.0.

After finally getting well, Lewis, a lion, plays doctor with his friend Angel. When Angel eats too many cookies in spite of Lewis's warn-ings, he gets sick. Full color pictures of "cute" animals accompany a very brief, bold-type text.

1602 *Strike Four!* Ill. by Mavis Smith. Viking Kestrel, hb and pap., 1988. ISBN 0-670-82033-4. SERIES: Hello Reading! SUBJECTS: Behavior—Bored—Fiction; Family life—Fiction; Sports—Baseball—Fiction. RL 2.0.

With nothing to do, Debbie tries tossing her ball in the house until she is told to do it elsewhere. She finally takes her ball and bat outside and practices hitting—until she breaks a window. A good, brief story and simple, colorful pictures combine to create an easy yet appealing book.

1603 *Surprise!* Ill. by Mary Morgan. Viking Kestrel, 1988. ISBN 0-670-8203-9. SERIES: Hello Reading! SUBJECTS: Birthdays—Fiction; Families—Fiction; Mothers—Fiction. RL 2.6.

Three young children get up very early and quietly prepare a breakfast tray of juice and cookies for their mother on her birthday. The text is very brief, relying on the pictures of the excited children and their rambunctious cat to help tell the story.

Ziegler, Sandra

1604 *A Visit to the Airport.* Photos. Childrens, 1988. ISBN 0-516-01488-9. SERIES: Visit to. SUBJECTS: Airports. RL 2.1.

An elementary school class tours the Milwaukee airport passenger terminal. The color photos and clearly written comments allow children to share their experience. Ziegler could have chosen more descriptive photos and coordinated them more carefully with the text.

1605 *A Visit to the Dairy Farm.* Photos. Childrens, 1987. ISBN 0-516-01496-X. SERIES: Visit to. SUBJECTS: Farm and country life. RL 2.0.

This tour of a dairy farm, in simple terms with color photos, can introduce a young reader to farming and milk production. The book is not put together very carefully and the photos do not always seem to correspond

Ziegler, Sandra (cont.)

to the text. In addition one photo appears twice—with two different captions.

1606 *A Visit to the Natural History Museum.* Photos. Childrens, 1989. ISBN 0-516-01489-7. SERIES: Visit to. SUBJECTS: Museums. RL 2.4.

Not an exciting visit to a museum but merely a walk from exhibit to exhibit in the Field Museum of Chicago. The book follows an elementary school class as they explore and learn bits of information about the museum. The photos are either from the museum or stiffly posed pictures of the class.

Ziner, Feenie, and Thompson, Elizabeth

1607 *Time.* Photos. Childrens, hb and pap., 1982. ISBN 0-516-41651-0. SERIES: New True. SUBJECTS: Concepts—Time. RL 1.9.

In the first part of this book, the reader learns that long before modern-day clocks were invented, people measured time using shadow sticks, sundials, candles, and ropes. The second part of the book describes how to tell time with modern-day clocks. Full color photos, a glossary, and an index are included.

Zion, Gene

1608 *Harry and the Lady Next Door.* Ill. by Margaret B. Graham. Harper & Row,

hb and pap., 1960. ISBN 0-06-026852-2. SERIES: I Can Read. SUBJECTS: Humorous stories; Music—Fiction; Pets—Dogs—Fiction. RL 2.0.

Harry, a white dog with black spots, tries one thing after another to get the lady next door to stop her terrible high-pitched singing. A popular picture-book character, Harry is familiar to most children. This good story is combined with simple humorous pictures.

Zweifel, Frances W.

1609 *Bony.* Ill. by Whitney Darrow, Jr. Harper & Row, 1977. ISBN 0-06-027071-3. SERIES: I Can Read. SUBJECTS: Animals—Squirrels—Fiction; Pets—Wild animals—Fiction. RL 2.3.

Kim rescues an orphaned baby squirrel, names her Bony, and raises her in his home. Finally grown and behaving like the wild animal she is, Bony is reintroduced to the wild. Whimsical pencil drawings add humor to a situation that does not always end so happily.

1610 *Pickle in the Middle and Other Easy Snacks.* Ill. by author. Harper & Row, 1979. ISBN 0-06-027073-X. SERIES: I Can Read. SUBJECTS: Cookery. RL 3.1.

Without having to cook, children can use this recipe book to create 26 snacks. The instructions occasionally call for expensive items like sweetened condensed milk or dates. Many of the recipes are very sweet but most are nutritious. Appealing illustrations help to explain the instructions.

SUBJECT INDEX

Subject heads are to nonfiction works unless designated with the word "Fiction." To make this index easier to use, "Fiction" cross-references can refer to both fiction and nonfiction headings. When a cross-reference does not have the label "Fiction," that cross-reference applies solely to nonfiction works. *Note:* Numerals refer to entry numbers, not page numbers.

ANIMALS—Turkeys—Fiction

Baker, Betty
The Turkey Girl, 63

ANIMALS—Turtles

Cromie, William J.
Steven and the Green Turtle, 334
Harrison, David
Little Turtle's Big Adventure, 542
Selsam, Millicent E.
Let's Get Turtles, 1308
Serventy, Vincent
Turtle and Tortoise, 1333

ANIMALS—Turtles—Fiction

Christian, Mary B.
Devin and Goliath, 293
Hoban, Lillian
The Case of the Two Masked Robbers, 601
Stick-in-the-Mud Turtle, 604
Turtle Spring, 605
Murdocca, Sal
Tuttle's Shell, 998
Van Woerkom, Dorothy
Harry and Shellburt, 1507

ANIMALS—Vultures

Stone, Lynn
Vultures, 1466

ANIMALS—Walruses—Fiction

Bonsall, Crosby
What Spot?, 168
Hoff, Syd
Walpole, 628
Stevenson, James
Winston, Newton, Elton, and Ed, 1458

ANIMALS—Whales

Martin, Louise
Whales, 909
Mizumura, Kazue
The Blue Whale, 969
Patent, Dorothy H.
All about Whales, 1088
Petty, Kate
Whales, 1113

Posell, Elsa
Whales and Other Sea Mammals, 1139
Ricciuti, Edward R.
Catch a Whale by the Tail, 1180

ANIMALS—Whales—Fiction

Roy, Ron
A Thousand Pails of Water, 1249
Wolcott, Patty
Pirates, Pirates Over the Salt, Salt Sea, 1564

ANIMALS—Wolves

Spanjian, Beth
Baby Wolf, 1439

ANIMALS—Wolves—Fiction

Friskey, Margaret
Indian Two Feet and the Wolf Cubs, 460
Van Woerkom, Dorothy
Meat Pies and Sausages, 1509

ANIMALS—Woodchucks

McNulty, Faith
Woodchuck, 868

ANIMALS—Woodchucks—Fiction

Stanovich, Betty Jo
Hedgehog Adventures, 1448
Hedgehog Surprises, 1449

ANIMALS, ZOO—Fiction

McInnes, John
Leo Lion Paints It Red, 850
Pape, Donna L.
Count on Leo Lion, 1054
Thaler, Mike
There's a Hippopotamus under My Bed, 1480

Anteaters—Fiction

SEE Animals—Anteaters—Fiction

Ants—Fiction

SEE Animals—Ants—Fiction

Apaches

SEE Native Americans—Apaches

Arbor Day

SEE Holidays—Arbor Day

Argumentative—Fiction

SEE Behavior—Argumentative—Fiction

Armadillos—Fiction

SEE Animals—Armadillos—Fiction

ART AND ARTISTS

Clark, Ann N.
Little Indian Basket Maker, 304
Hamsa, Bobbie
Fast Draw Freddie, 536
Radford, Ruby
Robert Fulton, 1176
Venezia, Mike
Van Gogh, 1513

ART AND ARTISTS—Fiction

McPhail, David M.
Lorenzo, 869

ARTS AND CRAFTS

Rockwell, Harlow
I Did It, 1224
Look at This, 1225

ARTS AND CRAFTS—Fiction

McInnes, John
Goodnight Painted Pony, 847

ASIAN AMERICANS—Fiction

McDaniel, Becky B.
Katie Can, 842
Katie Couldn't, 843
Katie Did It, 844

ASTRONOMY

Berger, Melvin
Stars, 137

BEHAVIOR—Brave—Fiction (cont.)

Wolcott, Patty
  Beware of a Very Hungry Fox, 1560

BEHAVIOR—Bullying—Fiction

Carlson, Nancy
  Loudmouth George and the Sixth-Grade Bully, 249
Dinardo, Jeffrey
  Timothy and the Big Bully, 382

BEHAVIOR—Curiosity—Fiction

Moore, Lilian
  Little Raccoon and the Outside World, 982

BEHAVIOR—Decisive—Fiction

Weiss, Ellen
  Millicent Maybe, 1528

BEHAVIOR—Efficient—Fiction

Krasilovsky, Phyllis
  The Man Who Tried to Save Time, 749

BEHAVIOR—Excuses—Fiction

Carlson, Nancy
  Loudmouth George and the Big Race, 246
  Loudmouth George and the Cornet, 247

BEHAVIOR—Fiction

McDaniel, Becky B.
  Katie Did It, 844
McKissack, Patricia, and McKissack, Fredrick
  Messy Bessey, 862
Mooser, Stephen, and Oliver, Lin
  Tad and Dad, 988
Sadler, Marilyn
  The Very Bad Bunny, 1270

Thomson, Pat
  Good Girl Granny, 1485
Wood, Audrey
  Tugford Wanted to Be Bad, 1571

BEHAVIOR—Generous—Fiction

Wagner, Ken, and Olson, Mary C., eds.
  The Lion Who Couldn't Say No, 1518

BEHAVIOR—Greedy—Fiction

Manushkin, Fran
  Buster Loves Buttons!, 880
Van Woerkom, Dorothy
  Tit for Tat, 1512

BEHAVIOR—Honest—Fiction

Carlson, Nancy
  Harriet and the Garden, 242
Skurzynski, Gloria
  Honest Andrew, 1426

BEHAVIOR—Lying—Fiction

Elliott, Dan
  Ernie's Little Lie, 416
Sleator, William
  Once, Said Darlene, 1427

BEHAVIOR—Manners

Parish, Peggy
  Mind Your Manners, 1076

BEHAVIOR—Manners—Fiction

Christian, Mary B.
  Go West, Swamp Monsters, 295
Marzollo, Jean, and Marzollo, Claudio
  Ruthie's Rude Friends, 922
Skurzynski, Gloria
  Honest Andrew, 1426
Smath, Jerry
  The Housekeeper's Dog, 1429
Wiseman, Bernard
  Don't Make Fun!, 1546

Yolen, Jane
  Sleeping Ugly, 1585

BEHAVIOR—Obedient—Fiction

Gackenbach, Dick
  Hattie Be Quiet, Hattie Be Good, 467
Hurd, Edith T.
  Johnny Lion's Book, 655

BEHAVIOR—Responsible—Fiction

McArthur, Nancy
  Pickled Peppers, 833
Porte, Barbara Ann
  Harry in Trouble, 1130
Roy, Ron
  Awful Thursday, 1247
Schick, Eleanor
  Joey on His Own, 1279
Shortall, Leonard
  Steve's First Pony Ride, 1395

BEHAVIOR—Running away—Fiction

Brenner, Barbara
  Nicky's Sister, 201
LaFarge, Phyllis
  Joanna Runs Away, 762
Robins, Joan
  Addie Runs Away, 1202

BEHAVIOR—Selfish—Fiction

Smath, Jerry
  The Housekeeper's Dog, 1429

BEHAVIOR—Sharing

Corey, Dorothy
  Everybody Takes Turns, 328

BEHAVIOR—Sharing—Fiction

Carlson, Nancy
  Harriet's Halloween Candy, 245
Holl, Adelaide
  Small Bear Builds a Playhouse, 640

Chipmunks—Fiction
SEE Animals—Chipmunks—Fiction

Chippewas
SEE Native Americans—Chippewas

Christmas—Fiction
SEE Holidays—Christmas—Fiction

CIRCUSES
Denzel, Justin
Jumbo: Giant Circus Elephant, 376
Edwards, Anne
P. T. Barnum, 411

CIRCUSES—Fiction
Brandenberg, Franz
What Can You Make of It?, 183
De Brunhoff, Laurent
Babar's Little Circus Star, 346
Dolch, Edward W., and Dolch, Marguerite P.
Circus Stories, 386
Hillert, Margaret
Circus Fun, 581
Hoff, Syd
Ida the Bareback Rider, 620
Julius, 622
Manushkin, Fran
Hocus and Pocus at the Circus, 881
McInnes, John
On with the Circus!, 851
Olson, Mary C., ed.
Fly, Max, Fly!, 1038
Quackenbush, Robert
Detective Mole and the Circus Mystery, 1161
Wiseman, Bernard
Morris and Boris at the Circus, 1551

CITY AND COUNTRY LIFE—Fiction
Heide, Florence
Lost and Found, 570

CITY AND TOWN LIFE
Jacobs, Leland B.
Playtime in the City, 672

CITY AND TOWN LIFE—Fiction
Bozzo, Maxine Z.
Toby in the Country, Toby in the City, 173
Harrison, David
Case of the Missing Frog, 541
Hoff, Syd
Barney's Horse, 612
Holl, Adelaide
Sylvester: The Mouse with the Musical Ear, 643
Kaye, Marilyn
Will You Cross Me?, 698
Kotzwinkle, William
Up the Alley with Jack and Joe, 745
LaFarge, Phyllis
Joanna Runs Away, 762
McInnes, John
The Chocolate Chip Mystery, 846
How Pedro Got His Name, 849
Poulin, Stephane
Have You Seen Josephine?, 1142
Schick, Eleanor
Rainy Sunday, 1281
Wolcott, Patty
I'm Going to New York to Visit the Queen, 1563

Classification
SEE Animals—Classification

CLEANLINESS—Fiction
McKissack, Patricia, and McKissack, Fredrick
Messy Bessey, 862
Ziefert, Harriet
A Clean House for Mole and Mouse, 1592

CLOCKS
Abisch, Roz
Do You Know What Time It Is?, 1

CLOCKS—Fiction
Bram, Elizabeth
Woodruff and the Clocks, 174

CLOTHING—Fiction
Thomson, Pat
The Treasure Sock, 1489

Clouds—Fiction
SEE Weather—Clouds—Fiction

CLUBS—Fiction
Alexander, Sue
Seymour the Prince, 11
Bonsall, Crosby
The Case of the Hungry Stranger, 162
Coerr, Eleanor
Mixed-Up Mystery Smell, 315
Lawrence, James
Binky Brothers and the Fearless Four, 773
Binky Brothers, Detectives, 774
Myrick, Mildred
Secret Three, 1003
Robert, Adrian
The "Awful Mess" Mystery, 1200

CODES AND SECRET MESSAGES—Fiction
Myrick, Mildred
Secret Three, 1003

COLLECTING AND COLLECTORS—Fiction
Manushkin, Fran
Buster Loves Buttons!, 880

Colonial period—Fiction
SEE United States—Colonial period—Fiction

Color—Fiction
SEE Concepts—Color—Fiction

Communication
SEE Animals—Communication

DOCTORS AND NURSES (*cont.*)

Greene, Carla
Doctors and Nurses: What Do They Do?, 507
Kessler, Ethel, and Kessler, Leonard
Our Tooth Story: A Tale of Twenty Teeth, 712

DOCTORS AND NURSES— Fiction

Quackenbush, Robert
Calling Doctor Quack, 1159

Dogs—Fiction
SEE Animals—Dogs—Fiction; Pets—Dogs—Fiction

Dolls and dollhouses—Fiction
SEE Toys—Dolls and dollhouses—Fiction

Dolphins—Fiction
SEE Animals—Dolphins— Fiction

Donkeys—Fiction
SEE Animals—Donkeys— Fiction

Dragonflies
SEE Animals—Dragonflies

DREAMS—Fiction

Bonsall, Crosby
Piggle, 166
Hurd, Edith T.
No Funny Business, 660
Neasi, Barbara
Sweet Dreams, 1006

DRUGS AND DRUG ABUSE

Seixas, Judith S.
Alcohol: What It Is, What It Does, 1300
Drugs: What They Are, What They Do, 1301

Ducks—Fiction
SEE Animals—Ducks—Fiction

Eagles—Fiction
SEE Animals—Eagles—Fiction

Ears—Fiction
SEE Human body—Ears— Fiction

Earthworms
SEE Animals—Earthworms

Easter—Fiction
SEE Holidays—Easter—Fiction

ECUADOR—Fiction

Gramatky, Hardie
Bolivar, 500

Efficient—Fiction
SEE Behavior—Efficient— Fiction

EGYPT, ANCIENT

Donnelly, Judy
Tut's Mummy: Lost and Found, 397
Milton, Joyce
Secrets of the Mummies, 953
Scott, Geoffrey
Egyptian Boats, 1297

Electric power failures— Fiction
SEE Blackouts—Electric power failures—Fiction

ELECTRICITY

Berger, Melvin
Switch On, Switch Off, 139

Elephants—Fiction
SEE Animals—Elephants— Fiction

EMERGENCIES

Older, Jules
Don't Panic: A Book about Handling Emergencies, 1035

EMERGENCIES—Fiction

Rockwell, Anne, and Rockwell, Harlow
Blackout, 1221
Out to Sea, 1223
Stevens, Carla
Anna, Grandpa, and the Big Storm, 1451
Ziefert, Harriet
Jason's Bus Ride, 1595

EMIGRATION AND IMMIGRATION—Fiction

Sandin, Joan
The Long Way to a New Land, 1274

EMOTIONS

Behrens, June
How I Feel, 92
Sheehan, Cilla
The Colors That I Am, 1392

EMOTIONS—Anger—Fiction

Keller, Beverly
Don't Throw Another One, Dover, 700

EMOTIONS—Fear—Fiction

Berenstain, Stan, and Berenstain, Jan
Bears in the Night, 112
Brandenberg, Franz
A Robber! A Robber!, 181
Carlson, Nancy
Harriet and the Roller Coaster, 243
Caseley, Judith
Molly Pink, 268
Lexau, Joan M.
I Hate Red Rover, 797
Lobel, Arnold
Owl at Home, 815
Low, Joseph
Benny Rabbit and the Owl, 823
Marzollo, Jean
Cannonball Chris, 915
Phillips, Joan
Tiger Is a Scaredy Cat, 1116

FISHING—Fiction (cont.)

Firmin, Peter
Basil Brush Goes Boating,
434
Marzollo, Jean
Amy Goes Fishing, 914
Winnick, Karen
Sandro's Dolphin, 1539

FLAGS

Fradin, Dennis
The Flag of the United States,
448

Flies—Fiction
SEE Animals—Flies—Fiction

Flowers—Fiction
SEE Plants—Flowers—Fiction

Flying animals
SEE Animals—Flying

FOLKLORE

Bowden, Joan C.
Strong John, 172
Carrick, Malcolm
Happy Jack, 258
Christian, Mary B.
Lucky Man, 298
Dolch, Edward W., and Dolch,
Marguerite P.
Lion and Tiger Stories, 388
Once There Was a Bear, 390
Once There Was a Monkey,
391
"Why" Stories, 394
Evans, Katherine
The Boy Who Cried Wolf, 423
Huber, M. B.
It Happened One Day, 651
Lobel, Anita
The Straw Maid, 806
Patterson, Lillie
Haunted Houses on Hallow-
een, 1090
Schwartz, Alvin
In a Dark, Dark Room and
Other Scary Stories, 1294
Van Woerkom, Dorothy
Meat Pies and Sausages,
1509
Old Devil Is Waiting: Three
Folktales, 1510

FOLKLORE—Africa

Arnott, Kathleen
Dragons, Ogres, and Scary
Things: Two African Folk-
tales, 48
Spiders, Crabs, and Creepy
Crawlers: Two African Folk-
tales, 49
Dolch, Marguerite P.
Stories from Africa, 396
McKissack, Patricia
Monkey-Monkey's Trick, 856
Porter, Wesley
About Monkeys in Trees,
1134

FOLKLORE—Black Americans

Bang, Molly G.
Wiley and the Hairy Man:
Adapted from an American
Folktale, 78
Hayward, Linda
Hello, House!, 567

FOLKLORE—China

Bang, Molly G.
Tye May and the Magic
Brush, 77
Rockwell, Anne
Big Boss, 1211

FOLKLORE—Denmark

Bason, Lillian
Those Foolish Molboes!, 86
Kent, Jack
Hoddy Doddy, 706

FOLKLORE—England

O'Connor, Jane
The Teeny Tiny Woman, 1032
Shub, Elizabeth
Seeing Is Believing, 1413

FOLKLORE—Europe

Dolch, Edward W., and Dolch,
Marguerite P.
Folk Stories, 387

FOLKLORE—France

Wahl, Jan
Drakestail, 1519

FOLKLORE—Germany

Shub, Elizabeth
Clever Kate, 1412

FOLKLORE—Hawaii

Funai, Mamoru
Moke and Poki in the Rain
Forest, 466

FOLKLORE—India

Bang, Betsy
Tuntuni the Tailor Bird, 76
Wheeler, M. J.
Fox Tales, 1532

FOLKLORE—Indonesia

Boegehold, Betty
Small Deer's Magic Tricks,
156

FOLKLORE—Ireland

Shub, Elizabeth
Seeing Is Believing, 1413

FOLKLORE—Japan

Porter, Wesley
The Magic Kettle, 1135
Van Woerkom, Dorothy
Sea Frog, City Frog, 1511

FOLKLORE—Latvia

Van Woerkom, Dorothy
Tit for Tat, 1512

FOLKLORE—Mexico

Baker, Betty
No Help at All, 58
Evans, Katherine
One Good Deed Deserves An-
other, 427
Lazarus, Keo F.
Billy Goat in the Chili Patch,
776

FOLKLORE—Native Ameri-
cans

Baker, Betty
Three Fools and a Horse, 62

GHOST STORIES (*cont.*)

Patterson, Lillie
Haunted Houses on Hallow-een, 1090
Peters, Sharon
The Goofy Ghost, 1102
Quackenbush, Robert
Sheriff Sally Gopher and the Haunted Dance Hall, 1172
Rockwell, Anne
A Bear, a Bobcat, and Three Ghosts, 1209
The Bump in the Night, 1212
Schwartz, Alvin
In a Dark, Dark Room and Other Scary Stories, 1294

GIANTS—Fiction

Baker, Betty
All-by-Herself, 55
Coville, Bruce, and Coville, Katherine
The Foolish Giant, 331
Holl, Adelaide
George the Gentle Giant, 636
Yolen, Jane
The Giants' Farm, 1583
The Giants Go Camping, 1584

GIFTS AND GIFT-GIVING—Fiction

Gelman, Rita Golden
Hey, Kid!, 479
Numeroff, Laura J.
The Ugliest Sweater, 1026

Giraffes—Fiction
SEE Animals—Giraffes—Fiction

Goats—Fiction
SEE Animals—Goats—Fiction

Gorillas—Fiction
SEE Animals—Gorillas—Fiction

GRANDPARENTS—Fiction

Brenner, Barbara
Beef Stew, 199
Cazet, Denys
Saturday, 272

Eugenie, and Olson, Mary C.
Kittens for Keeps, 422
Goldman, Susan
Grandma Is Somebody Special, 497
Keller, Beverly
Don't Throw Another One, Dover, 700
Lapp, Eleanor J.
The Mice Came in Early This Year, 766
Lexau, Joan M.
I Hate Red Rover, 797
McCully, Emily A.
The Grandma Mix-Up, 841
Minarik, Else H.
A Kiss for Little Bear, 956
Little Bear's Visit, 959
Neasi, Barbara
Listen to Me, 1005
Numeroff, Laura J.
Does Grandma Have an Elmo Elephant Jungle Kit?, 1025
Pomerantz, Charlotte
Buffy and Albert, 1129
Shortall, Leonard
Just-in-Time Joey, 1394
Stevens, Carla
Anna, Grandpa, and the Big Storm, 1451
Thomson, Pat
Can You Hear Me, Grandad?, 1484
Good Girl Granny, 1485
Van Leeuwen, Jean
Oliver, Amanda, and Grandmother Pig, 1501

Grasshoppers—Fiction
SEE Animals—Grasshoppers—Fiction

GRAVITY

Selsam, Millicent E.
Up, Down and Around: The Force of Gravity, 1315

Greedy—Fiction
SEE Behavior—Greedy—Fiction

Groundhog Day—Fiction
SEE Holidays—Groundhog Day—Fiction

Groundhogs
SEE Animals—Groundhogs

GROWING-UP

Freschet, Berniece
Possum Baby, 459
Goennel, Heidi
My Day, 493
Hurd, Edith T.
Mother Kangaroo, 659

GROWING-UP—Fiction

Benchley, Nathaniel
Running Owl the Hunter, 101
Boegehold, Betty
Here's Pippa Again, 153
Pippa Pops Out!, 155
Dauer, Rosamund
Bullfrog Grows Up, 341
Eastman, Philip D.
Are You My Mother?, 406
Hoban, Lillian
Arthur's Honey Bear, 597
Krensky, Stephen
Lionel-at-Large, 752
Kwitz, Mary D.
Little Chick's Story, 761
McDaniel, Becky B.
Katie Couldn't, 843

Growth and development—Fiction
SEE Animals—Growth and development—Fiction

Guinea Pigs
SEE Pets—Guinea Pigs

Gymnastics—Fiction
SEE Sports—Gymnastics—Fiction

GYPSIES—Fiction

DeLage, Ida
Beware! Beware! A Witch Won't Share, 352

Hair—Fiction
SEE Human body—Hair—Fiction

HAIRCUTTING—Fiction

Davis, Gibbs
Katy's First Haircut, 343
Quin-Harkin, Janet
Helpful Hattie, 1173

Showers, Paul
Listening Walk, 1402

SENSES—Touch

Hatch, Shirley C.
Wind Is to Feel, 550
Showers, Paul
Find Out by Touching, 1399

SEX ROLES

Wandro, Mark, and Blank,
Joani
My Daddy Is a Nurse, 1521

SEX ROLES—Fiction

Carlson, Nancy
Making the Team, 250
dePaola, Tomie
Oliver Button Is a Sissy, 379
Klein, Monica
Backyard Basketball Superstar, 739
Krasilovsky, Phyllis
The Man Who Cooked for Himself, 747
Lewis, Thomas P.
Clipper Ship, 791
Shecter, Ben
Hester the Jester, 1390
Waddell, Martin
The Tough Princess, 1517

SHADOWS

Cartwright, Sally
Sunlight, 265
Schneider, Herman, and
Schneider, Nina
Science Fun with a Flashlight, 1283

SHADOWS—Fiction

Hamilton, Virginia
Jahdu, 534
Kent, Jack
The Biggest Shadow in the Zoo, 705

Shape
SEE Concepts—Shape

Sharing—Fiction
SEE Behavior—Sharing—
Fiction

Sharks
SEE Animals—Sharks

Sheep
SEE Animals—Sheep

SHELLS

Sorrells, Dorothy
The Little Shell Hunter, 1436
Victor, Joan B.
Shells Are Skeletons, 1514

SHERIFFS—Fiction

Osborne, Mary P.
Mo to the Rescue, 1046

SHIPS—Fiction

Lewis, Thomas P.
Clipper Ship, 791

SHOPPING—Fiction

Claverie, Jean
Shopping, 307
Ross, Pat
M and M and the Big Bag, 1238
Schick, Eleanor
Joey on His Own, 1279
Thomson, Pat
My Friend Mr. Morris, 1486

Shoshoni
SEE Native Americans—
Shoshoni

Shrews—Fiction
SEE Animals—Shrews—Fiction

Shyness—Fiction
SEE Behavior—Shyness—
Fiction

SIBLING RIVALRY—Fiction

Boegehold, Betty
Three to Get Ready, 157
Brenner, Barbara
Nicky's Sister, 201
Carley, Wayne
Puppy Love, 238
Chorao, Kay
Ups and Downs with Oink and Pearl, 292

Keller, Beverly
Don't Throw Another One, Dover, 700
Leech, Jay, and Spencer, Zane
Bright Fawn and Me, 777
McDaniel, Becky B.
Katie Can, 842
McNulty, Faith
The Elephant Who Couldn't Forget, 867
Minarik, Else H.
No Fighting, No Biting!, 960
O'Connor, Jane
Lulu and the Witch Baby, 1029
Olson, Mary C., ed.
This Room Is Mine!, 1041
Roche, P. K.
Webster and Arnold and the Giant Box, 1208
Stevenson, James
Winston, Newton, Elton, and Ed, 1458
Van Leeuwen, Jean
Amanda Pig and Her Big Brother Oliver, 1498
Tales of Oliver Pig, 1503
Weiss, Nicki
Menj, 1531

SIBLINGS—Fiction

Boegehold, Betty
Three to Get Ready, 157
Bonsall, Crosby
The Day I Had to Play with My Sister, 164
Bronin, Andrew
Gus and Buster Work Things Out, 206
Carlson, Nancy
Harriet and Walt, 244
The Perfect Family, 252
Castiglia, Julie
Jill the Pill, 269
Chorao, Kay
Oink and Pearl, 291
Dinardo, Jeffrey
Timothy and the Big Bully, 382
Heilbroner, Joan
The Happy Birthday Present, 573
Hoban, Lillian
Arthur's Funny Money, 595
Arthur's Honey Bear, 597
Arthur's Pen Pal, 599
Arthur's Prize Reader, 600

TITLE INDEX

Note: Numerals refer to entry numbers, not page numbers.

ILLUSTRATOR INDEX

If an author is other than the illustrator, the author's name appears in parentheses after the title of the work. *Note:* Numerals refer to entry numbers, not page numbers.

Marshall, Richard
T-Ball Is Our Game (Gemme, Leila B.), 480

Martin, Clovis
Bugs! (McKissack, Patricia, and McKissack, Fredrick), 860
I Am (Milios, Rita), 951
Sweet Dreams (Neasi, Barbara), 1006
Who Is Coming? (McKissack, Patricia), 858

Martin, Diane
A Gerbil for a Friend (Pape, Donna L.), 1055

Martin, Dick
Play Ball (Hillert, Margaret), 585

Masheris, Robert
Dogs Have Paws (Ross, Jan), 1236

Massie, Diane R.
The Komodo Dragon's Jewels, 923

Mathieu, Joe
Big Bird Says: A Game to Read and Play Featuring Jim Henson's Sesame Street Muppets (Lerner, Sharon), 778
Ernie's Little Lie (Elliott, Dan), 416
It's Easy! (Hautzig, Deborah), 554
Plants Do Amazing Things (Nussbaum, Hedda), 1028

Mawicke, Tran
Captain: Canada's Flying Pony (Hall, Lynn), 529

McCaffery, Janet
Waza Wins at Windy Gulch (Coerr, Eleanor), 316

McCann, Gerald
Once There Was a Bear (Dolch, Edward W., and Dolch, Marguerite P.), 390

McClung, Robert M.
Horseshoe Crab, 838
Ladybug, 839

McCully, Emily A.
The Boston Coffee Party (Rappaport, Doreen), 1177
Finding Out with Your

Senses (Simon, Seymour), 1418
The Grandma Mix-Up, 841
The Halloween Candy Mystery (Markham, Marion M.), 886
Lulu and the Witch Baby (O'Connor, Jane), 1029
Lulu Goes to Witch School (O'Connor, Jane), 1030
No Help at All (Baker, Betty), 58
Partners (Baker, Betty), 59
Tree House Town (Miles, Miska), 944

McKie, Roy
Bennett Cerf's Book of Animal Riddles (Cerf, Bennett A.), 274
Bennett Cerf's Book of Riddles (Cerf, Bennett A.), 276
Eye Book (LeSieg, Theo), 781
The Hair Book (Tether, Graham), 1476
In a People House (LeSieg, Theo), 782
More Riddles (Cerf, Bennett A.), 277
The Nose Book (Perkins, Al), 1099
Snow (McKie, Roy, and Eastman, Philip D.), 853
Ten Apples Up on Top (LeSieg, Theo), 785
The Tooth Book (LeSieg, Theo), 786
Would You Rather Be a Bullfrog? (LeSieg, Theo), 788

McLean, Sammis
Uncle Boris and Maude (Sharmat, Marjorie W.), 1379

McPhail, David M.
Lorenzo, 869
Snow Lion, 870

McQueen, Lucinda
Beware of a Very Hungry Fox (Wolcott, Patty), 1560
The Cake Story (Wolcott, Patty), 1561

McRae, Rodney
The Trouble with Heathrow, 872

McVay, Tracy
A Bunny Ride (DeLage, Ida), 353

Good Morning, Lady (DeLage, Ida), 356
Squirrel's Tree Party (DeLage, Ida), 363

Meadway, Clifford
Tractors (Rickard, Graham), 1190

Meddaugh, Susan
Blue Sun Ben (Marzollo, Jean, and Marzollo, Claudio), 918
Red Sun Girl (Marzollo, Jean), 916
Ruthie's Rude Friends (Marzollo, Jean, and Marzollo, Claudio), 922
Too Short Fred, 933

Meisel, Paul
Monkey-Monkey's Trick (McKissack, Patricia), 856

Merkling, Erica
Ginger's Upstairs Pet (Ryckman, John), 1259
Puppy Love (Carley, Wayne), 238

Merryweather, Jack
Cowboy Sam and Freddy (Chandler, Edna W.), 278
Pony Rider (Chandler, Edna W.), 279

Michel, Guy
The Birthday Cow (Merriam, Eve), 936

Miller, Bill
M Is for Move (Shiefman, Vicky), 1393

Miller, J. P.
A Birthday Present for Mama: A Step Two Book (Lorian, Nicole), 822
Little Turtle's Big Adventure (Harrison, David), 542
Lucky Bear (Phillips, Joan), 1114

Miller, Marilyn
Stars (Berger, Melvin), 137
The Tide (Cartwright, Sally), 266
Wind Is to Feel (Hatch, Shirley C.), 550

Milord, Jerry
Molly and the Slow Teeth (Ross, Pat), 1244

Three Fools and a Horse
(Baker, Betty), 62

Ruffins, Reynold
Camels: Ships of the Desert
(Waters, John F.), 1522

Russell, Jim
Noah and His Ark (Storr,
Catherine), 1469

Ruth, Rod
These Islands Are Alive (May,
Julian), 932

Saltzberg, Barney
What to Say to Clara, 1273

Salzman, Yuri
The Man Who Entered a Contest (Krasilovsky, Phyllis),
748

Sandin, Joan
Clipper Ship (Lewis, Thomas
P.), 791
Daniel's Duck (Bulla, Clyde
R.), 210
Hill of Fire (Lewis, Thomas
P.), 792
The House of a Mouse
(Fisher, Aileen), 438
*The Long Way to a New
Land*, 1274
Small Wolf (Benchley, Nathaniel), 104
Woodchuck (McNulty,
Faith), 868

Sandland, Reg
The Town That Moved
(Finsand, Mary J.), 432

Santoliquido, Dolores
Secrets of the Mummies (Milton, Joyce), 953

Santoro, Christopher
*Animals Build Amazing
Homes* (Nussbaum,
Hedda), 1027

Schaffert, Arthur
Atoms (Berger, Melvin), 133

Schick, Alice
Just This Once (Schick, Alice, and Schick, Joel),
1277

Schick, Eleanor
Home Alone, 1278
Joey on His Own, 1279
Neighborhood Knight, 1280
Rainy Sunday, 1281
Summer at the Sea, 1282

Schick, Joel
Derek Koogar Was a Star
(Hall, Malcolm), 531
Farley, Are You for Real? (Allen, Marjorie N., and Allen, Carl), 36

Schneider, Howie
Gus the Bus (Cossi, Olga),
329

Schramm, Ulrick
Let's Find Out about Sound
(Knight, David), 741

Schroeder, Ted
*Beware! Beware! A Witch
Won't Share* (DeLage, Ida),
352
The Dog That Took the Train
(Meeks, Esther), 934
*Here Comes Mirium, the
Mixed-Up Witch* (Carley,
Wayne), 234
What Does a Witch Need?
(DeLage, Ida), 365

Schucker, James
Little Black, a Pony (Farley,
Walter), 429

Schumacher, Claire
Cat Games (Ziefert, Harriet),
1591

Schweninger, Ann
*Amanda Pig and Her Big
Brother Oliver* (Van
Leeuwen, Jean), 1498
Amy Goes Fishing (Marzollo,
Jean), 914
More Tales of Amanda Pig
(Van Leeuwen, Jean), 1499
Oliver, Amanda, and Grandmother Pig (Van Leeuwen,
Jean), 1501
Tales of Amanda Pig (Van
Leeuwen, Jean), 1502

Scott, Jerry
Elephant on Skates (Olson,
Mary C., ed.), 1037

Scrace, Carolyn
Let's Look at Rain (Dineen,
Jacqueline), 383

Sendak, Maurice
Father Bear Comes Home
(Minarik, Else H.), 955
A Kiss for Little Bear
(Minarik, Else H.), 956
Little Bear (Minarik, Else
H.), 957

Little Bear's Friend (Minarik,
Else H.), 958
Little Bear's Visit (Minarik,
Else H.), 959
No Fighting, No Biting!
(Minarik, Else H.), 960

Senior, Helen
Potato (Watts, Barrie), 1526

Servello, Joe
*Up the Alley with Jack and
Joe* (Kotzwinkle, William),
745

Seuling, Barbara
Just Me, 1334

Seuss, Dr.
Cat in the Hat, 1335
Cat in the Hat Comes Back,
1336
Foot Book, 1337
Fox in Socks, 1338
Green Eggs and Ham, 1340
Hop on Pop, 1341
*I Can Read with My Eyes
Shut!*, 1343
*Mister Brown Can Moo! Can
You?*, 1344
Oh, Say Can You Say?, 1345
*Oh, the Thinks You Can
Think!*, 1346
*One Fish Two Fish Red Fish
Blue Fish*, 1347
*There's a Wocket in My
Pocket!*, 1348

Sewell, Marcia
*The Man Who Tried to Save
Time* (Krasilovsky, Phyllis), 749
Poor Boy, Rich Boy (Bulla,
Clyde R.), 211

Shannon, Kenyon
Once There Was a Monkey
(Dolch, Edward W., and
Dolch, Marguerite P.), 391

Sharp, Gene
Hi, Clouds (Greene, Carol),
511
Listen to Me (Neasi, Barbara), 1005
Over-Under (Matthias, Catherine), 928
Please Wind? (Greene,
Carol), 513
Purple Is Part of a Rainbow
(Kowalczyk, Carolyn), 746
Shine, Sun! (Greene, Carol),
515

READABILITY INDEX

The readability levels in this index range from 1.0 to 4.0 and off Spache scale. Using the criteria established for including a title (see Preface) and relying on our experience and judgment, rather than strict adherence to readability levels, allowed for the inclusion of books such as *The Berenstains' B Book*, which tested beyond the first and second grade level. *Note:* Numerals refer to entry numbers, not page numbers.

READING LEVEL 1.0

Cohen, Caron L.
  Three Yellow Dogs, 317
Greene, Carol
  Snow Joe, 516

READING LEVEL 1.1

Hillert, Margaret
  Happy Birthday, Dear Dragon, 583
  Little Puff, 584
  The Witch Who Went for a Walk, 590
Lillegard, Dee
  Where Is It?, 803
McKissack, Patricia
  Who Is Who?, 859

READING LEVEL 1.2

Berenstain, Stan, and Berenstain, Jan
  Bears on Wheels, 113
Carley, Wayne
  The Witch Who Forgot, 239
Greene, Carol
  Please Wind?, 513
Grey, Judith
  What Time Is It?, 518
Hillert, Margaret
  Circus Fun, 581
  Play Ball, 585
  Run to the Rainbow, 586
  What Is It?, 588

Kim, Joy
  Come On Up!, 731
  Rainbows and Frogs: A Story about Colors, 732
Milios, Rita
  I Am, 951
Wolcott, Patty
  Pirates, Pirates Over the Salt, Salt Sea, 1564
  Super Sam and the Salad Garden, 1565

READING LEVEL 1.3

Corey, Dorothy
  Everybody Takes Turns, 328
DeLage, Ida
  Good Morning, Lady, 356
Hillert, Margaret
  Come Play with Me, 582
  Who Goes to School?, 589
Kessler, Leonard
  Hickory Dickory Dock, 721
LeSieg, Theo
  Ten Apples Up on Top, 785
McKissack, Patricia
  Who Is Coming?, 858
Minarik, Else H.
  Cat and Dog, 954
Petrie, Catherine
  Joshua James Likes Trucks, 1109
Wolcott, Patty
  Beware of a Very Hungry Fox, 1560

READING LEVEL 1.4

Berenstain, Stan, and Berenstain, Jan
  Old Hat, New Hat, 130
Eastman, Philip D.
  Are You My Mother?, 406
Harrison, David
  Wake Up, Sun, 543
Hillert, Margaret
  Snow Baby, 587
Hurd, Edith T.
  Come and Have Fun, 653
McInnes, John
  Goodnight Painted Pony, 847
Minarik, Else H.
  Father Bear Comes Home, 955
Mooser, Stephen, and Oliver, Lin
  Tad and Dad, 988
Olson, Mary C., ed.
  Big Ride for Little Bear, 1036
Peters, Sharon
  Puppet Show, 1104
Wolcott, Patty
  I'm Going to New York to Visit the Queen, 1563

READING LEVEL 1.5

Berenstain, Stan, and Berenstain, Jan
  Bears in the Night, 112
  Big Honey Hunt, 124

READING LEVEL 2.6

READING LEVEL 2.7 (cont.)

Patent, Dorothy H.
All about Whales, 1088

Perera, Thomas B., and
Orlowsky, Wallace
Who Will Clean the Air?,
1096

Rappaport, Doreen
The Boston Coffee Party,
1177

Rice, Eve
*Mr. Brimble's Hobby and
Other Stories*, 1182

Richardson, Joy
*What Happens When You
Eat?*, 1186

Rosen, Ellsworth
Spiders Are Spinners, 1228

Rosenbloom, Joseph
*Deputy Dan and the Bank
Robbers*, 1229

Ross, Pat
*M and M and the Santa Se-
crets*, 1241

Rowland, Florence W.
Amish Wedding, 1246

Sandin, Joan
*The Long Way to a New
Land*, 1274

Schick, Alice, and Schick, Joel
Just This Once, 1277

Seixas, Judith S.
*Junk Food: What It Is, What
It Does*, 1302

Selsam, Millicent E., and
Hunt, Joyce
*A First Look at Animals with-
out Backbones*, 1318
A First Look at Dinosaurs,
1322
A First Look at Leaves, 1325

Seuss, Dr.
*Mister Brown Can Moo! Can
You?*, 1344

Sharmat, Marjorie W.
*Nate the Great Stalks Stu-
pidweed*, 1373
Sophie and Gussie, 1375

Shaw, Evelyn
Elephant Seal Island, 1385

Simon, Seymour
*Turtle Talk: A Beginner's
Book of LOGO*, 1423

Sitomer, Mindel, and Sitomer,
Harry
Circles, 1425

Spanjian, Beth
Baby Raccoon, 1438

Stanovich, Betty Jo
Hedgehog Adventures, 1448

Tobias, Tobi
Maria Tallchief, 1490

Victor, Joan B.
Shells Are Skeletons, 1514

Waddell, Martin
The Tough Princess, 1517

Wright, Mildred W.
*Henri Goes to the Mardi
Gras*, 1572

Yolen, Jane
The Giants' Farm, 1583

Zarins, Joyce A.
Toasted Bagels, 1588

Ziefert, Harriet
So Hungry!, 1600

READING LEVEL 2.8

Adams, Florence
Mushy Eggs, 2

Adler, David A.
*Redwoods Are the Tallest
Trees in the World*, 7

Alexander, Sue
*More Witch, Goblin, and
Ghost Stories*, 10

Aliki
My Hands, 27

Applebaum, Stan
*Going My Way: Nature's
Hitchhikers*, 46

Baker, Donna
I Want to Be a Pilot, 65

Baker, Eugene
*I Want to Be a Basketball
Player*, 67

Bang, Molly G.
*Wiley and the Hairy Man:
Adapted from an American
Folktale*, 78

Barr, Jene
What Will the Weather Be?,
81

Barrett, Judi
*I'm too small. YOU'RE TOO
BIG*, 82

Bason, Lillian
Those Foolish Molboes!, 86

Baynton, Martin
Fifty Gets the Picture, 89

Behrens, June
*Juliette Low: Founder of the
Girl Scouts of America*, 95
Look at the Sea Animals, 96

Berger, Melvin
Energy from the Sun, 134

Bishop, Ann
Merry-Go-Riddle, 141

Bishop, Bonnie
No One Noticed Ralph, 142

Blassingame, Wyatt
*Pecos Bill Catches a
Hidebehind*, 150

Boegehold, Betty
Pippa Pops Out!, 155

Branley, Franklyn M.
*The Planets in Our Solar Sys-
tem*, 187
The Sun: Our Nearest Star,
191

Burt, Denise
Our Family Vacation, 217

Carley, Wayne
*Here Comes Mirium, the
Mixed-Up Witch*, 234

Carlson, Nancy
Arnie and the Stolen Markers,
240
The Mysterious Valentine,
251
The Talent Show, 253

Carrick, Malcolm
Mr. Tod's Trap, 259

Cebulash, Mel
*Basketball Players Do Amaz-
ing Things*, 273

Chlad, Dorothy
*Stop, Look, and Listen for
Trains*, 289

Coerr, Eleanor
Jane Goodall, 313

Craig, M. Jean
Spring Is Like the Morning,
333

DeLage, Ida
The Old Witch's Party, 361

dePaola, Tomie
The Kids' Cat Book, 378

Dolch, Edward W., and Dolch,
Marguerite P.
Once There Was a Monkey,
391

Dorros, Arthur
Feel the Wind, 400

Evans, Katherine
*One Good Deed Deserves An-
other*, 427

Fitz-Gerald, Christine
I Can Be a Mother, 440

Friskey, Margaret
*The True Book of the
Moonwalk Adventure*, 463

Gage, Wilson
The Crow and Mrs. Gaddy,
473

READING LEVEL 3.1

SERIES INDEX

Under each series title entries are arranged by author, then title and entry number. No distinction has been made where publishers share the same series title.

All about You

McNamara, Louise G., and Litchfield, Ada B.
Your Busy Brain, 865
Your Living Bones, 866

American Folktales

Blassingame, Wyatt
Pecos Bill and the Wonderful Clothesline Snake, 149
Pecos Bill Catches a Hidebehind, 150

Animal Friends

Anders, Rebecca
Dolly the Donkey, 42
Lorito the Parrot, 43
Winslow the Hamster, 44
Johnson, Sylvia A.
Elephants around the World, 685
Lions of Africa, 686
Penney and Pete the Lambs, 687

Animal Life Stories

Royston, Angela
The Deer, 1250
The Duck, 1251
The Fox, 1252
The Otter, 1253
The Penguin, 1254
The Tiger, 1255

Animals in the Wild

Serventy, Vincent
Kangaroo, 1331
Koala, 1332
Turtle and Tortoise, 1333

Basic Vocabulary

Dolch, Edward W., and Dolch, Marguerite P.
Circus Stories, 386
Folk Stories, 387
Lion and Tiger Stories, 388
Lodge Stories, 389
Tepee Stories, 393
"Why" Stories, 394

Begin to Read with Duck and Pig

Kessler, Ethel, and Kessler, Leonard
The Big Fight, 710
Pig's Orange House, 713

Beginning Readers

Long, Ruthanna
Tiny Bear Goes to the Fair, 818

Beginning Science

May, Julian
Rockets, 931

Beginning to Learn About

Allington, Richard L.
Colors, 37
Hearing, 38
Allington, Richard L., and Krull, Kathleen
Reading, 39
Spring, 40
Time, 41

Beginning to Read

Chittenden, Margaret
When the Wild Ducks Come, 285
Granowsky, Alvin; Tweedt, Joy A.; and Tweedt, Craig L.
Chicken Salad Soup, 501
Who Said That?, 504
Hillert, Margaret
Run to the Rainbow, 586
Judson, Clara I.
Christopher Columbus, 694
Meeks, Esther
The Dog That Took the Train, 934
Ridlon, Marci
A Frog Sandwich: Riddles and Jokes, 1191
Kittens and More Kittens, 1192
Ross, Jan
Dogs Have Paws, 1236
Smith, Susan M.
No One Should Have Six Cats, 1431
Taylor, Sydney
The Dog Who Came to Dinner, 1474

Read Aloud and Easy Reading

Read-Aloud/Read-alone